D1167433

Here's What the Reviewers Say...

"Your book... was done with a great deal of care and respect. I highly recommend this book not only to tourists but also to Puerto Ricans who haven't taken the time to know their homeland. I know I will be using this book on my next trip! ... thank you for a job well done!" *Willie Colon, internationally known salsa trombonist, songwriter, and vocalist*

"Each title in this fine series shares a similar format: extensive background on the island's history, economics, and politics, flora and fauna, and culture and religion; the daily practicalities of life (e.g., recycling requirements, boating conduct, buying land); what to see and do." *Library Journal*

"... one of the best writers about the Caribbean region... " *Travel Books Review*

"Get off the beaten path with *The Adventure Guide to Puerto Rico*. ... In addition to the resorts and gourmet restaurants, the guide helps you find local eateries and inexpensive guesthouses, and profiles the less visited islands of Culebra and Mona." *Caribbean Travel and Life*

Other Books by Harry S. Pariser from Hunter Publishing

Jamaica: A Visitor's Guide, 3rd Ed.. 1-55650-703-8 $15.95
Explore Belize, 4th Ed. (formerly *Adventure Guide to Belize*)
1-55650-785-2 $16.95
Adventure Guide to Barbados, 2nd Ed. 1-55650-707-0 $15.95
Adventure Guide to Costa Rica, 3rd Ed. 1-55650-722-4 $16.95
Adventure Guide to the Virgin Islands, 4th Ed. 1-55650-746-1 $16.95
Adventure Guide to the Dominican Republic, 2nd Ed.
1-55650-629-5 $14.95

Available in bookstores nationwide, or directly from the publisher. To order, send a check for the title(s) desired plus $3 shipping & handling to: Hunter Publishing, Inc., 130 Campus Drive, Edison, NJ 08818

Adventure Guide to Puerto Rico

3rd Edition

Harry S. Pariser

HUNTER PUBLISHING

Hunter Publishing, Inc.
130 Campus Drive, Edison NJ 08818
(908) 225 1900, (800) 255 0343
Fax (908) 417 1744
e-mail: hunterpub@emi.net

In Canada
1220 Nicholson Rd., Newmarket, Ontario
Canada L3Y 7V1, (800) 399 6858

ISBN 1-55650-749-6

©1997 Harry S. Pariser (3rd Edition)

Maps by Lissa K. Dailey and Kim André

Cover photo: *San Juan Gate* (Bob Krist, PRTC)
Back Cover: *Folkloric Festival – Children in Traditional Dress* (Bob Krist, PRTC)
Photos provided by Hill & Knowlton
for the Puerto Rico Tourism Company (PRTC)
or by author, as indicated.
Coqui drawing on page 11 by Jennifer Ewing.

For complete information about the hundreds of other travel guides and language courses offered by Hunter Publishing, visit our Web site at:
www.hunterpublishing.com

2 3 4 5

Contents

MAPS

CHARTS

ABOUT THE AUTHOR

After graduating from Boston University with a B.S. in Public Communications in 1975, Harry S. Pariser hitched and camped his way through Europe, traveled down the Nile by steamer, and by train through Sudan. Visiting Uganda, Rwanda, and Tanzania, he then traveled by ship from Mombasa to Bombay, and on through South and Southeast Asia before settling down in Kyoto, Japan. There he studied Japanese and ceramics while teaching English to everyone from tiny tots to Buddhist priests. Using Japan as a base, he traveled through other parts of Asia: trekking to the vicinity of Mt. Everest in Nepal, taking tramp steamers to Indonesian islands like Adonara and Ternate, and visiting rural China. He returned to the United States in 1984 via the Caribbean, where he researched two travel guides: *Guide to Jamaica* and *Guide to Puerto Rico and the Virgin Islands,* published in 1986. In 1996, Mr. Pariser received a Silver Award in the Lowell Thomas Travel Journalism Competition, sponsored by the Society of American Travel Writers Foundation, for his book *Adventure Guide to Barbados, 2nd Edition.* He currently lives in San Francisco, California. Besides traveling and writing, his other pursuits include print-making, painting, cooking, hiking, photography, reading, and listening to music – especially jazz, salsa, calypso, and African pop. He may be contacted by e-mail at vudu@jps.net or can be visited on the Internet at http://www.catch22.com/~vudu/.

ACKNOWLEDGMENTS

Thanks go out to mapmaker and editor Lissa Dailey, David A. Castelveter, John Turner, Pasquale Rex, Geoffrey E. Aronson, Dr. Virginia L. Richmond, Gail Burchard, Juan P. Sierra, Michael Giessler, Kathy West, Edna E. Pérez Toledo, Myrna L. Robles, Marty, Kristina A. Felbeck, Richard Druitt, Sherril Labovich, Awilda Elias, Wendy Marrero, Joan W. Burns, Cindy Roberts, Arthur Rosenfeld, Tom Hess, Tamara Orengo González, Roberto Parrilla, Linda Williams, Jan E. Bonnet, Santiago Oliver, and Ken Coughlin. A final thank you goes to my mother, who always worries about me.

WE LOVE TO GET MAIL

Things change so rapidly that it's impossible to keep up with everything. Like automobiles, travel books require fine tuning if they are to stay in top condition. We need input from readers so that we can continue to provide the best, most current information possible. Please write to let us know about any inaccuracies or new information. Although we try to make our maps as accurate as possible, errors can occur. If you have suggestions for improvement or places that should be included, please let us know.

READER'S RESPONSE FORM
Adventure Guide to Puerto Rico, 3rd Edition

I found your book:

Your book could be improved by:

The best places I stayed in were (explain why):

I found the best food at:

Some good and bad experiences I had were:

Will you return to Puerto Rico?

If so, where do you plan to go? If not, why not?

I purchased this book at:

Please include any other comments on a separate sheet. Mail to Harry S. Pariser, c/o Hunter Publishing, 130 Campus Drive, Edison NJ 08818 USA; fax to (561) 546 7986 or e-mail comments to the author at vudu@jps.net.

A NOTE ABOUT PRICING

The rates listed are generally high season or are valid for the entire year. They do not include the 7% accommodation tax (9% at hotels with casinos) unless specified otherwise. Rates are given as a guideline only and are approximate; price fluctuations can and will occur. For current rates, contact the hotel in question. Listing of a hotel does not constitute a recommendation. All transportation times and carriers are subject to change. Be sure to confirm departures ahead of time. Hotel addresses are completed with "Puerto Rico."

ABBREVIATIONS

Av. – *avenida*, avenue
C. – *calle*, street
Carr. – *carretera*, road
d – double
E – east, eastern
ha – hectare(s)
km – kilometer

m – meter
N – north, northern
pw – per week
rt – round trip
S – south, southern
s – single
W – west, western

☎ AREA CODE
As of March 1996, the area code
for Puerto Rico was changed to 787.

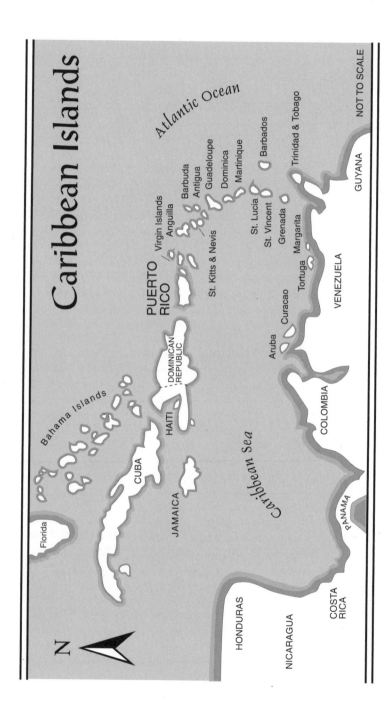

Caribbean Islands

N

Florida

Bahama Islands

CUBA

JAMAICA

HAITI

DOMINICAN REPUBLIC

PUERTO RICO

Virgin Islands

Anguilla

St. Kitts & Nevis

Barbuda

Antigua

Guadeloupe

Dominica

Martinique

St. Lucia

Barbados

St. Vincent

Grenada

Margarita

Trinidad & Tobago

Tortuga

Curacao

Aruba

Atlantic Ocean

Caribbean Sea

HONDURAS

NICARAGUA

COSTA RICA

PANAMA

COLOMBIA

VENEZUELA

GUYANA

NOT TO SCALE

Introduction

Despite the fact that Puerto Rico has been part of the territorial United States since 1898, most Americans know little or nothing about the island. Yet Puerto Rico is one of the most exotic places in the nation – a miniature Latin America set in the Caribbean. And San Juan was a thriving town when Jamestown was still an undeveloped plot of land. A very attractive island, Puerto Rico contains numerous forest reserves, beaches, ancient indigenous sites, an abundance of historical atmosphere, and the only tropical National Forest in the US. Sadly, the vast majority of visitors get stuck in the tourist traps of Condado and never experience the island's charms.

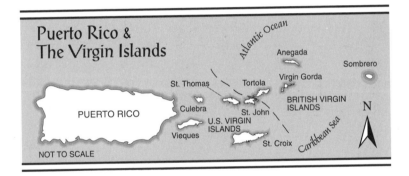

Puerto Rico & The Virgin Islands

Atlantic Ocean

Anegada

Sombrero

St. Thomas

Tortola

Virgin Gorda

PUERTO RICO

Culebra

St. John

BRITISH VIRGIN ISLANDS

N

Vieques

U.S. VIRGIN ISLANDS

St. Croix

Caribbean Sea

NOT TO SCALE

The Land

The islands of the Caribbean stretch in a 2,800-mile (4,500-km) arc from the western tip of Cuba to the small Dutch island of Aruba. The region is sometimes extended to include the Central and S. American countries of Belize (the former Colony of British Honduras), the Yucatán, Surinam, Guiana, and Guyana. The islands of Jamaica, Hispaniola, Puerto Rico, the US and British Virgin Islands, along with Cuba, the Caymans, and the Turks and Caicos islands form the Greater Antilles. Early geographers gave the name "Antilia" to hypothetical islands thought to lie beyond the equally imaginary "Antilades." In general, the land is steep and volcanic in origin: chains of mountains run across Jamaica, Cuba, Hispaniola, and Puerto Rico, and hills rise abruptly from the sea along most of the Virgin Islands.

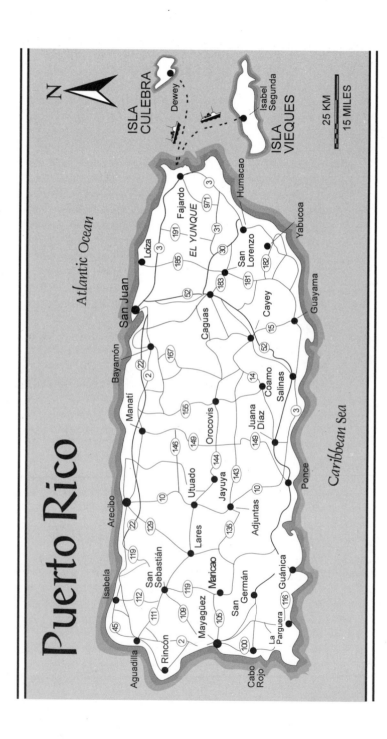

Puerto Rico

Atlantic Ocean

Caribbean Sea

ISLA CULEBRA

Dewey

ISLA VIEQUES

Isabel Segunda

25 KM

15 MILES

Aguadilla
Isabela
Rincón
Arecibo
Manatí
San Juan
Bayamón
Loíza
Fajardo
Humacao

45
111
112
119
2
129
22
119
109
105
100
135
10
146
155
167
22
2
52
185
191
3
971
3

San Sebastián
Mayagüez
Maricao
San Germán
La Parguera
Cabo Rojo
Guánica
Lares
Utuado
Adjuntas
Jayuya
Orocovis
Juana Díaz
Ponce
Coamo
Salinas
Caguas
Cayey
San Lorenzo
Yabucoa
Guayama

116
100
135
10
143
144
149
149
14
15
52
181
182
183
30
31
3

EL YUNQUE

Geography

Smallest and most easterly of the Greater Antilles, Puerto Rico's 3,435 sq miles (8,768 sq km – roughly the size of Connecticut, Crete, or Corsica) serve as one of the barriers between the waters of the Caribbean and the Atlantic: the N coast faces the Atlantic while the E and S coasts face the Caribbean. The Virgin Islands lie to the E; to the W the 75-mile-wide (121-km) Mona Passage separates the island from neighboring Hispaniola. The seas off the coast are peppered with numerous cays and some small islands. The small archipelago of Culebra and the island of Vieques lie off the E coast, while the even smaller Mona lies to the W. An irregular submarine shelf, seven miles at its widest, surrounds the island. Two miles off the N coast the sea floor plummets to 6,000 ft (1,829 m); the Milwaukee Deep, one of the world's deepest underwater chasms at 28,000 ft (8,534 m), lies 45 miles (72 km) to the N.

The nearly rectangular island runs 111 miles (179 km) from E to W and 36 miles (58 km) from N to S. Numerous headlands and indentations punctuate its coastline. Puerto Rico is the tip of a huge volcanic mass. The coastal plain, an elevated area of land that rings the island, encircles the mountainous center. Two mountain ranges, the Luquillo and the Cordillera Central, cross the island from E to W. The Sierra de Luquillo in the E contains El Yunque ("The Anvil"), which reaches 3,843 ft (1,171 m). A smaller range, the Sierra de Cayey, is in the SE. Cordillera Central, a broader *sierra* to the W, contains Cerro De Punta which, at 4,398 ft (1,319 m), is the highest peak on the island.

Spectacular shapes along the NW of the island are the result of karstification – a process whereby, over a million-year period, heavy rains seeping through the primary structural lines and joints of the porous limestone terrain carved huge caves, deep sinkholes, and long underground passages. As a result, the island is honeycombed with caves – one of the most extensive cave systems in the Western Hemisphere. Of some 220 caves, only the Camuy caves have been commercially developed. There are a total of 57 rivers and 1,200 streams on the island. Commercially valuable minerals include iron, manganese, coal, marble, gypsum, clay, kaolin, phosphate, salt, and copper.

One final feature on the landscape that will not escape the notice of many visitors is the military presence. Some 13% of the land is occupied by the US military.

Climate

With an average temperature of 73°F during the coolest month and 79°F during the warmest, the island has a delightful climate. Located within the belt of the steady NE trade winds, its mild, subtropical climate varies little throughout the year. Winter temperatures average 19° warmer than Cairo and Los Angeles, 7° warmer than Miami, and 4° warmer than Honolulu. Temperatures in the mountain areas average eight to 10° cooler than on the coast. Lowest recorded temperature (40°F) was measured at Aibonito in March 1911. Only five days per year are entirely without sunshine. Rain, which usually consists of short showers, is most likely to occur between June and October. The N coast gets much more rain than the S, with San Juan receiving 60 inches per year as compared with Ponce's 30 inches. Trade winds produce the greatest amount of rain in the mountain areas, with El Yunque averaging 183 inches (4,648 mm) per year, falling in some 1,600 showers.

PUERTO RICO CLIMATE CHART

	Daily Average Air Temp. °F	Rainfall Days	Rainfall Inches
January	80	20	4.3
February	80	15	2.7
March	81	15	2.9
April	82	14	4.1
May	84	16	5.9
June	85	17	5.4
July	85	19	5.7
August	85	20	6.3
September	86	18	6.2
October	85	18	5.6
November	84	19	6.3
December	81	21	5.4

Hurricanes

Cast in a starring role as the bane of the tropics, hurricanes represent the one outstanding negative in an otherwise impeccably hospitable climate. The Caribbean as a whole ranks third worldwide in the number of hurricanes per year. These low-pressure zones are serious business. Property damage from them may run into the hundreds of millions of dollars.

A hurricane begins as a relatively small tropical storm, known as a cyclone when its winds reach a velocity of 39 mph (62 kph). At 74 mph (118 kph) it is upgraded to hurricane status, with winds of up to 200 mph (320 kph) and ranging from 60-1,000 miles (100-1,600 km) in diameter.

A small hurricane releases energy equivalent to the explosions of six atomic bombs per second. A hurricane may be compared to an enormous hovering engine that uses the moist air and water of the tropics as fuel, carried hither and thither by prevailing air currents – generally eastern trade winds which intensify as they move across warm ocean waters. When cooler, drier air infiltrates as it heads N, the hurricane begins to die, cut off from the life-sustaining ocean currents that have nourished it from infancy. Routes and patterns are unpredictable. As for their frequency: "June – too soon; July – stand by; August – it must; September – remember." So goes the old rhyme. Unfortunately, hurricanes are not confined to July and August. Hurricanes forming in Aug. and Sept. typically last for two weeks, while those that form in June, July, Oct., and Nov. (many of which originate in the Caribbean and the Gulf of Mexico) generally last only seven days.

Approximately 70% of all hurricanes (known as Cabo Verde types) originate as embryonic storms coming from the W coast of Africa. Fortunately, they are comparatively scarce in the area around Puerto Rico. Since record-keeping began in 1508, 76 hurricanes have wreaked havoc on the island. Four of the most recent hurricanes with serious consequences have been San Felipe (1928), San Ciprian (1932), Santa Clara (1956) and Hurricane Hugo (1989). The latter lashed the island with 140 mph winds. Hurricane Marilyn devastated St. Thomas in 1995, also causing major damage to Culebra, Vieques, and the eastern part of the island.

Natural Areas

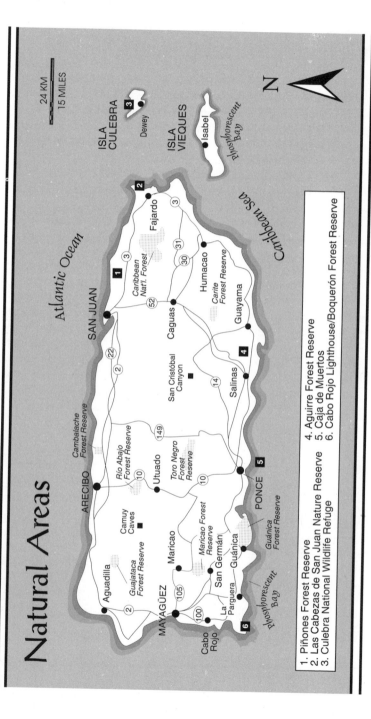

Atlantic Ocean

SAN JUAN

ARECIBO

Cambalache
Forest Reserve

Río Abajo
Forest Reserve

Utuado

Toro Negro
Forest
Reserve

San Cristóbal
Canyon

Caguas

Caribbean
Nat'l. Forest

Fajardo

Aguadilla

Guajataca
Forest Reserve

Camuy
Caves

Maricao

Maricao Forest
Reserve

San Germán

Guánica

Guánica
Forest Reserve

PONCE

MAYAGÜEZ

Cabo
Rojo

La
Parguera

Phosphorescent
Bay

Humacao

Carite
Forest Reserve

Guayama

Salinas

Aguirre Forest Reserve

Caja de Muertos

Caribbean Sea

ISLA
CULEBRA

Dewey

ISLA
VIEQUES

Isabel

Phosphorescent
Bay

24 KM
15 MILES

N

1. Piñones Forest Reserve
2. Las Cabezas de San Juan Nature Reserve
3. Culebra National Wildlife Refuge

4. Aguirre Forest Reserve
5. Caja de Muertos
6. Cabo Rojo Lighthouse/Boquerón Forest Reserve

Flora & Fauna

Puerto Rico's central location in the northern Caribbean, together with its variations in elevation, rainfall, and soil, have served to stimulate the development of a varied plant life. These variations account for five differing areas of natural vegetation: humid sea forest or marshland, humid wood forest, the humid tropical forest found in the center of the island, the subhumid forest along the NW coast, and the thorny dry forest on the S coast. Although 75% of the island was covered by forest a century ago, today it's only 25%, with a bare 1% of the forest retaining its virginity. Natural ground cover can be found in the Caribbean National Forest (El Yunque) and the forest reserves of Puerto Rico. Although a considerable number of the 3,355 species of flora are indigenous, many have been introduced from neighboring islands.

Trees & Tropical Vegetation

TREES: Altogether, there are 547 native species of trees, with an additional 203 naturalized species – an incredible variety for such a small area. Native trees include the *ceiba*, or silk cotton tree; famous for its enormous size, it may live 300 years or more. Masks and eating utensils have traditionally been made from the gourd of the *higuero* or calabash tree. Now rare, the *guayacán* (lignum vitae) has some of the densest wood in the world: it's so heavy that it sinks in water! It was once used interchangeably with money. Masts and prows in Spanish and Dutch ships were made from the wood; *guayacol*, an extract, was considered a remedy for cholera. As the trees take centuries to grow, supply could not keep up with demand. You can identify the tree by its compound dark green leaves, mottled peeling bark, and blue flowers.

Introduced more than two centuries ago, the Dominican mahogany has been used in furniture making and in carpentry work. The *campeche* yields a red to black dye whose active ingredient, haematoxylin, can be used in treating dysentery; it was once exported to Europe. Its deciduous, compound leaves have small heart-shaped leaflets, and its gray fissured trunk is often fluted at its base. Its fragrant yellow blooms produce oblong flat pods. The orange fissured bark of the *mabí* is fermented to make a form of root beer; its evergreen leaves are smooth on top but hairy underneath. Distantly related to the coca, the *indio* produces blooming masses of small white flowers. The unopened leaves of the Puerto Rican hat palm are still put to use in weaving fine hats and baskets, but the *ausobo*, a type of ironwood used for ceiling beams during the Colonial era, has virtually disappeared. Having whorled leaves with spines at their base, yellow-brown bark, and white flowers, the *ucar* has been widely used for fenceposts; the yellow-shouldered blackbird commonly nests in its branches. Easily recognized by its peeling red bark, the gumbo-limbo produces a latex that has been used for incense, glue, and medicine. Its saplings have been planted in alignment to form living fences. The graceful *alelí* produces a large white flower. Its long, thin evergreen leaves are popular with yellow-and-black caterpillars.

Imported trees include the Australian casuarina, the cassia, the Mexican *papayuelo*, the Indo-Malayan coconut palm, the mango, and the tamarind. Ornamental vines and shrubs include bougainvillea, *carallita*, jasmine, hibiscus, shower of orchids, gardenia, thunbergia, poinsettia, and croton. Found along the coast, the sea grape has round, leathery leaves; it produces an edible, grape-like purple fruit.

CACTI: Any visitor to the island's drier areas will notice the proliferation of cacti and other scrub vegetation. Cacti were classified into a single genus comprising 24 species by Linnaeus in 1737. The name is Greek for "the bristly plant." The oldest fossilized cactus remains are found in Colorado and Utah and date from the Eocene Era some 50 million years ago. Cacti have evolved to suit a hot, dry climate. Their need to reduce surface area – in order to deter evaporation and protect it from the sun's rays – have resulted in flattened, columnar, grooved, bumpy, globular, and barrel-shaped plants. Evolution has transformed their leaves into spines and their branches into areoles – localized regions that carry spines and/or bristles. The stems are responsible for photosynthesis. Shade and light diffusion is provided by bumps, warts, ribs, spines, and hairlike structures. These structures also serve to hinder evaporation and hold dew. Its thick, leathery flesh stores water effectively, is resistant to withering and can endure up to a 60% water loss without damage. Stomata (apertures) close during the day to prevent water loss, but reopen at night. Blossoms generally last for only one day, and nearly all depend upon animals for pollination.

varieties: Named for its distinctive shape, the pipe organ cactus is generally found in the island's driest areas. The barrel-shaped Turk's Cap is capped with red flowers, while the prickly pear is a small, rapidly spreading cactus that has innumerable spines and yellow flowers. The dildo cactus has tall hollow stems that are used for food storage by birds. The squat melon cactus is pollinated by hummingbirds. It has pink flowers and fruit; its shallow spreading root system serves to capture water.

CACTUS-RELATED PLANTS: These plants have adapted to high temperatures and a lack of water by converting their leaves into spines. The large century plant has a rosette of thick spiked leaves at its base and sends up a 10-to 20-ft stalk. It blooms after 20 years and then dies. The indigenous peoples of the Caribbean mixed its fiber with cotton and used the resulting cord to weave hammocks. The aloe is a single-stalked succulent renowned for its healing properties. It is native to Africa and the Mediterranean.

HELICONIAS

Famous worldwide as an ornamental, the heliconia (*platanillo*), lends bizarre color and shape to the tropical landscape. The name of these medium to large erect herbs comes from Helicon, a mountain in southern Greece believed to have been the home of the muses. They are a member of the order known as the Zingiberales, and there are thought to be around 200-250 species. Relatives within this category include the banana, the birds-of-paradise, the gingers, and the prayer plants.

The family name Zingiberales comes from the Sanskrit word *sringavera*, which means "horn shaped" in reference to the rhizomes. Each erect shoot has a stem and leaves that are frequently (although not always) topped by an inflorescence with yellow or red bracts. Each inflorescence may produce up to 50 hermaphroditic flowers. Leaves are composed of stalk and blade and resemble banana leaves. Flowers produce a blue colored fruit which has three seeds. In Puerto Rico you're most likely to find heliconias near rivers and along roads; they thrive in light gaps. Most are found in the tropical lowlands or in middle-elevation or cloud forest habitats. Lured by the bright colored flowers and bracts, hummingbirds arrive to pollinate the blooms. The birds spread pollen as they fly from flower to flower in search of nectar.

MANGROVES: Mangrove forests are found along the coasts; these water-rooted trees serve as a marine habitat sheltering sponges, corals, oysters, and other members of the marine community around its roots – organisms which in turn attract a variety of other sealife. Some species live out their lives in the shelter of the mangroves and many fish use them as a shelter or feeding ground; lobsters use the mangrove environs as a nursery for their young. Above the water level, they shelter seabirds and are important nesting sites. Their organic detritus, exported to the reef by the tides, is consumed by its inhabitants, providing the base of an extensive food web. Mangroves also dampen high waves and winds generated by tropical storms. Mangroves have also functioned as hurricane shelters for boats.

By trapping silt in their roots and catching leaves and other waste material that decomposes to form soil, the red mangroves act as land builders. Eventually, the red mangroves kill themselves off by building up so much soil that the black and white mangroves take over. White mangroves have light-green fleshy leaves, with glands that allow the tree to excrete excess salt. Meanwhile, the red mangroves have sent out progeny in the form of floating seedlings – bottom-heavy youngsters that grow on the tree until reaching six inches to a foot in length. If they drop in shallow water, the seeds touch bottom and implant themselves. In deeper water they stay afloat and, crossing a shoal, drag until they lodge. Named after their light-colored bark, the white mangroves are highly salt tolerant. If growing in a swampy area, they produce pneumatophores, root system extensions which grow vertically to a height that allows them to stay above the water during flooding or tides and carry on gaseous exchange. The black mangrove also produces pneumatophores, as well as a useful wood. The buttonwood, smaller than the others, is not a true mangrove but is found on the coasts where no other varieties are found. It is named for its round, hard fruits. Three-quarters of the island's mangrove forests have been destroyed by development.

Animal Life

Except for bats, dolphins, and sea cows, Puerto Rico has no indigenous mammals. One extinct species is the multicolored mute dog, which the Native Americans liked to fatten up and roast. Cows, pigs, mongooses, and horses were all imported by the Spanish. Although there was once a great demand in the Spanish Antilles for Puerto Rican horses and cattle, this industry has almost died out. *Paso Fino* and *anadura* horses are still held in high esteem; the former can walk at a pace that enables a rider to carry a full glass of water in his hand and not spill a drop. There are over 7,000 *Paso Fino* horses on the island. Mongooses, imported from India to combat rats and now-extinct poisonous reptiles, have propagated to the point where they too have now become an agricultural pest.

BIRDLIFE: Puerto Rico has approximately 200 species of birds, including the Puerto Rican grackle, the kingbird, the petchary, several species of owls, and the Puerto Rican sharp-shinned and West Indian red-tailed hawks. Once a million strong, the colorful Puerto Rican parrot now hovers near extinction, surviving only in the outback areas of El Yunque.

The endangered Puerto Rican nightjar, nearly invisible, its brown coloration disguising it in the brush, rests during the day. The pearly-eyed thrasher, nesting in cliffsides and cave ceilings, is another species popular among birders. The iridescent green Puerto Rican mango hummingbird lives in evergreen forests and feeds on nectar with its curved beak. Among the smaller birds are the onomatopoetically named *pitirre* and the *reinita* ("little queen") which hangs out around kitchen windows and tables. The Puerto Rican whippoorwill *(guaibaro pequeño)*, Puerto Rican tody *(San Pedrito, medio peso, papagallo)*, Puerto Rican woodpecker *(el carpintero)*, the Puerto Rican grosbeak *(el comeñame)*, and the Puerto Rican emerald hummingbird *(el zumbadorcito)* are other species of note.

REPTILES & AMPHIBIANS: If Puerto Rico can be said to have a national animal, it must be the diminutive *coquí*. This 1½-inch (36 mm) streamlined treefrog has bulging eyes, webbed fingers and toes with 10 highly efficient suction discs, and smooth, nearly transparent beige skin. Its cry is enchanting, so sweet that it's sometimes mistaken by newcomers for that of a bird. Once thought to be only a single species, the *coquí* actually comes in 16 varieties. Its evening concert has won it a special place in the hearts of Puerto Ricans all across the island. In El Yunque, where they may be as thick as 10,000 per acre, studies have shown that the *coquís* climb trees nightly (where they find varied and more plentiful food sources) and then jump out at dawn chirping co-quí-quí and co-co-quí-quí as they land.

A rather different type of animal, the protected giant tortoise is closely related to its more famous cousins on the Galapagos. Culebra's population of giant leatherback turtles, which come ashore to lay

Coquí

their eggs, stand in danger of extinction. The leatherback, black with very narrow fins, gets its name from the black leathery hide which covers its back in lieu of a shell. Reaching up to six ft (two m) in length and weighing as much as 1,600 lbs. (700 kg), its chief predator has been the poacher. Another endangered species, the green turtle, has been plagued by mysterious tumors.

INSECTS AND SPIDERS: Some 15,000 species of insects include a vast variety ranging from the lowly cockroach to 216 species of butterflies and moths. *Mimes* are tiny, biting sand flies. The *guaba*, the local tarantula, is one of about 10 spiders on the island. Another is the *araña boba* or "silly spider." The bite of the centipede, which grows up to 15 inches (38 cm) long, will prove traumatic if not fatal.

Sealife

Humpback Whales

Migrating every fall from the polar waters through the passage between Puerto Rico and the Virgin Islands where they breed, these marine mammals may be sighted offshore near Humacao and also near Rincón. Overhunting during the early to mid-19th century has endangered them; they have been internationally protected since the mid-1960s. They range in length from 30 to 40 ft (12-15 m). Acrobatically inclined, humpbacks leap belly-up from the water, turn a somersault, and arch backwards, plunging headfirst back into the watery depths with a loud snapping noise. When making deep dives, these whales hump their backs forward and bring their tails out of the water.

In addition to diving, male whales love vocalizing. Their moans, cries, groans, and snores are expressed in songs lasting up to 35 minutes. These can be heard by their comrades many miles away! The probable reason for the tunes is to attract mates. Up until the time of the first recording in 1952, stories of fishermen hearing eerie songs through their boat hulls were widely disbelieved.

Humpbacks feed on small fish, plankton, and shrimp-like crustaceans – all of which they strain from the water with their baleen. They may devour as much as a ton per day during the feeding season (in the far N) in order to build up blubber for the long trip S to the Caribbean. Distinguished by their very long pectoral fins, scalloped on their forward edges, as well as by large knobs on their jaws and head, humpbacks are black-bodied with a white coloration on their underbelly.

Calves are born one at a time, light gray in color and weighing a ton, but virtually without blubber. Mothers move in close to land for nursing. (*Never* disturb a mother and calf). A calf feeds off of one or two teats, ordinarily lodged in slits, and drinks as much as 190 liters (50 gallons) of milk daily. The milk is the consistency of yogurt and has a 40-50% fat content, in contrast to the 2% fat in human milk. Calves become adults at between four and eight years of age; humpbacks have managed to keep their boudoir practices out of the limelight, and no one has ever observed them mating. Their life span is unknown, and this may not be determined until the middle of the next century (when the first litter of monitored cows, born in 1975, dies out).

Other Marine Life

FISH: Species of fish include the leather jacket, sawfish, parrotfish, weakfish, lionfish, big-eye fish, bananafish, ladyfish, puffer, sea-bat, sardine, mullet, grouper, Spanish and frigate mackerels, red snapper, eel, barracuda, and a variety of sharks.

ECHINODERMATA: Combining the Greek words *echinos* (hedgehog) and *derma* (skin), this large division of the animal kingdom includes sea urchins, sea cucumbers, and starfish. All share the ability to propel themselves with the help of "tube feet" or spines. Known by the scientific name *astrospecten*, starfish *(estrella de mar)* are five-footed carnivorous inhabitants that use their modified "tube-feet" to burrow into the sea. Sluggish sea cucumbers ingest large quantities of sand, extract the organic matter, and excrete the rest. Crustaceans and fish reside in the larger specimens.

Avoid trampling on that armed knight of the underwater sand dunes, the sea urchin. Consisting of a semi-circular calcareous (calcium carbonate) shell, the sea urchin is protected by its brown, pointed barbs. It uses its mouth, situated and protected on its underside, to graze by scraping algae from rocks. Surprisingly to those uninitiated in its lore, sea urchins are considered a gastronomic delicacy in many countries. The ancient Greeks believed they held aphrodisiacal and other properties beneficial to health. They are prized by the French and fetch four times the price of oysters in Paris. The Spanish consume them raw, boiled, in *gratinés*, or in soups. In Barbados they are termed "sea eggs," and the Japanese eat their guts raw as sushi. Although a disease in recent years has devastated the sea urchin population, they are making a comeback. **contact:** If a sea urchin spine breaks off inside your finger or toe, don't try to remove it: you can't! You might try the cure people use in New Guinea. Take a blunt object to mash up the spine inside your skin so that it will be absorbed naturally. Then dip the wound in urine; the ammonia helps to trigger the process of disintegration. It's best to apply triple-antibiotic salve. Avoiding contact is best. Sea urchins hide underneath corals, and wounds are often contracted when you lose your footing and scrape against one.

SPONGES: Found in the ocean depths, reddish or brown sponges are among the simplest forms of multicellular life and have been around for more than a half-billion years. They pump large amounts of water between their internal filters and extract plankton. There are numerous sizes, shapes, and colors, but all can be recognized by their large, distinctive openings. Unlike other animals, they show no reaction when disturbed.

CNIDARIANS: The members of this group – anemones, corals, jellyfish, and hydroids – are distinguished by their simple structure: a cup-shaped body terminating in a combination mouth-anus which is encircled by tentacles. While hydroids and corals (covered later in this section) are colonial, jellyfish and anemones are individual. The name of this group derives from the Greek word for another of its common characteristics: stinging capsules, or nematocysts, used for defense and for capturing prey. Hydroids spend their youth as solitary medusas, later settling down in colonies that look like ferns or feathers. Some will sting, and the best known hydroid is undoubtedly the Portuguese Man-of-War; its stinging tentacles can be extended or retracted. There have been reports of trailing tentacles reaching 50 feet. It belongs to the family of *siphonophores*, free-floating hydroid colonies that control their depth by means of a gas-filled float. The true jellyfish are identifiable by their domes, which vary in shape. Nematocysts are found in both the feeding tube and in their tentacles. Also known as sea wasps, box jellies have a cube-shaped dome; a single tentacle extends from each corner. They have a fierce sting. If you should get stung by any of the above, get out of the water and peel off any tentacles. Avoid rubbing the injured area. Wash it with alcohol and apply meat tenderizer for five to 10 minutes. The jellyfish season runs from August to October. Solitary bottom-dwellers, sea anemones are polyps with no skeleton. They use their tentacles to stun prey and force it to their mouths. Shrimp and crabs, immune to their sting, often find protection nearby. The tentacles may retract for protection when disturbed. One type of anemone lives in tubes buried in the muck or sand. Their tentacles emerge to play only at night.

MANATEES

The manatee (*manati*), popularly known as the sea cow, can occasionally be sighted offshore near Humacao. Once ranging from S America up to N Carolina, their numbers have dwindled dramatically. They move along the ocean floor (at a maximum pace of six mph) searching for food, surfacing every four or five minutes to breathe. Surprisingly, as the manatee's nearest living relative is the elephant, the creature was thought to be the model for the legend of the mermaid – perhaps because of the mother's habit of sheltering her offspring with her flipper as the infant feeds or perhaps because some sailor had an overactive imagination. Weighing 400-1,300 lbs (181-590 kg), the pudgy creature is covered with finely-wrinkled gray or brown skin decorated with barnacles and algae; it may reach 12 ft (four m) in length. Although to you they may appear ugly with their small eyes, thick lips, bristly muzzles, and wrinkled necks, they are affectionate, kissing each other and sometimes swimming flipper-to-flipper. They dwell in lagoons and in brackish water, eating as much as 100 lbs of aquatic vegetables per day. Strictly vegetarian, their only enemy is man, who has hunted them for their hides, oil, and meat. They have been hunted by privateers – who used the skin to make oarlocks and horsewhips – and by the Maya, who speared them and dragged them ashore to die from their wounds. Archaeological remains suggest that they have been hunted off the Florida coast for a minimum of 8,000 years.

The manatee is definitely an endangered species. Although hunting has been curtailed, dangers, such as being sliced by a powerboat, remain. Off of Florida, manatees have been dying of a mysterious ailment. Manatees (*Trichecus sp.*) are related to the dugong (*Dugong dugon*), a similar aquatic mammal found in the Indo-Pacific region. Another relative, the Steller's sea cow, was exterminated by Russian sealers. Discovered in 1741, none were left just 27 years later. There are five subspecies of manatees: the Floridian, the Antillean, the West Indian, the African, and the Amazonian. The last is the most distinctive owing to its smaller size, an irregular white patch on its stomach, and its lack of fingernails.

CRUSTACEANS: A class of arthropods, crustaceans are distinguished by their jointed legs and complex skeleton. The decapods (named for their five pairs of legs) are the largest order of crusta-

Flora & Fauna

ceans. These include shrimp, lobsters, and crabs. The ghost crab (*ocypode*) abounds on the beaches, tunneling down beneath the sand and emerging to feed at night. Although it can survive for 48 hours without contacting water, it must return to the sea to moisten its gill chambers as well as to lay its eggs, which hatch into planktonic larvae. The hermit crab carries a discarded mollusc shell in order to protect its vulnerable abdomen. As it grows, it must find a larger home, and you may see two struggling over the same shell.

DINOFLAGELLATES: These microorganisms are a variety of protozoans known as "whippers" – single-celled animals with one or more tiny projecting flagella that function as lashes or whips. Because multibillion-member blooms of dinoflagellates drain the surrounding water of dissolved oxygen, they poison the water for fish. Dinoflagellates luminesce only when disturbed. The glow of the species *Noctiluca milaris* dims when they are anesthesized, and these microscopic unicellular creatures have been found to possess a time clock that limits the intensity of their flashes to the late-night hours.

UNDERWATER HAZARDS AND CURES

Not a true coral, fire coral mimics its appearance; it may appear in many forms and has the ability to encrust nearly anything and take its host's form. Generally colored mustard yellow to brown, it often has white finger-like tips. As with coral wounds, you should wash the affected area with soap and fresh water, then apply a triple-antibiotic salve. Spotted scorpionfish, found on rocky or coral bottoms, are well camouflaged so it's easy to step on them. Although the Caribbean species is non-lethal, their bite can be quite painful. Another cleverly camouflaged denizen of the deep, the stingray will whip its tail if stepped on, driving its serrated venomous spine into the offender. If this happens, see a doctor. Bristle worms, fuzzy creatures with painful-when-touched defense mechanisms, have glass-like bristles that may break off in the skin. Apply tape to the skin and attempt to pull the bristles out; reduce the pain with rubbing alcohol. Moray eels, which have a tendency to bite whatever is thrust at them, have a tight grip and can be extremely difficult to dislodge. Always exercise caution before reaching into a crevice!

The Coral Reef Ecosystem

One of the least appreciated of the world's innumerable wonders is the coral reef. This is in part because little was known about it until recent decades. In many ways the reefs go beyond the limits of any wild fantasy conjured up by a science fiction novel. This is a delicate environment – the only geological feature fashioned by living creatures. Many of the world's reefs – which took millions of years to form – have already suffered damage from human contact. One of the most devilish of these is coral bleaching, thought to have come from either global warming or a thinning ozone level. The condition results from a dying off of the symbiotic algae that provides coral with its coloration.

Corals produce the calcium carbonate (limestone) responsible for the buildup of the island's offlying cays and islets as well as most of the sand on the beaches. Bearing the brunt of waves, they also conserve the shoreline. Although reefs began forming millenia ago, they are in a constant state of flux. Seemingly solid, they actually depend upon a delicate ecological balance to survive. Deforestation, dredging, temperature change, an increase or decrease in salinity, silt, or sewage discharge may kill them. Because temperature ranges must remain between 68° and 95°F, they are only found in the tropics and – because they require light to grow – only in shallow water. They are also intolerant of fresh water, and reefs do not form where rivers empty into the sea.

THE CORAL POLYP: Corals are actually animals, but botanists view them as being mostly plant life, while geologists dub them "honorary" rocks. Acting more like plants than animals, corals survive through photosynthesis: the algae inside the coral polyps do the work while the polyps themselves secrete calcium carbonate and stick together for protection from waves and boring sponges. A polyp, bearing a close structural resemblance to its relative the anemone, feeds at night by using the ring or rings of tentacles surrounding its mouth to capture prey (such as plankton) with nematocysts, small stinging darts.

The coral polyps appear able to survive in such packed surroundings through their symbiotic relationship with the algae present in their tissues: Coral polyps exhale carbon dioxide and the algae consume it, producing needed oxygen. Although only half of the world's coral species have such a symbiotic relationship with these single-celled captive species of dinoflagellates (*Gymnodinium microdriaticum*), these species – termed hermatypic corals – are the ones that build the reef. The nutritional benefits gained from their relationship with the algae enable them to grow a larger skeleton and to do so more rapidly than would otherwise be possible. Polyps have the ability to regulate the density of these cells in their tissues and can expel some of them in a spew of mucus should they multiply too quickly. Looking at coral, the brownish colored algal cells show through transparent tissues. When you see a coral garden through your mask, you are actually viewing a field of captive single-celled algae.

A vital but invisible component of the reef ecosystem is bacteria, microorganisms that decompose and recycle all matter, producing food for everything from worms to coral polyps. Inhabitants of the reef range from crabs to barnacles to sea squirts to multicolored tropical fish. Remarkably, the polyps themselves are consumed by only a small percentage of the reef's inhabitants. They often contain high levels of toxic substances and are also thought to sting fish and other animals that attempt to consume them. Corals retract their polyps during daylight hours when the fish can see them. Reefs originate as the polyps develop. The calcium secretions form a base as they grow; a single polyp can have a 1,000-year lifespan.

CORAL TYPES: Corals may be divided into three groups. The **hard** or **stony corals** (such as staghorn, brain, star, or rose) secrete a limey skeleton. The **horny corals** (for example sea plumes, sea whips, sea fans, and gorgonians) have a supporting skeleton-like structure known as a gorgonin (after the head of Medusa). The shapes of these corals result from the different ways in which the polyps and their connecting tissues excrete calcium carbonate. There are over a thousand different patterns – one specific to each species. Each also has its own method of budding. Found in the Caribbean, giant **elkhorn corals** may contain over a million polyps and live for several hundred years or longer. Then there are the **soft corals**. While these too are colonies of polyps, their skeletons are made of soft organic material, and their polyps always have eight tentacles instead of the six or multiples of six found in the stony corals. Unlike the hard corals, soft corals disintegrate after death and do not add to the reef's stony structure. Instead of depositing limestone crystals, they excrete a jelly-like matrix imbued with spicules (diminutive spikes) of stony material; this jelly-like substance gives these corals their flexibility. Sea fans and sea whips exhibit similar patterns. The precious black coral, prized by jewelers because its branches can be cleaned and polished to high gloss ebony-black, resembles bushes of fine gray-black twigs in its natural state.

COMPETITION: To the snorkeler, the reef appears to be a peaceful haven. The reality is that the fiercest competition has developed here. Although the corals appear static to the onlooker, they are continually competing with each other for space. Some have developed sweeper tentacles with an especially high concentration of stinging cells. Reaching out to a competing coral, they sting and execute it. Other species dispatch digestive filaments that eat the prey. Soft corals appear to leach out toxic chemicals called terpines that kill nearby organisms. Because predation is so prevalent, two-thirds of reef species are toxic. Others hide in stony outcrops or have formed protective relationships with other organisms – as in the classic case of the banded clown fish that live among sea anemones, protected by their stingers. The cleaner fish protect themselves from larger fish by setting up stations at which they pick parasites off their carnivorous customers. Mimicking the coloration and shape of the feeder fish, the sabre-toothed blenny is a false cleaner fish that takes a chunk out of the larger fish and scoots off!

CORAL LOVE AFFAIRS: Not prone to celibacy or sexual prudery, coral polyps reproduce sexually and asexually through budding; a polyp joins together with thousands or even millions of its neighbors to form a coral. (In a few cases, only one polyp forms a single coral). During sexual reproduction polyps release millions of their spermatozoa into the water. Many species are dimorphic, with both male and female varieties. Some practice internal, others external fertilization. Still others have both male and female polyps. As larvae develop, their "mother" expels them and they float off to found a new coral colony.

UNDERWATER FLORA: Most of the plants you see underwater are algae, primitive plants that can survive only underwater because they do not have the mechanisms to prevent themselves from drying out. Lacking roots, algae draw their minerals and water directly from the sea. Calcareous red algae are very important for reef formation. Resembling rounded stones, they are 95% rock and only 5% living tissue. Sea grasses are land plants returned to live in the sea. They are found in relatively shallow water in sandy and muddy bays and flats; they have roots and small flowers. One species, dubbed "turtle grass," provides food for turtles. In addition, seagrasses help to stabilize the sea floor, maintain water clarity by trapping fine sediments from upland soil erosion, stave off beach erosion, and provide living space for numerous fish, crustaceans, and shellfish.

PUERTO RICAN REEFS: Most common are fringing reefs, which occur close to shore, perhaps separated by a small lagoon. Elongated and narrow bank or ribbon reefs are offshore in deep water. Atolls and barrier reefs are absent. Fringing reefs exist at Seven Seas Beach in Las Croabas, Fajardo and along several other offshore cays in the NE corner of the island; at Guayama and Salinas; near Caja de Muertos Island off the coast from Ponce; at La Parguera; and off the coast of Mona Island. Bank reefs exist near Culebra and Vieques.

EXPLORING REEFS

Coral reefs are extremely fragile environments. Much damage has been done to reefs worldwide through the carelessness of humans. Despite their size, reefs grow very slowly, and it can take decades or even hundreds of years to repair the effects of a few moments. Do nothing to provoke moray eels; they may retaliate when threatened. Watch out for fire corals, recognizable by the white tips on their branches. They can inflict stings. In general, look but don't touch.

History

Through the 19th Century

PRE-EUROPEAN HABITATION: Believed to have arrived 5,000-20,000 years ago on rafts from Florida via Cuba, the Arcaicos or Archaics – food gatherers and fishermen – were the first settlers. Little evidence of their habitation survives. The Igneri, a sub-group of Northern South America's Arawaks, are thought to have reached the island as early as 200 B.C. They were agriculturists who brought tobacco and corn with them. Last to appear and most culturally advanced, the Taínos arrived from the S between AD 1,000 and 1,500. These copper-skinned, dark-haired people were expert carvers (in shell, gold, stone, wood, and clay) and skilled agriculturalists, cultivating cassava, corn, beans, and squash. They gave the island the name of Borinquen, "Land of the Noble Lord," after the creator Yukiyu who was believed to reside in the heart of the present-day Caribbean National Forest.

EUROPEAN DISCOVERY: During his second voyage in 1493, Columbus stopped off at the island of Santa Maria de Guadalupe.

Here, he met 12 Taíno women and two young boys who said that they wished to return to their home on the island of Boriquen (Puerto Rico). Columbus took the Native Americans along with him as guides. On Nov. 19, the Native Americans, spying their home island, leapt into the water and swam ashore. Columbus named the island San Juan Bautista ("Saint John the Baptist") after the Spanish Prince Don Juan. The island was colonized under the leadership of Juan Ponce de León in 1508, and he was appointed governor in 1509. Soon, Franciscan friars arrived with cattle and horses; a gold smelter was set up and production begun.

On Nov. 8, 1511, this first settlement was renamed Puerto Rico ("Rich Port") and a coat of arms was granted. King Ferdinand distributed the island's land and the 30,000 Taínos among the soldiers. Under the system of *repartimiento* ("distribution"), Native Americans were set to work in construction and in the mines or fields. Under a similar system, termed *encomienda* ("commandery"), they were forcibly extracted from villages and set to labor for a *patrón* on his estate. Although, in return, the Native Americans were supposed to receive protection and learn about the wonders of Catholicism, this system was a thinly disguised form of slavery. Ultimately, it led to the extinction of the native inhabitants as a distinct racial and cultural group. The Native Americans tragically assumed that these newcomers, owing to their remarkable appearance and superior technology, were immortal. A chieftain decided to put this theory to the test, and a young Spaniard, Diego Salcedo, was experimentally drowned while being carried across the Río Grande de Añasco in the NW part of the island. When he did not revive after three days, the Taínos realized their mistake, at which point they killed nearly half the Spaniards on the island. The revolt was put down, however, and many Taínos fled to the mountains or neighboring islands. Most were freed by royal decrees in 1521, but it was too late: they'd already been absorbed into the racial fabric.

With the depletion of both Taínos and gold, a new profit-making scheme had to be found. That proved to be the new "gold" of the Caribbean: sugar. The first sugar mill was built in 1523 near Añasco, and the entire economy changed from mining to sugar over the next few decades. The first Portuguese slavers, filled to the brim with captive Africans intended to provide agricultural labor, arrived in 1518.

The city of Puerto Rico was moved to the site of present-day San Juan, which name it took, and the entire island in turn was renamed Puerto Rico. Puerto Rico became one of Spain's strategic outposts in the Caribbean. Ignoring the economic potential of the island,

History

hard-nosed military commanders appointed by Madrid treated the island as if it were one huge military installation. An attack by Sir Francis Drake's fleet in 1595 was repelled, but the English Count of Cumberland launched a successful invasion in 1598. Harsh weather conditions, coupled with the effects of dysentery, caused him and his troops to exit shortly thereafter. The Dutch besieged San Juan in 1625; defeated, they did succeed in torching a great deal of the city. With the island forbidden to trade except within the Spanish Empire, a brisk inter-island business in contraband goods (ginger, tobacco, and cattle hides) developed during the mid-16th century. In April 1797, the British, under the command of Abercrombie, led an unsuccessful attack against San Juan.

THE NINETEENTH CENTURY: The Puerto Rican political scene was divided into loyalists, liberals, and separatists. In March 1812 a new constitution, more liberal than the previous one, was approved and Puerto Ricans became Spanish citizens. With the arrival of Canary Islanders, Haitians, Louisiana French, Venezuelans, and black slaves, Puerto Rico became a lively potpourri of cultures. As the population exploded, a new nationalism – a distinct sense of being Puerto Rican – began to emerge. From 1825 to 1867 the island was governed by a series of ruthless, despotic military commanders known as the "Little Caesars." During the 1850s, Ramón Emeterio Betances became the leader of the separatist movement and founded the Puerto Rican Revolutionary Movement in Santo Domingo. At midnight on Sept. 23, 1868, several hundred rebels marched into and took over the town of Lares.

Hearing news of the revolt, the government placed reinforcements at nearby San Sebastian, and the rebels took to the hills. A guerilla war ensued and lasted a month. This was the famous *Grito de Lares* ("The Cry of Lares"). Even though this first (and only) attempt at rebellion failed, it is cited by *independentistas* as a major event in Puerto Rican history. In 1869, Puerto Rico sent its first representatives to the Cortes, the Spanish House of Representatives.

A law abolishing slavery became effective on March 22, 1873, though "freed" slaves had to continue toiling for their masters for another three years as indentured laborers; full civil rights were granted five years later. Led by Luis Muñoz Rivera, the Autonomous Party was formed in 1882. On Nov. 28, 1897, Prime Minister Sagasta signed a royal decree establishing "autonomy" for Puerto Rico, though on paper only. A side effect of the pressure by the US on Spain to grant autonomy to Cuba and prevent a war, the charter actually made few fundamental changes in the island's status. Included in the package was voting representation in the two houses of the Spanish Cortes (legislature). However, it allowed the King of Spain to appoint the island's governor, who in turn was authorized to suspend any constitutional guarantees, to control the legislature's output (and even suspend it if necessary), and to appoint seven of the 12 members of the Legislative Council (the Senate). The charter was never actually ratified by the Spanish parliament.

The 20th Century

AMERICAN ANNEXATION: In the furor (spurred on by American newspaper barons Hearst and Pulitzer) over the explosion of the battleship *Maine* on February 15, 1898, President McKinley declared war with Spain. In July, just as the new government had begun to function, Gen. Nelson A. Miles landed on the island at Guánica with 16,000 US troops. The Puerto Rican campaign of the Spanish-American War lasted only 17 days and was described by one journalist as a "picnic." On Dec. 10 , 1898, under the Treaty of Paris accords signed by the United States and Spain, Puerto Rico was ceded to the US. With no consultation whatsoever, the Puerto Ricans overnight found themselves under American rule after nearly 400 years of Spanish occupation. Intellectuals on the island had high expectations from the US government; after all, Gen. Miles had promised "to give the people of your beautiful island the largest measure of liberty (and) to bestow upon you... the liberal institutions of our government." Naturally, this meant attempting to make the Puerto Ricans as "American" as possible, up to and including changing the name to "Porto" Rico – in order to make it easy to spell! Hopes for independence were dashed, however, as two years of military rule were followed by the Foraker Act. In effect from 1900 to 1916, the act placed Puerto Rico in an uncertain purgatory with the government a mix of autocracy and democracy. Americanization continued by importing teachers who taught classes entirely in English – an unsuccessful tactic. Requests by island leaders for a plebiscite to determine the island's status were ignored. In 1909, enraged by the provisions of the Foraker Act, the Puerto Rican House of Delegates refused to pass any legislation at all. This protest brought no change in status and, by the beginning of WW I, there was widespread talk of independence.

CITIZENSHIP: To secure the island as a strategic defense bastion and assure a ready supply of "raw materials" for the slaughter mills of Europe, Puerto Ricans were granted American citizenship by the Jones-Shafroth Act. Under this bill, which President Woodrow Wilson signed into law on March 2, 1917, Puerto Ricans automatically became US citizens unless they signed a statement rejecting it. If they refused, they stood to lose a number of civil rights, including the right to hold office, and would then be designated aliens. Naturally, only a few refused. Another request two years later for a plebiscite also failed. In 1922, local politician Antonio Barceló tried a new approach: he proposed an association that would be modeled after the Irish Free State. The bill died in committee. The same year marked the formation of the Nationalist Party.

THE 1930s DEPRESSION: High unemployment, political anarchy, and near starvation reigned as the Depression years of the 1930s hit Puerto Rico even harder than the mainland. Pedro Albizu Campos, a Harvard Law School graduate and former US Army officer, emerged as head of the new Nationalist Party. After members of the party turned to violence, followed in turn by police brutality and oppression, Campos and seven of his followers found themselves in jail in Atlanta, Georgia. On March 21, 1936, after a permit to hold a Palm Sunday parade was revoked by the government at the last moment, Nationalists went ahead with it anyway. As *La Bourinquena* played in the background, police opened fire on protestors, innocent bystanders, and fellow policemen. This event, known as *La Masacre de Ponce*, resulted in the deaths of 20 and the wounding of 100 persons.

THE STERILIZATION CAMPAIGN: A little-known episode in Puerto Rican history is the sterilization campaign launched by the government. A 1937 law legalized contraception and sterilization (under the direction of a eugenics board). A mover and shaker behind the program was physician Clarence Gamble, a leader in the stateside eugenics movement and an heir to the Proctor and Gamble fortune. An active campaign was launched during the mid-1940s as health department workers touted the benefits of *la operación* in rural areas. The operation (including its irreversibility) was often ill explained, and consent was obtained from women in labor or just after childbirth. A 1947 survey disclosed that more than 25% of the sterilized women regretted their decision. Catholics and *independentistas* teamed up in the 1950s to fight the campaign; the government, in turn, denied the existence of any organized effort to sterilize women. The sterilization law was repealed in 1960. However, some 35% of Puerto Rican women of child bearing age had been sterilized by 1965; some two-thirds of this number were in their 20s. In 1989, more than 40% of the women between 15-49 had had their tubes tied.

LUIZ MUÑOZ MARIN: Luiz Muñoz Marin, son of Luis Muñoz Rivera, and his Popular Democratic Party (PDP) came to power in 1940 with a 37% plurality. Perhaps the dominant figure in all of Puerto Rican history, Muñoz presided over the governmental, economic, and educational transformation of the island. He served for eight years as Senate majority leader before becoming the island's first elected governor in 1948. After his election, he changed from being pro-independence to pro-commonwealth. On Oct. 30, 1950, there were *independentista* uprisings on the island. That same week, *independentistas* opened fire outside Blair House, President Truman's temporary abode in Washington, D.C. Resistance leader Pedro Albizu-Campos was charged with inciting armed insurrection and imprisoned.

COMMONWEALTH STATUS: On June 4, 1951, Puerto Ricans approved a referendum granting commonwealth status to the island. As the only alternative was continued colonial status, many Puerto Ricans failed to show up at the ballot box. In a second referendum the new constitution was approved, and commonwealth status (*Estado Libre Asociado* or "free associated state") was inaugurated on July 25, 1952. While the new status superficially resembled that of a state of the Union, Puerto Ricans still paid no income tax and were forbidden to vote in national elections or elect voting representatives to Congress. In 1954, two Puerto Ricans (New York City residents) wounded five Congressmen when they opened fire in the House of Representatives in Washington. In 1964, Muñoz stepped down, and Roberto Sánchez Vilella became the island's second elected governor.

A plebiscite sponsored by the *Populares* was held on July 23, 1967, although the statehooder Luis A. Ferré and *Independentista* Hector Alvarez Silver bolted to form their own parties. The buoyant economy, coupled with strong support for commonwealth status by the ever-influential Muñoz, caused a record turnout (with 65.9% of the eligible voters participating) in which 60% of the voters supported commonwealth status, 39% were for statehood, and .06% favored independence. This plebiscite's results were tainted by US government interference – documented in a report during the Carter administration. In 1968, Luis A. Ferré, head of the newly created New Progressive Party (NPP), was elected governor, and he began to push actively for statehood.

On Sept. 26, 1969, when an *independentista* was jailed for one year for draft evasion, college students set fire to the ROTC building at Río Piedras. In the aftermath, seven students were suspended and marches and counter-marches degenerated into riots.

CERRO MARAVILLA: Carlos Romero Barceló of the New Progressive Party won the governorship over the Popular Democratic Party's Hernandez Colón by 43,000 votes in 1976 and by a 3,000-vote margin in 1980. After the polls closed in 1980, Commandant Enrique Sanchez, security chief in charge of polling and a Romero henchman, refused for hours to turn over the ballots to the counting authorities. What happened to the ballots in that time remains a mystery. On July 25, 1978 security forces shot and killed two *independentistas* atop Cerro Maravilla, Puerto Rico's highest peak, which is topped with communications towers. Apparently, two youths, Arnaldo Dario Posado and Carlos Soto Arrivi, were lured by undercover agent Gonzalez Malaveto to the mountaintop to plant explosives. It is believed that the youths, one mentally disturbed and the other a teenager, were enticed there and then shot in order to discredit the independence movement. Though no one will ever know the exact truth because there has been such an extensive cover up, the official government story has been thoroughly discredited. In addition, seven former police officers involved in the case have since been sentenced to 20-30 years each on charges of perjury and obstructing justice. Three officers remain to be tried for first-degree murder for their involvement in the slayings.

The FBI has admitted attempting to cover up the incident, and it is believed that the agency may have been in on the operation all along. Disclosure of possible involvement by members of his administration or by Romero himself in the entrapment at Cerro Maravilla was a major contributing factor in his 1984 defeat to the PDP's Rafael Hernandez Colón. The first primary gubernatorial contests held in the island's history were in June 1988 between San Juan Mayor Balthasar Corrada del Río and Romero Barceló. Corrada won but went on to lose the November 1988 election to Hernandez Colón. In 1990, Hernandez proposed selling the government-owned telephone company and using the proceeds (after paying off its $1 billion in debt) to create two "perpetual funds" of $1 billion each. One would have been used to improve public services (such as sewage and drinking water) and the other would have been earmarked for secondary education. Approval of the proposal would have required passage of a constitutional amendment. The sale never materialized. The offer was withdrawn in

1991 because there were no buyers at the price of $3 billion, which amounted to $3,000 a line! Early in 1992, a knife-wielding man attacked Gov. Hernandez at a Dorado hotel; he was not harmed.

THE 1992 ELECTIONS: In November Dr. Pedro Rosselló and the NPP won the elections by securing 49.9% of the vote in a three-way contest. The 47-year-old pediatrician faced the PDP's Senator Victoria "Melo" Muñoz, the daughter of former Gov. Luis Muñoz Marin and Fernando Martín, who was the Puerto Rican Independence Party's (PIP) candidate. While Martín garnered just 79,000 votes (4.2%), Muñoz gained 45% of the vote. Former governor Carlos Romero Barceló was elected Resident Commissioner.

THE ROSSELLO ADMINISTRATION: By the end of his first month in office, Rosselló had already signed into law a measure restoring English as an official language along with Spanish. This came despite a 100,000-strong rally held in Old San Juan protesting the measure. This repealed an earlier PDP statute that made Spanish the only official language. He also removed "Commonwealth of Puerto Rico" from the government stationery masthead and substituted "Government of Puerto Rico," following an NPP tradition. In 1993, he moved towards a controversial "community-school" concept which met strong protest from teachers who saw in it a move towards privatizing the educational system.

In 1993, a distressing new chapter was added to Puerto Rican history when National Guard troops began occupying public housing projects in Bayamón, Río Piedras, Hato Rey, Arecibo, Cayey, Humacao, Ponce, Mayagüez, and other municipalities where drugs were actively sold at *puntos* (drug distribution points). After taking over the project, the guardsmen handed out pens, pencils, erasers, and other school equipment bearing the Guard's logo as well as the slogan "Say No To Drugs." Around 20 projects had been occupied by the end of Aug., and the government planned to occupy 10% of the island's 332 housing projects by the end of the year. Fences and access controls with bulletproof guardhouses have been constructed. As the guards withdraw, a permanent police presence will be maintained.

This policy, known as *mano dura* (hard hand) has come under sharp attack. Critics decry the militarization of the island as an unfortunate precedent and point out that the island-wide homicide rate has not decreased and that the dealers have been dispersed rather than stopped. While many housing project residents say they feel more secure, others worry about the future. There is a plan to erect a wall around Lloréns Torres (a housing project completely occupied by the national guard and police in a March 1996 raid). This would effectively turn the project into a prison camp, and residents say they will tear down any such wall (proposed as an "ornamental fence"). One final criticism is that the people at the top of the drug pyramid, who apparently pose as respectable members of the Commonwealth's business community, are never apprehended; in a sense, the invasion of the housing projects is a war against the poor.

Another disturbing tendency was instituted that same year – controlled access to private urbanizations in which only those who lived there or had a valid reason for visiting were permitted entry. Residents collectively paid for the guards, although the Commonwealth Supreme Court ruled that residents opposing controlled access did not need to pay the monthly fees for the system.

Rosselló signed a controversial voucher initative into law in Sept. 1993. It provides $1,500 in credits that would allow students to transfer to private schools with subsidies from the government. These funds may be used for books, uniforms, tuition, and/or tutoring. The Puerto Rican Teachers Association has filed a lawsuit in which they allege that the voucher program breaches the constitutional separation of church and state. Budgeted at $10 million, the program has now expanded islandwide. Public schools are credited with the funds directly, and private schools bill the government. Credits are available only to families making $18,000 per year, a figure selected because it matches teachers' base salaries. Families must fund all expenses above the $1,500 threshold.

THE SCHOOL VOUCHER CONTROVERSY

Puerto Rico introduced a $10 million educational scholarship and voucher program in 1993. In order to qualify, families must have an annual income of below $18,000. Each child may receive a $1,500 voucher which may be used to transfer between public schools, from public to private schools, and from private to public school. The voucher may also be used by gifted teenagers in high school who wish to take college courses. Although some 15,000 students are participating in the program, the San Juan Supreme Court has ruled that part of the program is unconstitutional because voucher use means that public funds are paid directly to private educational institutions. The $18,000 limit on income was set because it is the average teacher's salary. The voucher program remains in place while the case is under appeal.

IMPORTANT DATES IN PUERTO RICAN HISTORY

1493: 19 Nov., Columbus "discovers" the island of Puerto Rico on his second voyage, naming it San Juan Bautista.

1508: Juan Ponce de León is appointed governor and founds Caparra, the first settlement.

1509: Government seat is moved and named Ciudad de Puerto Rico.

1521: The capital is renamed San Juan while the entire island takes the name Puerto Rico.

1530: Having exhausted the gold supply, many colonists migrate to Peru in search of new plunder, while those remaining become farmers.

1595: Sir Francis Drake unsuccessfully attacks San Juan.

1598: The Count of Cumberland captures San Juan, holds it for seven months.

1625: 24 Sept., attack by a Dutch fleet is repelled but not before its troops sack the city.

1631: Construction begins on El Morro.

1680: Ponce is founded.

1760: Mayagüez is founded.

1775: Population reaches 70,000, including 6,467 slaves.

1778: Private ownership of land is granted by the Crown.

1790: British attack and pull out after a one-month siege.

1800: Island population estimated at 155,406.

1821: First of a series of 19th-century slave rebellions takes place in Bayamón.

1822-37: Tyrannical rule of Governor Miguel de la Torre, Spanish Commander defeated by Bolivar in Venezuela in 1821.

1833: Blacks forbidden to serve in the military.

1859: Patriot and leader Luis Muñoz Rivera born.

1860: Population reaches 583,308.

1868: The *Grito de Lares* revolt occurs.

1873: Abolition of slavery.

1891: *Independentista* leader Pedro Albizu Campos is born.

1897: 25 Nov., autonomy granted by Spain.

1898: 25 July, American troops land at Guánica and establish control.

1899: 11 Apr., Spain cedes Puerto Rico to the US under the Treaty of Paris.

1900: Under the Foraker Act, Puerto Rico becomes a US territory; an American-led civil administration replaces the millitary.

1917: 2 Mar., the Jones Act makes Puerto Ricans US citizens.

1937: 12 Mar., the "Ponce Massacre" occurs when police fire on an *Independentista* parade, killing 19 and injuring 100.

1938: Attempted assassination of Gov. Winship.

1942: Tugwell, last US governor, appointed.

1950: Public Law 600 permits Puerto Rico to draft constitution. *Independentistas* attack La Fortaleza; riots result. Attempted assassination of Truman on Nov. 1, wounding five Congressmen. Campos and others jailed.

1965: Abolishment of literacy test under the Civil Rights Act.

1967: Commonwealth status wins approval by 60.5% in a referendum.

1972: Roberto Clemente, Pittsburgh Pirate and island hero, dies in a plane crash while on an earthquake relief mission to Managua, Nicaragua.

1973: Bishop of San Juan, Luis Aponte Martinez, appointed Cardinal by Pope Paul VI.

1989: Hurricane Hugo hits the island and causes extensive damage.

1993: Support for "enhanced" Commonwealth status upheld in a plebiscite.

THE 1993 PLEBISCITE: In 1993 Puerto Ricans were given a chance to choose among three options: enhanced commonwealth backed by the PDP, statehood backed by the New Progressive Party, or independence backed by the Puerto Rican Independence Party. Each was identified by a simple geometrical symbol: a rectangle represented commonwealth, a circle stood for statehood, and a triangle represented independence. While Reagan and Bush appeared in TV commercials extolling the statehood option, commonwealth forces warned that the island would lose its language, culture, 936 benefits, and – most distressingly – its Olympic team. One strong opponent of statehood was political right-wing pundit Pat Buchanan. Statehood advocates argued that entry into the US would decrease unemployment, thin the bloated bureaucracy (22% of total employment), and substitute two senators and six congressmen in place of the current non-voting Congressional representative. The estimated 100,000 pro-independence voters were divided between the more radical faction favoring abstention and the rest who advocated participation. Congressional polls conducted in 1991 by the firm Analysis Inc. indicated that statehood lacked sufficient votes for passage. The enhanced commonwealth forces won the plebiscite by a margin of 48.4% to statehood's 46.2%. After the Commonwealth "victory," the New Progressive Party announced that it would not provide public funds to the Popular Democratic Party to lobby Congress for changes in the Commonwealth status. While the government claimed that providing such funds would be unconstitutional, House Minority Leader José Enrique Arrarás alleged that Gov. Rosselló is "drunk with power" and that his "attitude is a cheap one that evokes the pampered child who, when he's not allowed to play, threatens to take away the bat and ball."

On the ballot, the PDP had promised to immediately propose to Congress the reformulation of Section 936 (see "Economy") to ensure the creation of more and superior jobs; protection for island agricultural products other than coffee (which is already protected); and extending Supplementary Security Income (SSI) to Puerto Rico and obtaining Nutritional Assistance Program funding equal to that received by the states. So far these proposals have not been submitted to Congress, probably because the Republican-controlled body would be unreceptive to these changes. Full food stamp funding along with SSI would cost an additional $1.5 billion annually.

The plebiscite has been followed by three years of stalling. In 1996 opportunistic Alaskan Republican Congressman Don Young introduced a bill promising to call for a plebiscite in 1998 which would force Puerto Ricans to choose between statehood or independence. After an outcry, it was decided to add commonwealth to the plebiscite, rendering it a rehash of the 1993 vote! The bill's outcome remains uncertain at present.

THE OIL SPILL: On Jan. 7, 1994, the oil tank barge *Morris J. Berman* ran aground 16 miles from shore. While it was being towed a line broke (for the second time that morning) and the boat sank and settled on a reef. It spilled more than 26,000 of its 35,000-barrel contents onto the beaches. The oil spill cleanup cost the government around $65 million, a figure representing two-thirds of the entire amount set aside by Congress for such spills.

1996 EVENTS: At hearings for the Young bill (see above) in San Juan, rallies were mobilized by both parties; *popularistas* (PDP members) outnumbered NPP members by two-to-one. At a conference in 1996 in San Juan, Drug Enforcement Agency Chief Tom Constantine announced that he believes over 1,000 drug-trafficking and money-laundering groups operate in Puerto Rico and import 84 tons of cocaine valued at more than $20 billion. Of this, 20% remains for sale on the island. According to Constantine, heroin is also now being smuggled through the island and 64% of all violent crimes on the island in 1995 have been linked to drug trafficking. He maintained that Puerto Rico is becoming a "bloody playground" and that the Columbia drug cartels make the American mafia families look like schoolchildren in comparison.

In a speech to the conference, *San Juan Star* reporter Manny Suárez pointed out that, while 10-20% of all shipments are interdicted, the profits are so enormous that "all a major importer has to do is to land about 5 to 10%of the shipments to have a money-making operation.... Interdiction is a failure.... (Great Britain) treat(s) addicts like sick people and we throw them in jail. Perhaps we should look at the British model to see what we could learn from it."

Government

There is possibly no other island of its size where politics is as hot an issue as it is in Puerto Rico. In spite of the fact that elections determine nothing save who will deliver what slice of the political patronage, Puerto Ricans eat, drink, sleep, and breathe politics. Some even consider politics to be Puerto Rico's national sport. In addition, Puerto Rico has one of the most curious political systems in the world. Although it's a colony of the US, the island has commonwealth rather than colonial status. Puerto Ricans have both US citizenship and freedom of travel to and from the States. Puerto Ricans may be drafted, yet they may not vote in US elections. Undoubtedly, the ambivalence of Puerto Rico's status is unequaled anywhere in the world.

Administrative Organization

The Puerto Rican government is divided into executive, legislative, and judicial branches just as on the mainland. Governors are elected for a four-year term. The executive branch is extremely powerful and governors appoint more than 500 executive and judicial branch officials. The bicameral legislature consists of a 27-member *Senado* (Senate) and a 51-member *Camara de Representantes* (House of Representatives). In order to prevent one party from dominating the legislature, both houses may be increased by additional minority party members when any one party gains more than two-thirds of the seats in an election. In this situation, the number of seats may be increased up to a maximum of nine in the *Senado* and 17 in the *Camara*. These "at large" seats are apportioned among party members according to the electoral strength of each minority party. Spanish is the language used in both houses, as well as throughout the courts. Puerto Rico's Supreme Court heads the unified judicial system. Contested decisions made by the Court may be reviewed by the US Supreme Court. Puerto Rico is also part of the Federal District Court System. Instead of being divided into counties, Puerto Rico is sectioned into 78 municipalities, many of them mere villages. Each has a mayor and municipal assembly elected every four years. Technically a congressman, Puerto Rico's nonvoting Resident Commissioner sits in the US House of Representatives in Washington, D.C. Unlike other congressmen, he is elected only once every four years and represents a constituency seven times as large as the average.

The Question Of Status

The single most important and hotly debated issue in Puerto Rico centers on the issue of political status. There are three distinct possibilities for Puerto Rico's future status. One would be the continuation of the present commonwealth status in its current or modified form. The second is statehood. The third and least likely would be independence.

Modification of the commonwealth status would involve granting more autonomy to the island government while retaining ties with the US. Autonomy would be granted over trade tariffs, immigration, the minimum wage, and federal grants, and would be coupled with exemption from ICC and FCC regulations. Elevation to statehood, on the other hand, would require a severe economic transition. Chase Manhattan and Citibank, which provide most of the island's financing, would find themselves in violation of interstate banking regulations and would have to close their operations there. Income tax, now paid only to the local government, would have to be turned over to the federal government. Statehood would also mean forfeiture of tax-exempt status for Puerto Rico's industries.

Support for statehood is growing, not because the islanders have an explicit wish to enter the American mainstream, but because the politicians are selling the story that it will bring increased revenues and more money. The coconut palm is the symbol of the New Progressive Party, and its leaders assure followers that *los cocos* (dollars) will rain down on them after statehood is achieved. However, there is little incentive for the US Congress to grant Puerto Rico statehood status. Statehood is controversial not only because most Puerto Ricans cannot speak English fluently, but also because Puerto Rico's large population and high birth rate would give it more congressional representatives than 20 other states.

Independence, the third and least likely alternative, is supported by a small but vocal minority. There has long been serious talk of independence in Puerto Rico, but as things stand now popular support is lacking. One reason is that Puerto Ricans fear the political and economic chaos that independence might bring. The independence movement in Puerto Rico has a long tradition of using terrorist tactics, which has resulted in official government repression. Attacks include the Nov. 1979 ambush of a US Army bus on the island in which two were killed and three wounded. The island is of such strategic military importance and is so economically tied to the US that a meaningful change in status is unlikely under the prevailing political and economic conditions.

Political Parties

If Puerto Rico's political status seems confusing, so are the vast number and varied politics of its many *partidos* (parties), some of which hardly engender enough support to be worthy of the name. There is no dominant party in Puerto Rican politics; instead, there are a number of factions, none of which ever receives majority support. The two major political parties are the *Partido Popular Democratico* (Popular Democratic Party or PPD), headed by Governor Rafael Hernandez Colón, and the *Partido* Progresivo Nuevo (New Progressive Party or PPN), led by Carlos Romero Barceló. Each has half a million hard-core supporters, out of a total two million registered voters. The Popular Democratic Party supports continued maintenance of commonwealth status provided it is revised to allow more autonomy. The PPN's Carlos Romero Barceló, nicknamed *El Caballo* ("the horse") by his detractors because he is allegedly stubborn, ruthless, and macho, served as governor from 1976-84. His party supports statehood for the island, but because Americanization is seen as a prerequisite, he and his party, whose members are dubbed *"estadistas"* ("statehooders") are frequently regarded as enemies of Puerto Rican culture. Current Governor Dr. Pedro Rosselló is also a PPN *estadista*.

Former San Juan Mayor Hernan Padilla's Puerto Rican Renewal Party is a PPN splinter party with 300,000 supporters. There are also two independence parties; the larger is the socialistic Puerto Rican Independence Party, formed in 1946 and led by Rubén Berríos-Martinez. The other is the Puerto Rican Socialist Party, which was established in 1971 as an outgrowth of the Pro Independence Movement that was founded in 1946. Led by Juan Mari Bras, the Pro Independence Movement advocated independence by any means. It was superseded in Oct. 1993 by the New Independence Movement (NIM), headed by Rev. Eunice R. Santana. It advocated a boycott of the 1993 plebiscite and differs from the former organization in that it avoids Marxist-Leninist affiliation. It recognizes the importance of struggle by labor unions, feminists, environmentalists, and others to tranform the conditions of life for these groups. Bubbling below the surface are the *Fuerzas Armadas de Liberación Nacional* (FALN) and the *Macheteros*. While the FALN terrorizes targets on the mainland, the *Macheteros* confine themselves to such island targets as the San Juan Power Station and Fort Buchanan. They claim responsibility for the Sept. 1983 robbery of the Wells Fargo terminal in West Hartford, Connecticut, which netted $7 million and is said to be the second largest heist in US history.

Economy

Background

Much is made of the economic "miracle" that is taking place in Puerto Rico. It's true that in 1992 Puerto Rico's GNP reached $23.62 billion; not only is this the Caribbean's highest, but it is billions above Cuba's, even though that country has a much larger area and three times the population. Per capita gross product (personal income) for 1992 was $6,626 and average family income was $22,896 – the highest in the Caribbean after the US Virgin Islands but only 47% of Mississippi's, the nation's poorest state. Yet, Puerto Rico's economy is troubled. Now economically interdependent with the US to the point of absurdity, the entire economic structure has undergone a thorough transformation since the US invasion in 1898. At that time Puerto Rico was a subsistence-level agricultural society largely dependent upon crops like sugar, coffee, and tobacco. While these are still of some importance to the economy, the overriding emphasis today is on manufacturing (which pays the highest wages: $10.48 ph on the average), with tourism coming second. Consumer debt among Puerto Ricans ranks high. In 1991, consumer debt (which excludes mortgages) comprised 47% of disposable income, a figure which compares unfavorably with the US (12%) and Japan (7%). In 1992, Puerto Ricans saved 1.22¢ for every dollar they earned; this compares with 4.6¢ in the US.

AMERICAN INVOLVEMENT: The history of the Puerto Rican economy is the story of the US economic presence in Latin America rendered in microcosm. After cession by Spain, the US financial barons deemed the Puerto Rican coffee crop, once the major generator of income, unprofitable. Devastated by the 1899 hurricane, coffee farmers were refused a loan by the Executive Council set up by the Americans to rule the island. As a consequence, the coffee economy was soon supplanted by sugar, and American companies were quick to establish themselves. By 1930, 60% of the banking and 80% of the tobacco industry were under the control of American interests, and by 1935, nearly 50% of all lands operated by sugar companies were under the control of four big American concerns. Although a law had limited farms to 500 acres, these giants had an average of 40,000 acres each under their control! This trend has continued to the point where the small cane farmer has virtually disappeared, replaced by the large sugar corporations like those of the Serralles family empire. The 1930's depression period hit Puerto Rico extremely hard and resulted in the decline of the sugar, needlework, and tobacco industries. At the end of WW II, fewer than 10% of Puerto Rico's workers held industrial jobs. In order to modernize the island and spur the sluggish economy, Fomento, the Economic Development Administration, was set up to attract industry. The island's 1950 hourly wage of 40¢ was more attractive to employers than the $1.50 average wage stateside. A high rate of unemployment reduced the prospects for potential strikes.

Recent Events

OPERATION BOOTSTRAP: By offering 10-30 year tax exemptions and low wages, this program has managed to lure 2,000 manufacturing plants to the island. Nearly 400 of these are operated by "Fortune 1,000" corporations. Needless to say, these companies are not here for altruistic reasons: they are here because, despite high power and shipping costs, tax incentives make the island a paradise for profitable investment. Under Section 936 of the IRS Code, American companies pay no federal taxes on profits earned in Puerto Rico. Although Congress acted in 1982 (and again in 1994) to slightly modify this section, US companies still earn billion-dollar profits (see more information in the box on the next page). The Treasury Department charges that the law has become a boondoggle, because it allows firms to reap huge profits while creating only a minimal amount of employment. Through a system known as "transfer pricing," corporations pay an inflated price for products purchased from their Puerto Rican subsidiary, thus reducing their US profits on paper and their taxable income along with it. The Treasury estimates that 50% of the tax-exempt income in Puerto Rico in 1980 was generated by this and other nefarious means such as transferring ownership of patents and trademarks to the island.

If Section 936 should ever be repealed, Puerto Rico Industrial Development Co. head Antonio Colorado estimates that 25-50% of all industrial firms will leave the island. In addition, the 21 companies planning to build "twin plants," which would link Puerto Rican plants with those in other Caribbean nations, have threatened to abandon their plans should the section be repealed.

Sadly, imaginative alternatives are lacking. The best scheme would be to transform 936 into a wage-based tax credit, which would in effect subsidize the hiring of workers in Puerto Rico. This would discourage corporations (such as pharmaceuticals) from setting up shop in Puerto Rico just to reap tax benefits, while rewarding companies that bring high-wage jobs here.

THE 936 CONTROVERSY

Section 936 has its origins in Operation Bootstrap, known on the island as "Manos a la Obra" ("Let's Get to Work"). The Industrial Incentives Act of 1947 exempted manufacturers establishing new facilities from payment of property and income taxes for a 10-year period. Although Section 931 of the US International Revenue Code had been legislated in 1921, it was not applied in Puerto Rico until 1948. It provided exemption from profits repatriated by a US based foreign company after the end of this 10-year period. Lobbying resulted in Section 931 being replaced by Section 936 as part of the Tax Reform Act of 1976. Whereas previously corporate profits repatriated before tax were subject to Federal taxes, Section 936 exempted corporations from taxes. However, it also required subsidiaries to reinvest retained earnings within the Commonwealth. Although 936 has been successful in promoting industrial development, it has also had its shortcomings.

One major defect is that corporations moving to Puerto Rico are capital-intensive rather than labor-intensive, which means that they provide few jobs for low-skilled workers. Many have charged that the results do not justify the enormous tax breaks reaped by corporations and the resulting loss in revenues to the US Treasury. Whatever the results may be to the island, 936 has been continually under assault for decades, and it appears that it will eventually be phased out. House Republicans, in particular, are calling for its revocation. Dr. Pedro Rosselló, the current governor, has opposed the continuance of 936, a stance which may cost him the 1996 election. Sadly, imaginative alternatives are lacking. The best scheme would be to transform 936 into a wage-based tax credit, which would in effect subsidize the hiring of workers in Puerto Rico. This would discourage corporations (such as pharmaceuticals) from setting up shop in Puerto Rico just to reap tax benefits while rewarding companies that bring high-wage jobs here.

At present, total hourly labor costs on the island in manufacturing are half as high as in the States as a whole. Puerto Rico was intended to serve as a model to show what the miracle drug of capitalist investment can do for an undeveloped economy under the right circumstances. In these terms, Operation Bootstrap must be seen as a failure. Although US investments in Puerto Rico are now the second largest in all of Latin America (after Venezuela), the economy is in bad shape. While the economy has kept expanding, employment has not. The explanation for this is very simple: capital intensive, rather than labor intensive, industries have been transplanted to Puerto Rico. For example, pharmaceutical companies do pay their workers more, but use relatively less labor. General Accounting Office figures disclose that in 1987 pharmaceutical firms gained more than $3 billion in Section 936 tax credits, a figure which translates to $70,000 per worker or $2.67 in government credits for each dollar dispensed in wages by the firms!

Although Operation Bootstrap brought an average GNP growth of 5.2% from 1950-1979 after accounting for inflation according to the US General Accounting Office, growth has declined to only 3.3% annually since 1983. The 1990 Census put median household income at $8,895, compared to $30,000 in the States. While only 6.1% of US households earn less than $5,000 per year, 29.9% of Puerto Rican households do.

THE CARIBBEAN BASIN INITIATIVE: Popularly known as CBI, this 1983 Reagan administration scheme allows any firm with a Puerto Rican plant to open a support facility in an eligible Caribbean nation and receive tax breaks. Because wages in these unionless countries are abysmally low and exploitive (50-70¢ ph), businesses can reap added profits.

Economic Sectors

MANUFACTURING: Tax exemptions and other advantages have lured 24 pharmaceutical companies to the island; Puerto Rico produces 7% of the world's total supply of pharmaceuticals, and *all* of America's birth control pills. Figures for the year 1973 show that US firms produced $500 million worth of drugs on the island. A Chase Manhattan study of the top seven firms showed that they saved more than $66 million because of their tax-exempt status; Lilly and Searle alone saved over $33 million that year. These days, the tax break is estimated to be some $3 billion and may represent a subsidy of $100,000 for each job. Some $10 billion (in 1990 dollars) were lost to the US Treasury during the 1980s. In 1993, the congressional budget reduced the tax exemption to 60%, and it is scheduled to drop to 40% by 1998.

Besides savings on taxes, companies also avoid safety inspections: Puerto Rican men working in the birth control pill factories have begun to grow breasts after handling estrogen, some have had radical mastectomies, and others have become impotent. In the States, this would cause an outrage, but in Puerto Rico it has passed almost unnoticed.

At this point, the industry accounts for some 21,000 direct jobs or 14% of all employment in manufacturing. Its exports and imports exceeded $9.2 billion in fiscal 1992 or nearly a third of the total for trade. Manufacturing accounts for some 17% of total employment and generates 38.7% of the GNP and some $180 million in tax revenues, in addition to providing jobs in the construction, trade, and service industries. More than one-third of all manufacturing jobs are still in apparel and textiles. Many of these goods are destined for the US; the shoe industry ships 20 million pairs stateside each year.

The island is also the world's largest producer of rum. Excise taxes on each case of rum sold in the US are rebated to Puerto Rico's Treasury. In 1982 this totaled $210 million, or 10% of the island's revenues. However, more than half of the molasses used in its manufacture and most of the rum is exported in bulk and bottled on the mainland in order to keep down costs. To produce all of these goods, Puerto Rico uses incredible amounts of electricity, most of it generated by imported oil, making the island more dependent on foreign oil than any of the 50 states.

TOURISM: A growing sector, the tourism "industry" continues to increase its influence on the economy. Despite the tragic fire at the Dupont Plaza Hotel in Condado that claimed 96 lives on Dec. 31, 1986, hotel occupancy rates have continued to rise. In fiscal 1991, tourism expenditures reached $1.4 billion, topping one billion for the third consecutive year. Tourism contributed approximately 6% of the gross domestic product and provided direct and indirect employment for some 60,000. Since 1985, more than $500 million has been invested, and total visitation has risen by more than 60%, with an 11.3% increase in cruise ship passengers and a 40% increase in daily flights. Hotel capacity is set to rise to 12,000 rooms; presently there are approximately 8,500. Wages in the hotel industry average around $7.50 ph.

MINING: Although the original impetus for Spanish conquest of the island was gold, mining is no longer a major industry. Even though rich copper deposits have been discovered in the Lares-Utuado-Adjuntas area in the heart of the Cordillera Central, a drop in the world copper price, coupled with the determined opposition of environmentalists and *independentistas*, has so far kept the multinationals at bay.

Prospects for the Future

It is unlikely that Puerto Rico's economy will improve in the near future. The sixth largest customer of US goods, Puerto Rico purchases some $4.5 billion annually in manufactured products from the States. This represents $3.5 billion in gross income for American business and workers, and employment for 200,000 Americans. This does not include, however, the profits stemming from transport of goods and people, from financial and banking transactions, and from insurance and advertising. In 1982, $4.1 billion in federal funds was sent to Puerto Rico: $2.4 billion for personal transfers (such as food stamps and Medicare), and the rest for functions such as immigration, customs, and the military, the island's single largest employer. This sum has held steady over the years.

Indeed, the relationship between Puerto Rico and the US resembles the proverbial one between the worker and the company store. Instead of company bills of promise, the Puerto Ricans shop with *cupones*. Some $100 million in food stamps reach 53% of the populace and comprise 10% of the total distributed nationwide. Although Puerto Ricans pay more for food and the cost of living in general is higher, federal subsidies make life comfortable. Rather than having the Puerto Ricans themselves pay for these subsidies or taxing the companies who reap immense profits, the American taxpayer is forced to foot the bill!

Currently, unemployment continues to rise. While the official figure hovers around 13%, unofficial estimates are higher. Teenage unemployment has soared to 60% (although a number are now employed in the crack trade). Including the men who have given up looking for work, the *ociosos voluntarios* (voluntary idle), there are more than 300,000 unemployed. As Puerto Rico cannot compete with Mexico or the Dominican Republic in terms of low wages, the island's future depends upon skilled labor. Yet the 1990 Census found 42% of Puerto Ricans to be functionally illiterate.

Agriculture

Like the economy in general, the agricultural situation in Puerto Rico has been in constant flux since the US occupation in 1898. Sugarcane, once the backbone of the economy and still a major crop, has become an economic drain. The government buys most of the crop and operates its own sugar mills but, even with subsidies, the $4.25 minimum wage dictates that the cost cannot compete with neighboring nations like the Dominican Republic, where labor (imported from Haiti) is $2.50 pd. The government loses money on every pound of sugar, and this industry is little more than a costly, outmoded public employment program. Devastated by the 1899 and 1928 hurricanes, coffee production is now down to 30 million pounds per year and is raised by 13,000 farmers. Once another flourishing crop, tobacco's production levels continue to decline, and the largest processing plant shut its doors in 1977. The government neglect of agriculture in favor of industry since WWII has served to guarantee that local products are ignored in favor of expensive imports from the States. The percentage of farmers in the workforce has plummeted from 35% to 5%, and 80% of all food is imported. Imported canned vegetables are favored over local produce, and citrus fruit is flown in from California and Florida while local fruit rots on the trees. Other imports include such staples as frozen meat, butter, eggs, and pinto beans. To its credit, the government is trying to reverse this trend by offering tax and other incentives to spur production. Locally grown rice is now being marketed by the government under the name *Arroz D'Aqui* ("rice from here"). In spite of these measures, it will be decades, if ever, before the island can feed itself.

The People

Caribbean culture is truly creole culture. The word "creole" comes from *criar* (Spanish for "to bring up" or "rear"). In the New World, this term came to refer to children born in this hemisphere, implying that they were not quite authentic or pure. Later, creole came to connote "mixed blood," but not just blood has been mixed here – cultures have been jumbled as well. Because of this extreme mixture, the Caribbean is a cultural goldmine. The culture of a specific island or nation depends upon its racial mix and historical circumstances. Brought over on slave ships where differences of status were lost and cultural institutions shattered, the slaves had to begin entirely anew. In a similar fashion, but not nearly to so severe a degree, the European, indentured or otherwise, could not bring all of Europe with him. Beliefs were merged in a new synthesis born of the interaction between different cultures – African and

European. Today, a new synthesis has arisen in language, society, crafts, and religion.

The Influence of Other Cultures

NATIVE AMERICAN INFLUENCE: Although the Native Americans have long vanished, their spirit lives on in tradition, in the feeling of dramatic sunsets, and in the wafting of the cool breeze. Remaining cultural legacies include foods (*achiote*), place names (Mayagüez, Utuado, and Humacao, to name a few), words (such as "hammock" – an Indian invention), and native medicines still in use. Even the Indian name for the island, Borínquen, is still popular, and *La Borinqueña* is the national anthem. Many Spanish towns were built on old Indian sites; the *bateyes* of the Native Americans became the plazas of the Spanish. There are numerous archaeological sites, most notably those at Utuado and Tibes, and Old San Juan has a museum devoted to the island's Native Americans. Jayuya has an annual Indian Festival and an outlying museum.

AFRICAN INFLUENCE: This was the strongest of all outside influences on those islands with large black populations. Arriving slaves had been torn away from both tribe and culture, and this is reflected in everything from the primitive agricultural system to the African influence on religious sects and cults, mirroring the dynamic diversity of W. African culture. Puerto Rico was a special case in that there were never a large number of slaves imported, and all escaped slaves from other islands who landed on its shores were granted freedom. However, the island still reflects a strong African influence that shows up in religion, music, language, food, and other areas.

SPANISH INFLUENCE: Spain was the original intruder in the area. The Spaniards exited Puerto Rico in 1898, following 400 years of influence, and the island's culture is still predominantly Spanish, as are neighboring Cuba and the Dominican Republic. Most Caribbean islands, whether the Spaniards ever settled there or not, still bear the names Columbus bestowed on them 500 years ago. Although other European influences have had a powerful effect, Spanish continues to be the predominant language in the islands once controlled by Spain. Major Spanish architectural sites remain in the old parts of San Juan and in Santo Domingo, the capital of the Dominican Republic.

Important Historical and Archaeological Sites

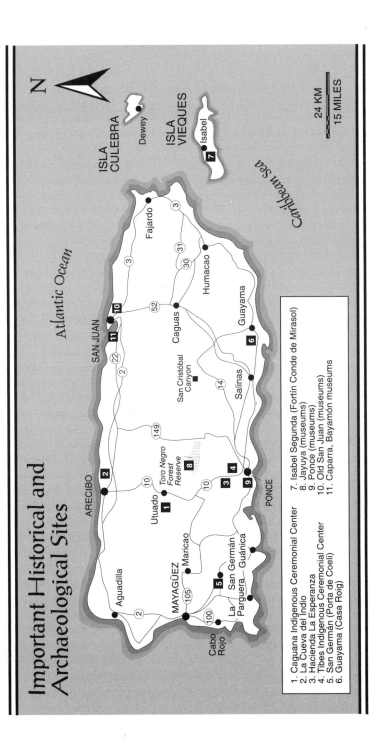

1. Caguana Indigenous Ceremonial Center
2. La Cueva del Indio
3. Hacienda La Esperanza
4. Tibes Indigenous Ceremonial Center
5. San Germán (Porta de Coeli)
6. Guayama (Casa Roig)
7. Isabel Segunda (Fortín Conde de Mirasol)
8. Jayuya (museums)
9. Ponce (museums)
10. Old San Juan (museums)
11. Caparra, Bayamón museums

AMERICAN INFLUENCE: The history of the US is inextricably linked with the Caribbean in general and Puerto Rico in particular. American influence in Puerto Rico predates American occupation. Television (especially cable), the proliferation of malls, and fast food continue to have their effect, as have the migration and return of Puerto Ricans to the mainland.

The Puerto Ricans

Like so many of the neighboring islands, Puerto Rico has forged a unique racial and cultural mix. The original inhabitants of the island, the Taíno Native Americans, were forced into slavery. Some escaped into the mountains, where they intermarried with the local Spanish immigrant subsistence farmers. The offspring from those unions, the *jibaro*, the barefoot-but-proud peasant, have come to be regarded as a symbol of the island. The name itself comes from the *Jivaro*, a fiercely independent tribe of Amazonian Native Americans; they lived a highly individualistic and rugged existence. Residing in *bohios* (thatch huts), they were virtually self-sufficient and skilled in the production of crafts. With the urbanization and industrialization which have marked the 20th century, the *jibaros* have dwindled in number, to emerge as a folk hero much like the American cowboy. Black slaves, although never arriving in the numbers that they did on surrounding islands, added another important ingredient to the racial-cultural stew.

But Puerto Rico's complex cultural blend doesn't stop there. French families arrived from Haiti and Louisiana in the late 18th and 19th centuries. Loyalist Spaniards and Venezuelans sought refuge here from newly independent Latin American republics. A flourishing sugar economy attracted Scottish and Irish farmers. After abolition, farmers and laborers emigrated from Spain's NW province of Galicia and the Canary Islands. Chinese coolies were imported in the 1840s to help build roads, and numbers of Italians, Corsicans, Germans, and Lebanese also arrived. American expatriates founded an Episcopal church in Ponce in 1873, and many more arrived after the American annexation in 1898. Cubans fleeing Castro arrived in the 1960s, as did Dominicans following the 1965 upheavals. Both of these have had a powerful influence: the Cubans on top of the social stratum, the Dominicans on the very bottom. All of the diverse ethnic groups, intermarrying and multiplying, have helped forge modern Puerto Rican culture.

Currently, some 9% of the population were not born on the island, and Dominicans continue to mount rickety *yolas* (small boats) and risk drowning and shark attacks to cross the dangerous Mona Passage. Paying up to $500 each, the smuggling has proved a popular and profitable business: there are an estimated 100,000-300,000 Dominicans on hand at any one time! Soon after arrival, they pick up a stolen or forged birth certificate and learn to talk like Puerto Ricans. Then, it's a simple matter to migrate to the States.

POPULATION: With 3.76 million people, Puerto Rico is one of the most crowded islands in the world. Its population density of over 1,000 persons per square mile is higher than in any of the 50 States. And still another two million Puerto Ricans live within the continental United States. In fact, more Puerto Ricans reside in New York City than in San Juan. Most of them have been compelled to migrate by economic necessity; in recent years, however, declining economic opportunities in the States have reversed the trend and many Puerto Ricans are now returning to the island. The population is expected to pass 3.9 million by 2005, and the elderly will increase as a proportion of the overall total.

SOCIAL VALUES: Of course, no single description fits all Puerto Ricans; there are too many kinds of people for one mold to apply. And the impact of American colonialism, coupled as it has been with transmigration from the States, has had an immense effect. Social values are undergoing a rapid transformation as the economic base switches from agriculture to industry and manufacturing. Speaking in terms of the traditional culture, however, Puerto Ricans live in a tightly-knit, class-structured society. Very conscious of their roles within that society, they submit passively to it.

This attitude, which some have termed fatalistic, has deep historic roots. The centuries-old feudal system of social relationships under which the island has been governed continues to this day. Hacienda owners traditionally held immense power over the *agregados,* the landless peons on their properties, and the Puerto Rican version of Catholicism has also worked to keep the peasants' aspirations in check: the world has been seen as ruled by supernatural forces, basically benevolent but beyond man's control. *"Acepto lo que Dios me mande"* ("I accept whatever God will offer me") has been a common expression for generations, as is *"¡Ay Bendito!,"* short for "Blessed is the Lord," but whose actual meaning is closer to "Ah, woe is me." This sense of resignation seems to pervade social interactions: Puerto Ricans are reluctant to say no, and direct confrontations are avoided. One tries to do things *a la buena*, "the nice way."

Resistance is undertaken via the *pelea monga* (literally "the relaxed fight") or passive non-cooperation. Puerto Ricans are very gregarious, but they are also highly independent. Their sensitivity to criticism, and their awareness that individual aims may best be achieved through collective efforts, helps keep them in line. One's expectations in life and one's behavior are formed and controlled by the ever-watchful eyes of one's peers. Social mobility is limited; behavior expected of persons at each class level is clearly defined and taught from birth. All of these factors combine to help the society run smoothly. Puerto Ricans in general accept their situation; the sense of being small, anonymous and not in direct control of their lives alleviates frustration and works to reinforce traditional customs and conventions.

COMPADRAZGO: Literally "co-parentage," this important practice of social bonding resembles the system of godparents found in the States, but is much more solemn. Selected when a child is baptized, *compadres* and *comadres* can be counted on to help out financially in a pinch. A poor farmer may seek out a rich employer to be his child's *compadre*. The employer will assent because he knows that this will tighten the bonds between himself and his employee. Or such a relationship may be sought merely to cement a close friendship between males.

MALES IN THE SOCIETY: Although Puerto Rico is indisputably a male-dominated society (as are all Latin cultures), men raised in the traditional culture have tended to be very immature. Women have been instructed to search for a mate who is *serio* (serious), but such men are rare because they are raised to be insecure and unstable. Much effort is made to form "*de confianza*" (confidential) relationships with other men, and exhibitionism is one way to do this. Fighting, heavy drinking, betting, and sexual prowess have historically been viewed positively by traditional male society. Sexual experience, both premarital and extramarital, is mandatory for establishing and maintaining one's *macho* status. In Puerto Rico's highly structured pecking order, women are at the bottom.

FEMALES IN THE SOCIETY: Women have been carefully groomed for their role from an early age. Soon after birth their ears are pierced and they begin wearing clothes, whereas their brothers may run around naked for some years. They are carefully separated from contact with the opposite sex; this guarding intensifies as the girls reach puberty. Traditionally, women were considered eligible for marriage at 15 or 16. All chances for girls and boys to meet were carefully controlled. Before *noviazgo* (engagement) there was little chance for them to talk to each other. *Noviazgo* differed from its English equivalent in that it implied a very serious commitment to marry and, accordingly, was very difficult to break. During the period of *noviazgo* the couple were never left alone; the assumption was that they were not to be trusted. Rather than spending the time trying to get to know each other better, the woman was expected only to learn how to accommodate herself to the will of her future husband.

Even today, Puerto Rican society fosters a cult of virginity: the woman must be a virgin at marriage. The husband's authority is paramount in the home; the wife controls little money and has no right to make decisions. Husbands dictate; wives submit. Obedience rather than communication is of paramount importance. Because the man has taken her virginity, he owes her support and fair treatment. On the other hand, the wife has been forbidden to associate with any other man, even on a casual basis. Women have simply not been trusted around men. However, these days attitudes are changing rapidly. Among younger couples there is much better communication between husband and wife, and her status has improved tremendously. The problems of sexual discrimination, however, still remain.

ATTITUDES TOWARDS AMERICANS: Puerto Ricans are among the most hospitable people on Earth. A foreigner will not be long in a bar before someone is buying him a drink and conversing with him. However, a *gringo* may rest assured that he will always be regarded as a *gringo*. Although Puerto Ricans are American citizens and one-third of all Puerto Ricans live in the US, the visiting North American will be called *Americano*. Puerto Ricans are clearly doubtful and confused about their political identity, as soon becomes evident in conversation. Puerto Ricans returning from the States are termed *Neoricans* and never completely readmitted into the society.

RACIAL ATTITUDES: As in all of the Caribbean islands, racial prejudice is part of a lingering colonial legacy. Although most Puerto Ricans have at least a pinch of *negrito* blood running through their veins, it is not socially desirable to admit it; the undesirability of being black stems from the fact that the blacks were once slaves. While the apartheid system of the American South never took root here, and Puerto Ricans do not believe in a biological inferiority of blacks, blacks are nevertheless stereotyped as being lower class and it is difficult for them to rise within the society.

Traditionally, upper and middle-class islanders have been the most concerned about *limpieza de sangre* (purity of blood). In the past, trials to prove purity of blood were conducted before an upper-class couple could marry. Today, although prejudice remains, it has been moderated over time: an upper-class man, for example, may marry a mulatto woman without much censure, but she may never be fully accepted by the wives of his associates. Factors such as economic position and social standing now tend to override racial considerations. Still, the darker child in a family may win less praise from his parents and be more likely to be teased by his brothers and sisters. Interestingly enough, the term *negrito*, as used in society, is a term of endearment, implying a sense of community or communal belonging, while *blanquito* ("little white") usually implies the opposite. The latter term has historical roots: *Peninsulares*, islanders born in Spain, held a higher rank than *criollos*, Spaniards born on the island. Today, this term is still used in reference to the elite. The vast majority of Puerto Ricans today are neither black nor white, but *trigueno*, tan or swarthy in color.

Language

Spanish is the norm throughout the island. Although many Puerto Ricans can speak English, the more Spanish the visitor can speak, the better: outsiders who can speak Spanish are more readily accepted by locals. The Spanish here is laden with borrowed English (*el coat* for example), local idioms, and numerous Indian and African words. When speaking with Puerto Ricans, keep in mind that the "*tu*" form of address connotes a high degree of familiarity; don't jump from the more formal "*usted*" until the relationship warrants it. "S" sounds are muted and may even disappear at the end of syllables (as in *graciah* instead of *gracias* and *loh* instead of *los*). The "ll" and "y" sounds are pronounced like the English "js." Spanish words which end in ado (such as *pescado*) are generally pronounced as if the d is silent. And the terminal "e" sound is often truncated (as in *noch* instead of *noche*).

☞ **Traveler's Tip.** Cayey University offers a summer course (in June) in "Conversational Spanish and Puerto Rican Culture." Students receive 2½ hrs. of classroom instruction and 1½ hrs. of language lab for four days a week over six weeks. There's one excursion per week, and housing is available. Tuition is $600 and includes excursions, lab fees, and medical insurance. Write Conversational Spanish and Puerto Rican Culture, University of Puerto Rico, Cayey University College, Ave. Antonio Barceló, Cayey, PR 00736; ☎ 738-4445, 738-2161 (ext. 2146, 2031, 2232); or fax 263-5882.

Religion

Catholicism & Protestantism

CATHOLICISM: Although Puerto Rico is predominantly Catholic, its brand is a far cry from the dogmatic religion practiced in Italy. Distance, combined with the elitist attitudes of the all-Spanish clergy who chose to support slavery and exclude locals from the priesthood, have altered the religion here. Puerto Ricans have selected the rules and regulations they wish to follow while conveniently ignoring the rest. To them, being a good Catholic does not mean being dogmatic. Many strict Catholic couples, for example, have civil or consensual marriages and practice birth control.

PROTESTANTISM: Many other sects have proliferated here as well. Chief among these is Protestantism. Although the religion had reached the island prior to 1898, the US invasion spurred a rapid increase in its popularity. Facilitated by the separation of church and state decreed in the US Constitution, its emphasis on the importance of the individual, so much more in keeping with present-day society than the Catholic emphasis upon dogmatic ritual, won it many new converts. Also, because it provides the rural and urban poor a sense of emotional security in the face of a rapidly changing world, evangelical fundamentalism has gained in popularity. Presently, some 1,500 evangelical churches dot the island, and missionaries are sent to Europe and Africa to propagate the faith.

Spiritualism

As in other Latin areas, Catholicism has been lightly seasoned with a mixture of African and native Indian traditions. For example, the African influence on the costumes and statues in Loíza Aldea's patron saint festival is unmistakable, as is the dark-colored flesh of the Virgin of Monserrate. Some go so far as to claim that spiritualism (*espiritismo*) is the real religion of Puerto Rico. Illegal under Spanish rule, spiritualism surfaced only in this century. Many middle-class Catholics, while remaining formally within the confines of Catholicism, practice spiritualism at home. Few Protestants, on the other hand, are spiritualists because the stress on application of day-to-day ethical choices inherent in Protestantism runs counter to the spiritualist belief that one's fate is affected by outside influences or by acts committed in a past existence.

Spiritualism is steeped in native Indian religion and folklore. The Taínos believed that *jipia* (spirits of the dead) slept by day and roamed the island by night, eating wild fruit and visiting relatives. Food was always left on the table because easily insulted *jipia* might haunt one's dreams at night if left unfed. Although many no longer know where the belief comes from, plastic fruit is still left atop refrigerators to appease hungry *jipia*. Folk beliefs continue to predominate among country folk. Many still believe in the *mal de ojo* or "evil eye." Although its possessor may be unaware of its power, one covetous glance upon a child, adult, or animal is believed to cause sickness or even death. Children have been traditionally protected by a bead-charm bracelet.

Spiritualism is also closely connected with folk medicine and healing. You should not mix "cold" things with "hot," or touch "cold" things when you are "hot." Otherwise you risk suffering *empache* or *espasmo*, stomach cramps or muscular disturbances. "Cold" food, banana or pork for example, must never be mixed with hot food like red meat or manioc. Never wash clothes in a "cold" area while you are "hot," and avoid taking a cold bath after getting heated up through physical exercise. *Botanicas*, the supermarkets of spiritualism, sell plants, herbs, oils, rubbing water, and spiritualist literature.

SANTOS **CULTS**: Another complement to Catholicism is the half-magical cult of the saints or *santos*. Most households have an image of one or two of these (see "Arts and Crafts"), usually St. Anthony and one of the Virgins. These are grouped together with the family crucifix and designated as the "Holy Family." Saints are selected in accordance with one's needs, and reciprocation is mandatory if devotions are to continue. The relation between saint and worshipper is one of *promesa* (promise or obligation); promises are made by the devotee and carried out if wishes are granted by the saint. Certain goods are offered to the saint, who is expected to reciprocate by providing prosperity and good fortune. Gamblers and drinkers offer up dice, cards, pennies, small glasses of rum, lottery numbers, and pictures of beautiful women to their patron San Expedito. If the saint does not respond, the icon may be beaten and kicked out of the house. Rituals of devotion, termed *rosarios*, are held to obtain relief from sickness or give thanks for recovery after an illness. Traditional events involving mass participation, such as the Rosario de la Cruz (see "events" under "Bayamón") and the *rogativa* or candlelight procession, are on the wane, as are *veladas*, or pre-funeral wakes in which neighbors gather at the home of a dying community member to render assistance in case of need.

Arts & Crafts

Puerto Rico's art reflects its cultural diversity. With a growing coterie of young, dynamic artists, the island also has an indigenous crafts tradition with roots in European, African, and Taíno traditions. The best places to see art (and antiques) are in San Juan's numerous art galleries. A good assortment of crafts can be found at the Folk Arts Center on C. Cristo near the chapel in Old San Juan. Other shops are located inside Sixto Escobar Stadium near the Caribe Hilton and inside Plazoleta de la Puerta across from Terminal Turismo in Old San Juan. Crafts are sold every weekend along Callejón de la Capilla in Old San Juan as well as in El Centro market inside Condado Convention Center. Annual crafts fairs are held on the grounds of the Bacardi Rum Plant, Cataño, San Juan, and in Barranquitas. By far the best way to see local crafts, however, is by checking out the island craftspeople in their workshops. Hammock-making is centered in and around San Sebastian. Hats are made in Agua and Moca. Other Puerto Rican crafts include ceramics, masks, musical instruments, wooden replicas of birds and flowers, and macramé. Two of the most important craft traditions, *santos* and *mundillo*, are described below. For information on visiting crafts shops all around the island contact Acte Cestero (☎ 721-2400, ext. 2201) at the Puerto Rico Tourism Company.

SANTOS: Among the oldest and certainly the most impressive of Puerto Rican traditional crafts are *santos*, eight- to 20-inch-tall figurines representing saints, carved of capa or cedar wood, stone, clay, or gold. While the oldest date back to the 16th century, the *santero's* craft is a continuation of the indigenous Indian tradition in which small statues (*zemi*) were placed in every home and village as objects of veneration. Thus, the carving of *santos* seems to be linked to the pre-Columbian era. Just as every town had its patron saint, so every home had its *santos* who would offer protection. And just as some people substitute a TV service for a visit to church, so Puerto Ricans substitute *santos* worship for the traditional Mass.

Santeros, skilled carpenters using handmade tools, carved the statues out of wood, using natural dyes and sometimes even human hair to decorate them. Natural dyes were subsequently replaced by oils; the initial full-figure design was later joined by carvings of busts and group figures. Saints most commonly represented include the various Virgins (Pilar, Monserrate, Carmen, etc.) and the male saints (Jose, Rafael, Peter the Apostle, etc.). Accompanying symbols render them easily identifiable. Just as Rafael carries his spear and fish trademark, so the Virgin of Monserrate holds the baby Jesus on her lap and Saint Anthony is always shown with the infant Jesus and a book. Most popularly represented of the group figures are the Three Kings; others include the Nativity, the Trinity, and biblical scenes. Most remarkable of all the *santos* is the carving of the *mano poderosa* ("powerful hand"), a hand with five fingers terminating in intricately carved miniature images of various saints.

Although *santos*-making reached its artistic peak around the turn of the 20th century, *santeros* still practice their art at various locations all over the island. The best collections of antique *santos* may be seen in Old San Juan. The *santos* possess a singularly attractive and simple solemnity which remains as freshly inspiring today as the day they were carved. Unfortunately, it's difficult to find *santos* of similar quality being carved today and, new or antique, they are expensive.

MUNDILLO: A Spanish import, this type of lacemaking derives its name from the wooden box *mundillo* frame on which it is worked. It is also known as bobbin lace or pillow lace because its threads are wound on bobbins, and its patterns are anchored to pillows. Today, this technique of bobbin lacemaking, which has a 500-year tradition, can be found only in Spain and in Puerto Rico. *Torchon*, or beggar's lace, was the technique first introduced and the one which still predominates today. Originally poorly made and of low quality, it has evolved into a highly intricate and delicate art form. The two traditional styles of lace bands are *entredos*, which have two straight borders, and *puntilla* with a straight and scalloped border. Although the craft once seemed destined to disappear from the island, today it is undergoing a revival. Probably the foremost instructor in San Juan is Maria A. Capella Ricci. One place to see *mundillo* is at the Puerto Rico Weaving Festival held annually at the end of April in Isabela. Otherwise, check the Centro de Artes Populares (Folk Arts Center, ☎ 724-0700) on Calle Cristo for information on shops which make and sell *mundillo*.

ART AND ARTISTS: Expanding quickly after a belated start, Puerto Rican art has grown to include a wide range of artistic media, including mural art, innovative ceramics, and poster art. The story of Puerto Rican art begins with painter José Campeche (1751-1809); indeed, painting on the island can hardly be said to have existed before him. His works, which deal exclusively with religious themes, are easily identified through their characteristic style. A self-trained artist who mixed his own pigments, Campeche is today recognized as one of the great artists of the Americas.

The next painter to hit the big time was Francesco Oller (1833-1917). Studying art in France and Spain, he returned to the island to create many masterpieces. Known as the first Latin American impressionist, this contemporary of Pissarro and Cézanne was commissioned by King Alfonso of Spain to be Court Painter for six years.

An artistic renaissance took place during the 1950s when many artists returned to the island after studying in the States. During this period, poster art emerged as an important medium of artistic expression. Another art form which has gained popularity in recent years is the mural. Mural art, which draws on everything from complex Taíno symbology to religious themes, decorates the sides of buildings of all sizes and shapes. Modern Puerto Rican artists of note include Carlos Irizarry, Carlos Osorio, Julio Rosado del Valle, Rafael Turfino, Lorenzo Homar, Carlos Raquel Riviera, and Julio Rosado del Valle.

Music & Dance

Although many legacies of European, African, and Taíno traditions survive in Puerto Rico, none are as expressive of cultural feeling or as illustrative of intercultural blending as music and dance. The story of Puerto Rican music begins with the Taíno. At least one instrument, the *guiro* or *guicharo*, a hollow, notched, bottle-shaped gourd played with a wire fork, has been handed down by the Native Americans, and musicologists speculate that the *areytos* (Indian dance tunes) have also influenced the development of Puerto Rican music. Besides the Native Americans, Spanish influence is also evident in the design of musical instruments. Puerto Ricans have transformed the six-string Spanish guitar into four different instruments: the *tiple, cuatro, bordonua,* and *requinto,* which differ in shape, pitch, and number of strings. The 10-string *cuatro,* so named because it is tuned in fourths, is the most popular instrument today. Other instruments include the *maracas,* round gourds filled with small beans or pebbles, and the *tambor,* a hollowed tree trunk with an animal skin stretched on top. Bands of troubadours once traveled from town to town like European wandering minstrels.

> ☞ **Traveler's Tip**. Puerto Rico is a good place to stock up on CDs – especially if your taste runs towards Latin music. In addition to local stores, Spec's, a Miami-based chain, has opened up in a number of locations island-wide. Cuban salsa bands, whose releases may be hard to find elsewhere, are well represented. While you won't find CDs or cassettes any cheaper (and used CD stores are as yet nonexistent), you *will* save because there is no sales tax.

FOLK MUSIC: Varied and multifarious. The *seis* is probably the liveliest and most popular of all Puerto Rican music. Originally limited to six couplets, its more than 40 versions, composed of eight-syllable lines, range from contemporary to century-old standards. While some are representative of particular areas (*seis Bayamones* from Bayamón, for example), others are representative of the way the music is danced. Their names may derive from the area or region where the dance originated, the style of dance, or the composers or most famous performers. A story set to song, the *decima* may carry a deep message. *Decimas* are strictly metered into 10-line stanzas controlled by eight-syllable lines and alternating rhyme structure.

   Another of the more popular forms of Puerto Rican music is the *danza*. Created in the 1850s, its refined, classical score resembles a minuet; the *danza* is a uniquely Puerto Rican musical interpretation of this Spanish Caribbean form. Juan-Morel Campos, known as the father of the *danza*, is the best-known early composer. Unlike the Cuban *contradanzas* (the model for the Puerto Rican danzas), his compositions have a Chopinesque feel to them. The most famous composer of popular music is Rafael Hernandez, who died in 1966. Known for such hits as "El Cumbanchero" and "Lamento Borincano," Hernandez is idolized on the island.

BOMBA Y PLENA: These two most famous types of music coupled with dance are usually grouped together, although in reality they are totally different forms. While the *plena* possesses the elegance and coquetry of the Spanish tradition, the *bomba* has the beat of Africa. Though the origin of both the *bomba* and the *plena* is uncertain, some maintain that their arrangements were influenced by the Taíno *areytos* (epic songs danced to by the Native Americans); certainly both are a mixture of European and African influences – although African elements predominate in the *bomba*. Some say that the *plena* was brought to the island by a couple from St. Kitts. Historians do agree, however, that the *plena* first emerged in Ponce.

Once an important social event, the *bomba* provided the working people the only available relief from the monotonous drudgery of everyday life. Usually on Saturday or Sunday nights or on special occasions and festivities, the dance was performed in a circle. The soloist stood next to the drums, and the chorus stood behind the singer. While the soloist sang, the chorus provided the harmonies. The dancer, entering in front of the drums, performed the *piquete* (coquettish dance) before saluting the drums and exiting. The *bomba* is really a dialogue between drummer and dancer. The first drummer (*repicador*) challenges the dancer to a duel while the second drummer maintains the basic rhythmic pattern. The dance lasts as long as the dancer can successfully challenge the drummer. Unlike similar dances found elsewhere, the drummer follows the dancer rather than vice-versa.

The different rhythms of the *bomba* (the *Cunya, Yuba, Cuende, Sica, Cocobale, Danua, Holande,* etc.) represent the diverse ethnic roots of the dance. While the first five are African names, the latter two represent adaptations of Danish and Dutch styles learned from arriving immigrants. Another style, *Lero,* is an adaption of the French circle dance, *le rose.* Today, the bomba is performed only in lower-class black communities, and most Puerto Ricans have no contact with it.

CLASSICAL MUSIC: Interest in classical music has grown over the years in Puerto Rico, and the island has its own symphony orchestra and conservatory. A great inspiration was cellist and conductor Pablo Casals, who retired at age 81 to the island, his mother's birthplace, to spend his last years there. Each year, generally in June, the month-long Casals Festival draws artists from all over the world to perform his music. The most notable native classical musician was master pianist Jesus Maria Sanroma (1902-1984), who toured and recorded internationally. A friend and collaborator of Casals, he promoted both symphonic music on the island and the *danza*, recording, editing, and performing the latter. Puerto Rico is also the birthplace of famed operatic tenor Antonio Paoli (1872-1946), who performed for Czar Nicholas II of Russia, Kaiser Wilhelm of Germany, and the Emperor Franz Joseph of Austria. The latter bestowed upon him the title of Court Singer. After earning and spending an estimated $2 million, Paoli returned home to the island in 1922, where he taught music to the island's youth. Other famous Puerto Rican opera singers include Pablo Elvira and Justino Diaz.

MODERN MUSIC: Although born and bred in New York's Caribbean melting pot, *salsa* (Spanish for "sauce") and the Dominican-originated *merengue* blare from every car stereo and boom box on the island. El Gran Combo, comprised of 13 or so members and led by pianist Rafael Ithier, who is the band's only remaining original member, is one of Puerto Rico's contributions to the *salsa* scene. They have recorded more than 60 albums. Major *salsa* figures of Puerto Rican extraction include pianists (and brothers) Charlie and Eddie Palmieri, trombonist Willie Colón, percussionist Ray Barretto, and timbale wizard Tito Puente. Born in Ponce, José "Cheo" Feliciano is one of the most famous island-born *salsa* singers.

MERENGUE AND MURDER

The Commonwealth's police chief Pedro Toledo alleged that the NYC-produced *El Venao*, a merengue tune about an unfaithful wife shot by her husband, is responsible for a rash of shootings on the island. Composer Ramon Orlando, a fervent evangelical Christian who answers his phone with the phrase "Christ Loves You," insists that the lyrics are simply a complaint about infidelity. The word *venao* is a contraction of *venado* ("deer" or "venison") and is used to describe naive adulterers. Although the song became one of the island's top hits for 1995, members of the religious right asked stations to remove it from their playlist. Thankfully, most stations refused to heed the call.

Despite ambivalence regarding its Dominican roots, *merengue* also has quite an audience. Although there have not been any homegrown *merengue* stars in the past, this has changed and Los Sabrosos Del Merengue and Prime Tono Rosario are Puerto Rican merengue stars. Unfortunately, rap music is also popular here; rap singer Fransheska, the "Queen of Rap," is one of the most popular stars. Her music is styled "meren-rap," and she has recorded four albums that have stormed the charts throughout Latin America. The most popular Puerto Rican male rap star is probably Vico-C. Pop. Music rendered in Spanish also commands a large audience.

Festivals & Events

The Latin nature of the island really comes to the fore in its celebration of festivals and holidays. Puerto Ricans know how to relax and have a good time. Although the centuries-old custom of midday siesta is in danger of extinction, *Viernes social* or "social Friday" is still popular. Every Friday men gather to eat *lechon asado* (roast pig) and gossip and gamble at local roadside stands. Most other celebrations, however, are in a religious vein. Many of these are famous, including those at Hormigueros and Loíza; the Festival of St. John the Baptist in San Juan on June 24 is one long night of partying. Every town on the island has its **fiestas patronales** or patron saint festival. They always begin on a Friday, approximately 10 days before the date prescribed. Although services are held twice a day, the atmosphere is anything but religious. Music, gambling, and dancing take place on the town plaza, and food stalls sell local specialties. On the Sunday nearest the main date, *imajenes* or wooden images of the patron saint are carried around the town by four men or (sometimes) women. Flowers conceal supporting wires and the base is tied to the platform to prevent it from falling.

A generally somber atmosphere prevails during **Holy Week** (*Semana Santa*), the week surrounding Easter, when processions and pageants are held island-wide. **Las Navidades** or the Christmas season, which stretches from Dec. 15 to Jan. 6, is the liveliest time of the year. Marked by parties and prayers, it's a time to get together with friends. Everyone heads for *el campo* ("the country") to join in celebrating the occasion with friends and loved ones. Out in the countryside, groups of local musicians known as *trulla* roam from house to house singing *aguinaldos*, or Christmas carols. *Nacimento* (nativity scenes) are set up in homes and public places, the most famous being the one near San Cristóbal fortress in Old San Juan. On *Nochebueno* (Christmas Eve) most people attend midnight Mass (*Misa del Gallo*) before returning home to feast on the traditional large supper known as *cena*. On Jan. 6. *Epiphany* or Three Kings Day is celebrated. The night before, children traditionally place boxes of grass under their beds to await the arrival of the Three Kings, Gaspar, Melchior, and Baltazar. After the camels have eaten all the grass, the kings leave presents in the now empty boxes. On the day itself, the Three Kings are put up in front of the Capitol, and candy and toys are given away on the grounds of El Morro fortress in Old San Juan.

PUERTO RICO FESTIVALS & EVENTS

Jan. 1	New Year's Day
Jan. 6	Epiphany or Three Kings Day; traditional day of gift-giving
Jan. 11	Birthday of Eugenio De Hostos, Puerto Rican educator, writer, and patriot (half-day)
Jan. 15	Martin Luther King Day (half-day)
Jan. 18-20	San Sebastian Street Fiesta in Old San Juan. Crafts, shows, arts, games, processions, dancing, and *paso fino* horses on display.
Feb.	Washington's Birthday (half-day, movable)
March 22	Emancipation Day
April	Good Friday (movable)
April 16	José de Diego's Birthday
May	Memorial Day (movable)
June 24	St. John the Baptist Day
July 4	Independence Day
July 17	Luiz Muñoz Rivera's Birthday
July 25	Commonwealth Constitution Day
July 27	Dr. José Celso Barbosa's Birth
Sept.	Labor Day (movable)
Oct.	Columbus Day (movable)
Nov. 11	Veteran's Day
Nov. 19	Puerto Rico Discovery Day
Nov.	Thanksgiving (movable)
Dec. 25	Christmas Day

FESTIVALS BY TOWN

☐ JANUARY

Aguada	Velorio de Reyes
Añasco	Festival Mayuco
Bayamón	Fiesta de Reyes
Cagua	Fiesta de Reyes
Camuy	Velorio de Reyes
Cidra	Cabalgata de Reyes Magos
Coamo	Actividad Dia de Reyes
Dorado	Festival de Reyes
Florida	Festival de Reyes
Guánica	Verbena San Antonio Abad
Mayagüez	Festival de Reyes
Mayagüez	Festival del Blanco y Negro
Mayagüez	Nuestras Fiestas Patronales
Sabana Grande	Festival de Reyes
San Juan	Festival de la Calle San Sebastián
San Juan	Festival de Teatro de Muñecos
San Juan	Festival de Teatro Titere
San Juan	Festival Folklorico International
San Lorenzo	Trulla de Reyes
San Sebastián	Festival de la Novilla
San Sebastián	Nuestras Fiestas Patronales
Toa Baja	Fiesta de Reyes

☐ FEBRUARY

Arecibo	Carnaval Arecibeño
Arroyo	Carnaval de Cristobal Sanchez
Camuy	Carnaval Río Camuy
Cidra	Festival Teatro Myrna Vazquez
Coamo	Nuestras Fiestas Patronales
Dorado	Carnaval del Plata
Guayama	Festival de la Candelaria
Humacao	Festival de la Pana
Jayuya	Festival Jibaro del Tomate
Lajas	Festival Internacional Chiringa
Lajas	Nuestras Fiestas Patronales
Loíza	Festival del Buren
Loíza	Nuestras Fiestas Patronales
Manatí	Nuestras Fiestas Patronales
Mayagüez	Festival Nacional de la Danza
Ponce	Festival de Carnaval Ponce de León
Quebradillas	Festival de la Chiringa
Sabana Grande	Gran Verbena Petatera
Salinas	Carnaval Abey

San Juan	Festival de Carnaval
San Juan	Festival de Claridad
Vega Alta	Carnaval Vegalteño
Vieques	Festival Cultural
Yauco	Festival del Café

☐ MARCH

Cabo Rojo	Festival de los Cuarentes
Cabo Rojo	Festival del Pescao
Coamo	Semana Santa
Guánica	Festival de la Independencia
Gurabo	Nuestras Fiestas Patronales
Juana Díaz	Carnaval del Mavi
Lajas	Feria Agropecuaria
Las Marías	Festival Fundacion Pueblo
Maricao	Fiesta de Acabe del Café
Quebradillas	Nuestras Fiestas Patronales
San Juan	Festival de Teatro Puertorriqueña
San Lore.	Festival La Chiringa
Vega Alta	Festival de la Caña
Guayanabo	St. Patrick's Day Parade

☐ APRIL

Adjuntas	Festival del Gigante
Aguadilla	Fiestas San Antonio
Arroyo	Festival Negra
Cayey	Feria Regional de Artesanias
Cidra	Festival de la Educacion
Comerio	Carnaval de Primavera
Dorado	Festival de Teatro Infantil
Guánica	Festival del Pescao
Guayama	Festival Pionero Artesana
Guayanil	Festival La Chiringa
Guaynabo	Nuestras Fiestas Patronales
Humacao	Fiesta de Bomba y Musica
Juana Díaz	Festival Sapo Toro
Luquillo	Festival de Playa
Rosario	Festival Añasco's Anón
Sabana Grande	Festival del Soberao
San Juan	Feria de Artesania Feminina
San Juan	Orchid Show
Vieques	Festival Plenero

☐ MAY

Adjuntas	Festival de la Cidra
Aguadilla	Verbena de Corrales

Añasco	Festival de Teatro
Arecibo	Nuestras Fiestas Patronales
Bayamón	Nuestras Fiestas Patronales
Cabo Rojo	Festival del Ostión
Cabo Rojo	Festival del Tejido de Sombrero
Caguas	Festival del Coqui
Camuy	Nuestras Fiestas Patronales
Carolina	Nuestras Fiestas Patronales
Coamo	Actividad Madre Ejemplar
Coamo	Tradicionales Rosarios de Cruz
Dorado	Festival de Cruz
Fajardo	Festival de Bomba y Plena
Guayama	Carnaval Deportivo
Guayama	Festival de Primavera
Guayama	Rosario de la Cruz
Guayanilla	Festival de la Cruz
Guayanilla	Festival de Playa
Hormigueros	Fiesta de la Dulce Caña
Hormigueros	Semana de Segundo Ruiz
Isabela	Festival del Tejido
Juana Díaz	Semana Lloreniana
Lajas	Festival Piña Cabezona
Mayagüez	Carnaval Mayagüezano
Moca	Festival del Camarón
Morovis	Festival del Camarón
Peñuelas	Nuestras Fiestas Patronales
Ponce	Festival de Cruz
Ponce	Festival Playa de Ponce
Rincón	Festival del Coco
Sabana Grande	Nuestras Fiestas Patronales
San Germán	Festival de la Caña
San Juan	Concurso Nacional de Trovadores
San Juan	Concurso Nacional del Cuatro
San Juan	Concurso Nacional del Guiro
San Juan	Festival de Cruz
San Juan	Festival de la Musica Puertorriqueña
San Juan	Semana de la Danza
Santa Isabela	Festival del Mango
Toa Alta	Nuestras Fiestas Patronales
Toa Baja	Festival Arte y Cultura
Utuado	Feria de Artesania

❑ JUNE

Aguada	Festival de Playa Noche San Juan
Aguadilla	Festival Playero
Aguas Buenas	Festival de la Rosa
Añasco	Festival del Merengue
Barceloneta	Festival de Verano

Barranquitas	Nuestras Fiestas Patronales
Caguas	Noche de San Juan
Camuy	Dia de San Juan
Cataño	Noche de San Juan
Ceiba	Nuestras Fiestas Patronales
Coamo	Actividad Padre Ejemplar
Coamo	Festival de la Juventud
Comerío	Festival Jibaro
Corozal	Carnaval San Juan Bautista
Corozal	El Carnaval de Corozal
Culebra	Nuestras Fiestas Patronales
Dorado	Nuestras Fiestas Patronales
Guánica	Festival Jueyero
Guayama	Festival Populares
Guyama	Nuestras Fiestas Patronales
Guayanilla	Festival del Marisco
Guayanilla	Festival Virgen del Carmen
Guaynabo	Dia Nacional de la Salsa
Isabela	Nuestras Fiestas Patronales
Lajas	Festival de Chiringa y Tiguero
Lajas	Festival de la Chiringa
Loíza	Festival Bomba y Plena
Maricao	Nuestras Fiestas Patronales
Maunabo	Nuestras Fiestas Patronales
Naguabo	Festival Diplo
Narajito	Festival Artes y Cultura
Narajito	Festival San Antonio
Orocovis	Nuestra Fiestas Patronales
Salinas	Festival del Pescao
San Juan	Festival Casals
San Juan	Festival de Verano
San Juan	Nuestras Fiestas Patronales
Santa Isabela	Carnaval del Juey
Toa Baja	Nuestras Fiestas Patronales
Vega Alta	Festival del Panapen

❑ JULY

Adjuntas	Nuestras Fiestas Patronales
Aguadilla	Festival del Atun
Aguadilla	Festival del Pescao
Aguadilla	Festival Musica de Verano
Aguadilla	Verbenas
Aibonito	Festival de Flores
Aibonito	Nuestras Fiestas Patronales
Arecibo	Festival Playero
Arroyo	Nuestras Fiestas Patronales
Barceloneta	Nuestras Fiestas Patronales
Barranquitas	Feria Nacional de Artesanias

Bayamón	Ann. José Celso Barbosa
Bayamón	Festival de Artesanias
Bayamón	Festival del Chicharrón
Cabo Rojo	Cruce de Bahia de Boqueron
Cabo Rojo	Festival del Melon
Cabo Rojo	Nuestras Fiestas Patronales
Cabo Rojo	Retorno a la Arena
Camuy	Festival Playero Penon Brusi
Carolina	Festival de la Caña
Cataño	Nuestras Fiestas Patronales
Cidra	Festival Tradicionales
Cidra	Nuestras Fiestas Patronales
Coamo	Aniversario de Coamo
Coamo	Festival Deportivo y Musical
Comerio	Festival El Jobo
Comerio	Festival La Paila
Culebra	Nuestras Fiestas Patronales
Fajardo	Nuestras Fiestas Patronales
Guánica	Desfile 25 de Julio
Guánica	Nuestras Fiestas Patronales
Guayanilla	Carnaval del Pueblo
Hatillo	Nuestras Fiestas Patronales
Lajas	Festival del Pescao
Loíza	Festival de Santiago Apostol
Manatí	Festival de Los Manatí
Mayagüez	Festival del Seco
Morovis	Nuestras Fiestas Patronales
Orocovis	Festival del Camaron
Patillas	Festival Monte y Mar
Ponce	Festival de Bomba y Plena
Río Grande	Nuestras Fiestas Patronales
Santa Isabela	Nuestras Fiestas Patronales
Toa Baja	Festival Playero
Vega Alta	Festa de la Piña
Vega Alta	Paseo de la Virgen
Vieques	Nuestras Fiestas Patronales
Villalba	Nuestras Fiestas Patronales

❏ AUGUST

Añasco	Festival Sta. Rosa de Lima
Barranquitas	Festival Viva Mi Calle
Cayey	Nuestras Fiestas Patronales
Cayey	Reconocimiento al Jibaro P.R.
Coamo	Festival La Flor
Coamo	Festival Macuya
Coamo	Semana Nacional Afuera
Comerío	Nuestras Fiestas Patronales

Culebra	Carnaval Deportivo
Dorado	Festival de la Cocolia
Fajardo	Festival de Piel de Seda
Juncos	Carnaval Valenciano
Juncos	Ferias Junqueñas
Mayagüez	Carnaval
Mayagüez	Festival del Mango
Patillas	Nuestras Fiestas Patronales
Ponce	Festival de la Quenepa
Rincón	Nuestras Fiestas Patronales
Salinas	Nuestras Fiestas Patronales
San Juan	Aniversario del Mercado de Ar.
San Juan	Festival de Ceramica
Toa Baja	Festival Banda de Musica

☐ SEPTEMBER

Aguas Buenas	Nuestras Fiestas Patronales
Añasco	Festival del Chipe
Arecibo	Festival Folklorico Arecibeño
Camuy	Feria de Artesano
Coamo	Festival Jardines de Santa Ana
Coamo	Festival Madrileño
Fajardo	Fiesta Tipica El Paraiso
Florida	Nuestras Fiestas Patronales
Hormigueros	Nuestras Fiestas Patronales
Jayuya	Nuestras Fiestas Patronales
Juana Díaz	Nuestras Fiestas Patronales
Juncos	Nuestras Fiestas Patronales
Lares	Festival de Lares
Moca	Festival del Cuatro
Moca	Nuestras Fiestas Patronales
Naranjito	Nuestras Fiestas Patronales
Orocovis	Feria Artesania
San Germán	Festival del Anón
San Juan	Festival Cultural del Niño
San Juan	Festival de Bomba
San Juan	Festival of Inter-American Arts
San Juan	Sinfonica de Puerto Rico
San Lorenzo	Festival Bordado y Tejido
San Lorenzo	Nuestras Fiestas Patronales
Toa Baja	Aniversario de Levittown
Trujillo	Nuestras Fiestas Patronales
Utuado	Nuestras Fiestas Patronales
Vega Baja	Nuestras Fiestas Patronales
Vieques	Festival Casabe
Yauco	Nuestras Fiestas Patronales

◻ OCTOBER

Aguada	Festival del Juey
Aguada	Nuestras Fiestas Patronales
Aguadilla	Nuestras Fiestas Patronales
Aibonito	Festival de la Montaña
Añasco	Festival del Chipé
Arroyo	Festival del Pescao
Caguas	Nuestras Fiestas Patronales
Canóvan	Nuestras Fiestas Patronales
Ceiba	Festival de la Raza
Ciales	Nuestras Fiestas Patronales
Cidra	Festival Desc. de P.R.
Cidra	Festival Talento Pitri
Coamo	Festival de Bomba y Plena
Corozal	Festival del Platano
Corozal	Nuestras Fiestas Patronales
Florida	Festival Cultural Río Encantado
Guánica	Festival Cultura
Guayama	Feria Artesania y Musica
Guayama	Festival Cultural Luis Pales Matos
Guaynabo	Carnaval Mabo
Jayuya	Festival Indigena
Lajas	Festival Gallistico
Lares	Festival Almojabana
Lares	Festival Hacienda Rabano
Luquillo	Festival de Platos Tipicos
Luquillo	Nuestras Fiestas Patronales
Naguabo	Nuestras Fiestas Patronales
Río Piedras	Nuestras Fiestas Patronales
San Germán	Nuestras Fiestas Patronales
San Juan	Festival de la Musica
San Juan	Festival de Teatro Internacional
San Juan	Garden of P.R. Opening
Toa Baja	Festival de la Zafra
Yabucoa	Nuestras Fiestas Patronales

◻ NOVEMBER

Aguada	Feria de Artesanias
Aguada	Festival Desc. de P.R.
Aibonito	Festival de la Montaña
Barceloneta	Festival Folklorica
Cayey	Festival Tierra Adentro
Cidra	Festival Paloma Sabanera
Coamo	Festival la Yuca
Coamo	Festival Musical y Deportivo
Culebra	Festival de Artesania

Dorado	Accion de Gracia
Dorado	Festival de P.R.
Fajardo	Festival de Chiringa
Humacao	Festival de Santa Cecilia
Isabela	Festival de Gallo
Las Marías	Nuestras Fiestas Patronales
Maunabo	Festival Platano
Mayagüez	Feria Regional De Artesanias
San Sebastián	Expo Arte
Santa Isabela	Carnaval del Pavo
Villalba	Festival Areyto

☐ DECEMBER

Adjuntas	Festival Navideño
Añasco	Festival de la Bellas Artes
Arroyo	Festival Musica Puertorriqueña
Cabo Rojo	Festival de la Paleta
Coamo	Parrandas Navideñas
Dorado	Festival de Navidad
Guánica	Festival Navidad
Guayama	Verbenas
Guayanil.	Nuestras Fiestas Patronales
Hatillo	Festival de las Mascaras
Humacao	Nuestras Fiestas Patronales
Juana Díaz	Festival Puertorriqueñas
Juana Díaz	Festival Santos Reyes
Lares	Nuestras Fiestas Patronales
Las Piedras	Nuestras Fiestas Patronales
Manatí	Festival Navideño
Maunabo	Festival de Navidad
Mayagüez	Apertura Epoca de Navidad
Mayagüez	Festival de Navidad
Orocovis	Encuentro Nacional Santeros
Ponce	Nuestras Fiestas Patronales
Sabana Grande	Festival de Trovadores
Sabana Grande	Festival del Buren
Sabana Grande	Festival del Petate
San Germán	Festival de Navidad
San Juan	Criollisimo Ballet
San Juan	Festival Infantil Arlequin
San Juan	Festival Old San Juan Christmas
San Juan	Iluminacion de Belen
San Juan	Navidades (Christmas Events)
Toa Baja	Fiesta de Navidad
Utuado	Fiesta de Navidad
Vega Alta	Nuestras Fiestas Patronales

Transport

By Air

Although the days of bargain basement flights are over, it's still possible to visit Puerto Rico relatively cheaply. And though the only really cheap way to get there is to swim, you can still save money by shopping around. A good travel agent should find the lowest fare for you; if he or she doesn't, find another agent, or try doing it yourself. If there are no representative offices in your area, check the phone book – most airlines have toll-free numbers. In these days of airline deregulation, fares change quicker than you can say *"Minuto,"* (minute) so it's best to check the prices well before departure and then again before you go to buy the ticket. Advance purchase excursion fares, weekday and night flights, and one-way fares are among the options that may save you money. The more flexible you can be about when you wish to depart and return, the easier it will be to find a bargain. Whether dealing with a travel agent or with the airlines themselves make sure that you let them know clearly what it is you want. Don't assume that because you live in Los Angeles, for example, it's cheapest to fly from there. It may be better to find an ultrasaver flight to gateway cities like New York or Miami and then change planes. Fares tend to be cheaper on weekdays and during low season (mid-April to mid-December). You must now pay $12.50 additional in tax to fly in or out of San Juan airport, which works out to an extortionate $25 RT added to your ticket. Expect to pay around $350 RT from JFK, $400 RT from Chicago, and $620 RT from Los Angeles.

for San Juan: Flying to San Juan from Charlotte, Philadelphia, and (seasonally) from Orlando, USAir (☎ 800-842-5374) is one of the most important carriers serving the Commonwealth. On-board service is both congenial and attentive. USAir serves 40 states, and the 465 daily departures at Charlotte and 300 at Philadelphia offer numerous possibilities for connections. From the W coast, cities served include Seattle, Sacramento, Los Angeles, Orange County, and San Diego; Phoenix, Las Vegas, Denver, and Albuquerque are served from the SW; and most other major cities in other parts of the US are served as well. Members of the USAir Club can relax in any of its 27 lounges and clubs. These comfortable and placid retreats serve complimentary breakfast coffee, muffins, and juice. They also provide fax machine access, check cashing, free local phone calls, and other services. If you are interested in a package tour, you can contact USAir Vacations, ☎ 800-833-5436. Carnival flies from Miami, JFK, and Newark to San Juan and has connecting flights to destinations as diverse as Los Angeles, Manhattan (Kansas) and White Plains. Check with them for details. Delta flies directly from Atlanta, and TWA flies from NY. American Airlines also flies from NY and Miami to San Juan.

AIRLINES

Aeropostal Venezolana	☎ 787-721-2166
Aero Virgin Islands	☎ 787-791-1215
Air Caribe	☎ 787-791-6610
Air France	☎ 787-791-8282
Air Jamaica	☎ 787-724-2555
American, American Eagle	☎ 800-462-8455
	☎ 787-749-1747
British Airways	☎ 800-247-9297
	☎ 787-725-1575
BWIA	☎ 787-724-2555
Canadian International	☎ 787-791-4730
Caribbean Air Carrier	☎ 787-870-2680
Carnival	☎ 800-274-6140
	☎ 787-259-1010
City Wings	☎ 787-899-5920
Delta	☎ 800-221-1212
Dolphin	☎ 800-707-0138
Dominicana	☎ 787-724-7100
Flamenco	☎ 787-724-7110
Iberia	☎ 800-772-4642
	☎ 787-721-5630
LACSA	☎ 787-724-3330
LIAT	☎ 787-791-3838
Lufthansa	☎ 800-645-3880
	☎ 787-723-9553
Mexicana	☎ 787-722-8212
Northwest Airlines	☎ 800-225-2525
Prestige Aviation	☎ 787-742-3141
TWA	☎ 800-221-2000
	☎ 800-892-8466
United	☎ 800-241-6522
	☎ 800-538-2929
USAir	☎ 800-842-5374
Vieques Air-Link	☎ 787-722-3738

for Aguadilla: American flies to Aguadilla nonstop from New York and Miami.

for Ponce: American flies to Ponce nonstop from New York. Carnival Airlines flies daily from JFK and Newark to Ponce. Puerto Rico may also be reached by air from everywhere in the Caribbean except Cuba.

for Culebra and Vieques: Carib (☎ 800-981-0212) is the only airline flying directly from the international airport to Culebra. Flamenco (☎ 725-7707, 723-8110) flies to Culebra from Isla Grande and Fajardo, and Vieques Air Link (☎ 722-3736, 723-9882 in San Juan) flies to Vieques from Fajardo and Isla Grande.

excursions from Puerto Rico: As the island is a Caribbean hub, you might wish to combine your visit with trips to other islands. LIAT (791-3838; 800-981-8585) offers its Caribbean Explorer (three stops in 21 days for $250) and its Super Caribbean Explorer (up to 27 stops in 30 days for $367)

for the Virgin Islands: A number of small airlines fly to the American and British Virgin Islands.

for the Dominican Republic: American and Dominicana fly. In the past a ferry ran between Mayagüez and San Pedro de Macorís. There has been talk about restarting the service.

By Sea

Sadly, there's little passenger service between Puerto Rico and other Caribbean islands. In 1987 a hydrofoil ran to the Virgin Islands but, as it was designed more for use in rivers than at sea, it soon folded. Transport does run from St. John to Fajardo, but only a few times per month. So, unless you are willing to take a cruise ship – which not only costs more than flying but often isolates you from locals – there is no other regularly scheduled alternative. One potentially rewarding opportunity (if you can afford it) is to sail your own yacht to Caribbean waters and travel about on your own. Or fly to St. Thomas or Tortola and rent a yacht to sail to Puerto Rico. It's possible to crew on a boat coming over from Europe; most, however, head for the southern Caribbean, so you'd have to find a way N from there.

Transport

Tours

PACKAGE TOURS: As they say, all that glitters is not gold. This cliché may be old but it is certainly pertinent when it comes to package tours! If you want to have everything taken care of, then package tours are the way to go. But they do have at least two distinct disadvantages: almost everything has already been decided for you, which takes much of the thrill out of traveling, and you are more likely to be put up in a large characterless hotel (where the tour operators can get quantity discounts), rather than in a small inn (where you can get quality treatment). So think twice before you sign up. Also, if you should want to sign up, read the fine print and see what's *really* included and what's not. Don't be taken in by useless freebies that gloss over the lack of paid meals, for example.

BIRDING TOURS: Field Guides (☎ 512-327-4953, fax 512-327-9231; Box 160723, Austin, TX 78716-0723) offers worldwide tours. Their Puerto Rican tour (which also includes Jamaica) generally leaves in the Spring and focuses on El Yunque, Guánica, and Maricao. On the trip you may see such species as scaly-naped woodpeckers, pearly-eyed thrashers, elfin woods warblers, Puerto Rican todies, Puerto Rican lizard cuckoos, green mangos, or Puerto Rican nightjars.

TOUR OPERATORS

Angelo Tours	☎ 787-784-4375
Attabeira Educational Travel	☎ 787-767-4023
Cordero Caribbean Tours	☎ 787-799-6002
Faith Travel & Tours	☎ 787-257-8775
Gray Line	☎ 787-727-8080
Land & Sea Excursions	☎ 787-382-4872
Normandie Tours	☎ 787-722-6308
Rico Suntours	☎ 787-722-2080
Royal King Travel	☎ 787-724-0744
Sunshine Tour Guide	☎ 787-791-4500
Tour Co-op of PR	☎ 787-253-1448
Travel Service Inc.	☎ 787-724-6281
Turismo Internacional	☎ 787-721-1347
United Tour Guides	☎ 787-725-7605
VIP Coach & Tour	☎ 787-782-0435
Western Tourist Services	☎ 787-833-4328
Will Rey Tour	☎ 787-791-0666

ECO/ADVENTURE TOURS: If you're looking to get off the beaten track but want to do so in an organized fashion, you might consider one of the following companies offering outdoor activities in the Commonwealth.

ECO/ADVENTURE TOUR OPERATORS

- ❑ **AdvenTours,** ☎ 787-832-2016. Trips to natural and historic wonders. Customized packages available.

- ❑ **Adventuras Tierra Adentro,** ☎ 787-766-0470. Cave exploration and rappelling.

- ❑ **Encanto Ecotours,** ☎ 787-272-0005. Expeditions to see manatees, explore mangroves, raft, to Mona Island, and to go on a turtle nesting watch.

- ❑ **EcoAdventures,** ☎ 787-791-6053. Expeditions to Mona Island, Toro Negro, and scuba and snorkeling.

- ❑ **Expediciones Montaña Adentro,** ☎ 787-98-2723. Cave expeditions.

- ❑ **Paradise Island Ecotours,** ☎ 787-832-7933. Trips to various reserves, Culebra, and Caja de Muertos. Employs biologists as guides.

- ❑ **Tropix Tours,** ☎ 787-268-2173. Customized trips to Culebra, Vieques, and other locations. Bicycling tours.

Getting Around

You'll need to have patience! Always allow plenty of time to get to any island destination. City bus service in San Juan is cheap but painfully inefficient and slow. Around the island, there is no longer any regular passenger bus service. Unscheduled but cheap rural services run all over the island, including along the mountain road from Arecibo (Carr. 10) down to Ponce. *Públicos* are Ford vans with seats that serve as shared taxis. A cheap and convenient form of transportation, they can be picked up or left at any point. Identifiable by the letter "P" on the license plate, their route is listed on the windshield. Unfortunately, except for the San Juan-Ponce and other runs originating from San Juan, they cover only short hops between towns, which can mean changing vehicles innumerable times before reaching your final destination. Hitchhiking is slow

TRAVEL DISTANCES WITHIN PUERTO RICO

(top number – km; bottom number – miles)

	Aguadilla	Arecibo	Caguas	Cayey	Coamo	Fajardo	Guayama	Humacao	Manatí	Mayagüez	Ponce	San Germán	San Juan	San Sebastian	Yauco
Aguadilla		53	149	161	138	180	162	177	79	28	104	47	136	25	74
		33	93	101	86	112	101	110	49	17	65	29	85	16	46
Arecibo	53		96	108	91	127	133	124	26	72	82	93	83	41	82
	33		60	67	57	79	83	77	16	45	51	58	52	25	51
Caguas	149	96		26	61	54	53	28	70	172	95	152	35	137	126
	93	60		16	38	34	33	17	43	107	59	94	22	85	78
Cayey	161	108	26		35	80	27	54	82	146	69	126	52	148	100
	100	67	16		22	50	17	34	51	91	43	78	32	92	62
Coamo	138	91	61	35		115	42	89	65	111	34	91	80	113	65
	86	57	38	22		71	26	55	40	69	21	57	50	70	40
Fajardo	180	127	54	80	115		92	33	101	199	149	206	59	168	180
	112	79	34	50	71		57	21	63	124	93	128	37	104	112
Guayama	162	133	53	27	42	92		59	107	135	58	116	79	137	89
	101	83	33	17	26	57		37	66	84	36	72	49	85	55
Humacao	177	124	28	54	89	33	59		98	194	117	174	60	165	148
	110	77	17	34	55	21	37		61	121	73	108	37	103	92
Manatí	79	26	70	82	65	101	107	98		98	82	119	57	67	108
	49	16	43	51	40	63	66	61		61	51	74	35	42	67
Mayagüez	28	72	172	146	111	199	135	194	98		77	19	155	31	46
	17	45	107	91	69	124	84	121	61		48	12	96	19	29
Ponce	104	82	95	69	34	149	58	117	82	77		57	114	79	31
	65	51	59	43	21	93	36	73	51	48		35	71	49	19
San Germán	47	93	152	126	91	206	116	174	119	19	57		171	52	26
	29	58	94	78	57	128	72	108	74	12	35		106	32	16
San Juan	136	83	35	52	80	59	79	60	57	155	114	171		124	145
	85	52	22	32	50	37	49	37	35	96	71	106		77	90
San Sebastian	25	41	137	148	113	168	137	165	67	31	79	52	124		64
	16	25	85	92	70	104	85	103	42	19	49	32	77		40
Yauco	74	82	126	100	65	180	89	148	108	46	31	26	145	64	
	46	51	78	62	40	112	55	92	67	29	19	16	90	40	

but very possible and a good way to pass the time while waiting for buses.

Hiking

An alternative to local transport or renting a car is the **Fondo de Mejoramiento** (☎ 759-8366), a local travel organization that conducts tours to various spots of scenic, historical, and cultural interest. Participants are asked to refrain from gathering plants or littering. It sponsors an annual hike which traverses the entire 165-mile Panoramic Route from Maunabo to Mayagüez over the course of 16 weekend days. It has some 1,300 family members; annual dues are $13 per family. Each day trip costs $6 for individuals and $3 for students. Another organization offering hikes is the **Natural History Society** (☎ 728-1515, ext. 283); it also holds free monthly talks. **The Camping Association of Puerto Rico** charges annual dues of $20 for individuals and $25 for families. You must go on one trip before being admitted. Write Box 2738, Metropolitan Shopping Center, Hato Rey, PR 00919-2738. In Aibonito, the **Piedra Restaurant** (☎ 735-1034) offers free hikes through the Cristóbal Canyon leaving at 8:30 AM on the last Sat. of each month; reservations are required.

Renting A Car / Driving

The island's poor internal transportation system makes this an option you'll want to consider. If you don't have insurance, however, make sure you purchase coverage for the rental vehicle. All too often roads are poorly marked, so getting anywhere can be an adventure in itself! Be aware of Transit Law #126, requiring that every child under age four must be strapped into a protective seat. Puerto Rican law also prohibits the rental of scooters and motorbikes. Cars can be rented at the airport; a valid US driver's license is required. Expect to pay at least $25 per day, but weekend specials and a weekly rate may be available. Insurance is additional. Smaller companies frequently offer better deals. One of the best of these is **Charlie's** (☎ 791-1101, 726-6138). They have offices in both Condado and Isla Verde.

As you should do everywhere, read the contract thoroughly, especially the fine print. Ask about unlimited mileage, free gas, late return penalties, and drop-off fees. In general, it's preferable to avoid driving in San Juan. Not only is it congested, it has the highest rate of carjacking in the US: an average of 638 cars per month in

1992, surpassing LA and more than six times the number in New York City.

CAR RENTAL AGENCIES

(San Juan Unless Other City Noted)

AAA	☎ 787-791-1465
Afro	☎ 787-724-3720
Charlie's	☎ 787-728-2418
Discount	☎ 787-726-1460
L&M	☎ 787-725-8307
Leaseway	☎ 787-791-5900
Luchetti	☎ 787-725-8298
National	☎ 787-791-1805
Popular – Mayagüez	☎ 787-265-4848
Popular – Ponce	☎ 787-259-4848
Sánchez – Aguadilla	☎ 787-891-7777
Target	☎ 787-783-6592

---

times and distances: From San Juan it takes around 45 minutes to drive the 34 miles to Fajardo, 40 minutes to drive to Humacao (34 miles), 1½ hours to Guayama (44 miles), 1½ hours to Coamo (49 miles), 1½ hours to Ponce (70 miles), 2½ hours to San Germán (76 miles) 2 hours to Mayagüez (98 miles), 1½ hours to Aguadilla (81 miles), 2½ hours to Utuado, one hour to Arecibo (48 miles), and 30 minutes to Dorado (19 miles).

suggested routes: One advantage of renting a car is that you can explore remote routes which are poorly served by public transportation. It is highly recommended that you tour all or part of the Ruta Panorámica. Although improvements are being made, roads remain inadequately signed; driving can be confusing. Roads will flood easily in the back country during heavy rainstorms. Driving at night along mountain roads can be stressful. You may encounter traffic jams in small towns such as Yauco. It helps to know some Spanish for obtaining directions, but people are very helpful. Gas starts at around 25¢/liter (a bit over $1/gallon) and is cheapest in towns. A good map is a necessity. You'll have the best time if you don't set a rigid schedule for yourself and just play it by ear.

HIGHWAYS: Considering its size, Puerto Rico has an astounding number of major arteries to accommodate its million-plus vehicles. During the past 25 years, some 85 miles of new roads have been constructed and another 140 miles are planned. One major project currently underway is the construction of Carr. 66, a new highway which will parallel the 65th Infantry Road running from Río Piedras to Río Grande. Other projects include relocating Carr. 3 (running from Fajardo to Salinas), connecting Guayama with the Las Américas tollway at Salinas, completing the Ponce South Bypass which will extend the Las Américas tollway, extending the De Diego tollway from Dorado to Arecibo, constructing additional lanes on Carr. 2 between Arecibo and Ponce, relocating Carr. 167 from Bayamón to Comerio and Naranjito, improving Baldorioty de Castro Av. in San Juan, and conversion of a section of Carr. 17 to an expressway in Hato Rey. Now completed is a privately run toll bridge over the San José Lagoon, which links the Piñero Expressway to Baldorioty de Castro Avenue.

SPANISH FOR DRIVERS

Adelante	Ahead
Calle sin Salida	Dead end
Peligro	Danger
Desvio	Detour
Salida	Exit
Neblina	Fog
Lomo	Hill or bump
Desprendimiento	Landslide
A la Izquierda	To the left
Puenta Estrecho	Narrow bridge
Transito	One-way traffic
No Estacione	No parking
Cruce de Peatones	Pedestrian crossing
A la Derecha	To the right
Carretera Cerada	Road closed
Zona Escolar	School zone
Semaforo	Signal light
Resbala Mojado	Slippery when wet
Baden	Speed bump
Pare	Stop
Peaje	Toll station
No Vire	No turn

Transport

Internal Air Transport

Small airlines fly to the outlying islands of Vieques and Culebra; American Eagle flies daily from San Juan's international airport to Ponce and Mayagüez.

Ferries

Passenger ferries leave daily from Fajardo to Culebra and Vieques. Another ferry route of note is the Aquaexpress service running from Old San Juan to Cataño and Hato Rey. Intended largely for local residents, a passenger boat service (free) is available on Dos Bocas Lake.

Accommodations

Accommodations on the island are not cheap in general but, if you hunt around, you may find some bargains. Rates in this book generally do not include the 7% government tax. You might want to breeze by the tourist traps and explore other areas of the island where things are often significantly cheaper.

Centros Vacacionales are clusters of rental cottages situated at Boquerón, Cabo Rojo, Humacao, Maricao, and Arroyo. These are available to "bona fide family groups" for $20 per night with a minimum stay of two and a maximum stay of seven nights. From Sept. 1 through May 31 there's a special weekly rate of $100. For more information and a reservation form (apply 120 days in advance) write to Oficina de Reservaciones, Compania de Fomento Recreativo, Apartado Postal No. 3207, San Juan, PR 00904 (☎ 722-1771/1551, 721-2800 ext. 225, 275).

Attractive buildings set in lush surroundings, the government-run *paradores* were planned to be inexpensive inns originally. Now, they're moderately priced and normally empty during the week. (See chart). Reserve from the States by dialing ☎ 800-443-0266. You can also reserve in Old San Juan at 301 San Justo, ☎ 721-2400 or 721-2884. Call toll-free within the island at ☎ 800-462-7575. There are many campgrounds, but take care to ensure the safety of your gear.

PARADORES AT A GLANCE

These government-sponsored "country inns" are scattered all across the island. Prices listed are subject to fluctuation and are given as guidelines only. Charges for additional persons range from $8-$15 per room. For current prices and to make reservations, contact Paradores Puertorriqueños, Box 4435, Old San Juan, PR 00905; ☎ 800-443-0266 in the US and 800-462-7575 in Puerto Rico; fax 787-721-4698. **Note:** Paradores located in rural areas require your own transportation. All transportation times given are by private car.

❑ **Baños de Coamo,** ☎ 787-825-2239; fax 825-4739. s/d $50/$60. A half-hour's drive from Ponce and 1½ hours from San Juan (via the expressway). Facilities include 48 a/c rooms with private bath and balconies, restaurant, hot spring swimming pool, hot springs, tennis court, poolside bar.

❑ **Boquemar,** ☎ 787-851-2158; fax 851-7600. s/d $60/$65. In Cabo Rojo, Boqueron, off Carr. 307 and 103. Near Mayagüez, La Parguera, Puerto Real fishing village, and numerous beaches. Facilities include 41 a/c rooms with 2nd floor balcony and refrigerator, and a pool.

❑ **Casa Grande,** ☎ 787-894-3939; fax 724-4920. s/d $55. Located within a former coffee plantation on Carr. 612, relatively near Utuado. Facilities include 20 fan-equipped rooms, restaurant, pool, and hiking trails.

❑ **El Faro,** ☎ 787-882-8000; fax 882-1030. s/d $65/$70. A modern 32-room building set next to the former Ramey Air Force Base (and its golf course), which is some 2½ hours from San Juan. It has a restaurant, cocktail lounge, and pool, and its a/c rooms have cable TV, balconies, and phone.

❑ **Guajataca,** ☎ 787-895-3070; fax 895-3589. s/d $72-$73/$75-$83. Two hours on San Juan on Carr. 2, Km 103.8 near Quebradillas. Near beach, Lago Guajataca (bring fishing gear), and near Arecibo Observatory and Camuy Caves. Facilities include 38 a/c rooms with private bath and balconies facing the ocean, restaurant, pool, live music on weekends, telephone in room, and two tennis courts.

❑ **Hacienda Gripiñas,** ☎ 787-828-1717; fax 828-1719. s/d $50/$60. Located 2½ hours from San Juan on Carr. 527, Km 2.5 near Jayuya. Near Caguana Ball Park, petroglyphs, and Lago Caonilla (bring fishing gear). Facilities: 19 rooms with private bath (most with ceiling fans) in 200-year-old restored coffee plantation greathouse; pool; restaurant.

❑ **Hacienda Juanita,** ☎ 787-838-2550; fax 787-838-2551. s/d $55/$65. Located in former coffee plantation 2½ hours from San Juan on Carr. 105, Km 232.5 near the town of Maricao, fish hatchery, and Monte del Estado reserve. Facilities: 21 rooms with private bath, restaurant, lounge, hiking trails, tennis, volleyball and handball courts.

❑ **J.B. Hidden Village,** ☎ 787-868-8686/8687; fax 868-8701. s/d $70+. On Carr. 416 and three minutes from Carr. 2, it has 25 a/c rooms with balcony and cable TV, pool, conference center (holds up to 300), and restaurant (seafood and other dishes).

❑ **Joyuda Beach,** ☎ 787-851-5650; fax 265-6940. s/d $65/$85. This hotel has 41 a/c rooms with TV, phone and bath; some suites have sunset views. Facilities include restaurant and beach bar, beach volleyball, small children's playground, windsurfing, canoeing, and golfing (at the Club Deportivo). Cabins with kitchens are also available.

❑ **La Familia,** ☎ 787-863-1193; fax 860-5435. s/d $45-$52/$56-$65. In Las Croabas, this 22-room parador offers access to the area's attractions. Its a/c rooms have TV and refrigerator.

❑ **Oasis,** ☎ 787-892-1175; fax Ext. 200. s/d $52-$54/$58-$60. Located along Carr. 102 in San Germán 2½ hours from San Juan near La Parguera and Mayagüez. Facilities include 34 a/c rooms with private bath and color TV, restaurant, and convention hall.

❑ **Perichi's,** ☎ 787-851-3131; 851-0560. s/d $65-$70. Set in Joyuda, it has 25 a/c rooms with balconies, color TV, and phone. There's a pool, restaurant, banquet hall, baseball and basketball courts, and game room.

❑ **Perichi's,** ☎ 787-851-3131; 851-0560. s/d $60-$65. Located at Carr. 102, Km 14.3 in San Germán 2½ hours from San Juan, near many beaches and Mayagüez Mall. Facilities include 15 a/c rooms with private bath and balconies facing the sea, restaurant, basketball court, and dance music on weekends.

❑ **Posada Porlamar,** ☎ 787-899-4015; fax 899-6040. s/d $40/$55. Located 2½ hours from San Juan on Carr. 304 in Lajas near San Germán and La Parguera. There are 19 a/c rooms, restaurant, and kitchen facilities.

❑ **El Sol,** ☎ 787-834-0303; fax 265-7567. s/d $45+/$50+. Located at 9 East Mariano Riera, Plamer Street, Mayagüez. Facilities include 40 a/c rooms with private bath, cable color TV, continental breakfast, and swimming pool.

❑ **Villa Antonio,** ☎ 787-823-2645; fax 823-3380. One bdrm $50-$90/two bdrm $75-$95. Located 2½ hours from San Juan on Carr. 115, Km 12.3 in Rincon, the island's surf capital. Facilities include 50 a/c rooms (cabanas and one-bdrm s/d apartments), two tennis courts, and swimming pool.

❑ **Villa Parguera,** ☎ 787-899-3975; fax 899-6040. s/d $75/$85. Located on Carr. 304 in La Parguera, 2½ hours from San Juan. Facilities: 50 a/c rooms with private bath, restaurant, swimming pool, live floor show and dance music on weekends.

❑ **Vistamar,** ☎ 787-895-2065; fax 895-2294. s/d $61, $72, $85. Located on Carr. 113, Km 4 off Carr. 2, two hours from San Juan in Quebradillas near Guajataca and relatively near Arecibo Observatory and Camuy Caves. Facilities: 35 a/c rooms with private bath, restaurant, swimming pool, game room, tennis, volleyball, and basketball courts.

APARTMENT AND CONDOMINIUM RENTALS: These are best reserved in advance. **Heidi Steiger,** 2019 Cacique St., Santurce, PR 00911 (☎ 727-6248), rents high quality apartments in the Condado area. In Luquillo, to the E of San Juan, Playa Azul Realty (Box 386, Luquillo, PR 00673, ☎ 889-3425) rents studio, one- , two- , and three-bedroom apartments. Prices range from $300 pw ($800 pm) for a studio to $300 for a three-bedroom, two-bath for the weekend. Most are air conditioned; all come with fully equipped kitchens, have guard service, face the ocean, and have beach and pool facilities. BV Real Estate (☎ 863-3687, fax 860-4565; Box 1327 Fajardo, PR 00738) also offers short- and long-term rentals in the Fajardo and Luquillo areas. Vieques and Culebra rentals are listed under their specific sections.

☞ **Traveler's Tip.** A wise precaution is to call ahead. (See Traveler's Tip about phone cards on page 107.) If you're driving, you can always cruise around in the early afternoon and seek out a place to stay. If you're traveling in a group, you should be aware that some places charge by the room rather than the number of people, so this might be one way to keep costs down. Remember that the lower priced hotels offer better values, much more charm, *and* have a more interesting clientele. As one reader put it, "the travelers one encounters ...tend to be more interesting than the people in the Condado area or resorts like El Conquistador. The people who go to the traditional resort locales don't seem to have much interest in knowing anything about the landscape outside of the pool, the beach, the bar, and the casino."

Food & Drink

You'll find plenty of places to eat. There are cafeterias which serve everything from grilled cheese sandwiches to rice and beans, simple local restaurants, and their more expensive cousins which serve the most elaborate combinations of Spanish and other cuisines imaginable. In addition, there are the ubiquitous and ultra-popular fast-food joints (from Wendy's to Ponderosa to Burger King) and a proliferation of pizzerias. Combining African, Indian, and Spanish cuisine into something new and refreshingly different, food on the island provides a unique culinary experience. Although similar to Dominican, Cuban, and other Caribbean cuisines, it has its own distinct flavor. Seasonings used include pepper, cinnamon, fresh ginger, cilantro, lime rind, *naranja agria* (sour orange), and cloves. *Sofrito,* a sauce used to flavor many dishes, combines *achiote* (annato seeds fried in lard and strained) with ham and other seasonings. Many dishes are cooked in a *caldero,* a cast-iron kettle with a rounded bottom.

SNACKS: Street vendors and *cafeterias* sell a wide variety of tasty, deep-fried snacks. *Alcapurrias* contain ground plantain and pork, or (less commonly) fish or crab fried in batter. *Bacalaítos fritos* are fried codfish fritters made with the dried, salted cod imported from New England. *Amarillos en dulce* are yellow plantains fried in a sauce of cinnamon, sugar, and red wine. *Empanadas* are made with yucca or plantain dough stuffed with meat and wrapped in plantain leaves. *Pastelillos* are fried dough containing meat and cheese. They are sometimes made using fruit and jam; *empanadillas* ("little pies") are larger versions available on some parts of the island. *Pasteles* are made from plantain or *yautia* dough which has been stuffed with ground pork, garbanzo beans, and raisins, then wrapped in plantain leaves. *Pinonos* are a mixture of ground beef and ripe plantains dipped in a beaten egg batter and then fried. *Surullitos* or *sorullos* are deep-fried corn meal fritters. *Rellenos de papa* are meat-stuffed potato balls fried in egg batter. *Mofongo* is mashed and roasted plantain balls made with spices and *chicharron* (crisp pork cracklings).

SOUPS AND SPECIALTIES: Not particularly a vegetable-producing island, Puerto Rico nevertheless has its own unique *verduras* (vegetables), including *chayote* and *calabaza* (varieties of West Indian squash), *yuca* (cassava), *yautia* (tanier), *batata* (a type of sweet potato), and *name* (African yam). All are frequently served in local stews. *Asopao* is a soup made with rice and meat or seafood. *Lechon asado* or roast pig is an island specialty. Served in local *lechoneras,* it's tastiest when the pig's skin is truly crisp and golden. *Chicharron,* chunks of crispy pork skin, are sold alongside. Other pork dishes include *cuchifrito,* pork innards stew, *mondongo* (an African stew of chopped tripe), and *gandinga* (liver, heart, and kidneys cooked with spices).

Carne mechada is a beef roast garnished with ham, onion, and spices. Goat is also quite popular and *cabro* (young or kid goat) is considered a delicacy. *Fricase,* a dish made with stewed chicken, rabbit, or goat, is usually accompanied by *tostones,* plantains that have been fried twice. *Sopa de habichuelas negras* (black bean soup), is a popular dish, as are the standards *arroz con habichuelas* (rice and beans), and *arroz con pollo* (rice and chicken).

SEAFOOD: One of the most popular seafood items is actually imported from New England. *Bacalao* (dried, salted codfish) is cooked in several ways. *Bacalao a la Viscaina* is codfish stewed in rich tomato sauce. *Serenata* is flaked *bacalao* served cold with an oil and vinegar dressing and toppings like raw onions, avocados, and tomatoes. Although some seafood like shrimp must be imported, many others like *chillo* (red snapper), *mero* (sea bass), *pulpo* (octopus), and *chapin* (trunkfish) are available locally. Fish dishes served *en escabeche* have been pickled Spanish-style. *Ensalada de pulpo* is a tasty salad based on octopus. *Mojo isleño* is an elaborate sauce made of olives, onions, tomatoes, capers, vinegar, garlic, and pimentos. The most famous dishes are *langosta* (local lobster), *jueyes* (land crabs), and *ostiones* (miniature oysters that cling to the roots of mangrove trees). The damming of the island's rivers has brought about a decline of another indigenous delicacy, *camarones de río* (river shrimp).

CHEESE AND SANDWICHES: *Queso de hoja* is the very milky, mild-flavored, local soft cheese. It must be eaten fresh. It is often combined with the local marmalade, *pasta de guayaba* (guava paste). Many types of sandwiches are also available. A *cubano* contains ham, chicken, and cheese inside a long, crusty white bread. A medianoche ("midnight") contains pork, ham, and cheese.

DESSERTS: Puerto Rican desserts are simple but tasty. They include *arroz con dulce* (sweet rice pudding), *cazuela* (rich pumpkin and coconut pudding), and *bien-me-sabe* (sponge cake with coconut sauce), *tembleque* (coconut pudding), and *flan* (caramel custard). The last is an egg custard baked in a *baño de maría,* a set of two interlocking pans, one of which is filled with hot water. French in origin, *flan* is now widespread in the Spanish-speaking world. Ice cream is found islandwide. You can patronize Baskin Robbins or try the local ice cream, which often comes in fruit flavors and tends to be more like sherbet than true ice cream.

PUERTO RICAN FOOD A TO Z

Aguacate – avocado.
Alcapurrias – ground plantain and pork, fish, or crab fried in batter.
Amarillos en dulce – yellow plantains fried in a sauce of cinnamon, sugar, and red wine.
Arroz con dulce – sweet rice pudding.
Arroz con habichuelas – rice and beans.
Arroz con pollo – rice and chicken.
Asopao – soup made with rice and meat or seafood.
Bacalao a la Viscaina – codfish stewed in rich tomato sauce.
Bacalaítos fritos – fried codfish fritters.
Bien-me-sabe – sponge cake with coconut sauce.
Carne mechada – beef roast garnished with ham, onion, and spices.
Cazuela – rich pumpkin and coconut pudding.
Chapin – trunkfish.
Chicharron – chunks of crispy pork skin.
Chillo – red snapper.
China – the orange.
Coco frio – chilled drinking coconuts.
Corazón – custard apple, Jamaica apple, bullock's heart.
Cubano – sandwich containing ham, chicken, and cheese inside a long, crusty white bread.
Cuchifrito – pork innards stew.
Empanadas – yuca or plantain dough stuffed with meat and wrapped in plantain leaves.
Empanadillas – larger versions of pastelillos that are available on some parts of the island.
En escabeche – pickled Spanish-style.
Ensalada de pulpo – a tasty salad based on octopus.
Flan – caramel custard.
Fricase – a dish made with stewed chicken, rabbit, or goat.
Gandinga – liver, heart, and kidneys cooked with spices.
Guanábana – soursop.
Guineo – banana.
Jobo – hogplum.
Jueye – land crab.
Langosta – local lobster.
Lechón asado – roast pig.
Lechosa – papaya.
Malta – unique-tasting, non-alcoholic malt beverage made with barley, malt, cane sugar, corn grits, and hops.
Mamey – mammee apple; a brown, nearly round fruit
Mavi – local root beer made from tree bark.

Medianoche – a "midnight" sandwich containing pork, ham, and cheese.

Mero – sea bass.

Mofongo – mashed and roasted plantain balls made with spices and crisp pork cracklings.

Mojo isleño – an elaborate sauce that includes olives, onions, tomatoes, capers, vinegar, garlic, and pimentos.

Mondongo – an African stew of chopped tripe.

Naranja – the sour orange.

Níspero – sapodilla.

Panapen – breadfruit; roasted or boiled as a vegetable.

Parcha – passion fruit.

Pasta de guayaban – guava paste.

Pasteles – made from plantain or yautia dough which has been stuffed with ground pork, garbanzo beans, and raisins, then wrapped in plantain leaves.

Pastelillos – fried dough containing meat and cheese; sometimes made using fruit and jam.

Piña – pineapple.

Pinchos – shish kebabs

Pinonos – a mixture of ground beef and ripe plantains dipped in a beaten egg batter and then fried.

Piragua – shaved ice covered with tamarind or guava syrup served in a paper cup.

Plátano – plantain.

Pulpo – octopus.

Quenepa – "Spanish lime," a Portuguese delicacy about the size of a large walnut.

Queso de hoja – mild-flavored, local soft cheese.

Rellenos de papa – meat-stuffed potato balls fried in egg batter.

Serenata – flaked *bacalao* served cold with an oil and vinegar dressing and toppings like raw onions, avocados, and tomatoes.

Sopa de habichuelas negros – black bean soup.

Surullitos (sorullos) – deep-fried corn meal fritters.

Tamarind – tamarind.

Tembleque – coconut pudding.

Tostones – plantains that have been fried twice.

FRUIT: Although many fruits are imported from the US, Puerto Rico also grows a large variety of its own. Brought by the Spaniards in the 16th century, the sweet orange is known as *china* because the first seeds came from there. Vendors will peel off the skin with a knife to make a *chupon*, which you can pop into your mouth piece by piece. *Naranja* is the sour orange. *Guineos* or bananas, imported by the Spanish from Africa, come in all sizes, from the five-inch *niños* on up. Brought from southern Asia, the *plátano* or plantain is inedible until cooked. Puerto Rican *piñas* (pineapples) are much sweeter than their exported counterparts because they are left on the stem to ripen. The white interior of the *panapen* or breadfruit is roasted or boiled as a vegetable. Some bear small brown seeds, *panas de pepita*, that are boiled or roasted. Another fruit indigenous to the West Indies, *lechosa* or *papaya* is available much of the year.

The oval *parcha* (passion fruit) with its bright orange pulp was given its name by arriving Spaniards who saw its white and purple flowers as a representation of the Crucifixion in botanical form. It is high in vitamins A and C as well as iron. Coconut palms arrived in 1549 from Cape Verde, Africa via Dutch Guiana. Their nuts are chilled and served as *coco frio* (see below). You drink the water straight from the shell. The sour-tasting, green-skinned *guanábana* (soursop) can be used to make a delicious fruit drink; it is a native fruit, and can weigh as much as 10 lbs. A regional native, the *mamey* (mammee apple), is a brown, nearly round fruit which is high in pectin.

The *níspero* (sapodilla) is a fruit originally from the Yucatán. The *quenepa* or "Spanish lime" is a Portuguese delicacy about the size of a large walnut; its brittle green skin cracks open to reveal a white pit surrounded by pinkish pulp. It is related to the litchi nut, which is a prized Chinese fruit. The *corazón* (custard apple, Jamaica apple, bullock's heart) is a small, heart-shaped fruit that grows mostly in the wild. When cross-sectioned, the *caimito* (star apple), an Antilles native, has a star-shaped outline; its sweet pulp has a custard-like consistency. Island avocados (*aguacates*) are renowned for their thick pulp and small seeds. *Acerola*, the wild W Indian cherry, has from 20-50 times the vitamin C of orange juice. The little-known *jagua* (genipap or marmalade box) has a strong scent; many find it repugnant. Its dye was used by S American natives to tattoo their flesh and scientists have found it has antibiotic properties. The *tamarindo* (tamarind) is the fruit pod of a tree native to Africa and the Middle East; the tree is known for its long life – sometimes spanning two centuries. Its sticky pods are used to make a popular fruit drink. Known as the golden apple or Jew's plum, the *jobo de la India* has a delicious fruit used in marmalade and in juices. The related but smaller *ciruelo* (*jobito* or Spanish plum) is a Mexican native whose wood is often used for fenceposts. Enjoyed for its aromatic fruit more than its nut, the *pajuil* (cashew) grows wild. Its shell is poisonous.

DRINKS: Delicious fruit drinks are made from passion fruit and others. These are usually found at roadside stands in the countryside areas. Lotus is the government brand canned pineapple juice. (Some Puerto Ricans maintain it's the best thing the government does!) *Limber* (or *piragua*) is shaved ice covered with tamarind or guava syrup served in a paper cup; it's named after Charles Lindbergh, the famous pilot. Cool *cocos frios* or green drinking coconuts are available just about anywhere for around 75¢. Malta is a unique-tasting, non-alcoholic malt beverage made with barley, malt, cane sugar, corn grits, and hops. Mavi is a local root beer made from tree bark.

ALCOHOL: Blue laws are nonexistent in Puerto Rico; alcohol may be purchased anytime, anywhere. Locally brewed India and Medalla beers are available in seven- and 12-oz. bottles or in cans at every *colmado* or bar. Because brews were required to be sold in either 10 oz. cans or specially designed amber 12-oz. bottles, other brands were not readily available until recently. This law (designed to discourage imports) was repealed in 1992 after Heineken and Miller joined with a local distiller to challenge the law, and a beer war has resulted. Now also available are the extremely popular Miller Genuine Draft, Corona, Coors, Heineken, Bud, Michelob Golden Draft, Rolling Rock, Schlitz, Schaefer, and other brands. Premium beers such as Samuel Adams are also competing for market share.

Puerto Rico is the world's largest rum producer and accounts for 83% of US sales. Rum production began in the 16th century with production of *pintriche* or *cañita* (bootleg rum), a spirit that is still popular today. Under the Mature Spirits Act, white rum must be distilled for at least one year at a minimum of 180 proof and gold label (amber colored rum) for three years at 175 proof. Añejo, a special blend, requires six years. Although all of the 26 brands are roughly equivalent, Bacardi is the largest distiller on the island. (See "San Juan Bay and Cataño" under "Old San Juan" for tour information). Serralles (known for its Captain Morgan Spiced Rum and Don Q Rum) is the second largest. All other brands (such as the distinctive Barrilito) take raw rum from these two distillers and fabricate their own unique brands. Locals usually drink their rum with ice and water. Drinks such as *piña coladas* and banana daiquiris were developed especially for the tourist trade. *Piña coladas* are made by combining cream of coconut with pineapple juice, rum, and crushed ice.

Aside from alcohol, the most popular drink in Puerto Rico must be coffee. It is served either as *café* or *café con leche* (coffee essence with steamed milk) along with generous quantities of sugar. *Pocillo* or *café negro* is a demitasse cup of strong coffee served after dinner.

TIPS FOR VEGETARIANS: Puerto Rico is most definitely a carnivorous island, so the more you are able to bend or compromise your principles, the easier time you'll have. If you're a vegan (non-dairy-product user), unless you're cooking all of your own food, you will find it even more difficult, but fruits may be your salvation. The local rice and beans is a good staple, but it can get monotonous after a while, and the beans are often cooked with pork. Salads are also widely available, and there are Chinese restaurants as well. If you do eat fish, you should be aware that locals eat it fried and that it (along with dishes such as *tostones*, green fried plantains, may have been fried in lard or in the same oil as chicken or pork. If you eat a lot of nuts, plan on bringing your own because those available locally are expensive. The same goes for dried fruits such as raisins. As a final note, if preparing pasta dishes, you should note that tomato sauce sold in supermarkets frequently includes beef powder for flavor, so check the label carefully before purchasing. **note:** Places serving vegetarian food are listed frequently in the dining recommendations.

☞ **Traveler's Tip**. It's always a good idea to consider your eating habits when booking accommodations. For example, if you eat breakfast, you should think about what you may need or want to eat and when. Check to see when breakfast (or even coffee) will be available. Many hotels serve a complimentary breakfast, which is often continental. Consider whether this will satisfy you or not. Find out what other meals are available and how far it is to other restaurants. Vegetarians or those who simply shun meat and fowl will want to know if the restaurant will have anything for them to eat. Remember, it always pays to inquire before rather than after!

Sports & Sporting Events

Water Sports

Swimming

All the island's beaches must have unrestricted access by law. The island's *balnearios* provide lockers, showers, and parking. They are open Tues. to Sun., 9-5, summer, and 8-5, winter. A list of the major ones follows: **Playa Escambron**, Av. Muñoz Rivera, Puerto de Tierra; **Playa Isla Verde**, Carr. 187, Km 3.9 (both accessible by city bus); **Playa Punta Salinas**, Carr. 868, Km 1.2, Cataño; **Playa Sardinera**, Carr. 698, Dorado; **Playa Cerro Gordo**, Carr. 690, Vega Alta; **Playa Luquillo**, Carr. 3, Km 35.4; **Playa Seven Seas**, Carr. 987, Fajardo; **Playa Sombe**, Carr. 997, Vieques; **Playa Punta Santiago**, Carr. 3, Km 77, Humacao; **Playa Punta Guilarte**, Carr. 3, Km 128.5, Arroyo; **Playa Cana Gordo**, Carr. 333, Km 5.9, Guanica; **Playa Boquerón**, Carr. 101, Cabo Rojo; **Playa Añasco**, Carr. 401, Km 1, Añasco.

Scuba Diving & Snorkeling

Puerto Rico is an exceptionally fine place to do either. A large number of operations, many of which are Puerto Rican owned and managed, offer instruction and rentals. Operators from San Juan to Humacao can dive both their areas and more remote locations such as Culebra and Vieques. With an average underwater temperature of 80°, the visibility in many places is well over 100 ft, with 70 ft being an average. Owing to the frequent rainfall and freshwater runoff, Puerto Rican waters have a lower visibility than elsewhere in the Caribbean, but the runoff does attract a large number of fish, and it may be possible to see a manatee. Sharks are not a problem. Besides San Juan, scuba operations are also found in Isabela, Fajardo, at La Parguera, and on Culebra and Vieques.

dive spots: Popular locations off the coast of San Juan include Figure Eight Reef, the Molar, and Horseshoe Reef. Here you can find tunnels, overhangs, small caves (ranging down to 30 ft), and a number of lava rock formations housing everything from seahorses to banded coral shrimp. The many small islets off the coast of Fajardo, along with coral formations, underwater caves, and sunken sailboats, provide an excellent variety of dive spots. Names of sites here include Becerra

Reef, Corona, the North Shore, and the Slope. In addition, dives off of Culebra, Vieques, Icacos, Palominos, and Palomonitos are available. In this area you might spot everything from French angelfish to hairy hermit crabs to an octopus. Off of Culebra, there's a tugboat wreck and a coral zone called the "Impact Area." The latter is known for its arch formations. Offshore from Humacao, there are a number of sites, including Basslet Reef (35-60 ft in depth), and the Drift and the Canyon. Approximately five to seven miles offshore from La Parguera is an outer shelf where the sea bottom contours slope outward to form vertical walls. Here you can find a great variety of marine life from gorgonian corals to moray eels to dolphins and wall-lined sand trenches. Stingrays and eels are common at the Playground, the Trenches, and the Ninth Floor here. Phosphoresence occurs at Enrique Reef, which is just a few minutes offshore. Other opportunities lie near the pinnacle reefs and islets which are closer to land. In the NW, Crash Boat in Aguadilla is a popular dive site; Bajura in Isabela is known for its ring of coral caverns surrounding the 30-ft-deep Blue Hole. Reefs are also found off Mayagüez and off the beach next to Rincón's lighthouse. Isla Desacheo, a 260-acre uninhabited island about 15 miles from Rincón, offers clear water, reefs and caverns, and multitudes of fish. Mona and Monito also have great diving, but require a multi-day trip.

snorkeling and reefs: Good snorkeling spots are in Vieques, Culebra, off of Fajardo, and along the S coast. Ponce offers good diving in the horseshoe-shaped barrier reef (15-40 ft out from the offshore islands of Caja de Muertos, Cayo Cardona, Cayo Ratones, and Cayo Caribe), which stretches W from Ponce to Tallaboa. Puerto Rico's most unusual spot is an anchorage off Cayo Santiago (Monkey Island), from which you can snorkel in six-ft-deep water and watch macaque and rhesus monkeys. Coral reefs are found near La Parguera in the SW and off Caja de Muertos. Puerto Rico's best coral reefs are off Mona Island, a six-hour boat ride from the E coast.

Surfing & Windsurfing

SURFING: If you don't bring your own board, rentals are widely available. The most popular location is Rincón on the NW coast; the world championship was held here in 1968. Playa María nearby is the first of a series of surfing beaches that stretch around to Aguadilla and over to Isabela. Owing to the submerged rocks and high waves, this area is best left to the experienced. Others include Pine Grove in Isla Verde; Los Aviónes and La Concha in Piñones

(E of Isla Verde); Los Tubos next to Tortuguero Lagoon in Vega Baja (only during the winter); Jobos (near Isabela); and La Pared (to the E of Luquillo). Culebra's Ensenada Honda is another popular spot.

WINDSURFING: Different areas have different conditions. While ocean swells are found on the N shore, flat water sailing is available along the E and SW coasts. Long board and slalom conditions are found year round. Aficionados will prefer visiting in the winter when Atlantic storms cause swells. The most popular locations include Condado Lagoon (calm water, steady winds), the Ocean Park beaches, the area SE of Playa Luquillo on the NE shore, Boquerón (in the SW), and in Ensenada Honda on Culebra. Most major hotels rent equipment. The E end of Isla Verde is popular with advanced boardsailors. Contact **Lisa Penfield Windsurfing** (☎ 796-1234) here. La Parguera Bay has good slalom conditions. Nearby Cayo Enrique, while protected from the waves, is wide open to the winds.

On the NW shore, experts-only beaches include Jobos, Wilderness, and Surfers' beaches. Other good windsurfing spots in this area include Añasco, Boquerón, Crash Boat (Aguadilla), and the Shacks (Isabela). Windsurfing rentals are also available in Palmas del Mar (☎ 852-8114) in the SE. The PBA World Cup Tour is held annually in Isabela.

Deep-Sea Fishing

Thirty world records have been broken with fish caught from the island's seas. You can expect tuna, mackerel, yellow and blackfin tuna, bonefish, yellowfish, blue marlin, wahoo, and tarpon. While marlin are best caught from late Jan. through May, sailfish and wahoo can be caught in the fall, dorado (dolphinfish) from Nov. through early April, and yellow tuna, blackfin tuna, and skipjack (oceanic bonito) are caught year round. Half- and full-day charters are available. San Juan charters include **San Juan Fishing Charters** (☎ 723-0415, 781-7001, evenings); **Southern Witch Charters** (☎ 747-9247), **Marina Services of the Caribbean** (fax 723-2409), **Maragata Yacht Charters** (☎ 850-7548), **Castillo Watersports** (☎ 791-6195, 726-5752, evenings); and **Benítez Deep-Sea Fishing** (☎ 723-2292, 724-6265). Also try finding a charter at La Parguera in the SW and at Puerto Real near Mayagüez.

The Club Náutico International Billfish Tournament is held here in Sept. In its fourth decade, it is the longest running tournament of its kind in the world. The Cangrejos Yacht Club Blue Marlin Tournament takes place in Aug.

lake fishing: Rental equipment is not yet available, so bring your own! Try Lago Dos Bocas near Utuado, Lago Cidra, Lago Patillas, Lago Toa Vaca (in Villalba), Lago Yauco, and Lago Guajataca (in Quebradillas). Fish you might catch include catfish, peacock bass, largemouth bass, tilapia, and sunfish.

Sailing & Boating

Chartering a boat is another popular activity. Be prepared for a few discomforts: hand-held showers situated right next to the toilets are standard fare. Plan your itinerary at least six months in advance if you're interested in peak times like February, March, Easter, Thanksgiving, and Christmas. The poorest conditions for sailing run from the end of August through the middle of October. Bring dramamine if you get seasick.

The most useful book for yachting is *Yachtsman's Guide to the Virgin Islands and Puerto Rico*, published by Tropic Island Publishers (PO Box 611141, North Miami, FL 33161) which gives you in-depth sailing information. You can expect to spend $1,000-$2,000 pp for an eight-day/seven-night cruise with all meals, alcohol, and use of sports equipment included.

Boats can be rented at **La Playita Boat Rental,** 1010 Ave, Ashford, Condado (☎ 722-1607) and the **Condado Plaza Hotel Watersports Center** (☎ 721-1000, ext. 1361). Fajardo is now the major charter center. Boats can also be rented at Dorado, at Palmas del Mar near Humacao and at Puerto Real near Mayagüez. From La Parguera, you can charter a motorboat to explore the offshore cays.

marinas: The **San Juan Bay Marina** (☎ 721-8062) is at Stop 10, Ave. Fernández Juncos in Miramar. Set on Demajagua Bay on the E shore at Carr. 3 at Km 51.2, the **Puerto del Rey Marina** (☎ 860-1000) has slips for 700 boats and can accommodate vessels up to 200 ft. Also in Fajardo are the **Villa Marina** (☎ 728-2450, 863-5131) and **Puerto Chico Marina** (☎ 863-0834; Carr. 987). **Isleta Marina (Club Náutico de Puerto Rico)** (☎ 863-0370) is off the coast from Fajardo. The **Marina de Salinas** (☎ 752-8484) is on Carr. 52 in Salinas. The **Marina de Palmas** (☎ 852-6000, ext. 2551) is in Palmas del Mar, Humacao.

regattas: Initiated in 1981, the Discover the Caribbean Series is a major event for mono-hull sailing aficionados in Puerto Rico and throughout the Caribbean; it follows International Yacht Racing Union Rules. The three-day Velasco Cup Regatta and the Las Américas Regatta, held in Fajardo in March, mark the start of the Caribbean Ocean Racing Circuit. In July is the Budweiser Around Puerto Rico Race, which begins at El Morro in Old San Juan. On Labor Day is the Copa de Palmas held at the Palmas del Mar Resort. In October Fajardo hosts the three-day Kelly Cup Regatta.

power boat racing: Offshore power boat racing is quite popular, especially on the W coast from Mayagüez S to Boqueron Bay. While local races are held throughout the year, the biggest event is the Caribbean Offshore Race, an international event which often attracts celebrities. Contact **Offshore Power Boats** (☎ 787-6161) for information.

Land Sports

Tennis

The island boasts more than 100 courts and most of the large hotels provide pros. An abundance of courts are found around San Juan. San Juan Central Park, Calle Cerra, has 17 lighted courts (☎ 722-1646). Hotels with courts include Caribe Hilton, Carib Inn, Condado Beach, Condado Plaza, and El San Juan. Out on the island there are courts at the Dorado hotels and at Palmas del Mar Resort; Club Riomar in Río Grande; Hotel Copamarina (Guánica); at Punta Borínquen (Aguadilla); and at other locations. Tennis tournaments include the Bud Light Tennis Classic, the MCI National Championships, and the Puerto Rico Open. The Commonwealth also competes in the Davis Cup.

Golf

There are so many places to play that the island has been dubbed "Scotland in the Sun." The Hyatt Dorado Beach (☎ 796-1234, ext. 3710) offers two courses that were designed by Robert Trent Jones when Laurence Rockefeller owned the resort back in 1958. Clocking in at 7,500 yds. from the back and 72 par, the East Course is longer than the West Course, whose fairways extend for 6,913 yds. Spectacular ocean views can be found at holes 10 and 18.

Golf Courses

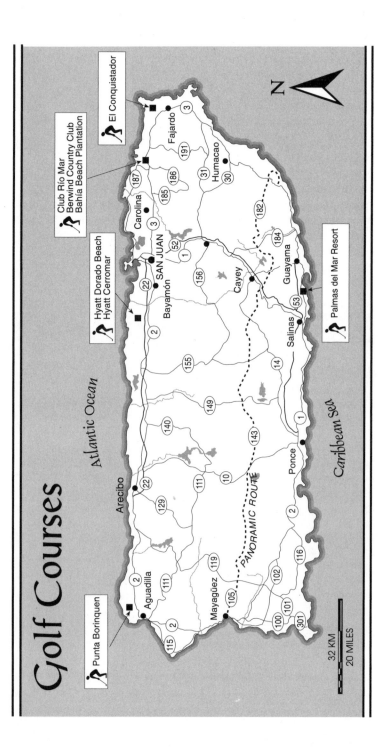

Atlantic Ocean

Caribbean Sea

N

32 KM
20 MILES

Punta Borinquen

Hyatt Dorado Beach
Hyatt Cerromar

Club Río Mar
Berwind Country Club
Bahía Beach Plantation

El Conquistador

Palmas del Mar Resort

Aguadilla
Mayagüez
Arecibo
Bayamón
SAN JUAN
Carolina
Fajardo
Humacao
Cavey
Guayama
Salinas
Ponce

PANORAMIC ROUTE

115
2
111
119
105
129
22
140
111
10
155
149
143
100
101
301
102
116
2
1
14
53
184
182
156
1
52
3
185
186
191
187
22
2
3
30
31

Other, less difficult Trent Jones courses are built on coastal plains at the **Hyatt Cerromar** (☎ 796-1234, ext. 3210). The North Course is 6,841yds. and the South Course extends for 7,047 yards.

In Río Grande on the E coast is the **Club Río Mar** (☎ 888-8815/8816), which is famous for its narrow, challenging 6,845-yd., par-72 course. Also in Río Grande, the Berwind Country Club (☎ 876-3056), a private club, opens for visitors on Tues., Thurs., and Fri. It has a 6,991-yard layout. The **Bahía Beach Plantation** course opened in 1992 (☎ 256-5600, fax 256-1035). Each hole is different.

Way over on the eastern tip is the new **El Conquistador** (☎ 863-1000) which boasts a par-72, 18-hole course designed by Arthur Hill. It has 6,700 yds. of fairways sandwiched between the Atlantic and the Caribbean.

In the island's SE, the course at **Palmas del Mar Resort** stretches out 6,991 yards. Its 350-yard par-4 11th is its most challenging hole. An 18-hole course is also located at Punta Borínquen.

Other courses include the **Luis Ortis** (☎ 786-3859, 787-7252) in the metropolitan area, the 18-hole **Punta Borinquen** in Aguadilla, the 9-hole **Aguirre Golf Course** on the S coast, and the Club Deportivo de Mayagüez.

Other Land Sports

HORSEBACK RIDING: This is available at Palmas del Mar Resort near Humacao, Santurce's Centro Equestre de Puerto Rico (☎ 728-4530), and at Hacienda Carabali (☎ 795-6351; Carr. 992, Km 4, Mameyes). Post time for **racing** at El Comandate (☎ 724-6060), to the E of San Juan in Canóvanas, is 2:30 on Sun., Wed., Fri., and holidays.

horse shows: Dulce Sueño, the Paso Fino Horse Show held in Guayama in February-March, and the Festival La Candeleria, held the first week in Feb. in the town of Manatí, are two of the best Paso Fino events. Other competitions include Bayamón's three-day Equi-Expo in Jan. and the **Copa Dorado** in April.

polo: Set on 25 acres bordering the Río Loíza, the Ingenio Polo Club (☎ 752-8181) hosts the Rolex Polo Cup in March.

BOWLING: There are a number of lanes scattered across the island. **Tower Lane Bowling** (40 lanes!) is in the San Juan suburb of Levitown, Paradise Bowling is in Hato Rey, **Ponce Bowling** is in Ponce, **Cupey Bowling** is in Trujillo, and **Western Bowling** is in Mayagüez. The week-long **Tirolcocos International Bowling Tournament** is held in June at Tower Lane Bowling.

CYCLING: The International Cycling Competition is held in Sabana Grande annually during the second week in May. The Tour Gigante de Puerto Rico is another major event. Contact the Cycling Federation (☎ 721-8755) for details.

MARATHONS: In its third decade and leading the pack, the 20-km San Blas Marathon (☎ 825-1094) takes place in Coamo in Feb. The 42-km Enrique Ramirez Marathon (☎ 899-1081) takes place in Lajas during April and qualifies runners wishing to compete in the Olympics and in the Central American Games. The 12-km Women's Marathon (☎ 892-3500) is an international race held in Guayanilla in Dec. The Modesto Carrion (☎ 734-2928) is in Juncos in Nov. Held in March, the Diet Pepsi Five Mile (☎ 734-2928) starts in San Juan's Central Park and finishes in Santurce. The 40-mile La Guadalupe Marathon (☎ 840-4141) is run in November in Ponce.
BASEBALL: The Caribbean League includes five teams; their season stretches from Oct. to March. In San Juan, you can see games by the San Juan Metros and the Santurce Crabbers at Hato Rey's Hiram Bithorn Stadium.

BASKETBALL: There's a six-team professional league as well as a 16-team amateur league. Obtain a current schedule from the Federación de Baloncesto.

VOLLEYBALL: Held during the last weekend in May, the National Beach Volleyball Tournament 2-on-2 is followed by the final event during the last weekend in June. This features the top 16 teams; it's followed in turn by the Caribbean Beach Tournament in Aug.

HIKING: The island is an excellent place to hike. Major locales include the Caribbean National Forest (El Yunque), Culebra, Carite Forest Reserve, Gúanica Forest Reserve, and Toro Negro Forest Reserve. Also, see the Hiking section on page 73.

Birdwatching

Despite the island's small size, there are 273 species of birds, 12 of them endemic. Good birding spots include the forest reserves, especially Guánica where you might see the Puerto Rican tody, the Puerto Rican tanager, the Puerto Rican lizard cuckoo, or the elusive and nocturnal Puerto Rican nightjar. In addition to being the only place on the island where you can see the endangered snowy plover, the Maricao Forest Reserve also is home to the Puerto Rican vireo and to scaly-naped pigeons. Puerto Rican parrots can be spotted only in the Luquillo Mountains and in the Caribbean National Forest. For more information, see Hiking on page 73, as well as specific entries in the travel section.

Cockfighting

Popular long before the construction of the first Puerto Rican court in 1764, this "sport" flourished until banned after the American occupation in 1898. It was prohibited on the grounds that it led to animal mistreatment and gambling. Naturally, cockfighting did not disappear – it went underground. Giving in to the inevitable, Gov. Robert Gore legalized the sport in 1933. He signed the "Rooster Law" with a feather from Justicia, a famous fighting cock. There are some 134 *galleras* (cockfighting arenas) which have attracted more than a million spectators annually. In rural areas, men and women are seated separately, with women high up in the back. The roosters are specially bred and pampered, and a *gallero* may spend 15 years refining his line. A champion bird can fight on for a few years. Roosters are entered according to weight, size and type of spurs used, and the starting bet may range from $100 to $5,000 and upwards. The rooster's natural spurs are generally cut off and a standard-length spur is attached with tape, thread, and wax. Although natural spurs that have been polished by an artisan can run as much as $300 per pair or more, plastic spurs (around $20) are the most popular ones used today. A fight is timed at 20 mins., and feathers fly frenetically for the duration. If you wonder who is winning, it's the one with the bloodiest spurs.

Practicalities

Basics

VISAS: All visitors from abroad (except Canadians) require a US visa. It's better to obtain a multiple entry visa and, if possible, to do so in your own country. Fill out forms perfectly; consular officials tend to be aggravatingly picayune.

☞ **Traveler's Tip.** Don't forget to bring a passport or driver's license with you. New FAA regulations – a clear violation of human rights – require you to show government-issued identification (which extends to a Social Security card or birth certificate) before boarding an airline. This measure is ostensibly designed to thwart terrorists.

CONDUCT: The more Spanish you speak the better. Keep in mind that, while Puerto Rico is part of the United States, Latin cultural mores prevail here. Men and women alike tend to dress conservatively. If you want to be accepted and respected, dress respectably. Bathing attire is unsuitable on main streets. Nearly a century of US colonial rule has had an effect here and you can expect some acrimony along with the hospitality. But, once people come to know you, they will accept you.

HEALTH: Medical care is usually on a first-come, first-served basis. Although the quality of medical and dental services is reasonably high, it's not quite up to mainland standards. Most physicians are centered in San Juan, Ponce, and Mayagüez. Hospital costs are slightly lower than in the States, and Medicare and all other Stateside hospitalization policies are honored. Equipped with 24-hour emergency service, the **Ashford Memorial Hospital**, 1451 Ashford Ave. in Santurce, has many English-speaking staff members. For help in obtaining a physician, call the **Medical Association** (☎ 725-6969) or check the Yellow Pages of the telephone directory under *Médicos Especialistas*. Either arrive with an adequate supply of any medications you may require, or bring your doctor's prescription with you.

Although diseases like malaria that had been a problem in the past have been eliminated, bilharzia, a disease spread by snails carrying the larvae of the parasite *schistosoma*, is something to watch out for. The chances of infection are remote, but it's best to be circumspect when bathing in freshwater pools near human habitation.

WHAT TO TAKE: Bring as little as possible, i.e., bring only what you need. It's easy just to wash clothes in the sink and thus save lugging around a week's laundry. Remember, simple is best. Set your priorities according to your needs. If you're planning on doing an exceptional amount of hiking, for example, hiking boots are a good idea. Otherwise, they're an encumbrance. With a light pack or bag, you can breeze through from one town to another easily. Confining yourself to carry-on luggage also saves waiting at the airport. See the chart below for suggestions and eliminate unnecessary items.

WHAT TO TAKE

CLOTHING
socks and shoes
underwear
sandals or thongs
T-shirts, shirts (or blouses)
skirts/pants, shorts
swimsuit
hat
light jacket/sweater

TOILETRIES
soap
shampoo
towel, washcloth
toothpaste/toothbrush
comb/brush
prescription medicines
Chapstick
other essential toiletries
insect repellent
suntan lotion/sunscreen
shaving kit
toilet paper
nail clippers
hand lotion
small mirror

OTHER ITEMS
passport and driver's license
traveler's checks
money belt
address book
notebook
pens/pencils

books/maps
watch
camera/film
flashlight/batteries
snorkeling equipment
extra glasses
umbrella/poncho
laundry bag
laundry soap/detergent
matches/lighter
frisbee/sports equipment

HIKING & CAMPING
internal frame pack
daypack/shoulder bag
foam sleeping bag
ripstop tape
tent/tent pegs
canteen
first-aid kit
binoculars
compass
hiking shorts/pants
candles/candle lantern
pocket knife
nylon cord
utensils
camping stove
can opener
food containers
spices, condiments
scrubbing pads
pots, pans
plastic wrap/aluminum foil

Practicalities

THEFT: This should not be a problem if you're careful. By all means avoid the slum areas of San Juan, don't flash money or possessions around and, in general, keep a low profile.

TRAVELING WITH CHILDREN: Puerto Rico is as safe as anywhere for children. Just take care that they are not overexposed to sun and get sufficient liquids. Remember to bring whatever special equipment you'll need. Disposable diapers and baby food are available but expensive. Be sure to inquire at your hotel as to extra charges for children and if they'll even be accepted. You can save money by dining at local restaurants. Finally, keep an eye on the kids while they're in the water. There are no lifeguards. Also, make sure that they apply sun protection.

☞ **Traveler's Tip. Teatro Circolo** (☎ 723-7612) at Calle de la Cruz 257 in Old San Juan, has performances geared towards children every Sun. at 1, 3, and 5. You'll see unicycling and pantomime. Admission is $3.

ENVIRONMENTAL CONDUCT: Dispose of plastics properly. Remember that six-pack rings, plastic bags, and fishing lines can cause injury or prove fatal to sea turtles, fish, birds, and other marine life. Unable to regurgitate anything they swallow, turtles and other sea creatures may mistake plastic bags for jellyfish or choke on fishing lines. Birds may starve to death after becoming entangled in lines, nets, and plastic rings. All of these items take hundreds of years to decompose and can do a lot of damage in the interim. Remember that the Caribbean National Forests and the Commonwealth's reserves were created to help preserve the environment and refrain from carrying off plants, rocks, animals, or other materials. Buying black coral jewelry also serves to support reef destruction, and turtle shell items come from an endangered species. On St. John remember not to feed the donkeys or to leave food within their reach. Environmental organizations are listed on pages 108 and 109.

undersea conduct: Respect the natural environment. Take nothing and remember that corals are easily broken. Much damage has already been done to the reef through snorkelers either standing on coral or hanging onto outcroppings. As stony corals grow at the rate of less than half an inch per year, it can take decades to repair the desecration caused by a few minutes carelessness. It's wise to keep well away just for your own protection: many corals will retaliate with stings and the sharp ridges can cause cuts that are slow to heal. In order to control yourself, make sure that you are properly weighted prior to your dive. Swim calmly and fluidly through the water and avoid dragging your console and/or octopus (secondary breathing device) behind you. While diving or snorkeling resist the temptation to touch fish. Many fish (such as the porcupine) secrete a mucous coating which protects them from bacterial infection. Touching them removes the coating and may result in infection and death for the fish. Also avoid feeding fish, which can disrupt the natural ecosystem. In short, look, listen, enjoy, but leave only bubbles.

RECYCLING IN PUERTO RICO

As this century draws to a close, Puerto Rico's environment is becoming more and more of concern, with good reason. In particular, the "garbage crisis" is looming large. The island generates 7,500 tons of garbage daily. Around 1,000 tons of this end up in San Juan's landfill. Presently covering 155 acres, it has grown to some 120 ft above sea level, and it may face closure in 1997. Around the rest of the island, half of the landfills were slated to be shut down on April 9, 1994 – extending an earlier deadline. Although Law 70 (the "Recycling Law") took effect in Sept. 1992, it has not had much enforcement clout. The law demanded that 35% of all solid waste be recycled by March, 1995, but currently less than 1/1,000th of one percent is recycled.

Things are, however, beginning to change. Some 50 business firms have begun to recycle materials. The Pueblo (☎ 757-0790) and Xtra supermarkets have launched a recycling campaign. In addition to offering specific collection days for recyclables, Pueblo accepts plastic bags for recycling provided that that they are clean and staple-free. Every second Saturday of the month, the Solid Waste Management Authority collects glass, plastic, newsprint and aluminum. There's also a Cans R' Us machine on the L side of the Caparra Shopping Center on Roosevelt Av. Operating 24 hrs., it pays 20¢ per lb. for aluminum cans; it is the first of 15 planned for the island.

The younger generation is also being schooled in recycling. The Museo del Niño has a room where children are taught to make useful things from recyclables, and the San Juan Dept. of Environmental Control has devised Gusto, a super-coqui mascot, who heads the "Recycle with Gusto" campaign. Gusto wears trendy recycled garb, including pull-tab sunglasses, a cap made from the plastic bottom of a soft drink bottle, sneakers with tire treads, and a cape fashioned from newspaper. If you inspect the cape with a magnifying glass, you can spot a recommendation to "recycle this newspaper."

Practicalities

BOATING CONDUCT: In addition to the behavior patterns detailed above, always exercise caution while anchoring a boat. Improperly anchoring in seagrass beds can destroy wide swatches of seagrass, which take a long time to recover. If there's no buoy available, the best place to anchor is a sandy spot which causes relatively little environmental impact. Tying your boat to mangroves can kill the trees, so it is acceptable to do so *only* during a storm.

In order to help eliminate the unecessary discharge of oil, maintain the engine and keep the bilge clean. If you notice oil in your bilge, use oil-absorbent pads to soak it up. Be careful not to overfill the boat when fueling. Emulsions from petrochemical products stick to fishes' gills and suffocate them, and deposits in sediment impede the development of marine life. Detergents affect plankton and other organisms, which throws off the food chain.

When you approach seagrass beds, slow down because your propeller could strike a sea turtle. Avoid maneuvering your boat too close to coral reefs. Striking the reef can damage both your boat and the reef. Avoid stirring up sand in shallow coral areas. The sand can be deposited in the coral and cause polyps to suffocate and die. If your boat has a sewage holding tank, empty it only at properly equipped marinas. Avoid using harsh chemicals such as ammonia and bleach while cleaning your boat; they pollute the water and kill marine life. Use environmentally safe cleaning products whenever possible. Boat owners should avoid paint containing lead, copper (which can make molluscs poisonous), mercury (highly toxic to fish and algae), or TBT. Finally, remember that a diver-down flag should be displayed while diving or snorkeling.

Suggested Itinerary

- ☐ **If you have 3 days:** Spend one day at the Condado, Isla Verde, or Luquillo beaches; one day in Old San Juan; and one day in El Yunque, Loíza, or exploring.

- ☐ **If you have 5 days:** Spend one day at the beach, one day in Old San Juan, one day in El Yunque or on a day trip, and spend two nights out on the island.

- ☐ **If you have one week:** Spend one day at the beach, a day in Old San Juan, one day in El Yunque or on a day trip, and spend some nights out on the island or on Vieques or Culebra.

- ☐ **Places not to be missed if you have time:** See the museums in Old San Juan and visit El Yunque, Vieques, Culebra, Coamo (hot springs); walk around and explore small towns like Aibonito, Barranquitas, or Jayuya; hike in one of the nature preserves such as Guanica; visit a National Trust site like Hacienda Buena Vista or El Faro; see the restored section of Ponce and the outlying archeological site at Tibes; visit Utuado's Caguana ceremonial ball court; and travel to coastal sites like Cabo Rojo.

PUERTO RICO TOURISM OFFICES

CALIFORNIA
3575 W. Cahuenga Blvd #560, Los Angeles CA 90068
☎ 800-874-1230, 213-874-5991; Fax 213-874-7257

FLORIDA
901 Ponce de Leon Blvd, Suite 604, Coral Gables, FL 33134
☎ 800-815-7391, 305-445-9112; Fax 305-445-9450

NEW YORK
575 Fifth Avenue, 23rd Floor, New York, NY 10017
☎ 800-223-6530, 212-599-6262; Fax 212-818-1866

SAN JUAN
Box 4435, #2 La Princesa Dr., Old San Juan Station PR 00902
☎ 787-721-2400, 787-721-2483; Fax 787-725-4417

UK
67-69 Whitfield St., London, W1P 5RL, UK
☎ 011-44-71-636-6558; Fax 011-44-611-724-089

GERMANY
Kreuzberger Ring 56, 6200 Wiesbaden, Germany
☎ 011-49-611-744-280; Fax 011-49-611-724-089

ITALY
Via San Vitale 25, 20038 Seregno (MI), Italy
☎ 011-0362-221763; Fax 011-0362-230412

FRANCE
5 bis, rue du Louvre, 75001 Paris, France
☎ 011-33-1-4477-8800; Fax 011-33-1-4260-0545

JAPAN
Shintkyo 913, 3-3-1, Marunouchi Chiyoda-Ku, Tokyo, 100 Japan
☎ 011-81-3-3213-5206-7

Money & Measurements

The monetary unit is the US dollar (called *"dolar"* or *"peso"*) which is divided into 100¢ (referred to as *"centavos"* or *"chavitos"*). Nickels (5¢) are referred to as *"vellons"* or *"ficha."* Quarters (25¢) are called *"pesetas."* If coming from abroad, it's better to change your money in a major US city or carry traveler's checks. Banks are open from 9-2:30, and ATMs (called ATH, "at any hour," here) are readily available; use the ones with private glass door entrances for security at night.

Measurements are a confusing mixture of American and metric. Gasoline and milk are both sold by the liter (*litro*). While road distances are given in kilometers, road speed signs and car speedometers use miles per hour. Land elevations are expressed in meters, but land is sold in units called *cuerdas*, equal to .97 acre. Weights are measured in pounds (*libras*) and ounces (*onzas*); a *tonelada* is a ton. *Pulgadas* are inches, and *pies* are feet. The Commonwealth operates on Atlantic Standard (Eastern Standard + one hour) time. When the Eastern US is operating on daylight savings, both are on the same time.

Shopping & Customs

SHOPPING: Opening hours vary but stores are generally open from Mon. through Sat., with some stores closing for an hour in the afternoon. Aside from local handicrafts, there isn't much to buy that can't be found cheaper (or at the same price) somewhere else. Some of the better buys are at the factory outlets (Farah, Hathaway, etc.) in Old San Juan. Jewelry is also a popular item in stores here, but know your prices at home. There's an import tax on photographic equipment and accessories, so bring your own. T-shirts make good souvenirs as do local coffee beans (about $4/lb. at Pueblo in Old San Juan). Rum is cheap and no import duties are charged if bringing it to the States, but other imported hard liquor is expensive and not worth bringing back. Ron de Barrilito, Bourget Creme de Cacao Liqueur, Coquito Trigo Coconut Creme Liqueur, and Bacardi Añejo are all examples of Puerto Rican liquors you can bring back. Rum is generally cheaper in town at the market than in the duty-free shops at the airport. Although heavy to carry, Lotus pineapple juice makes a unique gift. Parcha-flavored Tang is sold only on the island, as are traditional syrups made from tamarind, coconut, and guanábana, which are used to top shaved ice. Poultry and mangoes and most other citrus fruits are among the agricultural products prohibited from export to the States. You can bring breadnuts, avocados, plantains, quenapas, pineapples, and papayas. Citrus fruits must be inspected. You may also bring in dried or cured herbs, dried and preserved insects, cocoa beans, banana leaves, tamarind bean pods, dried and cleaned snail shells and seashells, and fresh cut or dried medicinal plants, and other such esoteric items. For details, call the quarantine division of the US Department of Agriculture in San Juan at 253-4505 or call your local customs office prior to departure.

☞ **Traveler's Tip.** If you would like to bring back a souvenir for your coffee-drinking friends, consider buying an eight oz. package of ground Puerto Rican coffee. Two brands with attractive labels (and taste to match) are Rioja and Adjuntas. These, along with others, should be obtainable in large and small food stores islandwide.

CANADIAN CUSTOMS: Canadian citizens may make an oral declaration four times per year to claim C$100 worth of exemptions which may include 200 cigarettes and 40 ounces of alcohol. In order to claim the exemption, Canadians must have been out of the country for at least 48 hours. A Canadian who's been away for at least seven days may make a written declaration once a year and claim C$300 worth of exemptions. After a trip of 48 hours or longer, Canadians receive a special duty rate of 20% on the value of goods up to C$300 in excess of the C$100 or C$300 exemption they claim. This excess cannot be applied to liquor or cigarettes. Goods claimed under the C$300 exemption may follow but merchandise claimed under all other exemptions must be accompanied.

GERMAN CUSTOMS: Residents may bring back 200 cigarettes, 50 cigars, 100 cigarillos, or 250 grams of tobacco; two liters of alcoholic beverages not exceeding 44 proof or one liter of 44 proof-plus alcohol; two liters of wine; and up to DM300 of other items.

Broadcasting & Media

TELEVISON, NEWSPAPERS, PERIODICALS: TV serves up a combination of the worst American programming rendered into Spanish and bad local imitations of the worst American programming. As is the case with radio and the press, it dishes up AP and UPI stories as news. There are a number of daily papers: The English-language tabloid the *San Juan Star* is the least partisan. Superficial and bland, its magazine format provides little investigative reporting. Even its editorials are borrowed. It does have a few good journalists, however, including Melanie Lenart and

Laura Randall. *El Nuevo Dia* is the personal property of Luis A. Ferré Enterprises. The almost comically grotesque *El Vocero*, the newspaper of the masses, is full of really gory, bloody murders, many of which are featured on the cover. There are also a number of free publications, including the monthly *Tropic Times*, which caters to nautical types in the Fajardo area. *San Juan* is a "city magazine" published once every six weeks by the *San Juan Star*. It has good political coverage and some amusing articles. *La Era de Ahora* is a Spanish-language new-age monthly which features ads for "professional rebirthers," overpriced yoga workshops, the latest idiotic James Redfield tome, and the like. *Tu Salud* is a natural foods advertising tabloid. *Puerto Rico Breeze* is the island's bilingual gay advertising tabloid.

PUERTO RICO ON THE INTERNET: Although the World Wide Web is still developing, there are a number of places you can access information on Puerto Rico. We are listing a few of them here, but you should use your browser's web search features to locate others.

Caribbean Internet Service, located in San Juan, is an Internet provider. You can contact them at ☎ 787-728-3992 or 1-800-59-CISCO, or visit them on the Internet at **http://www.Caribe.net/**. Datacom Caribe, Inc. also offers Internet services; visit them at **http://www.coqui.net/** for more information.

PUERTO RICO ON THE INTERNET

- ❏ **http://www.catch22.com/~vudu/** is the author's web site address; it has information about Puerto Rico, Guánica National Forest, and Culebra.

- ❏ **http://www.iprnet.org/IPR/** will bring up **The Institute for Puerto Rican Policy**; it's an interesting place to visit and may be the best Puerto Rican site on the web!

- ❏ **http://www.where2stay.com/islands/islands/puertorico.html** will give you information on accommodations.

- ❏ **http://www.usc.clu.edu** has information about **Universidad del Sagrado Carazon.**

- ❏ **http://www.golfweb.com/gws/tgws.html** is the address for **GolfWeb**. Search for state: PR to get info on golf courses in Puerto Rico.

- ❏ **http://fortaleza.govpr.org/** is maintained by the Puerto Rican Government.

- ❏ **http://hpprdk01.prd.hp.com/** is sponsored by Hewlett-Packard Puerto Rico, and contains island facts, the latest weather report, photos, and recipes.

- **http://www/upr.clu.edu/home.html** contains information about the **University of Puerto Rico**. Their Mayagüez campus can be accessed at **http://www_rum.upr.clu.edu/**; the Geology Department has its own site at **http://qualibou.upr.clu.edu/**.

- **http://coqui.metro.inter.edu** and **http://ponce.inter.edu** are run by the **Inter American University;** the sites listed are for the Metropolitan and Ponce campuses, respectively. You can find news from Puerto Rico in their gopher server at **gopher://ponce.inter.edu.** Information and images of the **Tibes Indian Cermonial Center** can be found at **http://ponce.inter.edu/tibes/tibes.html.**

- **http://www.worldwide. edu/ci/puerto_rico/** is maintained by the **World Wide Classroom** and contains mailing addresses of Puerto Rico's universities.

- Information on cultural activities in *"El Cuarto del Quenepon"* may be obtained at **http://www.upr.clu.edu/cuarto/quenepon.html.** This page features Puerto Rican artists around the world, articles, electronic publications, a calendar of activities, and announcements of cultural events.

- **http://www.pixi.com/~boricua/** has Puerto Rican music.

- **http://www.cu-online.com/~maggy/pr.html,** maintained by Magaly Rivera **(maggy@prairienet.org)**, also has information on Puerto Rico.

- **http://www.odci.gov/94fact/country/196.html** or **<gopher://hoshi.cic.sfu.ca/0/dlam/cia/all/Puerto_Rico** brings you to the **CIA World Factbook Sheet** about Puerto Rico.

- **http://www.pitt.edu/~alvarez/elecciones/pr/** lists results from the 1992 general elections, the 1993 status plebiscite, and the 1994 Constitutional Amendments referendum.

Entertainment

The liveliest nightlife is found in Old San Juan. The Puerto Rico Tourism Company's LeLoLai VIP card may be purchased for $10 at authorized travel agencies and hotels (Condado Plaza, Condado Beach, Caribe Hilton Regency, and La Concha). It gives access to a different tour or musical event daily. Outside of the metropolitan area, things tend to be quieter, but Ponce has some relatively good nightlife. There are a number of annual music festivals such as the **Heinecken Jazzfest** held each May (generally over Memorial Day Weekend) in Parque Muñoz Marín and the **Michelob Dry Jazz and Latin Music Festival** at Bellas Artes in June. During the fall months, the **Noches Borinqueñas** offers a series of island-wide open-air free concerts by such artists as Roy Brown.

GAMBLING: Casinos are found in San Juan, Ponce, and Mayagüez; they are mostly in large hotels. The Puerto Rican Tourism Company has been operating slot machines since 1974; machines in the 20-odd casinos raked in some $900 million in 1995. You'll find blackjack, roulette, craps, and baccarat here. The island's lottery, which was first held in 1814, is a venerable way to throw some hard-earned cash down the drain. Approximately 300,000 tickets are sold weekly by some 15,000 licensed agents and 3,000 vendors. They receive some $70 million annually in commission for their efforts. Each of the 49 weekly drawings offers a $150,000 prize; $1 million is dispensed thrice annually. There are thousands of computerized lottery terminals islandwide, dispensing Loto and *Pega Tres* ("Pick Three") tickets. With the latter, you select a three- or six-digit number with a $1 minimum which has a 1:1,000 chance of winning a $500 prize.

The system is designed to tap on the *bolita*, the underground lottery. Some $136 million was garnered by this government-perpetuated scam in fiscal 1994-1995. With less favorable odds, Loto is not as popular. Income tax is withheld and prizes are dispensed over a number of years as opposed to all at once. Puerto Ricans also bet some $300 million on horses in 1995. You can buy a ticket for as little as 35¢. Pools allow you to select three two-race combinations or a six-race combo.

☞ **Traveler's Tip.** To calculate odds in a slot machine multiply the number of stops exponentially by the number of reels. For example, a machine with 22 stops (pictures of cherries and the like) should be multiplied four times (22 x 22 x 22 x 22) to produce odds to win the top prize at 1:234,256. Most machines have 22, 32, 64, or 72 stops. Odds are much better on a three-reel, 22-stop machine (1:10,648) than on a four-reel, 72-stop machine (1:26,873,856). A machine with a top prize of $10,000 delivers that in coins, not dollars! If you hit the jackpot, you will be paid by check and the money will be reported to the government. All of the "Progressive Jackpot" machines are identically programmed and have the same chance of winning. If you're playing these, put down the total number of coins allowable for the maximum jackpot return.

BETTING: Thoroughbreds race at the El Comandante racetrack on Sun., Wed., and Fri.

Services & Organizations

PHONE SERVICE: Phone service is run by the Puerto Rico Telephone Authority, which was created in 1974 to own and run the Puerto Rico Telephone Company (PRTC). With more than a million access lines, Puerto Rico has one phone for every three persons. Cellular service is available through the PRTC and Cellular One Puerto Rico. Although the pay phone is still 10¢, service is deplorable and it can cost as much to call from one side of the island to the other as it does to call the States. To use a pay phone, wait for a dial tone *before* inserting money. The number for local information (if it's not busy!) is 411. For intra-island calls – more expensive than calling the same number from the States – dial the number; to call outside Puerto Rico, dial 1 plus the area code and number; for credit card or third-party calls, dial 0. 800 and 888 numbers may be reached by dialing 1 first. For information in English, see the Blue Pages in the center of the telephone directory. Available in some hotels and other locations, Go/Fax telephone stations provide fax service; you need to use a credit card. The island's **area code** is now 787, which took effect in March 1996.

> ☞ **Traveler's Tip.** Because of the extortionate cost of intra-island calls, the most economical thing to do is to buy a prepaid phone card (sold in drugstores and convenience stores) either before or after your arrival. This can allow you to call anywhere, anytime for 25¢/minute or less. Rates are lower after 5 PM and on weekends.

MAIL: Postal service is reliable. Have mail sent c/o General Delivery, San Juan, PR 00936; this is the General Post Office on Ave. Roosevelt in Hato Rey. Tourist information centers are in Old San Juan at La Casita (Pier 1), Condado (next to the Condado Plaza Hotel), in Ponce at Plaza Las Delicias, and at the San Juan and Aguadilla international airports. Be sure to pick up a copy of *Que Pasa*, the free quarterly guide to Puerto Rico.

ORGANIZATIONS: The island's oldest and best known non-profit organization is the **Conservation Trust** (☎ 722-5882; Box 4747, San Juan, PR 00902-4747), which has been responsible for the preservation of forests, beachfronts, marshes, a canyon, and a coffee plantation over the past two decades. Originally funded by contributions from a petroleum refinery and the petrochemical industry channeled through Fomento, funding now comes via the profits of US manufacturing subsidiaries that operate under section 936 of the IRS code. Over 14,000 acres have been preserved so far, and $8 million has been invested. The Trust's latest victory has been the acquisition of 164 acres fronting the Bahía Ballena on the S coast, which had been slated for a Club Med. It was acquired in 1992 after a 20-year battle. Individual memberships are $30 per year and include a newsletter subscription, a free pass to one of the two Trust sites, and a discount at the gift shops on purchases over $20. **Earthwatch** is an organization that allows you to visit Puerto Rico and to participate actively in valuable research. Volunteers contribute financially and receive an unusual experience at the same time. One current project is studying the life cycle of the mongoose at the Cabo Rojo Wildlife Refuge. For more information, ☎ 800-776-0188. The **PEN Club** (☎ 724-0859/4669), which hosts an annual literary competition, can be reached at Apt. 11 N, C. Hernández 721, Miramar, PR 00907.

ENVIRONMENTAL GROUPS

Campers Association of Puerto Rico, ☎ 787-760-1422
Caribbean Environmental Information, ☎ 787-751-0239
Caribbean Standing Network, ☎ 787-899-2048, ext. 800; 462-8124
Citizens for the Conservation of the Environment of Aguada,
    ☎ 787-868-4656
Commission of Justice and Peace, ☎ 787-765-0606
Committee of Guaynabo Neighbors for the Well-Being of the
    Environment, ☎ 787-731-7225
Committee of Yabucoa Citizens for Quality of LIfe, Inc.,
    ☎ 787-893-1567
Committee to Save Guánica, Inc., ☎ 787-821-2302
Committee to Save the Environment of Guayanilla, ☎ 787-835-2341
Committee to Save the Environment of Juncos, ☎ 787-734-4491
Conservation Trust of Puerto Rico, ☎ 787-722-5834

Ecological League of Rincón – Carlos Gaston/Sandra Riós Miranda,
☎ 787-823-5646/823-3663

Environmental Coalition of Puerto Rico, ☎ 787-765-4303, 767-0820

Environmental Organization of Yuguiyú – Mary Casillas,
☎ 787-889-6212

Grateful Bed and Breakfast Rainforest Action Network –
Marty Soucie, ☎ 787-889-4919

Highland Friends of the Environment, ☎ 787-828-1449

Mayagüez Citizens for Health & Environment, ☎ 787-265-6266

Missión Industrial of Puerto Rico, ☎ 787-765-4303

Natural History Society of Puerto Rico, ☎ 787-726-5488; 728-1515,
ext. 283

Neighbors United for a Better Environment – Angel G. Quiles/
George Flores, ☎ 787-743-2413/744-6250

New Dawn Association, ☎ 787-787-9391

Organization of the Environmental Communities of the East,
☎ 787-893-7803

Puerto Rican Association of Water Resources, ☎ 787-729-6951

Puerto Rican Conservation Foundation, ☎ 787-763-9875

Scientific and Technical Services, Inc., ☎ 787-759-8787/8675

Vieques Conservation and Historical Trust, ☎ 787-741-8850

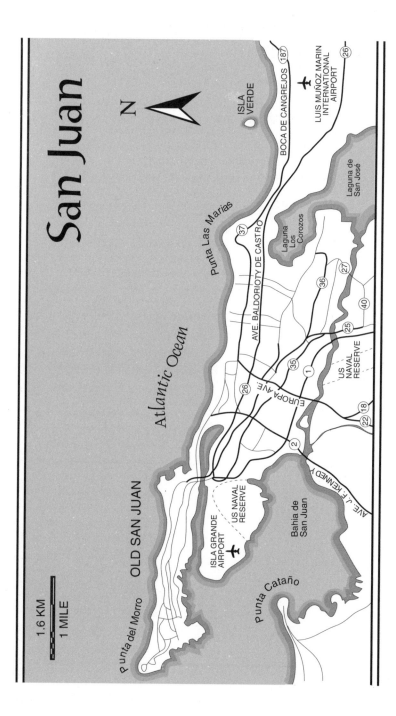

San Juan

N

1.6 KM
1 MILE

Punta del Morro

OLD SAN JUAN

Atlantic Ocean

Punta Las Marias

ISLA GRANDE AIRPORT

US NAVAL RESERVE

Bahia de San Juan

Punta Cataño

AVE. J. F. KENNEDY

AVE. BALDORIOTY DE CASTRO

EUROPA AVE.

Laguna Los Corozos

Laguna de San José

BOCA DE CANGREJOS

ISLA VERDE

LUIS MUÑOZ MARIN INTERNATIONAL AIRPORT

US NAVAL RESERVE

(187)

(26)

(37)

(36)

(27)

(40)

(25)

(35)

(1)

(26)

(2)

(18)

(22)

San Juan & Environs

As the second oldest city in the Americas (after Santo Domingo) and oldest city in the territorial United States, San Juan presents two distinct faces to the world. One is a vast, sprawling collection of towering concrete monoliths, freeways with crazy drivers, and bleak but functional housing projects with attractive murals painted on their sides. If it appears to have grown too fast, it has.

Its other face is that of Old San Juan, which retains the original flavor of the city – what the rest of the city must have been like before the svelte skyscrapers arrived. The metropolitan area of San Juan is divided and subdivided into a number of districts, many of which overlap, and it's nearly impossible to say where one stops and another begins. Sprawling Metropolitan San Juan (pop. 1.6 million) reaches out to touch the municipalities of Bayamón, Canovanas, Carolina, Cataño, Guaynabo, Loíza, Toa Baja, and Trujillo Alto. More than one-third of all Puerto Ricans live in this concentrated 300-sq-mile area, the island's economic, political, social, and cultural capital.

ARRIVING BY AIR: All international flights (and some domestic) arrive at **Luis Muñoz Marín International Airport** which is located on the easternmost side of town. Moneychangers, banks, coin lockers, bookstores, and other facilities are at the refurbished airport. In a separate building are a rum-tasting bar and the government-operated tourist information service. The girls here are content to sit and gaze off into the distance, read newspapers, or sample scratch-and-sniff ads in fashion magazines, but they will help if cornered. Be sure to pick up a copy of *Que Pasa* and any other material they may have.

If you don't have too much luggage, you may catch the a/c A7 bus (25¢) which runs via Isla Verde to Old San Juan. Another bus runs from the airport to Condado; you may change there to the T7, which will also take you into Old San Juan. Be prepared for a **long** wait and make sure that you have the right stop: one each on the same side goes towards Old San Juan (and Isla Verde and Condado) and towards Carolina. You should be at the stop marked "San Juan" on the upper level. Otherwise, there are always plenty of taxis (see the box on the next page). Be **sure** that they put the meter on! Limousines also run from out front. Service is very irregular so it's best to call the **Airport Limousine Service** (☎ 791-4745) to find out when the next one is leaving.

Completed in mid-1994, the Teodoro Moscoso Bridge, a toll road and bridge crossing San José, connects the airport with Hato Rey by linking up Av. Iturregui with Av. Baldorioty de Castro.

TAXIS IN SAN JUAN

❑ For trips leaving from the airport and the Tourism Piers in Old San Juan, a set flat-rate tariff applies. Rates from the airport are as follows: Old San Juan/Puerto de Tierra ($16), Condado/Miramar ($12), and Isla Verde ($8).

❑ All other trips are subject to metered rates. Rates are $1 plus 10¢ for each 1/13 of a mile. Each piece of additional luggage: 50¢. Waiting time: 10¢ per 45 seconds. 10 PM-6 AM: $1 surcharge. Trip minimum charge: $3. Tip is not included.

❑ For questions, suggestions, and complaints call the Public Service Commission at 756-1919.

GETTING AROUND: San Juan was originally served by streetcar lines. Although these have disappeared, streetcar stops are still used to identify locations. Watch for yellow obelisk posts or the upright metal signs (reading *Parada* or *Parada de Guaguas*) that identify bus stops. For reference purposes, Stop 8 is near Parque Muñoz Rivera in Puerto de Tierra; Stop 10 is in Miramar; Stop 18 is near Av. Roberto H. Todd; Stop 30 is the Fomento Building in Hato Rey; and Stop 40 is the University of Puerto Rico at Río Piedras.

The best thing that can be said about the bus system is that the buses are a/c. There are bus kiosks with ads that protect you from rain, but they offer no route map or other information. Although buses have digital readouts indicating their destinations, these may not be accurate so be sure to ask. Stops identify a specific area rather than a location. In an attempt to improve service, the bus service was split into two systems in 1990. The regular city buses are 25¢ (no transfers). Metrobus runs service (65¢) to Río Piedras every 5-15 minutes from 6AM to midnight. Otherwise, service is irregular and ends early in the evening. You can expect to wait. A new bus terminal has been built in the dock area. Other terminals are at Río Piedras, Country Club, Cataño, and Bayamón. The most frequented route is outbound on Av. Ponce de León and inbound (towards Old San Juan) on Av. Fernandez Juncos. For specific information phone the **Metropolitan Bus Authority, ☎** 767-7979 or **Metrobus, ☎** 763-4141.

note: An 11.8-mile, 16-station light rail system, the Tren Urbano, is under planning. The $935 million project is scheduled for completion by 2004, and will be able to handle some 115,000 riders daily. Most of the system will be above ground. New projections show that fares will cover only around a third of the operating costs between 2002 and the end of 2006; this figure is based on a 75¢ fare (three times the current bus price). This means that the Dept. of Transportation may have to subsidize losses of as much as $140 million over this five-year period. The first segment, which will run between Bayamón and Santurce, is budgeted at $1.1 billion. Unfortunately, in the meantime nothing is being done to prop up the bus service – which is irregular, stops very early, and is incomplete, to say the least.

BUSES TO & FROM OLD SAN JUAN'S BUS TERMINAL

Number	Route
I	Old San Juan/Río Piedras
2	Old San Juan/Condado/Calle Loíza/Bo. Obrero/Río Piedras
TI	Old San Juan/ Av. Ponce de León/C. Loíza/ IslaVerde/International Airport/Iturregui
MI	Old San Juan/Playa de Escambron/Old San Juan
M3	Old San Juan/Miramar/Condado/Old San Juan
A7	Old San Juan/Condado/Isla Verde/Piñones
M7	Old San Juan/Condado/Calle Loíza/Isla Verde/ International Airport/Iturregui
8	Old San Juan/Puerto Nuevo/Plaza Las Americas/San Patricio/Río Piedras
M2	Old San Juan/Condado/Miramar/Old San Juan

Another alternative is to ask around about *públicos,* which run from Old San Juan through several metropolitan area destinations, including Río Piedras and Bayamón. Metered taxis charge $1 initially with 10¢ for each additional 1/13 mile. Be sure they put down the meter; San Juan taxi drivers are, according to no less an authority than the former Tourism Company Executive Director Miguel Domenech, *estafadores* or "thieves." You should note that it may be difficult to get a taxi out of Old San Juan on Sat. night. A series of free open-air wheeled trains, manufactured by a California specialty vehicle company, traverse some of the streets of Old San Juan. These are useful for a rest or for getting your orientation, but their tortoise-like pace makes them an inefficient and cumbersome way to get around. A better idea is to use your feet. Assuming you are in halfway decent physical condition, no place in Old San Juan is beyond walking distance. Walking is definitely the best way to savor the atmosphere of the place, and you'd miss many things by getting around any other way. (The Condado area is similarly compact and may also be covered on foot). The section on sights which follows is arranged sequentially from El Morro to San Cristóbal, allowing the entire old town to be systematically and thoroughly explored.

USEFUL PHONE NUMBERS IN SAN JUAN & PUERTO RICO

American Airlines	☎ 800-981-4757
Banco Popular	☎ 723-0077
Better Business Bureau	☎ 759-5400
British Airways	☎ 725-1575
CaribAir	☎ 800-981-0212
Carnival Airways	☎ 800-724-7386
Delta Airlines	☎ 800-221-1212
Dept. of Natural Resources	☎ 724-3724
Dolphin	☎ 800-707-0138
Encanto Ecotours	☎ 272-0005, 800-272-7241
Flamenco	☎ 723-8110, 725-7707
Kiwi	☎ 800-538-5494
LACSA	☎ 800-225-2272
LIAT	☎ 800-981-8565
Medical emergency	☎ 754-2222;
outside San Juan:	☎ 754-2550
Northwest	☎ 800-225-2525
Police	☎ 343-2020 or 911
Tourist Information	☎ 791-1014, 791-2551, 722-1709
Travelers' Aid	☎ 791-1054/1034
United	☎ 800-241-6522
USAir	☎ 800-842-5374
Vieques Air Link	☎ 722-3736
Weather	☎ 253-4588

CAR RENTAL: There are numerous agencies; some of the larger ones are listed below.

CAR RENTAL COMPANIES

AAA	☎ 791-1465
Afro	☎ 724-3720
Ambassador	☎ 726-6982
Avis	☎ 721-4449
Budget	☎ 791-3685
Charlie's	☎ 728-2418
Discount	☎ 726-1460
Hertz	☎ 791-0840/0085, 725-2027/5537
L & M	☎ 725-8307; 800-666-0807; fax 791-6104
Leaseway	☎ 791-5900
Luchetti	☎ 725-8298
National	☎ 791-1805
Puerto Rico Rental	☎ 727-7724, 723-1722
Quality Car Rental	☎ 791-6350/3554
Romero	☎ 767-3059
Target	☎ 728-1447/1464
Thrifty	☎ 253-2525

San Juan Area

Old San Juan

For the amount of history, culture, and atmosphere that is packed into its seven-square-block area, no place in the territorial US can begin to touch Old San Juan. Perched on the western end of an islet bordered on the N by the Atlantic and on the S and W by a vast bay, the town is connected to the mainland by the historic San Antonio Bridge. When seen from the harbor, the town takes on the appearance of a gigantic amphitheater with its ramparts and castles forming the outer walls. Colonial Spain is alive and well here. The brilliantly restored architecture complements what was well-preserved to begin with. Old San Juan is not a place to hurry through: it cannot be seen in a day and can barely be appreciated in a week. Like a cup of the finest Puerto Rican coffee, it must be savored and sipped slowly.

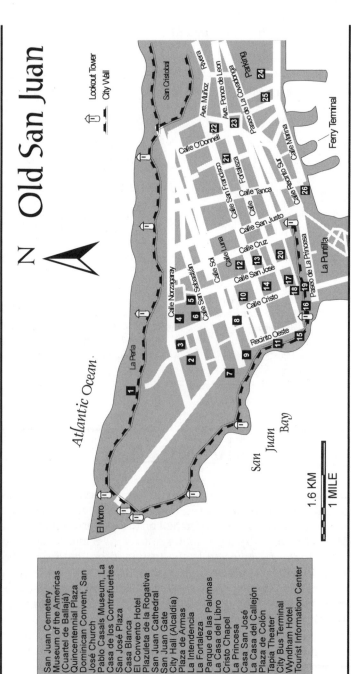

N Old San Juan

🏛 Lookout Tower
- - - City Wall

Atlantic Ocean

San Juan Bay

El Morro
La Perla
San Cristobal
Ave. Muñoz Rivera
Ave. Ponce de Leon
Paseo de La Covadonga
Parking
Calle O'Donnell
Calle San Francisco
Fortaleza
Calle Tanca
Calle Marina
Calle Recinto Sur
Calle San Justo
Calle Luna
Calle Cruz
Calle San José
Calle Sol
Calle San Sebastián
Calle Norzagaray
Calle Cristo
Recinto Oeste
Paseo de La Princesa
La Puntilla
Ferry Terminal

1.6 KM
1 MILE

1. San Juan Cemetery
2. Museum of the Americas (Cuartel de Ballajá)
3. Quincentennial Plaza
4. Dominican Convent, San José Church
5. Pablo Casals Museum, La Casa de los Contrafuertes
6. San José Plaza
7. Casa Blanca
8. El Convento Hotel
9. Plazuleta de la Rogativa
10. San Juan Cathedral
11. San Juan Gate
12. City Hall (Alcaldía)
13. Plaza de Armas
14. La Intendencia
15. La Fortaleza
16. Parque de las Palomas
17. La Casa del Libro
18. Cristo Chapel
19. La Princesa
20. Casa San José
21. La Casa del Callejón
22. Plaza de Colón
23. Tapia Theater
24. City Bus Terminal
25. Wyndham Hotel
26. Tourist Information Center

Stroll through the streets and take in the local color. See men playing dominoes, girls hanging out on the street corners waiting for marriage, groceries being hauled up to a second floor balcony with basket and rope. Get acquainted with the local characters: watch the crippled man on crutches who suddenly begins to move at top speed as soon as he is out of the sight of tourists. Or, if you're lucky, you might see the man who occasionally brings his pet snake out for a walk, holding it coiled in his hand and startling his unaware friend seated in a café. Or you might see the drunk singing a soliloquy on a streetcorner. Quite incongruous given the colonial backdrop, Old San Juan has become a favorite with the rollerblade set as well as with joggers! With some 5,000 residents, the panorama of people and events is constantly changing. Feed the pigeons in Parque de las Palomas or take in the view from the top of El Morro or San Cristóbal. With the exception of the obnoxious police, nobody hassles anybody in Old San Juan. Enjoy.

☞ **Traveler's Tip.** The best days to plan a visit to Old San Juan are from Wed. to Fri. Many museums are closed on Monday and Tuesday, and numerous cruise ships dock on these two days as well. On weekends the town tends to jam up as *SanJuaneros* come in for R & R.

HISTORY: Founded as a military stronghold in 1510, San Juan Bautista became a flourishing and attractive settlement by the end of the 19th century. It was originally called Puerto Rico and the island was called San Juan. On the way back to Spain, a cartographer mixed up the map labels. Although the town lacks an historic hospital, university, or any of the other significant architectural structures found in Santo Domingo, its buildings nonetheless have a distinctive charm and appeal of their own. After the American invasion in 1898, Old San Juan deteriorated. Most of it became a red-light district until 1949, when the seven-block downtown was declared a historical zone. Beginning in 1955, the Institute of Puerto Rican Culture, under the highly imaginative and insightful leadership of Ricardo Alegria, began the tremendous task of restoring the old buildings and homes in this historical area. Restoration of private residences was encouraged by legislation, which granted five- to 10-year tax exemptions to owners of buildings that had been partially or fully restored, and offered bank loans with liberal terms for performing restorative work.

Rather than becoming a pretentious museum piece, Old San Juan is a living historical monument where the past and present intermingle freely. The area has been designated as a United Nations

World Heritage Site, and an additional $100 million has been pumped into the historic zone in the past few years. One new development is the widening of C. Marina, which has been paved with cobblestones. Created from a former parking lot, the $16 million Quincentennial Plaza commemorates Columbus' "discovery." Two needle-shaped columns on its highest spot point to the North Star. It also has a fountain with 100 streams; three flights of stairs symbolize the next 300 years.

GETTING HERE: To get to Old San Juan from Isla Verde or the airport follow Carr. 26 to the W; this road merges into Carr. 25 at the San Antonio Bridge. Watch for signs reading "San Juan" or "Old San Juan" along the road. Continue along Carr. 25; the Capitol will be on your L; Fort San Cristóbal will be on your R. Note that public parking is extremely limited. The best place to park is the public parking lot at La Puntilla. If traveling here from the Condado area, it's better to take a bus.

Old San Juan Sights

FUERTE SAN FELIPE DEL MORRO (EL MORRO)

A walkway leads up to this dramatic structure, which is the most impressive legacy of the Spanish empire in Puerto Rico. If you're here on a weekend, you'll find Puerto Ricans relaxing: babies in strollers, tots pedaling tricycle-like machines, a zillion colorful kites flying, the works. Along with its sister structure in Havana, Brimstone Hill on St. Kitts (British), and Haiti's La Citadelle, El Morro is one of the premier forts in the Caribbean. Invincible from attack by sea during its time, it is now administrered by the National Park Service. It's open daily from 9-5 and there is no admission charge; call for information on free guided tours (☎ 729-6960).

Enter the small but cool museum and see the exhibits. The rooms on the fifth level were used as living quarters. The doors were made of ultrahard ausobo wood, which is now a protected species. See the carefully labeled spots where *The Forge*, *The Kitchen*, and *The Latrine* once were. The steep and dark triangular staircase, once an emergency passage, leads to the gun emplacements. Be sure to watch your step on the way down. The cannons on the Santa Barbara Bastion, also on the upper level, were found in the sea.

THE FORT'S HISTORY: Built to protect San Juan Harbor, gateway for supply ships headed to Spain's many colonies to the W and S, construction (in 1539) was spurred after recurring attacks by royally commissioned pirates and Carib Indian raids. The site of the fort was moved several times before the present outer fortification was completed in 1584. It was not completed in today's form until 1783, 199 years later, through the efforts of two Irishmen (O'Reilly and O'Daly), by which time about 40,000 man-years had been spent building the fortifications and city walls. Sir Francis Drake, pursuing a cargo of gold pesos being temporarily stored in the fortress vaults, struck on Nov. 22, 1584, and was repulsed. In 1598 the Earl of Cumberland attacked the Santurce area of San Juan with his 20 ships. Fighting tooth and nail, the Spanish, weakened by dysentery, held out for two weeks before surrendering. Cumberland and his forces were delirious with pleasure until they too succumbed to dysentery, followed by an epidemic of yellow fever. After just four months of control, the English sailed away, leaving 400 of their comrades buried. In 1625, the fortress was attacked by the Dutch, but this time the Spanish survived the attack and began work on San Cristóbal on the other side of town, to provide further defense. An attack by British Lt. General Abercromby in 1797 failed (see "Plazuleta de la Rogativa," page 124), and the last attack came during the Spanish-American War, when El Morro's batteries returned fire on US Admiral Sampson's fleet. El Cañuelo, which can be seen across the bay, was constructed to ward off hostile landings on the W side. The present structure was rebuilt in stone in the 1660s. Since 1977, $33 million has been spent on repairs to the fortress, including filling in cavities gouged by the sea under the Santa Elena bastion and under the N wall. A 750-ft-long breakwater, constructed by Pennsylvania's Maitland Construction Company at a cost of $7.88 million, was completed in October 1990. About 176,060 tons of stone were used in its construction.

NEAR EL MORRO: The **Polvorín de Santa Elena** (Santa Elena Gunpowder Magazine), is a chimney-topped structure to the L of the entrance. The **Escuela de Artes Plásticas** (School of Fine Arts) is an interesting place to walk by. Containing two attractive patios, the former **Asilo de Beneficiencia** (Home for the Poor) dates from the 1840s. It now houses the headquarters of the Institute for Puerto Rican Culture (☎ 724-0700), which has some small galleries with changing exhibits that are well worth a visit. It's open daily 9-5. The new **Parque de Beneficiencia** is in the background.

San Juan Area

FUN FACTS ABOUT EL MORRO & SAN CRISTÓBAL FORTS

❏ While El Morro was built to stave off sea attacks, San Cristóbal was designed to stave off land invasions.

❏ The white flag with the jagged red cross you see flying is the Cross of Burgundy, a Spanish military flag used during the 16th-18th centuries to identify forces loyal to the Spanish crown.

❏ English troops occupied El Morro for six weeks in 1598.

❏ Although the forts were modified constantly, it took an estimated half century to complete El Morro and around 25 years for San Cristóbal.

❏ San Cristóbal is much larger than El Morro. It covers 27 acres and is the largest Spanish constructed New World fortification.

❏ There are no secret tunnels connecting the fortresses with other edifices in the city.

❏ The forts' moats *never* held water. Their purpose was to protect the bottom of the walls from enemy cannon fire.

CEMETERIO DE SAN JUAN

Dramatically situated below towering El Morro, this cemetery contains the graves of such prominent Puerto Ricans as Pedro Albizu Campos and José de Diego. The circular neoclassic chapel, dedicated in 1863, is a most unusual architectural edifice. Note its eerie stained-glass reflection. Full-size weeping widows, realistically cut from marble, stand and kneel over graves. Long rows of tombs are set into the wall Etruscan-style, while faded and frayed Puerto Rican flags fly over graves. As space is at a premium, the grave of a less distinguished relative may be dug up and the bones transferred in order to make way for a new arrival. Legendary *independentista* Pedro Albizu-Campos is interred here. It's worth a visit, but stay clear at night or risk finding a knife at your throat.

LA PERLA

Elegant by comparison to the slums which line the banks of the Martín Peña Channel, this slum, situated along the Atlantic to one side of Cemeterio de San Juan, is a crowded group of houses that stretch from just below the remains of the colonial wall down a steep slope to the filthy beach below. Most houses have TVs (even satellite dishes) and other conveniences, while the better part of the slum is served by electricity, water and sanitation service. The area is a center for drug trade and other activities; it is recommended that you not come here unless it's with a local you trust. Bring nothing of value. La Perla is the place where Oscar Lewis penned his classic study of prostitution and poverty, *La Vida.*

CASA BLANCA

One of the gems of Old San Juan. Entering through the gates at 1 San Sebastián, a cool courtyard with a garden and beautiful chain of fountains is to the left. (You may also enter via the doorway across from Casa Rosada on the city wall side). Straight ahead is a house which has been restored to resemble a 17th-century noble-man's home, with simple but beautifully designed antique furniture and attractive white rooms. It also contains a small ethnographic museum which features a miniature replica of a Taíno village. Even older than La Fortaleza, this house was designed to be given to Ponce de León as a reward for his services. Ponce, however, went off to search for the fountain of youth in Florida and, meeting his end from an Indian's poisoned arrow, never returned. A hurricane destroyed the original structure and it was replaced by another in 1523. It still stands today and has been incorporated into the original. In 1779, after more than 250 years residence, Ponce de León's descendants sold it to the government, which expanded the structure for use as housing for military troops and engineers. Taken over by the US military in 1898, it was vacated in 1967 and declared a National Historical Monument the following year. Its library has a superb collection of Caribbean literature in Spanish and English. The complex (☎ 724-4102) is open Tues. to Sat., 9-noon, 1-4:30; $2 admission to the museum ($1 for children). Guided tours are available.

EL CONVENTO DOMINICANO

At C. Norzagaray 98, dominating Plaza San José, is the former Dominican Convent. Built in 1523 on land donated by Ponce de León, it's one of the major historical buildings in the city. After the closure of all convents in 1838, it was converted to a barracks.

San Juan Area

Following the American occupation, this was the center of the US Antilles Command until its termination in 1966. Carefully restored, it is now a showcase for cultural events. Concerts are held on occasion in the huge paved courtyard that lies below the beautiful arcaded galleries lined with carved wooden railings. You can see music lessons being given here on Sat. mornings. In the future, it will house the city's fine arts museum.

MUSEO DE ARTE Y HISTORIA

This former marketplace, located on C. Norzagaray (corner McArthur) was restored by the City of San Juan in 1979; it now serves as a cultural center which holds periodic exhibitions. Future plans are to transform it into a San Juan Historical Museum. It's open Tues. to Sun., 10-4, when it has exhibitions; ☎ 724-1875.

MUSEO DE LAS AMÉRICAS

Cuartel De Ballajá

This building once housed the Spanish troops and their families. Recently restored, the imposing structure still is largely empty. Most of it is a museum awaiting exhibits to fill it. There are a number of beautiful brass water fountains, which don't function owing to a lack of pressure. Set on the second floor, the **Museo de Las Américas** (open Mon. to Fri, 10-4, Sat. and Sun. 11-5; ☎ 723-8772) is intended eventually to cover the hemisphere's cultural development. So far only one gallery is open. Inaugurated in 1992, the **Artes Populares de Las Américas** contains an extensive folk art collection representing the full range of the Americas – from Paraguay to Cuba, Brazil to Haiti and Bolivia. There are old pictures of Puerto Rican villages, a phenomenal carved gourd from Peru, folk art from the US including carved whirligig dancers and a rooster weathervane, indigenous clothing from S America, musical instruments, including a harp from Venezuela, a Puerto Rican *cuatro* or 10-stringed guitar, a rustic tin banjo from Haiti, and a collection of masks from all over. Naturally enough, many of the exhibits relate to religion, some of them dealing with the influences of African religions on the New World. There are offerings to the dead from Mexico, an *abakua* (devil) costume from Cuba, a model *capilla campesina* (countryside chapel), and *manos poderosas* (powerful hands) from Puerto Rico – one of them topped by a group of women. Another room shows the artifacts found in Barrio Bállaja. There are several other rooms on this floor housing special exhibits.

Across the street, the offices of the **Institute for Puerto Rican Culture** have displays, including pictures of petroglyphs. Its E door opens onto the **Plaza del Quinto Centenario.** Raised, and reached by a series of steps on each side, this plaza has a fountain with 100 jets and a large pillar reaching to the stars. As previously mentioned on page 118, the $16 million Quincentennial Plaza commemorates Columbus' "discovery."

IGLESIA DE SAN JOSÉ

Oldest church still in use in the Americas, San José Church was built by Dominican friars as a monastery chapel. Originally dedicated to St. Thomas Aquinas, it was renamed by Jesuits who took it over in 1865. The Gothic ceilings are unequaled in this hemisphere. The church is most famous for what is missing or moved; most of the items currently on display have been donated. Ponce de León's tomb, after a 350-year rest, was moved to the cathedral. His coat of arms can still be seen to the left of the main altar. The famous Flemish masterpiece, The Virgin of Bethlehem, brought to the island in 1511, was stolen (and presumably deflowered) in 1972. During the 1898 US Navy bombardment, a cannonball crashed into one window and mysteriously disappeared; the chapel, crypt, and convent remained untouched. The church is right on Plaza San José. It's usually open Mon. to Fri. 8-3 and Sat. 8-noon, but may be sometimes be closed during these times. Mass is celebrated Sun. at noon.

San Juan Area

MUSEO DE CASALS

This collection of memorabilia includes cellist Pablo Casals' medals, sweater, cello, domino set, a yellow plaster of Paris cast of his hands, and even his pipes – including one carved in the shape of Wagner! It also holds manuscripts, photographs, and an extensive videotape library upstairs consisting of tapes from the Casals Festival; they are played on request. Open Tues. to Sat., 9:30-5:30; ☎ 723-9185.

☞ **Traveler's Tip.** The Casals Festival draws performing artists from all over the world. It generally takes place in June. Contact the tourist board for more information.

CASA DE LOS CONTRAFUERTES

Museo del Grabado Latinamericano

Directly on Plaza San José at C. San Sebastián, next-door to the Museo de Casals, this museum may be the oldest private residence remaining in Old San Juan. The house was constructed in the early 18th century, and its name means "heavily buttressed." Inside, a pharmacy museum is on the first floor. A reconstructed 19th-century shop is filled with antique crystal and porcelain ·jars and bottles, mysterious vials, antique medicine ads, as well as other furnishings and objects characteristic of Puerto Rican pharmacies of the time. The Latin American Graphic Arts Museum, which occupies the second floor, contains a superb collection of Puerto Rican artists past and present. Particularly notable are the collection of works by Latin American engravers, along with prized works from the San Juan Biennial. Open Wed. to Sun., 9-4:30; ☎ 724-5477.

PLAZA DE SAN JOSÉ

Restored to its original condition by the Institute for Puerto Rican Culture and reconditioned during 1988, the Plaza is quiet and peaceful during the daytime. It was the liveliest place in town at night, until the Cardinal (who doesn't even live here) complained about the noise! The statue of Ponce de León, first governor of Puerto Rico, was cast using melted bronze cannons captured in the 1797 British attack.

PLAZULETA DE LA ROGATIVA

Designed and built by an Australian residing in Puerto Rico, this remarkable statue – which has a touching spiritual character to it – is located in a small plaza next to the sea wall near Caleta Las Monjas. It was donated by a citizens' group to mark San Juan's

450th birthday in 1971. The statue commemorates a legend concerning the siege of San Juan in 1797. After taking Trinidad on Feb. 17 of that year, Lt. General Abercromby proceeded to San Juan with 60 ships containing nearly 8,000 troops. With the British apparently preparing to close in for the kill, the governor, weakened by dysentery, asked the head bishop to arrange a *rogativa* (procession) through the streets. The bishop, in turn, asked that it be held in honor of Santa Catalina (St. Catherine) and Ursula. The evening candle and torch procession moved from Catedral de San Juan Bautista through the streets. Abercromby became alarmed when he saw the huge masses of torchlights and heard the frenzied continual ring of church bells increasing in tempo until midnight, despite the steady barrage from his ships. Concluding that the town was being supplied by troops from the countryside, he ordered the fleet to sail, giving rise to the legend that the city had been saved by Ursula and her cohorts.

LA FORTALEZA

At the end of C. Fortaleza stands the oldest executive mansion in the Western Hemisphere; it was in operation three centuries before the Washington White House had even been designed. Its name, meaning "The Fortress," derives from its original use. Though replaced by El Morro, it continued to serve as part of the city's defense system. The $2 million in gold and silver that Sir Francis Drake sought during his 1595 attack was kept here. Occupied twice (by the Dutch in 1625 and the British in 1898), it had to be rebuilt in 1640 after the Dutch left. Usage as a governor's mansion dates from 1639 and continues today. It was completely remodeled in 1846. Pass by the security guards to join a guided tour of the downstairs area. You must be dressed properly. It's open weekdays except holidays; ☎ 721-7000, ext. 2211, 2323, and 2358 for the tour times. Inside, visit Santa Catalina's chapel, descend into the dungeon, and note the Moorish garden with its 19th-century parish tiles. If you stick your hand in the water, you will surely be granted any wish you request.

CATEDRAL DE SAN JUAN BAUTISTA

San Juan's cathedral is set on C. Cristo across from Plazuleta de las Monjas and El Convento Hotel. Once a small, thatched-roof struc-

San Juan Area

ture when built in 1521, the cathedral was completed in its present state in 1852. The only holdovers from the earlier structure are the partially restored Gothic ceiling and the circular staircase. See the remains of that ardent Catholic Ponce de León, who rests in a marble tomb. The wax-covered mummy of St. Pio, a Roman martyr killed for his belief in Christianity, is encased in a glass box. He has been here since 1862. To his right is a wooden replica of Mary with four swords stuck in her bosom. There are many, many beautiful stained glass windows. It's open daily from 6:30-5.

MUSEO FELISA RINCÓN DE GAUTIER

At Caleta de San Juan 51 nearby stands a memorial to a living saint: Felisa Rincón de Gautier, once Mayor of San Juan (1946-68). The former home of this pompadoured dynamo has been turned into a small museum. Well worth a visit but notable more for its architecture than its contents, the attractive house contains displays of the keys to cities offered her, along with various medals. Altogether she received 131 decorations and was named Woman of the Americas in 1954 by the Union of the American Women of New York. It's open Mon. to Fri. from 9-4.

THE CHILDREN'S MUSEUM

(El Museo del Niño)

One of the most unusual places in Old San Juan is a recent arrival. The concept of founder Carmen Vega, it is an example of a positive American influence: Vega visited similar museums in the States and based this on them. The ground floor is designed with tiny tots in mind. There are mirrors your kids can write on, and you can watch little bundles of joy gleefully descending the fabric slide. You can put on your own puppet show. On the second floor is a dentist's office ("Visitemos al Dentista") where it's explained what a visit is all about. Without a doubt, the museum's highlight is the "Viaje a Través del Corazón," a trip through a pulsating heart. Take off your shoes, go up the stairway, pull back the fabric. As you descend past a row of blinking lights you'll hear the intense thumping. Stethoscopes to be used for listening to your own heart are also provided. In the working kitchen ("La Cocinita"), children learn how to make dishes such as pizza and bread. Various art projects are pursued in the art room, there's a miniature *colmado* where food is purchased with play money, a barbershop, shortwave station, and T-shirts for sale on the first floor. **note:** The museum is currently open only on Sat. and Sunday from 12:30-5; admission is $2. It was devastated by a fire in 1995, but is being rebuilt. The finished structure will likely resemble the museum described above.

CASA ROSADA

Near the Rogativa statue, this attractive house was built in 1812 to serve as a barracks; it later became an officers' quarters. Although closed at present, it has been remodeled with the intent that it may perhaps someday serve as a museum for Puerto Rican crafts.

PROVINCIAL DEPUTATION BUILDING

Recently restored, this building's cloister-like design is done up in late neoclassical style. Puerto Rico's first representative body, the Provincial Deputation, was housed here. They began doing business on July 17, 1898, after Puerto Rico was granted autonomy by Spain. The US invaded only two weeks later. It seems appropriate that the building's current occupant is the US Department of State. It's on C. San Francisco at C. San José and is open Mon. to Fri. 8-noon and 1-4:30; ☎ 722-2121.

PLAZA DE ARMAS

This relaxed square has pay telephones, supermarkets, small cafeterias, a fruit vendor, and a shaved ice cart. Representing the four seasons, the four statues presiding over the oblong plaza are more than a century old. Originally a marketplace (Plaza de las Verduras or Plaza of the Vegetables), it was designed to be the main plaza before Ponce de León moved the capital from Caparra. Used during the 16th century for military drills by local militia, it was also the center of local nightlife. Bands played and singles walked around the square or sat in rented chairs. When the locals were replaced by Spanish garrisons, their cry of "Present arms!" resulted in a name change to Plaza de Armas. Remodeled in 1988 under the administration of San Juan Mayor Baltasar Corrada, it is now so

San Juan Area

spanking new that it has lost much of its ambiance. The shade trees which once graced the plaza were felled in a misguided attempt by the architect to restore the plaza to what it was in the beginning of this century. Two recently restored historical landmarks are right on the plaza. The Intendancy Building, located on the corner of San José and San Francisco, was once the office of the royal Spanish Exchequer. It now houses Puerto Rico's State Department (☎ 722-2121). The Provincial Deputation building (see above) once housed the island's first representative body. Both are open Mon. to Fri. 8-noon, 1-4:30. Also on the plaza is a Pueblo supermarket. Kiosko 4 Estaciones has piña coladas ($1.25), tuna sandwiches ($1.50), coffee, and other fare. El Mesón Sandwiches offers pizza and baked potatoes, among other dishes.

ALCALDIA

The San Juan City Hall is right on Plaza de Armas. Construction of this building, designed along the lines of its counterpart in Madrid, began in 1602. It was finally completed, after many delays, in 1799. During the years when it functioned as a city hall, numerous important events took place here, including the inauguration of the first Puerto Rican legislature and the signing and ratification of the decree abolishing slavery. The last restoration was in 1975. A tourist information center is on the ground floor (formerly a jail) next to a small gallery with frequent exhibitions. Open Mon.-Fri., 8-4; ☎ 724-7171, ext. 2391.

CASA DE LOS DOS ZAGUANES

(Museo del Indio)

At C. San José 119, this building has a small but excellent collection of artifacts including some great *cemis* (ancestral figures); be sure to see the *cemi* de Santa Isabel. It's open Mon. to Fri. from 9-noon and 1-5.

CENTRO NACIONAL DE ARTES POPULARES Y ARTESANÍAS

Located at C. Cristo 253 in the former Museo de Bellas Artes, this tastefully restored 18th-century building originally donated by local citizens, now holds one of the island's best folk art shops. In addition to temporary exhibitions by local artists, there's a permanent collection of artists like Oller and Campeche. It's open Tues. to Sat. from 9:30-4:30; ☎ 723-2320.

LA CASA DEL LIBRO

This museum of rare books and illuminated manuscripts, housed in a beautifully restored 18th-century townhouse, opened in 1958. Its 5,000-book collection, said to be the best of its kind in Latin America, includes over 200 books that date back to the 16th century and manuscripts dating back 2,000 years. Other books are reference works on the graphic arts. Conveniently located at C. Cristo 255, it's open Tues. to Sat. (except holidays), 11-4:30.

LA CAPILLA DEL CRISTO

At the foot of C. Cristo stands what must be the smallest chapel in the Caribbean. It is dedicated to the Christ of Miracles, and there are at least two stories explaining its origin. One claims that it was originally just an altar that prevented people from accidentally falling over the wall into the sea. The other story is more involved. On June 24, 1753, a rider, participating in the annual patron saint festival, missed the turn at the end of C. Cristo and plunged into the sea. Miraculously, he was not injured, and the chapel was constructed to commemorate the event. In 1925 the city government planned to demolish the chapel, but after vehement public protest, the idea was abandoned. On Aug. 6 every year, the chapel's feast day, the Cardinal of Puerto Rico officiates at a High Mass. The chapel is open Tues. from 10-3:30.

PARQUE DE LAS PALOMAS

At the end of Cristo St., next to Cristo Chapel, is this small gem of a park, perched at the top of the city wall – a nice place to sit early in the morning. Hundreds of pigeons circulate between the trees and the fountain. Feathers fly about everywhere. Caution is advised because they are not toilet trained. A man sells snacks and birdseed at the entrance.

BASTION DE LAS PALMAS

Originally constructed in 1678 as a gun emplacement, it once served as an integral part of the city's defense system. Now it's a small park overlooking San Juan Bay. Grab some morning caffeine at the coffee shop on San José and come here for the view. The statue off to the side is of Venezuelan patriot Gen. Miranda, a comrade in arms of Bolivar against the Spanish. His liberal views led to his internment here.

CASA DEL CALLEJÓN

Set on a sidestreet between Tance and O'Donnell at Fortaleza, this 18th-century home was originally opened after restoration in 1965. It houses the **Museo de Arquitectura Colonial,** along with the **Museo de la Familia Puertorriqueña.** Downstairs are tiles, blueprints, fittings, and scale models of buildings restored under the auspices of the Institute of Puerto Rican Culture. A good introduction to Old San Juan. Exhibits upstairs show how the rich lived in Puerto Rico during the 19th century. It's open Tues. to Sun. from 9-12 and 1-4; ☎ 725-5250.

PLAZA DE COLÓN

Once much larger, this square was formerly named Plaza de Santiago after the gate of the same name. In 1893, to mark the 400th anniversary of Columbus' discovery of Puerto Rico, the plaza was renamed and a statue of the explorer unveiled. Ponce de León's statue was then moved to Plaza San José. The plaza was renovated in 1988. Nowadays, it's chiefly of interest for the nearby Tapia Theater.

FUERTE SAN CRISTÓBAL

A strategic masterpiece, this imposing fortress still dominates the E side of town. In its prime, it covered 27 acres and contained seven independent but interlocking units. Although much smaller now than its more famous cousin El Morro, it has a slightly less touristy atmosphere. It's nice to spend the morning sitting and relaxing on the upper level fortifications, taking in the view and getting some sun. Enter the fortress and find the visitor center, a former guardhouse, on the left. The small museum, located across from the administrative offices on the ground floor, has illustrations detailing how the fort was constructed, a scale model of the original fortification, and other exhibits.

A separate room, opened for groups or for individuals with the assistance of a ranger, displays a wonderful reproduction of a soldiers' barracks. The uniforms, muskets, and tableware are all made by craftsmen from models, and the twin facing rows of borderless bunk beds were still in use in Europe as recently as 50 years ago.

There's also a good gift shop on this level, and you can buy this book here. A Military Archives serves as a repository of information on Spanish Caribbean military history; it may be visited for research Mon. to Thurs., from 10-3. If you're visiting in 1998, the superintendent's office will have become a museum; it will feature reproductions of paintings that used the fort in their composition.

On the second floor is a series of low, concave arches and barren rooms. Downstairs, the bronze cannon on an artillery mount was brought down from Delaware, while the iron cannons, which deteriorate faster in the salt breeze, were taken from the ocean. Five 150,000-gallon cisterns are on the lower level, and another is on the uppermost level. Water was obtained by rope and bucket, and animals were prohibited inside the fort to prevent contamination. Now, the water is emptied into the sea. The statue of Santa Barbara, patron saint of the fort, also on the ground level, was venerated by the soldiers. The red-and-white flag flying from the upper level is the red cross of St. Andrew. In use from the 16th to 18th century, it symbolizes 400 years of Spanish culture in Puerto Rico. Check out the view of the Devil's Sentry Box., built during the 17th century at ocean level. A sentry posted here disappeared one night, leaving no trace save his armor, weapons, and clothes. He was thought to have been possessed by the devil. In actuality, he had run off with his girlfriend from La Perla, and they were found to be happily settled on a farm near Caguas years later. From this viewpoint it's possible to see whales migrating from November to January.

THE FORT'S HISTORY: After El Morro proved unable to defend the city, construction began on San Cristóbal in 1634 and continued for the next 150 years. The basic structure, however, had been completed and joined to the city walls by 1678. Like El Morro, it was built entirely with materials gathered from the shoreline. Irishmen O'Reilly and O'Day enlisted in the Spanish army and developed ideas for its construction. Incorporating the most advanced ideas of the time, the complex contained six small forts supporting a central core. These were interconnected via an amazingly complex arrangement of passageways, moats, tunnels, bridges, roads, ramps, and dungeons. To storm the central fortress, the enemy would have to take over the six outer forts under continuous fire. Explosives placed under the moats could be ignited if the enemy gained control. In 1898, San Cristóbal aimed its guns at an American Naval force, firing the first round in the Spanish-American War. After the American occupation, the US Army moved into the fort. In 1949 it was placed under the National Park Service and opened to the public in 1961. Open daily, 9-5; ☎ 729-6920 for information on guided tours.

PLAZA SALVADOR BRAU

This small plaza, also known as La Baradilla, was once the haunt of local politicians. Set next to the Iglesia San Francisco here, the Catholic Academy opened in 1920 and was condemned in 1964. It has been scheduled for condo conversion since the 1970s, but nothing has happened. If it is torn down, the plaza may be extended to cover it.

TERMINAL TURISMO

See tour boats come in at Old San Juan's Terminal Turismo. Take a stroll at night while the ships are in and watch the tourists. The cruise ship terminal offers free rum punches when the tourists arrive. Chauffeured by guayabera-sporting drivers holding walkie-talkies, the taxis outside whisk them off to Condado, depriving them of the opportunity to sample Old San Juan's wonderful nightlife. Across the street is **Intermodal,** a commercialized and expensive municipal crafts center. It replaced the former Plazoleta del Puerto in 1994. Inside the Tourism Pier is the small **Museo del Mar** (Museum of the Seas) which, in addition to its displays of maritime equipment and models, has wall murals detailing the lifestyle of the indigenous Taínos. At one of the docks here, you may see a Navy ship pull up: your tax dollars at work and play.

CASA DE RAMÓN POWER Y GIRALT

The 250-year-old home of the island's first representative to the Spanish parliament has been purchased (and has been beautifully restored) by the Conservation Trust. At 155 Tetúan, it's open Tues. to Sat., 10-4. It has a small but great gift shop and exhibits ranging from Taíno artifacts to stuffed cased birds with soundphones that allow you to hear their calls. Offices are in the back, and they should be able to help you with reservations at Hacienda Buena Vista (see page 261) or at Cabezas de San Juan (page 200). A stop won't take much time and is highly recommended.

EL ARSENAL

Built in 1800, this former naval station was the last place in Puerto Rico to be handed over after the 1898 US takeover. This is where the Spanish general waited for the ship which would return him and his men to Spain. Exhibitions are held here. Open Wed. to Sun., 9-noon and from 1-4; ☎ 724-5949.

LA CASITA

Built in 1937 for the Dept. of Agriculture and Commerce, this "little house" serves as a branch of the tourist board. From outside the Casita you can see San Juan Bay, the Caribbean's busiest container and cruise ship terminal. The pink **Aduana,** Custom House, is to your R. From here you can continue down the Paseo de la Princesa, which has been attractively landscaped; the fountain with its bronze sculptures affirms the island's cultural roots. It is a favored

San Juan Area

make-out spot for couples at night. *La Esperanza* (☎ 724-5590), a wooden ship, takes visitors on excursions around the bay.

LA PRINCESA

A former jail, this building serves as headquarters of the tourism institute and as a fine art gallery; it's open Mon. to Sat. from 9-5. It has the island's most ornate toilets. If you go through the rear doors and out to the R you can see the remains of prison cells. To the R from the entrance you can continue on to the restored *muralla* (city wall). Dating from the 1700s, it is made of sandstone blocks which may be up to 20 ft thick. It terminates at La Puerta de San Juan (San Juan Gate), which is the first of the three city gates built and the sole one remaining. Once the main gate for dignitaries and cargo entering the city, it now serves only to ornament the roadway which passes through it. During the 17th century sloops anchored in the small cove just N of La Fortaleza. New bishops and governors, entering the city through this gate, would be escorted under a canopy to the cathedral where a *Te Deum* Mass would be offered in thanksgiving for the safely completed voyage.

☞ **Traveler's Tip**. Paseo de la Princesa is an ideal place for a romantic sunset stroll.

San Juan Bay & Cataño

Acuaexpreso, the new Cataño ferry (☎ 788-1155), runs across San Juan Bay to the suburb of Cataño. En route it offers great views of El Morro and other historic buildings. You can pay the 50¢ fare with tokens or with two quarters. Board at Pier #2 next to Terminal Turismo in Old San Juan. Ferries leave every half-hour from 6 AM-9 PM. Another ferry, whose entrance is to the L (75¢) runs to the financial district of Hato Rey in 20 minutes; it has frequent problems despite the fact that each boat cost more than a million dollars to purchase. There's an ice cream shop and magazine store in the terminal building. The Cataño area has been plagued by government-imposed pollution problems. The Commonwealth operates the Palo Seco plant, which spews out a fine precipitate matter blamed for environmental problems, ranging from asthma to having furniture covered with a fine black soot.

BACARDI RUM FACTORY

The **Bacardi Rum Factory** (☎ 788-1500), on the outskirts of Cataño, offers free daily tours of its facilities and drinks on the house served under a huge yellow, bat-shaped canopy. (Bacardi's first distillery housed a colony of fruit bats, thus the logo). It's a long walk (45 minutes) to the entrance so it's better to take the minibus. While the minibus is a bit pricey ($1.25) for the distance concerned, you do arrive right in time for the start of the tour. If arriving on foot, a guard will open the gate; walk straight and then turn right. Orange and yellow train-buses carry visitors around the grounds. Although there are regular times posted, tours leave whenever there are sufficient passengers. Each section of the distillery has its own guide. You'll visit the distillery, the ersatz museum, and other sites. It'll seem more interesting if you take advantage of the free drinks *beforehand*. It's open Mon. through Sat. (excluding holidays) from 9-10:30 AM and noon-4 PM. Tours leave on the half-hour. A crafts fair is held here on the first and second Sundays in Dec., featuring work by over 200 craftsmen. Also in the vicinity of Cataño is Cabras Island. Formerly two separate islands, Cabras and Canuelo, they have been connected by a causeway. Here are the ruins of 17th-century Fort Canuelo and the remains of a leper colony. Great place for a picnic. Seafood restaurants are at Palo Seco nearby. Punta Salinas Public Beach is alongside Boca Vieja Bay near Levitown.

San Juan Area

Old San Juan Practicalities

ACCOMMODATIONS: Although Old San Juan is the best place to base yourself for exploring the metropolitan area, there's a dearth of hotels. **The Galeria** (☎ 722-1808), C. Norzagaray 204, is a small guesthouse run by a sculptress. Her work is on display, and the place has a charming medieval feel. Rates are $82 d, including breakfast. The 242-room **Wyndham Old San Juan Hotel & Casino** (☎ 800-WYNDHAM, 721-5100, fax 721-1111), 100 Brumbaugh at Portuario across from the cruise ship terminal, opened in late '96. Rates are from around $150 d on up; facilities include restaurant, health club, casino and rooftop pool. The **Gran Hotel El Convento** (☎ 800-468-2779, 723-9020, fax 721-2877) is a recently renovated 300-year-old Carmelite Convent, in the heart of the old town at C. Cristo 100 at Caleta de San Juan across from the Catedral de San Juan. Facilities include restaurant, casino, pool, sundecks, meeting facilities, and Jacuzzi. It's worth a visit even if you don't stay there.

low budget: The least expensive hotel in the old town is **Hotel Central** (☎ 722-2751), located at C. San José 202, just down the street from Plaza de Armas. It charges around $27 s or d for a room with a shared bath and $45 s or d with a private bath. You are correct in thinking that you won't get much for this price. Another alternative, recommended by readers, is the **Enrique Castro Guest House** (☎ 722-5436; Box 947, Old San Juan PR 00902), C. Tanca 205, which offers rooms for $20 d and $80 pw (a/c rooms are $120 pw). Don't expect much in terms of facilities here.

longer term: If staying for an extended period, ask around about renting a room or an apartment. One of the most pleasant places to stay is **The Caleta** (☎ 725-5347; San Juan, PR 00901), Caleta de las Monjas 11, which offers modest but fully furnished studio apartments (phone optional) right in the heart of town near the Rogativa statue. Above a coin laundry, it's quiet, friendly, safe, and secure, and manager Michael is friendly and hospitable. Expect to pay from around $400/mo. Daily rates may be available depending upon the vacancy situation. For more information/current rates write Michael Giessler at 11 Caleta de las Monjas.

FOOD: The streets are lined with various eating houses and restaurants ranging from the comparatively plush ones lining C. Cristo to budget eateries on the other side of the town. The best place to eat a healthy lunch is undoubtedly **Café Paris,** which is at C. Luna 277. It has artwork by local artists hanging on the walls, a front room facing the street with checkered tablecloths, and a rear patio area for more intimate dining. Rates are quite reasonable – just $5 for a set vegetarian lunch; it also serves juices, desserts, crepes (with maple syrup) and gourmet mountain coffee (also for sale). Owner Magali Santos maintains that she tries "to cook with love." Highly recommended and reasonable is **Gopal** (☎ 724-0229), a *restaurante vegetariano* run by a Hare Krishna-ized Puerto Rican family. Natural food dishes like *sopa de vegetales,* tortillas, spinach, broccoli, lasagna, and a variety of fresh fruit drinks (rather sugary) are lovingly dished out by Jayapatni and her family. Try the combination plate ($4.25 for a "small" plate). It's at C. Tetuan 201 B and is open from 7-3, Mon. to Friday. The spacious, elongated room features some great Indian miniature paintings that are well worth checking out. Saturdays at 4:30 you'll find free food, Bhagavad-Gita reading, and bhakti yoga practice.

For honest Puerto Rican home cooking try **El Jibarito**, Mr. and Mrs. Ruiz's place, at C. Sol 276. **Tasa de Oro**, corner of C. Tanca and C. San Justo, serves up rice and beans and other traditional foods. **La Galería**, C. San Justo 205, is an inexpensive eatery with Cuban and Puerto Rican fare. At C. San Justo 207, **La Mallorquina** (☎ 722-3261) serves traditional Puerto Rican cuisine including *asopao*, the house specialty. **Cafeteria Manolin,** C. San Justo 258 in back of the Banco Popular, serves reasonably priced food. Higher but still not unreasonably priced is **La Bombanera**, at C. San Francisco 259; it is well known for its coffee and sweets. A sign here proclaims *"Vendemos Café Expresso Solamente"* ("We only serve expresso"). It also serves seafood dishes. **Siglo XX**, C. Fortaleza 355, is a coffee shop-style restaurant serving dishes such as paella. Catering to a Puerto Rican crowd, it has counter service, breakfast specials, and both inexpensive and moderate prices. **Café La Mallorca**, bordering Plaza de Jibaro, serves good food at reasonable prices. **Butterfly People**, C. Fortaleza 152, serves lunch, offering quiche, sandwiches, and the like. It is furnished with batik and butterfly murals. **La Danza**, C. Fortaleza 56 at C. Cristo, advertises a $12 paella special for two that includes coffee, pastry, salad, and a small bottle of wine. However, after you are lured into the restaurant, you find that the price is actually $14, that the wine bottle has been refilled from another, that the paella is made with turmeric, not saffron, and that the service is a bit sullen. There are also other eateries lining Plaza de Colón that are inexpensive.

SNACKS, SANDWICHES, AND DRINKS: Just around the corner from C. Tetuán on C. San José, **Cafeteria Los Amigos** has the cheapest morning coffee in town along with inexpensive sandwiches made on Puerto Rican-style bread. It is one of the most atmospheric of all the local eateries: you might be in a small town in the hills. It's closed on Sun. Another local, inexpensive sandwich shop is at C. Mendez Vigo and Luna. **El Mesón** is at Plaza de Armas. At C. Fortaleza 364, **Cafeteria Safari** has daily specials. **Las Tertulias**, C. Cristo 105, has a pleasant atmosphere and offers sandwiches, shakes, and expresso. **Maria's**, C. Cristo 204, is famous for its delicious but pricey fresh frozen fruit drinks. An Italian restaurant across the street has pizza slices and other Italian food. Located on Plaza Colón and not inexpensive, **Café Berlin** (☎ 722-5205; C. San Francisco 407) serves drinks and innovative food (including vegetarian dishes) and has art exhibits. It generally has a good collection of newspapers to read. Another alternative is **Casa Papyrus** – a combination bookstore, record store, and café, located at C. Tetuán 357 across from the Teatro Tapia. Prices are moderate, and ths staff is friendly. A *heladeria* (ice cream parlor) on Plaza San José has inexpensive *batidas* (shakes) and cones. **Pueblo** has a branch on Plaza de Armas with whole coffee beans, cold beer, and everything else you might want. There's also an expresso and ice cream joint or two out on the plaza itself.

TOURISTY EATERIES: One local landmark is the busy **Hard Rock Café**, 253 Recinto Sur. A visit here is like being instantaneously transported back to the US mainland. The restaurant is a modern-day shrine to rock stars (some of them little known), and is more worth a visit to look at its walls rather than to "Save the Planet." Artifacts here include one of The Band's gold records, Guns and Roses memorabilia, Quicksilver Messenger Service posters, John Hartford's guitar, John and Yoko's Wedding Album, a Phil Collins gold record and autographed drum sticks. Prices are high and entrées are largely for committed carnivores, but there's a vegetarian burger for $7.50; coffee is $1.50. It's open daily, and there's a souvenir shop where you can add to your collection of Hard Rock Café T-shirts. Another eatery, rather mammarian in character, **Hooters** is right on Plaza Colón at C. San Francisco 413. Operating under the slogan "More than a Mouthful," this chain was given syndicated columnist Ellen Goodman's "Backlash Award" for 1993.

FORMAL FOOD: There are a large number of gourmet eateries here. **Il Perugino**, C. Cristo 105, serves gourmet Italian dishes. At C. Recinto Sur 306, **Al Dente** (☎ 723-7303) serves Sicilian food and fresh fruit drinks. Dishes include pasta alla pescatore and salmon served in garlic with roasted red pepper sauce. An appetizer cart is wheeled right up to your table. In addition to mannequins, it has abstract paintings, a large aquarium, and an antique Italian flag. Gourmet **Yukiyu** (☎ 721-0653, 722-1423), C. Recinto Sur 311, serves fresh sushi as well as seafood and meat. The **Royal Thai** (☎ 725-8424), C. Recinto Sur 315, offers curried lobster tail, red curry clam soup, and scallops served with tamarind sauce over cellophane noodles. It's owned and operated by a Thai woman. **Marisoll** (☎ 725-7454), 202 Cristo, is set in the patio of an old building and serves entrées like fresh salmon in a polenta crust with champagne buerre blanc. Located right on Plaza San José, **Patio de Sam** (☎ 723-1149), C. San Sebastián 102, serves a variety of local specialties including seafood crepes. **Bohemia**, C. San Sebastián 103, serves German dishes and has a beer garden. At C. San Sebastián 106, **Amadeus** (☎ 722-8635) serves traditional Puerto Rican cuisine as well as seafood and even rabbit. **Café Seda,** C. San Sebastián 150, offers gourmet Puerto Rican dishes like *mofongo*. At C. Cristo 202, **Il Perugino** (☎ 722-5481) is a very expensive, intimate eight-room

Italian bistro. At C. Cristo 250, **Ambrosia** (☎ 722-5206) features Italian daily specials. It offers $9-$12 entrées. At Callejón de la Capilla 312 (corner C. San Francisco), **El Mesón La Gran Tasca** (☎ 722-5322) offers Spanish tapas and other entrées. At C. Tetuán 367 behind the Teatro Tapia, **La Chaumiére** (☎ 722-3330) is a very popular, very expensive ($21 and up for entrées) gourmet French restaurant. **Chamo's**, C. Tanca 259, serves expensive seafood paella as well as lunchtime specials. At C. Norzagaray 424, **Amanda's** (☎ 722-1682) serves fish, vegetable dishes, and fruit frappés. At C. Fortaleza 317, **Tasca del Callejón** (☎ 721-1689) serves seafood, paella, and meat dishes. **Rick's American Café** (☎ 723-3982; C. Tetúan 364) serves an international menu that includes seafood. **Pito's Seafood** (☎ 724-4515), C. San José 56, serves every manner of seafood in gourmet fashion. **Don Corleone** (☎ 723-0408), C. Fortaleza 206, offers gourmet Sicilian cuisine. At C. Fortaleza 320, **Bistro Gámbaro** (☎ 724-4592) serves elaborate gourmet *prix fixe* cuisine in an intimate, elegant atmosphere. **Aló Bistro** (☎ 722-3731) is a "Soho-style loft" offering creative gourmet dishes. **Café San Juan Bistro**, C. Cruz 152, serves sandwiches, Puerto Rican dishes, and vegetarian food – all in an art gallery setting. **Café de Puerto** (only open to non-members for lunch) is near the cruise ship terminals, as is **La Isla Bonita**. **Shooters Waterfront Café** is at the San Juan Bay Marina, slightly out of town at 10 Fernandez Juncos.

FAST FOOD: Fast-food freaks can find relief at an unusually aesthetic **Burger King** (complete with waterfall), right on Plaza Salvador Brau, and a spacious **Taco Maker** at C. San Justo 255; the latter has a **Subway** (veggie subs also) located right across the street. **Pizza Hut**, **McDonalds**, and **Baskin Robbins** line C. Fortaleza. **Ponderosa** is at C. Tetuán and C. San Justo. There's also a **Kentucky Fried Chicken** around. (No, I don't have the exact address!)

ENTERTAINMENT: For its size, Old San Juan has a greater concentration and more variety of nightlife than any city in the United States. Cobblestone-lined streets are packed wall to wall with nightspots ranging from sleaze bars to elite discos. Its dynamic and unmistakably Latin environment gets wild at night – especially on weekends when cars pour in. Everyone is desperate to see and be seen in this modern version of the *paseo*, the traditional evening stroll along the plaza. Well-heeled couples promenade up and down C. Cristo. Fashionable clothes and tons of makeup are everywhere

San Juan Area

in evidence – with everyone heading up to the bar-lined streets surrounding the Plaza San José.

On the Plaza, in addition to the young middle-class bar scene, there are sometimes jams with conga bands or folk musicians. It has gotten so wild up here at times that the police have come and fired shots into the air. Plenty of action and atmosphere in the surrounding streets as well. Innumerable bars, scattered throughout the town, have pool tables, TVs, and pinball machines. Here you can drink a beer for as little as $1 or so. Yet another alternative is watching cruise ship passengers, especially in the evenings when you'll see women who look as if they are decked out for a cocktail party come to shop. You might see a guy with "Video Fun Day" written on his t-shirt taping teenyboppers from a ship who are doing their rendition of Arrow's "Hot, Hot, Hot."

information: Check the "Performance" section of the Thursday *San Juan Star*'s "Entertainment Guide" to find out what's going on. *Que Pasa* also has listings. Another way is to check for posters.

music and theater: El Quinqué (☎ 722-5378) has jazz on Thurs. evenings at 9. **Café La Violeta**, C. Fortaleza 56, features a dark, romantic environment that seems expressly designed for romantic tête-à-têtes. A pianist plays Thurs. to Sat. from 9-2 AM. **Tetuán 20**, C. Tetuán 255, features live guitar music Thurs. and Fri. evenings. Pianists perform nightly (10-3 AM) at **Café Alejandro**, on O'Donnel between Fortaleza and Tetuán. For formal theater, try the **Tapia**.

clubs: Things aren't what they used to be; the yuppification of the old town has clearly had an impact and there are now no good venues for live music. **Extasy** (☎ 725-7581), C. Cruz 251, is a gay disco with drag queens and the works. **The Steam Works** (☎ 725-4993), C. Luna 205, is a gay bath.

☞ **Traveler's Tip.** If you can speak Spanish, **Casa Papyrus** (☎ 724-6105/6555), C. Tetuan 357, has frequent book-readings and lectures.

BARS: There are a number of watering holes scattered around the old town. Up C. San José is **El Batey**, an *Americano* hangout which is open until the last cat goes home. One classic place is **Victor's**, just around the corner from Walgreen's and up the street. Very popular with locals, it was initially a grocery, and drinks are dispensed on the former shopping register's goods mover. **Don Pablo** is a colorful bar at C. Cristo 103 that has unusual artwork – the decor includes sexist Bud and Finlandia posters, a moose head covered with cobwebs, and video game machines. An attached laundry offers to wash your clothes as you booze and schmooze it up.

   discos: Lazer Videoteque is at C. Cruz 251 and **Neon's Videoteque** is at C. Tanca 203 (Wed. to Sat. from 10 PM). Both cater to a very decked-out, youthful crowd, including cruise ship passengers with vouchers. Out at Fernandez Juncos 521, **St. Tropez Pub** provides scantily clad diversions for well-heeled Puerto Rican males.

EVENTS AND FESTIVALS: Most of the island-wide festivities find their fullest expression here. A **Puppet Theater Festival** is held in Jan., as is an international folklore festival and the **San Sebastián Street Fiesta**; this popular street fair has everything from processions and dancing in the plaza to displays of Paso Fino horses. The streets are absolutely packed. **The Festival de Claridad** (Festival of Clarity) takes place in Feb. The **Festival de Teatro Puertorriqueño** (Festival of the Puerto Rican Theater) is held at the Tapia Theater in March. The **Fiesta de la Musical Puertorriqueña** is held inside the Dominican Convent in May. The **Heinecken Jazzfest** is held in May at Parque Muñoz Marín. The **Festival de Verano** (the Summer Festival) is in June, as are the **Michelob Dry Jazz and Latin Music Festivals** (held at Bellas Artes), and the **Casals Festival** (which attracts the top names in classical music). Centering on June 26, San Juan's most famous fiesta, its *fiestas patronales* dedicated to San Juan Bautista, is celebrated as inhabitants (including the mayor) flock to the sea for the traditional midnight dip, which is believed to wash away sin. A ceramics fair takes place in August. These events are subject to change, so check the latest issue of *Que Pasa* to find out what, indeed, is happening.

CRAFTS: Centro de Artes Populares (☎ 723-2320) is a crafts shop at C. Cristo 253. It's open Tues. to Sat. from 9:30-4:30; **Pacopepe**, corner of C. Recinto Sur and C. Tanca, sells t-shirts and other fashionware made with handpicked Peruvian cotton. For a selection of *mundillo* lace from all over the island, visit **Aguadilla en San Juan** (☎ 722-0578), C. San Francisco 352. Imported Mayan-woven handicrafts are sold at **Tata**, C. Cristo 202. You can also find crafts and craft-like items (spray can stencil art for example) at the night market near the Banco Popular. For information on visiting crafts shops all around the island contact Acte Cestero (☎ 721-2400, ext. 2201) at the Puerto Rico Tourism Company.

San Juan Area

ANTIQUES: José E. Alegria's handsome shop at C. Cristo 154 houses a fascinating collection of *santos* and pre-Columbian artifacts. **El Alcazar** (☎ 723-1229), C. San José 103, has two annexes and claims to be the largest antique shop in the Caribbean. It has a wonderful collection of antiques from all over the world.

> ☞ **Traveler's Tip.** On Old San Juan's "Noches de Galerías," held the first Tuesday of the month from Feb. to Nov., all of the art galleries hold simultaneous receptions from 7-11PM. Be sure to check it out if you're in town. It's one of those see-and-be-seen affairs.

FACTORY OUTLETS: Clothing is one of the best buys in Old San Juan. Several factory outlets sell discounted clothes made on the island. **Valu** is at C. San Francisco 208. **London Fog Factory Outlet Store** is at C. Cristo 156. **Pfaltzgraff**, a factory store with "bridal and gift registry," is at C. Cristo 205.

other clothing: Specializing in swimwear, **Wet** is at C. Cristo 252. For motorcycle gear try **Storm Riders** at C. Cruz 252.

SOUVENIRS: There are a number of unusual stores here. **Bovedá**, C. Cristo 209, has a unique collection of items. **Señor Frog's Official Store**, C. San Francisco 265, offers wonderfully inventive T-shirts as well as other souvenirs. **Barrachina**, C. Fortaleza 104, has free rum samples but higher prices than the supermarkets. **Hecho a Mano**, C. San Francisco 260, offers a fine selection of crafts. At C. Cristo 154, **Spicy Caribbee** offers a wide variety of sauces and other food items. For a most unusual selection of products, try **Condom Mania** at C. San Francisco 353. **DMR**, C. Luna 204, offers a beautiful collection of antique furniture reproductions. An **Artisan Fair** is held on Plaza Hostos on Sat. and Sun.

JEWELRY STORES: These include **London House** at C. San José 206; the **Silver Gallery** inside the Arcade Mall at C. Cristo 206; **Joseph Machina,** C. Fortaleza 101; **Leather & Pearls**, C. Cristo 202; **Barrachina's**, C. Fortaleza 104; **Rainbow Jewelery** at C. Fortaleza 105; **Maximo**, C. San Francisco 250; **Faro**, C. Fortaleza 357; **Gitana**, C. Fortaleza 304; **Catala** at Plaza de Armas; **Corsalina**, C. San Francisco 350; **Ramon Lopez**, C. Fortaleza 256; **One Stop Shopping**, C. San Francisco 302; **Nayor**, C. San Francisco 250; **Yas Mar**, C. Fortaleza 205; **Boveda**, C. Cristo 209; and **Joyeria Demel**, C. Fortaleza 261. For reproductions, try **Impostors**, C. Tetuán 200 (at C. Cruz).

ART GALLERIES: Puerto Rican artists are well represented in Old San Juan's many galleries. In addition to the exhibits held inside Casablanca, the Balaja, La Arsenal, the Alcaldía, and the Museo de Arte y Historia, there are a number of private galleries. **Sala de Arte**, an unusual gallery with great recorded music, is at C. San José 101. **Galería Botello**, which displays the works of the Spanish expatriate namesake as well as other artists, is at C. Cristo 208. **Galería Luigi Marrozzini** is at C. Cristo 156. **Galería M.S.A.** is at C. San Francisco 266. **Galería San Juan** is on C. Norzagaray at the corner of San C. Justo. **Fenn Studio/Gallery**, San José 58, represents local artists. **Galería Santa Bárbara**, C. Luna 277, houses a selection of old maps and illustrations. **Roberto Parrilla** (☎ 722-2732) exhibits his paintings at C. Luna 360. The **San Juan Art Students League** holds exhibits in a blue building in front of Iglesia San José.

BOOKS AND MUSIC: The Bookstore, which is excellent, is located near the corner of San José and Tetuán. Another alternative is **Casa Papyrus** – a combination bookstore, record store, and café – which is at C. Tetuán 357 across from the Teatro Tapia. Both stores should be carrying this book. **Saravá**, C. Tetuán 207, is one of the world's most attractively designed music stores. Set in a lovely old building, it has two stories with extensive CD collections – salsa, merengue, African, even New Age.

INFORMATION: Minimal tourist information is provided in offices in the **Alcaldía** (City Hall) on Plaza de Armas (☎ 724-7171), at the main offices in **La Princesa** (which is on the *paseo* of the same name), and at **La Casita**, a small renovated building near the end of C. Tanca at the waterfront. Don't expect to be helped unless you ask them.

SERVICES: The post office located at the corner of Recinto Sur and San Justo has been closed. An **ATH terminal** is at the Roig Bank at C. Cruz and C. Tetuán. **Pharmacies** are located on the Plaza de Armas and at the corner of C. Luna and C. Cruz. Newspapers (including *The New York Times*) are found at the former as well as near the post office. An a/c **library** is located inside Casa Blanca. **The Calling Station** (☎ 724-1124, fax 724-7072) is across from the Teatro Tapia at C. Tetuán 357. It does not have a minimum charge for calls, and it has copy, video telephone, video rental, and fax services. You can call the UK here for $1/min. It also contains **The Mailing Station,** which offers mailboxes, money orders, packing, and access to a full range of shipping services. A message board holds notes for cruise ship arrivés, and the cruise ship schedule is

San Juan Area

posted. Another similar operation, **Phone Home** (☎ 721-5431, fax 721-5497) is at C. Recinto Sur 257D and across from the PO. **Lamour Video**, C. San Justo 254, offers video rentals. At Plaza de Armas, **Puerto Rico Drugs** has Spanish-speaking computerized pulse machines, vitamins, postcards, music, magazines, and schlock to bring back to tasteless relatives. **Laundromats** are located at corner of C. Cruz and C. Sol, as well as next to La Caleta Apartments near the Rogativa statue and at Walter's up from Walgreen's on C. Cruz. If you wish to buy flowers for that hot date (or to soothe that angry wife, mistress, or girlfriend), **Anflora** flower shop is located at Calles Cruz and Sol.

banks: For changing money, using ATH (instant teller) machines, and cashing traveler's checks, the **Bank of Nova Scotia**, C. Tetuán 251, and the **Royal Bank of Canada**, C. Tetuán 204, are open Mon. to Fri. from 9-2:30. The **Caribbean Foreign Exchange** (☎ 722-8222) is at Tetúan 201 B.

WATERFRONT REHABILITATION IN OLD SAN JUAN

The **Barrio la Marina** project has been conceived as a way to revitalize Old San Juan and provide a point of entry for the nearly one million cruise ship passengers who visit Old San Juan annually. This $100-million public and private sector partnership, which extends over six acres and seven city blocks, is the first of its kind on the island. This waterfront rehabilitation project received an award for excellence in urban design from the American Institute of Architects. Construction began in 1992 and should be completed by early in the next century. Projects include the $30-million 242-room Wyndham Old San Juan Hotel & Casino; 200 condos; 100,000 square feet of retail space; over 50,000 square feet of office space, and more than 950 parking spaces; some 600 of these are located in a new garage building, which has now been completed. The remainder will be underneath the new residential structures. An overhead sky bridge will connect the Wyndham to the adjacent Isla Bonita, a shopping center.

Metropolitan San Juan

Puerta de Tierra

Literally named "Land at the Door," this compact area, once right outside the old city walls, was originally settled by freed black slaves. Nowadays, Puerta de Tierra contains US Naval Reserves, the Capitol and other governmental buildings. Avenida Ponce de León runs right through its center.

SIGHTS: Seat of the Puerto Rican bicameral legislature, the **Capitol** was constructed during the 1920s. Its magnificent dome, with its coat of arms, hangs over an urn displaying the 1952 constitution. It's open Mon. to Fri., 8:30-5. For guided tours, call 721-6040, ext. 253. The once-exclusive **Casino de San Juan**, constructed in 1917 for the Casino de Puerto Rico social club, has since been renamed the Manuel Pavia Fernandez Reception Center and converted to use by the State Department. It has recently been restored with marble floors and walls and a 12-foot chandelier (open Mon. to Fri., 8-4:30; ☎ 722-2121). A statue of patron saint San Juan Bautista, across from the Capitol and overlooking the small beach below, bears an uncanny resemblance to Mr. Natural, of underground comic book fame. Gracefully landscaped **Muñoz Rivera Park** contains a statue of its namesake which stands near **El Polvorín**, an ammunition depot and small museum. The park, which first opened in 1983, now has a **tram car** which runs one km and takes 6½ minutes. Muñoz Rivera is open from 9-5 Tues. to Sun. Eighteenth-century **Fort San Jerónimo**, entered from the rear of the Caribe Hilton, houses a museum featuring dummies wearing military uniforms of different eras, ship models, and other war material. It's open from Wed. to Sun., 9-noon and 1-4:30; ☎ 724-5949.

ACCOMMODATIONS: The least expensive is **Hotel Ocean Side** (☎ 722-2410), Av. Muñoz Rivera 54. Considered to be one of the outstanding examples of art-deco architecture to be found in the Caribbean, the **Radisson Normandie Hotel** (☎ 729-2929/3083, fax 729-3083) was restored in 1988. Originally constructed in 1939 by a prominent local engineer in honor of his French wife, it was intended to mimic the famous French ocean liner *Normandie*. Facilities include a beachside pool with terrace, two restaurants, ballrooms, and a corporate floor and business center. There are 180 a/c guest rooms (including 115 suites); each has cable TV, minibar, coffeemaker, phones, and hair dryers. Some have sitting rooms. Specially designed rooms for the disabled are also available. The hotel is set on Av. Muñoz Rivera at the corner of C. Rosales. Winter rates for rooms run from around $200 s and $210 d. A full American breakfast is included. For more information write Box 50059, San Juan, PR 00902; US/worldwide ☎ (800) 333-3333.

On the upper end is the **Caribe Hilton** (☎ 721-0303; fax 725-8849; Box 1872, San Juan, PR 00902), which is set on 17 acres. The island's oldest resort hotel, its earliest building dates from 1849. At one time visitors to the island came here directly from the airport and (aside from time spent shopping in Old San Juan), the hotel environs were as much of the island as they saw! It has 668 rooms and suites with balcony, mini-bar, and TV. Its facilities include a casino, two pools, six tennis courts, squash and racquetball courts, car rental and airline reservation services, health club, two non-smoking floors, and a number of restaurants and bars. Rates run from $295 s, $320 d up to $1,200 for the most expensive suite. For more information, ☎ 1-800-HILTONS in the US, (800) 268-9275 in Canada, 0800-289-303 in the UK.

FOOD: A preeminent place (and one you won't want to miss) is **El Roble**. With a deli out front and a large restaurant in the back, here you can find an assortment of everything from beer and cheese to Cuban cigars from Miami. El Amendro nougats from Spain are a delicacy as are *turrones*, the locally produced Christmas candies. Try to grab a slice of cheesecake after it comes out fresh from the oven. For $9 an entire can of peaches imported from Spain can be yours. Try *quesito*, a tasty cheese pastry. Pancho Romano and the *empanadas* (meat pies) are also recommended. Other restaurants include **Ponce de León Pizza Parlor**, **Restaurant La Imperial** (another deli), **Hao Hao** (Chinese fast food and ice cream), and the **Cathay**; all are along Av. Ponce de León. The **Delibank**, set inside the Citibank Tower at Ponce de León 2521, offers more than 40 sandwiches on your choice of bread.

dining: More expensive is the **Tasca** at Av. Muñoz Rivera 54. At Ponce de León 307, **La Bota** serves light dishes, including Puerto Rican food. At Av. Fernández Juncos 521, the **Latin American Café** has casual Cuban food. At Parada 7½ on Av. Muñoz Rivera, the cliffside **Dumas** (☎ 721-3550) serves up Spanish-influenced international cuisine. **Marisquería Atlántica** (☎ 722-0890), Lugo Viña 7 (also in Isla Verde), specializes in seafood, including paella and

Maine lobster. The **Escambrón Beach Club** (☎ 724-3344), behind the Normandie, is an inexpensive Puerto Rican restaurant and popular night spot.

hotel dining: The Radisson Normandie has the **Normandie Restaurant** (☎ 729-2929) which features dishes ranging from Chinese to Italian. In the Caribe Hilton, **El Batey del Pescador** (☎ 721-0303) has a variety of dishes; the seafood menu is expanded on Fri. evenings. In the same hotel and overlooking the sea, the very expensive **Peacock Paradise** serves Chinese and other cuisine. Also here, the **Rotisserie Il Giardino** serves N Italian and international dishes.

SHOPPING: Buy handicrafts at **Mercado de Artesanía Puertorriqueña** inside Parque Muñoz Rivera and at **Mercado Artesanía Carabalí**, Parque Sixto Escobar. The former is open only on Sunday. A number of small shops line Av. Ponce de León.

SERVICES: A postal station is located along Av. Ponce de León. The **Archives and General Library**, at Av. Ponce de León 500, has served as a library, cigar factory, and rum plant. It displays books and archives from the collection of the Institute of Puerto Rican Culture. Its small chapel might seem to be an unusual feature, but keep in mind that it was originally designed as a hospital. It's open Mon. to Fri. from 8-5 and is a great place to read otherwise expensive imported newspapers. Also try the small library inside the ornate **Biblioteca Atenea Puertorriqueña**, Av. Ponce de León.

tours: Sunshine Tours (☎ 800-955-6689) in the Radisson Normandie offers tours to El Yunque, the old town, Ponce, Camuy Caves, and a Shopper's Special to St. Thomas.

Miramar

This high-class residential area is just across the bridge from Puerta de Tierra. The many beautiful homes in Miramar include several by architect Antonin Nechodoma, whose work shows the marked influence of Frank Lloyd Wright. Yachts shelter at Club Naútico on the bay side of the bridge. **Isla Grande** is just beside Miramar to the W. Formerly a US Naval base, it is now the site of Isla Grande Airport (domestic) which has flights to Culebra and Vieques. A large number of birds can be seen in this area.

San Juan Area

ACCOMMODATIONS: Located at Av. Ponce De León 801, **Hotel Excelsior** (☎ 721-7400, fax 723-0068; San Juan, PR 00907) has a pool, bar, restaurant, sports complex, and tennis courts. The 140 a/c rooms and suites offer refrigerator, cable TV, and balcony; rooms with kitchenettes and two-room suites with kitchenettes are also available. It charges $113-$139 s, $128-$154 d. For more information, ☎ (800) 223-9815. The 48-room **Miramar** (☎ 722-6239, fax 723-1180; Santurce, PR 00907), Av. Ponce de León 606, is geared towards visiting businessmen; rooms are $35-$50. The 45-room **Olimpo Court** (☎ 724-0600, fax 723-0068), Miramar 603, offers a/c rooms; studios have kitchenettes. Rates start from $50. Next door at Av. Miramar 605, 50-room **Hotel Toro** (☎ 725-5150/2647) is geared to business travelers. Rates range from around $30 s, $42 d.

FOOD: Open until 9, the **Pueblo Supermarket** in the Miramar Caribbean Tower has the usual stuff, including bulk coffee beans. Av. Ponce de León and surrounding side streets are literally lined with places to eat. For sandwiches and expresso try the **Panadería y Reposteria** at the corner of Av. Miramar and Av. Ponce de León. At Ponce de León 604, **Café Fornos** (☎ 722-3120) serves Puerto Rican, Spanish, and other dishes including paella valenciana.

   hotel dining: D'Arco is at the base of Hotel Toro, Av. Miramar 605. In the Excelsior Hotel at Av. Ponce de León 801, award winning, very expensive **Augusto's** (☎ 725-7700) serves distinct dishes such as lobster ravioli along with a wide variety of wines. **Café Miramar** here is an expensive but informal coffee shop serving three meals daily and a Sun. brunch. The **Ali-oli** is also here.

ENTERTAINMENT: The **Fine Arts Cinema** (☎ 721-4288), Av. Ponce De León 654 , has high quality first run films. Other theaters are farther down the road in Santurce. The **Black Angus** is one of the local meat markets. The "hoofers" here have a lower incidence of AIDS than the street hookers nearby (because they insist that their customers use condoms). Other such clubs are in the vicinity.

SERVICES: The **Calling Station** (☎ 722-8085, fax 722-8066) is across from the Pueblo and next to the Banco Popular at Av. Ponce de León 655. It has copy, video telephone, and fax services, with no minimum charge. Many airline offices are based here, including Iberia, Viasa, Lufthansa, and Dominicana. The information service center for the **Dominican Republic** (☎ 725-4774) is at Miramar Plaza, Av. Ponce de León 954. The **French Consulate** is in Edificio Centro de Seguros, Suite 412, Av. Ponce de León 701.

ISLA GRANDE AIRPORT: Situated at the end of a long stretch of road near the tractor trailer "Sea Train" terminal sits small and funky Isla Grande, which served as the island's first international airport. Inside are a *cafeteria* and several airlines, including Flamingo (which flies to Culebra), and Vieques Air Link (which flies to Vieques and on to St. Croix). **Hill Aviation** (☎ 723-3385) offers helicopter tours of Old San Juan and beyond. **Isla Grande Flying School** (☎ 722-1180, 725-5760) rents small planes for solo and dual flying with a three-hour minimum. Fuel, oil, and liability insurance are included. Unfortunately, the only way to get to this airport is via a long, hot walk, your own wheels, or by taxi.

Santurce-Condado

Once the most exclusive area in the city, Santurce is now deteriorating rapidly as businesses move over to the neighboring financial district of Hato Rey. Condado, the tourist strip on the main bus route between Old San Juan and the rest of the city, is as near to a perfect replica of Miami Beach as you'll find in the Caribbean. Check out the scene if you must. If you want to escape from Puerto Rico, this is the place to do it. Avenida Ashford, once famous for its hookers, now hosts a nightly crowd of male prostitutes and drug pushers. Whatever you do, keep off the beaches at night, or risk a mugging.

San Juan Area

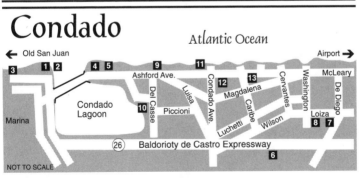

Condado
Atlantic Ocean

← Old San Juan   Airport →

Ashford Ave.

Condado Lagoon

Piccioni

Marina

Del Casse

Luisa

Condado Ave.

Magdalena

Caribe

Cervantes

Washington

McLeary

De Diego

Loiza

Luchetti   Wilson

NOT TO SCALE

(26) Baldorioty de Castro Expressway

1. Fort San Geronimo
2. Caribe Hilton
3. Regency Hotel
4. Condado Plaza
5. Regency Hotel
6. Fine Arts Center
7. Bell, Book and Candle
8. Pueblo Supermarket
9. Convention Center, La Concha
10. Tamana, Mirabel and Condado Lagoon hotels
11. Embassy, Atlantic Beach and Canario by the Sea hotels
12. Dutch Inn
13. Casablanca Guest House

history: Founded as Cangrejos (later San Mateo de Cangrejos), the area was the main agricultural and meat supplier to Old San Juan from the 17th century onwards. Inhabited mostly by freed slaves and Maroons (refugees from slavery on other islands), its name changed to Santurce. The bridge linking Condado with Puerto de Tierra was constructed originally in 1910 by two brothers (the Behns) who were early 20th-century immigrants from St. Thomas. The name (*Dos Hermanos,* "Two Brothers") of the current rebuilt and enlarged structure still refers to Hernand and Sosthenes who, after acquiring the Puerto Rican Telephone Company, went on to found ITT! C. Luchetti is named after their mother, Madame Luchetti. Av. Ashford's namesake is Dr. Bailey K. Ashford, who came to the island with the occupying American troops. He discovered that hookworms are the root cause of anemia. During the turbulent late 1950s in Cuba and after the revolution which followed, Condado was quick to soak up the tourists (and many Cubans) who fled, seeking a more hospitable environment.

sights: The area's most unusual "sight" must surely be the Tunel Minillas in Santurce. It's nicknamed the "carwash" because of its leaky roof. The **Museum of Contemporary Puerto Rican Art** (☎ 268-0049) is inside the Barat Bldg. in the Sacred Heart University which is off of Av. Ponce de León in Santurce; it's open Mon. to Fri. from 9-5.

beaches: To get to an okay beach, take the stairs to the R of the Convention Center. To reach a better one, head towards Santurce (in the direction of Isla Verde) and make a L on C. King's Court. Heading past the stoplight, you'll run right into the beach. This clean white sand beach is long and wide with palm trees.

CONDADO GUESTHOUSE ACCOMMODATIONS: Set off of C. Caribe 57, the **Casablanca Guest House** (☎/fax 772-7139; Condado PR 00907-3810) is an intimate, centrally located seven-room hotel set on C. Caribe 57, a side street off of Av. Ashford. The comfortable rooms have queen-size double beds, fans and radios; movie posters adorn the walls. It is run by affable Alex Leighton; coffee and donuts are served in the courtyard each morning. This is a good place to stay if you want to be in Condado yet wish to avoid the hustle and bustle. Rates start at $35 s and $45 d for the standard rooms and $45 s, $55 d for the superior rooms. Winter rates are $50 s, $60 d standard and $60 s, $70 d superior. Another good choice is the **Embassy Guest House** (☎ 725-8284/2400, fax 725-2400; Condado PR 00907), C. Seaview 1126, a street off of Vendig leading from Av. Ashford. It features rooms with a/c, fans, and cable TV starting at $45; more expensive rooms have kitchenettes, and a restaurant is just across the street. It is gay friendly. At Sea View 1125, **Aleli by the Sea** (☎ 725-5313/3895, fax 722-7823; Condado PR 00907) offers nine rooms starting at around $50 d with semi-private bath and a/c. Use of the shared kitchen and living room is included, as is a sundeck on the beach. The **Arcade Inn Guest House** (☎ 725-0668, 728-7524; Condado, PR 00901), C. Taft 8, has personal service. Rates start from around $50 s and $55 d. Down the street at C. Taft 53, the **Wind Chimes Guest House** (☎/fax 727-4153, 800-946-3244) is a restored Spanish-style villa. It has 12 rooms with a/c or fans. Cable TV and breakfast is included. Rates range from around $65.

CONDADO SMALLER HOTELS: A member of the International Gay Travel Association and right on the beach, the 37-room **Atlantic Beach** (☎ 721-6900, 722-3089, fax 721-6917; C.Vendig 1, Condado PR 00907), has a restaurant. Rates run around $90-$140. The 22-room **El Prado Inn and Apartments** (☎ 728-5925, 468-4521; 800-728-5925; fax 725-6978; Condado PR 00908), C. Luchetti 1350, is centrally located and offers a/c or fan rooms with private baths; continental breakfast is included. Rates run from $69 s, $79 d. The 48-room a/c **El Portal del Condado** (☎ 721-9010, fax 724-3714; Box 10133, San Juan, PR 00908), C. Condado 76, offers rooms with cable TV, radio, phone, and refrigerator; it's walking distance from the beach. Rates start from $95. At 1317 Ashford, the **El Canario Inn** (☎ 724-2793/3861, fax 722-0391; Condado PR 00907) has 25 rooms from $85. Rooms are a/c with phone and cable TV and rates include breakfast. The 40-room **El Canario By the Lagoon Hotel** (☎ 722-5058, 742-4276, fax 723-8590; Condado PR 00907), C. Clemenceau 4, charges from around $95. All rooms are a/c and have cable TV, phone, and balcony. Breakfast is complimentary. Completing the trio, the **El Canario By the Sea** (☎ 722-8640, fax 725-4921; Condado PR 00907), C. Condado 4, offers 25 a/c rooms with radio and cable TV. Rates run from $80 s, $95 d.

CONDADO LARGE HOTELS: Collectively marketed as **The Condado Beach Trio,** the Condado Beach Hotel & Casino (☎ 721-6090, fax 722-5062), El Centro, and La Concha (☎ 721-6090, fax 722-3200) combine to form a self-contained resort, casino, and multi-purpose activity center complex. Its 80,000-sq-ft El Centro is the Caribbean's largest convention and entertainment facility. It stands sandwiched between the 250-room Condado Beach and the 234-room La Concha. Rooms have cable TVs and phones; many have balconies. Facilities include two tennis courts, water sports,

San Juan Area

pools, restaurants, and casino and lounge (at the Condado Beach). Rooms go from $210 s and $240 d on up; La Concha charges from $155 s and $190 d on up. For reservations, ☎ 800-468-2775 for Condado Beach and ☎ 800-468-2822 for La Concha. Write La Concha at Box 4195, San Juan, PR 00902 and Condado Beach at Box 41226, San Juan, PR 00940.

At Av. Ashford 999, the **Condado Plaza Hotel & Casino** (☎ 721-1000, fax 722-7955; Box 1270, San Juan PR 00902) facilities include casino, fitness center, water sports center, nightclub, and piano bars. Most of its 550 a/c rooms have king-size beds, phones, individual climate controls, remote control cable TVs (equipped with "Spectravision"), and private terraces. More expensive rooms have Jacuzzis. Its Plaza Club is a "hotel within a hotel" and offers special services. There are a total of six restaurants, ranging from Chinese to Italian to NY-style pizza. Rates start from around $185 s, $205 d during the off-season and range up to a top of $1,100 s or d for the Plaza Club Suite during the peak season. In the US, ☎ 800-624-0420.

The **Regency Hotel** (☎ 800-468-2823, 721-0505, fax 722-2909; Box 364484, San Juan, PR 00936-4484), Av. Ashford 1005, has 127 a/c rooms have cable TV, refrigerator, and private balcony. Other facilities include pool, restaurant and banquet facilities, piano bar, and secretarial service. A private boardwalk connects with the Condado Plaza Hotel and its casino. A complimentary continental breakfast is served daily from 7-9 AM. Rates start at $105 s or d summer, $135 s or d winter. Superior rooms, studios, and one-bedroom suites are more expensive. The **Ramada Hotel Condado** (☎ 723-8000, fax 722-8230, 800-854-7854, fax 602-443-6543) is a 96-room a/c hotel located at Av. Ashford 1045. Facilities include a pool, restaurant, banquet facilities, and a Corporate Lounge. Rates start at $160 s or d. The $131 million **San Juan Marriott Hotel & Casino** opened in 1995 at Av. Ashford 1309, the site of the Dupont Plaza, which burned to the ground on New Year's Eve 1986. It has 529 rooms with casino, conference areas, pool, tennis courts, and a parking garage. Rates run from $270 s, $290 d. For information call the Marriott chain, ☎ (800) 228-9290.

With a choice of 233 rooms including 87 suites, the **Radisson Ambassador Plaza Hotel & Casino** (☎ 721-7300, fax 723-6151, US/worldwide 800-333-3333; Av. Ashford 1369, San Juan, PR 00907-9955) offers deluxe rooms complete with balconies, cable TV, radio, refrigerator, and sitting room. Its nine-floor suite tower has 87 two-room suites; each has a living room and bedroom as well as two TVs, three phones (one with fax), and personal computer modems. Facilities include four restaurants and lounges, casino, health spa, game room, and roof-top swimming pool. Rates start at $210 s and $220 d.

At C. Condado 55, the **Dutch Inn Hotel & Casino** (☎ 721-0810, fax 725-7895; 800-468-2014) has 144 rooms for around $110 s and $120 d. Overlooking the lagoon at C. Joffre 1, the 95-room a/c **Tamana Princess Hotel** (☎ 724-4160, 721-6072, fax 721-6782; Box 19355, San Juan, PR 00910) has a pool and rooms with cable TV. Other facilities are nearby. Rates run from about $65-140.

SANTURCE HOTELS: Hotels in Santurce include the **Hotel Capri**, Fernandez Juncos 902 (☎ 722-5663); **Hotel Colonial, Inc.**, Fernandez Juncos 1902 (☎ 727-1440); **Hotel Dos Hermanos**, Duffaut 263 (☎ 725-4349); **Hotel Metropol**, Ponce de León 1661; and the **Hotel San Jorge**, Av. Ponce de León 1700.

SANTURCE LARGE HOTELS: The **Hotel Pierre/Best Western** (☎ 721-1200, fax 721-3118; Box 12038, San Juan, PR 00914), De Diego 105 in Santurce, charges around $115 and up. The 184-room hotel has deluxe a/c rooms with TV and phone. For more information call (800) 528-1234. At C. Clemenceau 6, the 48-room **Mirabel Condado Lagoon** (☎ 721-0170, fax 724-4356; Box 13145, Santurce PR 00908) has five-star rooms priced from around $95.

CONDADO FOOD: At Av. Ashford 1018, **Aladdin** (☎ 721-7366) serves gourmet Middle Eastern dishes. The casual **Cadillac Café**, Av. Ashford 1021, serves deli sandwiches and Italian and meatball subs; it has work on the walls by local artists. **Gourmet Health Food**, Av. Ashford 1125, serves brown rice dishes as well as frappes. **Salud** (☎ 722-0911), Av. Ashford 1350, a natural health food restaurant and store, serves great food Mon. to Sat., 9-8 PM. The **Pattiserie Delicatessen**, Av. Ashford 1504, serves light dishes for lunch or dinner. **Via Appia**, Av. Ashford 1350, serves pizza, pasta, and sandwiches. Bordering the Plaza de la Libertad, **C'est La Vie!**, Ashford and Magdalena, serves a variety of tapas and other light fare. The **Salud Juice Bar** is at Av. Magdalena 1400. At Magdalena 1108, **Cielito Lindo** serves innovative and inexpensive Mexican dishes such as chicken with mole sauce. In the Centro Europa Bldg. on Av. Ponce de León, **Pizzeria Uno** serves deep-dish Chicago-style pizza as well as pasta and other dishes. At C. Vendig 105, **Sandy Beach** is a beachside café offering swordfish steaks and American dishes.

CONDADO DINING: Honoring famous entertainers in a multi-level club, the inexpensive **Hall of Fame** (☎ 721-5570), Av. Ashford 1020, serves tapas and dishes ranging from simple to elaborate. Simple yet atmospheric **Oasis Restaurant** (☎ 724-2005), Av. Ashford 1043, offers dishes such as shrimp in creole sauce and fresh red snapper. Offering innovative Italian cuisine, **Caruso** (☎ 723-6876), Av. Ashford 1104, is open daily. At Av. Ashford 1214, the **Chart House** (☎ 728-0110) serves seafood and meat dishes; mud pie is on the dessert menu. **Café Matisse**, Av. Ashford 1351, has dishes such as shrimp à la Matisse, and has a few sidewalk tables. **Marisquería La Dorada** (☎ 722-9583), 1104 Av. Magdalena at Ashford, serves gourmet Puerto Rican-style seafood and other dishes. A well-known gourmet restaurant, the **Ramiro** (☎ 721-9049) is at Magdalena 1100. **Antonio's**, in a converted mansion at C. Magdalena 1406 (☎ 723-7567), offers Spanish and other international specialties. At C. Magdalena 1108, the very expensive **Los Faisanes** (☎ 725-9076) serves a variety of international gourmet dishes. **Don Pepe** at C. Condado 72 offers dishes ranging from paella to eel; it is also expensive. Noted for its all-you-can-eat spaghetti nights (generally Mondays), **Molino Italiano** (☎ 721-1736) is at C. Condado 74. At C. Condado 106, very expensive **Compostela** (☎ 724-6088) serves gourmet specialties such as salmon tartare with caviar and salmon with mustard seed sauce. Popular **Ajili-Mójili** (☎ 725-9195) at C. Clemenceau 6 features Puerto Rican cusine and serves dishes such as *arroz con pollo*. It features dishes from all over the island and is considered to be one of the island's finest *criollo* restaurants. **Zabó** (☎ 725-9494) at C. Candida 14 specializes in New England clam chowder as well as a host of other dishes.

CONDADO HOTEL DINING: Lotus Flower (☎ 722-0940) inside the Condado Plaza, serves Dim Sum lunches as well as Szechwan and Hunan entrées. The Condado Plaza also has **La Posada** which provides 24-hr. service, informal dining, and a salad bar. Also in the Condado Plaza, **Tony Roma's** (☎ 722-0322) specializes in ribs. Another Condado Plaza restaurant, **Capriccio** (☎ 725-9236) serves a good selection of seafood, pasta, and other dishes. Informal **La Posada** is also here. Its offerings include a salad bar and a buffet breakfast. In La Concha Hotel, **Sirenas** (☎ 721-0690) serves California and Caribbean-style seafood. In the Regency Hotel, the **St. Moritz** (☎ 721-0999) serves fish and veal topped with exotic sauces. Open 24 hrs., the **Café del Arte** (in the Condado Beach Hotel) serves a variety of tapas, sandwiches, and salads. Also in the

Condado Beach Hotel, **Vivas Restaurant** (☎ 721-6090) serves very expensive "New World" cuisine. The informal **Adagio** (☎ 721-6090, ext. 1745) here offers N Italian cuisine. In the Ambassador Plaza, the very expensive and gourmet **Giuseppe Ristorante** (☎ 721-7300) serves N Italian cuisine. Set in the Ramada Hotel, the **Ocean View** (☎ 723-8000) serves a variety of local specialties. In the Hotel Tamaná Princess, the **Pikayo** (☎ 721-6194), C. Joffre 1, serves international dishes ranging from Cajun to Puerto Rican. The Marriott has **La Vista** (☎ 722-7000).

SANTURCE FOOD: There are innumerable places to eat, and the usual fast-food chains are everywhere in evidence. For Puerto Rican food try any *cafeteria*, or **Criollisimo**, 2059 Av. Edo Conde, Santurce; **Restaurant La Borincana**, 1401 Fernandez Juncos; **Delin's Café**, C. Antonsanti 1502; and **Restaurante El Ateneo**, Figueroa 610. Inexpensive and intimate, **La Buena Mesa**, Ponce de León 606, offers Puerto Rican food. **How Kow**, Magdalena 1408, features Cantonese and Szechuan dishes. For inexpensive Chinese dining you can also try **Honolulu**, Del Parque 413. The **Pabellón de las Artes** is on Plaza Juan Morel Campos at the Centro de Bellas Artes; it is designed for pre- or post-concert diners.

SANTURCE DINING: Specializing in Cuban cuisine, renowned **Metropol** is at De Diego 105. **Aurorita** (☎ 783-2899), De Diego 303, is an ultra-popular Mexican restaurant; mariachi bands serenade on weekends. **Mangére** (☎ 792-6748), De Diego 311, is one of the best Italian restaurants. At De Diego 316, **El Palacio de las Pastas** offers lunch specials as well as moderate-priced dinners. **El Paso,** De Diego 405, is an inexpensive Puerto Rican restaurant. At C. San Jorge 609, very expensive and gourmet **La Casona** (☎ 727-2717) is all mahogany and stained glass; its dishes include lobster salad. A popular seafood restaurant, **Fish & Crab** (☎ 781-6570) is at Matadero Rd. 301. **La Buona Lasagna** (☎ 721-2488), Diez de Andino 104, serves a wide variety of Italian dishes as well as organic Italian wines.

HOTEL DINING: In the Hotel Best Western Pierre, the **Petit Pierre** (☎ 721-2100) serves French-style seafood in an intimate setting. Also in the Best Western, the **Village Bake Shop** serves baked goods along with sandwiches and other light fare.

SUPERMARKETS: A large **Pueblo** is at 114 De Diego. Sample prices: bass filets $7.89/lb., potatoes 5 lbs./$2.79, onions 2 lb.

bag/$1.49, apples 3 lbs./$2.99, cauliflower $2.99/each, broccoli $1.99/each, carrots 5 lbs./$2.99, red bell pepper $2.99/lb., French bread $1.29/lb, apple cider $4.49/64 oz, carrot juice 32 fl oz/$3.69, papaya $1.19/lb, watermelon 89¢/lb., avocadoes 99¢/each, sugar $2.49/5 lbs., Yauco select coffee $10.99/10 oz, Mazola corn oil $2.49/48 oz., rice 3 lbs/85¢, lge. eggs/doz. $1.45, milk $1.54/half gallon, Minute Maid orange juice $3.99/64 oz, Häagen-Dazs ice cream $3.69/pint. It also has a deli and stand-up café with cut rate food. **Vega's Supermarket** is at **Hotel Condado Lagoon**, 6 Clemenceau, Condado. **Santurce Market** is on C. Canals.

ENTERTAINMENT: Egipto (☎ 725-4664), Av. RH Todd 1, is a disco designed to resemble an Egyptian temple. It plays no Latin music, has a minimum age for admission of 23, and caters to yuppies. It has a cigar bar, appropriate furnishings and decor, and two multi-level dance floors. Admission ranges from $10-20, and a yearly pass is $750. **Amadeus** is a disco inside El San Juan. The **Centro des Bellas Artes** (Performing Arts Center, ☎ 724-4751), largest and best of its kind in the Caribbean, is also the most attractive building in the entire area. Since it opened in 1981, the Center has featured internationally acclaimed musicians, ballet stars, opera and experimental dance performances, lectures, drama festivals, jazz concerts, and musical comedies. Student discounts are available. Be sure to get there early or buy tickets in advance if you want the cheaper seats. The Institute of Puerto Rican Culture may still be sponsoring a Sunday Concert Series (☎ 723-2686) on Sun. afternoons at 3. You may dine before or after events at the Bellas Artes Café on the premises. **Nuestro Teatro** presents plays dealing with Puerto Rican life and social realities. **The Greenhouse**, Ashford Av. 1200, has live entertainment from 11 on Wed., Sat., and Sun. nights. **Flamingo Road Bar & Restaurant** (☎ 723-0013), Av. Ashford 1313, has live bands on weekends. Touristic shows are put on regularly at the major hotels in the area; check *Que Pasa* for listings. **Divas** (☎ 721-8270), 1104 Ashford Av., is a "gentleman's club," code words for an upscale strip joint with trimmings. Condado is also a center for gay nightlife. **Vibration** bills itself as the "best men's cruising bar." It's at 51 Barranquitas in Condado. **La Laguna** (☎ 723-7386) is at 53 Barranquitas.

   cinema: In Santurce, the three-cinema **Metro** (☎ 721-4288) is at Ponce de León 1255, and the three-cinema **UA Paramount** (☎ 725-1103) is at Av. Ponce de León 1313.

SERVICES AND INFORMATION: Information about the island is available inside El Centro Convention Center on Av. Ashford. Located across from the Sheraton at Av. Ashford 1300, the **Virgin Islands Division of Tourism** (☎ 724-3816, 723-9215) offers information on the neighboring islands. Meet charming and helpful Mary Macaya de Gandía. **Bell, Book, and Candle**, Condado's leading bookstore, is at 102 De Diego. They have a fine selection of books. **Alianza Francesa** (Alliance Francaise) is at 206 Rosario, Santurce. They have a library and present films and other cultural events. The **Dutch Consulate** is at First Federal Savings, Stop #23, Av. Ponce de León.

The unisex **Muscle Factory** (☎ 721-0717), a gym, is at Av. Ashford 1302. **yoga:** Ragyi Shanti (☎ 722-9444, 725-5888; SwYakeen@aol.com) offers yoga classes in the area. **travel agencies:** Contact **Travel Network** (☎ 725-0960), 1035 Ashford; **Turismo Internacional** (☎ 721-1347), 1045 Ashford; or **Prime Market Travel** (☎ 791-3602/5151) in ESJ Towers over in Ocean Park. In the Dutch Inn, **Rico Suntours** (☎ 722-2040/2080) offers a wide variety of trips including ones to St. Thomas, to the racetrack, to the observatory, El Yunque, and Ponce. **car rental: Charlie's** (☎ 728-6525) is at Av. Ashford 890. Others are in the vicinity. **cycling: Bicycle Rental & Sales** (☎ 722-6288), 1122 Av. Ashford (across from Wendy's) offers rentals.

Ocean Park

This area, sandwiched between Santurce and Isla Verde, has a number of small hotels. The eight-room **Numero 1 on the Beach** (☎ 727-9687, ☎/fax 726-5010; Ocean Park, PR 00911), C. Santa Ana 1, offers two sundecks, a patio, and a pool with bar. Rates start from around $65 s, $80 d. The 12-room **Tres Palmas Guest House** (☎ 727-4617, fax 727-5434, Isla Verde, PR 00913), Park Blvd. 2212, offers attractive a/c bedrooms with separate entrances. There's a sundeck, Jacuzzi, pool, and shared cable TV. Food is served, breakfast is included, and major holidays see free feeds. Rates run around $60 and up. At Av. McLeary 1853, the 15-room **Beach Buoy Inn** (☎ 728-8119, 800-221-8119, fax 268-0037; Ocean Park, PR 00911) has a sunroof and garden patio. Rooms have color TV, a/c and fans, and a refrigerator. Rates run from around $60. The 19-unit **Hostería del Mar** (☎ 727-3302/0631, fax 268-0772; Ocean Park, PR 00911), C. Tapia 1, faces the beach and has rooms from $55 s, $85 d. The **Ocean**

San Juan Area

Park Beach Inn (☎/fax 728-7418, 800-292-9208), C. Elena 3, is gay friendly.

OCEAN PARK FOOD: At Tapia 1, **Hosteria del Mar** serves a variety of vegetarian dishes and offers a Sun. brunch. At María Moczó 57, **Mona's** serves Mexican food. Dining is also available in nearby **Punta Las Marias**, an area to the E of Ocean Park. Try the **Antique Café Museum** (☎ 727-6620), Loíza 2473, which serves US and Argentine dishes. It has more than a thousand antiques on display. **Mango's Café** (☎ 727-9328), Laurel 2421, is inexpensive (less than $10 for entrées) and serves Caribbean cuisine from both the English and Spanish speaking islands. They serve a mean veggie Rasta Burger. At C. Caoba 35 and open daily, **Che's** (☎ 726-7202) serves both Argentinian and Italian dishes. At C. Laurel 2413, the **Golden Unicorn** (☎ 728-4066) specializes in Szechwan cooking.

Isla Verde

Located to the W of the airport, Isla Verde is one of San Juan's main hotel areas. The area's development commenced with the opening of the San Juan Intercontinental in 1958. The hotel was managed by a subsidiary of now-defunct Pan Am, which influenced its location. After it was sold in 1961, five acres were promptly sold to the Loews Corp., which built the neighboring Americana (now called the Sands). Development has taken off from there. Isla Verde is convenient in terms of arriving and departing but does not offer much in terms of authentic Puerto Rican flavor.

ISLA VERDE GUESTHOUSES: Near the beach along Isla Verde's main drag, the **Borínquen Royal Guest House** (☎ 728-8400, fax 268-2411; Box 6241, Isla Verde, PR 00914) offers 12 a/c rooms with cable TV and phone for around $55 s and $70 d on up. At C. Rosa 4, the **Don Pedro Hotel** (☎ 791-2838; Isla Verde, PR 00979) has 17 rooms, a pool, bar, and restaurant. Rates run from around $75 d.

   in Villamar: The **Green Isle Inn** (☎ 726-4330, fax 268-2415; San Juan, PR 00979), C. Uno 336 , offers 36 rooms with a/c, TV, and phone, as well as free airport pickup. Rates start from around $50 s, $60 d. At C. Amapola 6, **La Playa** (☎ 728-9921; Isla Verde, PR 00979) is on the ocean and offers 15 a/c rooms with cable TV and phone. It has a bar and restaurant, and rates start at $50 s, $60 d. The 15-room **El Patio** (☎ 726-6298/6953; Isla Verde, PR 00979) offers a/c rooms and a communal kitchen. Rates start from $60.

The 46-unit **Casa Mathiesen Inn** (☎ 726-8662, 667-8860, fax 268-2415; San Juan, PR 00979), C. Uno 14, offers free transport to and from the airport. Rooms have a/c and fans, cable TV, and radio. The inn has a pool, restaurant, and bar. More expensive kitchenette rooms are available. Rates start from around $40.

ISLA VERDE SMALLER HOTELS: The **Hotel Casa de Playa** (☎ 728-9779, fax 727-1334, 800-829-3636; Isla Verde, PR 00979) has 20 units. Rooms with a/c and fan, cable TV, and phone start at $80; rates include breakfast. **The Empress Oceanfront** (☎ 791-3083; Isla Verde, PR 00913), Apapola 2, has a seafood restaurant. Rates run from around $150. Blue-and-white 59-room **Mario's Hotel and Restaurant** (☎ 791-3748/6868, fax 791-1672; Box 12366, Isla Verde, PR 00979), C. Rosa 2, offers free satellite TV in its rooms. Rates start at around $70. Located on the third floor of the airport, the 57-room **International Airport Hotel** (☎ 791-1700, fax 791-4050; Box 38087, San Juan, PR 00937) offers soundproof a/c rooms with TV and radio. Rates start from around $85.

ISLA VERDE LARGE HOTELS: On Carr. 187, the **Sands Hotel and Casino Beach Hotel** (☎ 791-6100; Box 6676 Loiza Station, Santurce, PR 00913) charges from $290 s and $305 d. Its facilities include 420 a/c rooms with private balcony/terrace, four restaurants (including the award winning **Guissepe's**), casino, watersports, and nearby golf and tennis. There's also an Executive Business Center. In the US and Canada, ☎ 800-443-2009, fax 809-791-8525, or telex 325-2299 SANDS PT. For group informatio, ☎ 800-544-3008. The 392-room a/c **El San Juan Hotel & Casino** (☎ 791-1000, fax 791-6985; Box 2872, San Juan, PR 00902), Av. Isla Verde, is San Juan's premier luxury hotel. It offers a "Cigar Bar" (with an attached cigar and pipe shop), 11-hole miniature rooftop golf course, jazz bar, French bistro, a conference center with meeting and banquet rooms, botanical garden, two pools, three Jacuzzis, and a health club/spa. For dining and snacks, there are numerous places to try: the rooftop **Margarita Bar, Yamato** (Japanese) restaurant nightclub/casino, **Scoops** ice cream parlor, **Back Street at Hong Kong** restaurant, and **Piccola Fontana** Italian restaurant. Entertainment venues include **Club Tropicoro** (an elegant 1930s dinner-style club with a flamenco show) and **Belle Epoque** salon (dancing and cabaret shows). There is 24-hour room service, a beach, and three tennis courts, as well as water sports such as windsurfing, scuba diving, snorkeling, and sailing. Rooms have individually controlled a/c as well as fans,

TV/VCR, radio, stereo tape deck/CD, bathroom TV, three tele-phones, and in-room bar. (One-story beachfront *casitas* are also planned). It charges from $295 s and $325 d during the high season. Renovated for $30 million in 1995, the hotel is under the management of the San Juan-based Williams Hospitality Group. For information and to book, call Leading Hotels of the World at ☎ 800-223-6800 or the hotel directly at 800-468-2818.

With 450 a/c rooms and studio apartments, the 17-story **ESJ Towers** (☎ 791-5151, fax 253-0428; Box 2200, Carolina, PR 00979) is directly on the beach next to El San Juan. Its attractively furnished condo apartments have fully equipped kitchens. Facilities include a restaurant/lounge, pool, fitness club, tennis courts, golf course, and watersports. Rates run from $130 s and $185 d. For more information ☎ 800-468-2026.

A $17-million **Hampton Inn** is expected to open in 1997. It will have 200 rooms, business center, meeting room, exercise rooms, pool and bar; local phone calls will be free and complimentary continental breakfast will be offered. The **Embassy Suites Hotel & Casino** will open in 1996 or 1997 and include a casino (*natch!*), a fitness center, pool and restaurant.

The 96-room **Travelodge of Puerto Rico** (☎ 728-1300, fax 727-7150; information 800-468-2028; Box 6007, San Juan, PR 00914) charges from around $90 s to $140 d in season. Deluxe executive-floor rooms have Jacuzzis. All rooms have a/c and cable TV. Set one block from the ocean and a 10-minute ride from the airport, the **Carib-Inn Tennis Club and Hotel** (☎ 791-3535, fax 791-0104, 718-235-9841, fax 718-235-0997; Box 12112, Loíza St. Station, San Juan, PR 00914) offers 225 a/c rooms with color cable TVs, phones, and balconies/porches. Facilities include eight tennis courts, adult and children's pools, spa, restaurant, convention facilities, and gam-bling arcade. Rates start at $70 s and $75 d for standard rooms and rise to $105 s and $110 d during the winter season. More expensive superior, deluxe, jr. suites, and regular suites are available. In Isla Verde on the beach, the **Holiday Inn Crowne Plaza** (☎ 253-2929, fax 253-2081; Box 38079, San Juan, PR 00937) offers standard rooms from around $185 s and $205 d. Its 254 a/c rooms and suites have cable TV. Facilities include two restaurants, theme casino, fitness center, nightclub, babysitting, pool, watersports, and nearby golf and tennis. For more information ☎ 800-468-4578.

ISLA VERDE FOOD: Mi Casita, at the Plazoleta de Isla Verde, serves inexpensive breakfasts as well as Puerto Rican dishes. At McLeary 1954, lively **Dunbar's** (☎ 728-2920) serves BBQ dishes and desserts. On Carr. 187, the informal **Oyster Bar** sells clams, oysters, and seafod salad. Open 24 hrs., **Duffy's**, Isla Verde 9, serves steaks and seafood dishes as well as all-you-can-eat spaghetti on Wed. evenings. **Chanteclair,** a small coffee shop on the Plazoleta, has innovative dishes and $8 lunch specials. At the Condado Racquet Club on C. Tartak, the **Hungry Sailor Restaurant** serves meat dishes. At Km. 1.3 on Carr. 187, **Lupi's** is a Mexican restaurant that doubles as a sports bar.

ISLA VERDE DINING: Marisqueria Atlántica (☎ 726-6654), C. Loíza 81 (also in Puerto de Tierra) specializes in seafood including paella and Maine lobster. In Isla Verde Mall, **Los Chiles** (☎ 253-3551) serves Mexican dishes. Inside Mario's Hotel, casual **Plaka** (☎ 791-3470) offers Greek food. With both outdoor and indoor dining, **Puerta al Sol** (☎ 268-7475), Loíza 2446, has Puerto Rican gourmet cuisine. In the Tropimar Beach Club, the gourmet **Casa del Mar** (☎ 791-0035) is a famed, very expensive restaurant which has a popular Sun. brunch. Offering Italian dishes and open daily, inexpensive **Freddo** is inside the Hotel Casa de Playa (☎ 728-9779). **Pizzaiolo,** a Brazilian-style pizzeria, is at Isla Verde 47. On Carr. 187 at Km.1.5, **Metropol** (☎ 791-4046) specializes in Cuban cuisine and is part of a chain of three. Expensive **La Scala** (☎ 791-3740), C. Rosa 2, has fine Italian cuisine. **Casa Dante** (☎ 726-7310), Isla Verde 39, serves its special version of *mofongo*. In Villamar at 35-A Marginal, **Pizzarella** (☎ 268-2433) serves a variety of imaginative gourmet pizzas from $10-21, depending upon size.

ISLA VERDE HOTEL DINING: Set in the Holiday Inn Crown Plaza, beachfront **Holly's Café** serves pasta, sandwiches, seafood, and other dishes. **Back Street Hong Kong** (☎ 791-1224) is located in El San Juan, in a pagoda that once formed part of the Hong Kong Pavilion at the 1962 World's Fair. It serves Chinese regional (Szechwan, Hunan, and Mandarin) cuisine. At El San Juan, **Piccola Fontana** (☎ 791-0966) serves N Italian cuisine and has wonderful seafood, and the highly regarded and very expensive **Dar Tiffany** (☎ 791-7272) serves seafood dishes (Maine lobster) as well as meat. In the Sands are **Café Tropical**, an open-air poolside restaurant and **Don Juan**, an intimate and very expensive bistro that serves dishes such as salmon over pineapple. Also in the Sands, the very expensive and intimate **Dumpling House** has a wide range of Chinese regional cuisines, and the very expensive **Valentino** (☎ 791-6100) serves N Italian dishes. Yet another Sands bistro is the very expensive **Reino del Mar,** offering seafood and meat entrées daily. With a special late-night menu in addition to salads, sandwiches, sea-food, and steaks, **Tucano Restaurant** is the least expensive restaurant found in the Sands. Inside the Empress Hotel, C. Apapola 2, the inexpensive **Sunny's Ocean View Terrace** serves BBQ dishes, crab and shrimp balls, and other seafood. An intimate family-style restaurant, **Marina** (☎ 728-3628), C. Marginal, specializes in Puerto Rican and other gourmet cuisine.

ISLA VERDE SHOPPING: At the corner of Los Gobernadores, the **Isla Verde Mall** has a wide variety of shops ranging from jewelers to optometrists to hair stylists. **Cool Runnings** here sells reggae discs and related items.

ISLA VERDE SERVICES: Charlie Car Rental (☎ 728-2418/2420, 791-1101) has its offices facing the Marbella del Caribe.

Hato Rey

Sometimes called the Golden Mile or the Wall Street of the Caribbean, Hato Rey is notable mainly for its skyscrapers, those lyrical concrete-and-steel paeans to the wonders of capitalist endeavor. The huge federal complex, the offices of Fomento, and the Western Hemisphere overseas headquarters of the Chase Manhattan Bank are all located here, as is the gigantic Bancos de Santander and its fiduciary compatriots. Without these, Hato Rey would be nothing more than a desolate, land-filled marsh.

GETTING HERE: Buses run from Old San Juan, and *Acuaexpreso* also has a ferry (75¢).

SIGHTS: Managed by the Puerto Rican Park Trust, the **Enrique Martí Coll Lineal Park** is named after a Puerto Rican environmentalist and businessman who passed on in 1992. When complete, it will extend for 11 miles and include biking, jogging, and hiking trails extending from Río Piedras to Old San Juan. You may access it via the 1½-mile elevated pedestrian walkway that extends around the perimeter of the Martín Peña Channel.

ACCOMMODATIONS: Hotel Europa (☎ 763-1524) is at C. Navarro 64 .

HATO REY FOOD: Naturalista y Vegetariano (☎ 758-6405) is at C. Duarte 205. At C. César González 553, **Booby's** is an inexpensive family-run restaurant serving Puerto Rican food. For buffet dining, **Gourmet To Go** (☎ 766-4079), Tnte. César González 437, serves innovative Puerto Rican dishes. At C. Barbosa 597, **La Guitarra** serves a variety of tapas and other Spanish dishes. For Puerto Rican food, **Metropolitan Restaurant and Coffee Shop** is at the Metropolitan Shopping Center. At Av. Ponce de León 507, **La Cueva del Chicken Inn** sells cock-a-doodle-doo in all formats. **bakeries: La Ceiba**, Ave. Roosevelt, is one of the best bakeries around.

HATO REY DINING: In the Royal Bank Center Lobby, **Yuan** (☎ 766-0666), appropriately named after the Chinese currency, offers very expensive Szechuan dishes for lunch and dinner daily. Specializing in Cuban cuisine, **Metropol** (☎ 751-4022) is at FD Roosevelt 124. **Hunan House** (☎ 252-8039), FD Roosevelt 141, also serves Szechuan dishes and offers inexpensive lunchtime specials. The **Yum Yum Tree** (☎ 753-7743), FD Roosevelt 131, serves Mandarin Chinese fare. At FD Roosevelt 164, **El Caney** (☎ 764-7559) has Puerto Rican dishes such as *mofongo relleno de mariscos* (stuffed mofongo). **La Trattoria** (☎ 764-4801) at FD Roosevelt 231 serves fresh pasta, seafood, and other dishes as well as "gourmet" pizza. The **Deli Restaurant Argentino**, FD Roosevelt 235, serves Italian, Puerto Rican, and Argentinian fare daily. El Paseo, FD Roosevelt 244, serves fine, inexpensive Puerto Rican dishes. At FD Roosevelt 254, **Los Chiles** (☎ 751-1747) has Mexican cuisine; *fajitas*, the house specialty, are prepared tableside. At FD Roosevelt 284, **Maxim de Puerto Rico** (☎ 796-1234) serves French and other international dishes. A deli restaurant, **La Canasta**, FD Roosevelt 313, serves a variety of salads and sandwiches. On the second floor at FD Roosevelt 315, **Don Andrés** (☎ 754-0232) offers Mexican food; the owner is a mariachi singer who entertains nightly. **La Trattoria**, FD Roosevelt 321, has homemade pasta, fresh "gourmet pizza" and seafood dishes. At FD Roosevelt 352, the gourmet and very expensive **Zipperle** (☎ 763-1636) has German, Puerto Rican, and Spanish dishes. **Margarita** (☎ 781-8452), FD Roosevelt 1013, serves Mexican dishes and has live music. **Porto Bello** (☎ 277-0911), FD Roosevelt 1144, serves gourmet Italian dishes. At FD Roosevelt 1247, **Mesón Gallego** (☎ 783-5866) serves paella and other Spanish fare. **Casa María** (☎ 793-8890), FD Roosevelt 1344, offers gourmet Mexican dishes.

Inexpensive **Viva Brazil** (☎ 758-5659), Queisqueya 13, serves up Brazilian fare with a flair. **El Cairo** (☎ 273-7140), Ensenada 352 at

FD Roosevelt, is an inexpensive Lebanese/Middle Eastern restaurant; stuffed cabbage is its house specialty. At América B-20, corner FD Roosevelt, **Restaurant y Marisquería Fruit de Mer** (☎ 764-5509) specializes in seafood. **Booby's** (☎ 753-8181), Tnte. César González 553, is an intimate, inexpensive Puerto Rican restaurant. **Jerusalem Restaurant** (☎ 764-3265), O'Neill 1-6, serves Arab dishes, including vegetarian entrées. It can supply belly dancers upon request. **El Chotis Taberna Española** (☎ 758-3086), O'Neill 187, offers a variety of tapas and other dishes. At Bolivia 52, the **Coachman Steakhouse** (☎ 753-8838) is a favorite with businessmen. **Casa Italia** (☎ 250-7388), at C. Domenech 275, serves a variety of Italian dishes. Offering Cantonese and Szechuan specialties, **Kimpo Garden** (☎ 767-0810), C. Jesús Piñero 264, serves lobster, chicken and other dishes. **Tokyo Grill** (☎ 754-7646), Muñoz Rivera 504, has *teppanyaki* tables and serves sushi. **Tapatío** (☎ 781-2006), at C. Jesús T. Piñero 1025, serves Mexican food. At C O'Neill 177, **Muelle 13** (☎ 767-7825) serves beef and seafood dishes. **Tango's** (☎ 759-8190), C. O'Neill 179, specializes in meat dishes. Romantic **Johnny's Restaurant** (☎ 763-2793), C. Domenech 208, has Puerto Rican-style seafood and other dishes. At Bolívar 59, **El Mesón de Porrón** (☎ 250-8156) is a Spanish-style restaurant with international and Puerto Rican dishes. **El Chotis Taberna Espanola**, C. 187 O'Neill, features Spanish cuisine. **El Belén** (☎ 282-6332) is a Middle Eastern restaurant that provides vegetarians with a wide selection; it's at Piñero 312A. **Bogart's Pub and Grill** (☎ 754-6878), C. Hostos 352, serves pub-type fare and has Bogart memorabilia galore. **Mesón Tropical** (☎ 751-7669), E Roosevelt 111, serves Spanish and international dishes and is known for its singing waiters.

SERVICES: The **General Post Office** is on Av. Roosevelt. Take a Hato Rey-bound bus from the terminal in Old San Juan. **Plaza Las Américas**, a gigantic shopping mall with some 200 stores, is a playground for the affluent. Branches of **Galería Botello** and **{Paréntesis}** are located upstairs, while **Thekes Bookstore** is on the first floor. All have good selections. Purchase handicrafts at the **Kiosko Cultural. Mother Earth**, on the second level here, has pricey health food products. Stop by here each March 21 for some cake when staff member Sallie celebrates her birthday. Suitably, it is also a recycling drop-off point for the Solid Waste Authority. Some 25 restaurants are also located at the remodeled La Terraza here on the third level. There's a **Sears,** and **Toys R' Us** is across the road. Since it opened in 1968, the mall has been graced with two historical events. Luís Muñoz Marín spoke here in 1972, and Pope

John Paul discoursed in 1984. At C. Federico Costa and C. Chardón, the **Plaza Acuática** (☎ 754-9500) offers water sports, a playground, and a miniature golf course; it's open weekends.

Río Piedras

This student area of the city has the University of Puerto Rico, the attractive Paseo de Diego (cheaper than the shopping malls), and a great market near the bus terminal. At the center of the campus stands the Roosevelt bell tower. Done up in a gaudy pink, it is Spanish-influenced but bears a passing resemblance to a South Indian Tamil Nadu Hindu temple. Theodore Roosevelt donated the money and so received the dubious distinction of having it named for him. See the three sculptured heads set in front of the bell tower. The campus has a laid-back atmosphere with students playing guitars and petting in the **José M. Lazaro Library**. Largest general library on the island, it contains the Juan Jiminéz Room, which displays memorabilia belonging to the famous Spanish expatriate poet. The small but intriguing **Museum of Anthropology, History, and Art** (☎ 764-0000, ext. 2452) next to the library features archaeological artifacts as well as special art exhibitions. It's open Mon., Tues., Wed. and Fri. from 9-4:30, Thurs. from 9-9, and Sat. from 9-3. Located on C. De Diego, the **Río Piedras Market** has fairly wide aisles numbered with signs showing the produce being sold. It is packed with fruits (pineapples, papaya, golden-skinned oranges), common and more exotic vegetables (*yuca, yautia*), and island spices (ginger, mint, cilantro). An arcade section sells clothes. The best time to visit is early morning when merchants and farmers unload trucks and pack booths. Savor the atmosphere. Set between Río Piedras and Trujillo Alto on the C. Marginal off the expressway, the **Casa-finca de Don Luis Muñoz Marín** (constructed circa 1930) has been restored and now functions as a small museum. It's at Km 181 on Carr. 181 and is open Wed. to Sun. from 9-3.

ACCOMMODATIONS: Gay friendly **Glorimar Guest House** (☎ 759-7304, 724-7440, fax 725-2400) is at 111 University Ave., three blocks from the university. It has daily, weekly, and monthly rates.

FOOD: Many cheap places to eat. **Esquina Universidad**, on the corner of Ponce de León and Gandara, is a popular student hangout. There's also the usual assortment of fast food places, including

San Juan Area

a **Taco Maker** at Ponce De León 1000. **Energy**, a health food store and restaurant, is at Av. Diego #2 (open Mon. to Sat., 9-3; ☎ 764-2623). **Sun y Cream**, at Ponce de León 1004, is a cheap Chinese restaurant which also serves ice cream. **Tomas Ice Cream**, across the street, is an attractive student meeting place. **El Isleño** (☎ 250-8046), at Lomas Verdes 1790 in Plaza Olmedo, is a good Puerto Rican restaurant. **Middle East** is at Padre Colón 207. **El Pacifico** (☎ 274-5756), C. 43 SE #893 at America Mirando, is a high quality, expensive seafood restaurant. A NY-style deli, **Howard's Deli and Pub** is set in the Caribe Shopping Center. At Muñoz Rivera 1000, **Café Valencia Restaurant** (☎ 764-3790) offers dishes such as paella. On Carr. 1 at Km 25.1, **Félix** (☎ 720-1626) is a family-run restaurant specializing in Puerto Rican home cooking, including seafood dishes. **Tacolandia** is at Las Vistas Shopping Center and offers a wide range of tacos including vegetarian items.

ENTERTAINMENT: The **Casals Festival** takes place on the University of Puerto Rico campus during May. The University also offers a cultural activities series featuring ballet and classical music performances and avant-garde films. For information, contact Actividades Culturales, ☎ 764-0000, ext. 2563/2567. The **El Señorial** (☎ 741-2387) offers a choice of four films daily.

SHOPPING: There are two shopping malls here – the **Reparto Metropolitano** and the **65 De Infanteria**.

BOOKSTORES: Librería La Tertulia (☎ 765-1148) corner of Amalia Marín and Gonzales, and **Libreria Hispanoamericano**, 1013 Ponce de León, are open Mon. to Saturday. Other bookstores are in Plaza Las Américas, Hato Rey.

AGRICULTURAL EXPERIMENTAL STATION: Operated by the University of Puerto Rico, it is still in Río Piedras but way off in the boonies near the intersection of Carr. 1 and Carr. 847. Pack a picnic lunch. The 140-acre **Botanical Garden** here is open Tues. to Sun. 9-5 (☎ 763-4408). There's no admission charge to visit this enchanting area, which includes an orchid garden with exotics like dendrobiums, epidendrums, vandas and a palm garden with 125 species. Broad paths traverse an incredible range of vegetation, from a flaming African tulip tree and croton bushes to endless varieties of palms and ferns. Woody lianas hang from trees. Cool off in one of several libraries and check in the Forest Service office for detailed info about El Yunque's rainforest.

Bayamón

A suburban municipality of San Juan, Bayamón has shifted from being an agricultural to an industrial community. It's still growing rapidly. More than 230,000 people and some 170 factories make their home here. The city is renowned for its *chicharrón*, a local delicacy (from the Spanish verb *achicharrar* ("to crisp"), which originated when slaves, given the skin torn from pigs by the Spaniards, hung them over the coals to dry. The grease dripped into the fire and the result was a crisp and curly morsel that is now one of the most popular Latin snacks.

GETTING HERE: Take bus no. 46 from San Juan or find one of the buses that occasionally run from near the PO in Old San Juan. Yet another alternative is to take the Cataño ferry (50¢) and then a *público*.

SIGHTS: Just before Bayamón on Carr. 2, Km 6.4 at Guaynabo, are the ruins of **Caparra**, the first colonial settlement on the island. Established by Ponce de León in 1508, it was abandoned for the Old San Juan site 12 years later. Only the masonry foundations, uncovered in 1936, remain. To the rear, a small museum contains Taíno artifacts and tools, weapons, and tiles found at the site (☎ 781-4795; open Tues. to Sat., 8:30-4:30). Inside the municipality itself, directly across from the City Hall, the immaculately landscaped grounds of **Central Park** contain a country house, which functions as a small museum, and the only locomotive train remaining in Puerto Rico, which runs through the grounds. This museum also displays artifacts excavated during archaeological digs at the site. **Junghanns Park**, several blocks to the W, features trees from all over the world which were planted by the local botanist of the same name.

Adjacent to Bayamon's plaza and in the heart of the historical zone, the former city hall contains the **Museo de Oller**, named after the famous local resident realist-impressionist painter (open Tues. to Sat., 9-4; ☎ 787-8620). This recently restored neoclassic building (dating from 1907) is painted in shades of blue, pink, and yellow – evocative of a San Francisco gingerbread house. Inside, the first level has one room dedicated to Francois Oller's portraits of local notables, with another room containing indigenous artifacts and a collection of Taíno skulls. The remaining rooms are largely devoted to the remarkable artwork of the local artist Tomas Batista. His work includes bronze and fiberglass busts and fossilized stones carved into the shape of gigantic seashells. The top floor contains gubernatorial and mayoral portraits by local artist Tulio Ojedo and a genuine mayoral desk belonging to the current mayor. It's obvious who was backing the museum. Another room illustrates the history of Bayamón complete with the making of *chicharrones* and the daily life of the *jíbaro*. There's even a shovel from the 1977 groundbreaking of a Union Carbide plant. The museum is completed with yet another room of Indian artifacts.

From the museum, enter the placid and tranquil **Paseo Barbosa**. Here, you might see a young girl standing and combing her boyfriend's hair as he sits on a bench. Or a mother sitting with her children, taking a break from shopping. Or pretty schoolgirls with plaid vests and white blouses parading through on their way to and from school. Continue along to the **Barbosa Museum** (open Mon. to Fri. 8-12, 1-5; ☎ 798-8191). The interior of the house contains antique furniture, small library, and memorabilia relating to José Celso Barbosa, journalist, physician, and political head of the pro-statehood Republican Party. **note:** It is temporarily closed, so call before visiting. The **Luis A. Ferré Parque de las Ciencias** (☎ 740-6868) a science park, is near downtown on Carr. 167 to the S of De Diego. It includes the Dr. Ventura Barnes Natural Science Museum, an amphitheater, the Space Rockets Plaza, the Planetarium, a native archeological museum, health pavilion, artificial lake, and a small zoo. It's open Wed. to Fri. from 8-4; Sat., Sun., and holidays from 10-6.

EVENTS AND FESTIVALS: The traditional *fiestas patronales*, titled *Fiestas de Cruz,* are held in early May. Although this event has its origin in the 18th century, many of the original traditions connected with it have been lost. Once held in a local house, the main event (carrying the cross up the nine steps) now takes place along the Paseo Barbosa. Traditionally, a nine-step altar is prepared and lavishly adorned with flowers and royal palm leaves; candles are placed on each step. After the recitation of *El Rosario Cantado de la Santa Cruz* each night, the cross is moved up one step higher until, on the ninth night, it reaches the top. Traditional refreshments like *guarapo de caña* (sugarcane juice) and *maví* are served at the end of each night's service.

Artisans' festivals are held throughout the year. Large concerts take place at the 23,000-seat Juan Ramón Loubriel Stadium here. Although the show sold out immediately despite ticket prices as high as $125, Madonna's "The Girlie Show," which was performed here in 1993, aroused great controversy. Charging that it would corrupt the young and promote pornography, Cardinal Luis Aponte Martínez wrote the Governor a letter asking him to speak out publicly against Madonna. He refused. Her appearance was marked by demonstrations. Madonna raised further ire by caressing a Puerto Rican flag during her performance. In retaliation, local clerics launched a campaign to hang black ribbons on trees in protest.

PRACTICALITIES: For information call **Bayamón Tourism Office** at 780-3056, ext. 280-281. Or visit them in their offices on the first floor of the surrealistically modern *Alcaldía*.

SHOPPING AND CRAFTS: Local craftspeople sell their wares in Central Park each Sunday. A feminist-run handicraft center, **El Centro Feminista**, is located at C. F No. 8 Hnas., Davilas, Bayamón. Anchored by a 40-lane bowling alley, the $6 million **Tower Lanes** shopping center affords you the chance to shop in the former property of drug dealers: It was confiscated from Jorge and Victor Torres who were convicted of drug trafficking and money laundering charges.

DOING IT DIFFERENTLY!

Many visitors to Puerto Rico miss out on a lot. Here are some suggestions to get more out of your trip:

☐ Plan in advance to visit either or both of the National Trust properties, **Hacienda Buena Vista** (page 261) or **Los Cabezas de San Juan** (page 200).

☐ Spend a day exploring Old San Juan. Don't make plans, just roam around and see what places you come across.

☐ Spend three or more nights in a place. Try to get to know the area. You can't see the entire island unless you have months available. Plan a picnic and have fun shopping at a local market. Check out small local bars and restaurants, many of which have great atmosphere.

☐ Don't try to go too far in a single day. Puerto Rico may not be large, but it takes a long time to get to places. The fun is being out of the car and not behind the wheel.

☐ Try to find a local festival or other event to participate in. Practice your Spanish!

San Juan Area

Vicinity of San Juan

San Juan can serve as an excellent base for becoming acquainted with the island, especially if you are renting (or have) your own vehicle. A good portion of the island may be comfortably explored in a day's excursion. Destinations like El Yunque, Loíza Aldea, and Humacao make good daytrips. There are also many small towns like **Gurabo, Guaynabo,** and **Cidra** (stay at **Hotel Flora del Valle,** Carr. 172, Km 7.4; tel 739-8864), which offer the visitor with limited time an inside look at Puerto Rican life.

TOURS, EXCURSIONS, AND CHARTERS: With offices poolside at La Concha in Condado, the **Island Safari** (☎ 723-4740, eve. 728-6606; Box 4195, San Juan, PR 00905) offers a bus trip past El Yunque and Luquillo and a trip on a dive party boat. It lasts all day and is priced at around $80 ($10 discount for advance cash payment); snorkeling equipment is included and a scuba dive is $25 extra. They also feature sailing trips on the *Fat Cat*, a catamaran that explores the San Juan area, and operate the Caribbean School of Aquatics, which offers dive instruction. **West Indies Charters** (☎ 887-4818) runs snorkeling trips from Villa Marina in Fajardo to Icacos, Palaminos, or Palominitos Island. **Group Services, Inc.** (☎ 724-5494/2504; Box 10354, Caparra Heights Station, San Juan, PR 00922) has a variety of excursions ranging from riding to hiking to tours. Operating out of Isla Verde's Laguna Gardens Shopping Center, **Mundo Submarino** (☎/fax 791-5764; Isla Verde, PR 00979) operates a full-service dive shop and has a variety of trips as well as scuba instruction. A 53-ft sailing catamaran, the *East Wind* (☎ 863-2821/4267; Box 664, Puerto Real, PR 00740) charges $45 pp ($10 add'l for RT transportation from San Juan) for trips from Fajardo's Villa Marina to an unnamed "tropical island." Lunch, snorkel gear, and some drinks are included. A 40-ft sailing catamaran, the *Spread Eagle* (☎ 863-1905/5875, fax 852-2443; Box 1740, Luquillo, PR 00773) also leaves from Villa Marina for the same price and a similar trip. **Captain Jack Becker** (☎ 860-0861) offers trips which take from two to seven passengers; snorkel gear is provided and "attorneys and kids tolerated." Scandinavian stewardesses are taken free of charge.

Operating out of C. Amapola 1 in Isla Verde but departing from Fajardo, **Captain Jayne Sailing** (☎ 774-1748; Isla Verde, PR 00979) runs a fleet of charter boats; skippers are also available. **Caribbean**

Divers: Fun Boats (☎/fax 722-7393; Box 5041, San Juan, PR 00936) is at Fajardo's Villa Marina. They operate a 53-ft catamaran. **Castillo Watersports** (☎ 791-6195/6100 ext. 344; eve. 726-5752, fax 726-6998; Doncella 27, Punta las Marias, Santurce, PR 00913) offers deep-sea and light tackle fishing. Their 46-ft catamaran, *Barefoot III*, has sailing, snorkeling, and a picnic for around $45 pp. Set next to Club Naútico at the San Juan Marina, **Caribe Aquatic Adventures** (☎ 724-1882, fax 723-6770; Box 2470, San Juan, PR 00902-2470) offers scuba instruction, wind surfing, and fishing, as well as a variety of cruises and trips. They also make a trip to a (not-quite) "deserted island." The *Makaira Hunter* (☎ 397-8028, 250-0140, ext. 18744, fax 768-2828; PMC Box 402, San Patricio Plaza, San Juan, PR 00920) is available for charter. Departing from Fajardo, *Erin Go Bragh* (☎ 860-4401, fax 863-8130) is a 50-ft sailing ketch that offers both short and long trips. In Puerto Del Rey Marina on Carr. 3, **Club Naútico Powerboats** (☎ 860-2400, fax 860-2401, 863-5253; Box Q, Fajardo, PR 00740) offers fishing, diving, and snorkeling trips. **Southern Witch/Fishing** (☎ 721-7335, 731-9252; HC-01, Box 20484, Caguas, PR 00625) operates a 22-ft boat with tarpon and reef fishing for one to four persons. **at Dorado:** For diving at Dorado, contact **Adventure by the Sea** (☎ 251-4923, fax 261-0946), C. 2J2, Santa Maria, Toa Baja, PR 00949 or the **Dorado Marine Center** (☎ 796-4645, 250-0140, ext. 2226, fax 796-7323; 271 Méndez Vigo, Dorado, PR 00646).

CAVE EXPLORATION: For the truly adventurous, **Aventuras Tierra Adentro** (☎ 788-5461; Box 1335, Cataño, PR 00963) takes groups of eight to 12 hikers through the Río Tamana's underground canyons. You float and walk through caves on your way to the campsite which is just below the Arecibo Observatory which you visit at sunset. On the second day, you must jump 25 ft into a pool and then descend another series of caves where you'll encounter bats and petroglyphs. Participants must supply wetsuits and snacks; everything else is provided. This trip costs $130. Other trips available include a visit to the Cueva Yuyú ($55) and descending by rope in the Cueva Resurgencia ($60).

Heading S

Caguas (pop. 173,961) is the largest inland town on the island. It has the **Antigua Alcaldía de Caguas** (dating from 1856) on C. Muñoz Rivera and the **Catedral Dulce Nombre de Jesús de Caguas** (1928) on C. Conchado; both are in front of Plaza Palmer. In the same area, the **Plaza de Recreo** (1950) is one of the best examples of Art Deco found in Puerto Rico. Doubling as the Museo Histórico de Caguas, the **Antigua Carnicería de Caguas** (☎ 746-0669; open from Mon. to Fri., 8:30-noon, 1-3:30) dates from 1871 and is one of the best examples of this type of building found on the islands. An attractive private residence is the **La Casita Verde** on C. Monseñor Berríos at C. Acosta. **Aguas Buenas** to the S is noted for its caves along Carr. 794. However, they have been found to be a source of histoplasmosis, a respiratory disease, and a visit is not advised.

ACCOMMODATIONS: For a tryst, you can try the **Hotel OK Executive** (☎ 789-9696), which offers a private disco and heart-shaped Jacuzzi in its suites; it's at Km 26 on Carr. 1 in front of Avon. **Hotel Villa Arco Iris** (☎ 741-9492), is on Carr. 698, Barrio Río Cañas. **Hotel The Rose** (☎ 747-1314) is on Carr. 175 at Km 1.3 in Barrio San Antonio. The **Bambu Motel** (☎ 747-9491) is on Carr. 796 at Km 27.2 in Río Cañas. At Gurabo to the NE,,**Hacienda Mirador** (☎ 737-3747, fax 737-4060), Carr. 942 in Jaguas Lomas, has 36 rooms, a restaurant, a swimming pool, and tennis courts.

DINING: You can dine near Caguas on Carr. 1 at **El Paraíso** (☎ 747-2012; Km 29.1), which offers Puerto Rican and international dishes, or at **Alameda** (☎ 743-9698), which has steak and seafood. Around 40 minutes by car from San Juan, **Papa Juan's Restaurant** (☎ 737-2227/4020) is a romantic dining getaway in Gurabo's Barrio Jaguas Lomas at the end of Carr. 942. Set dinners are around $20, there's a happy hour, and live music is featured on weekends.

Heading W To Dorado

Reachable either by car, limousine, or small plane, **Dorado** is the island's oldest resort town. **Hyatt Dorado Beach** and **Hyatt Regency Cerromar Beach** are famed for their pools, golf courses, and casinos. A free shuttle bus runs between the two resorts on the half-hour.

ACCOMMODATIONS: The a/c **Hyatt Regency Cerromar Beach** (☎ 796-1234, fax 796-4647; Cerromar Beach, Dorado, PR 00646), with 504 rooms and suites, offers scuba and snorkeling, tennis, bike rentals, a pool with three-story water slide, separate river pool, 21 tennis courts, jogging track, health club, a variety of restaurants, and a complimentary continental breakfast. Rates run from around $170-$430. The 298-room, two-story **Hyatt Dorado Beach**

(☎ 796-1234, fax 796-2022), which was originally designed to meet the specifications of Laurance Rockefeller, shares facilities with the Hyatt Cerromar Beach and has a windsurfing school. Rates run from around $160 d on up to $1,700. For more information on either hotel, ☎ (800) 233-1234, or write them at Dorado, PR 00646.

DINING: El Ladrillo, in town at C. Mendez 224, serves paella and other gourmet dishes. On C. Marginal parallel to Carr. 693 at Carr. 697 (Costa de Oro), **La Terraza** (☎ 796-1242) has a variety of seafood dishes. On Carr. 693 at Costa de Oro, **El Malecón** (☎ 796-1645) serves seafood, including lobster with creole sauce and parmesan. Set at Km 8.1 on Carr. 693 near the Hyatts, the expensive **Jewel of China** (☎ 796-4644) provides a feast of regional entrées. **Mangére**, which also has a branch in San Juan, serves Italian food. Others are **Los Naborias**, Carr. 690, and **La Familia**, Carr. 690 on the way to Playa Cerro Gordo.

HOTEL DINING: In the Hyatt Regency Cerromar Beach, set against a backdrop of gardens and waterfalls, expensive **Medici's** (☎ 796-1234) serves N Italian cuisine. In the same hotel are **Sushi Wong**, with Chinese and sushi dishes, and **Swan Café**, serving light meals. In the Hyatt Dorado Beach, expensive **Su Casa Restaurant** (☎ 796-1234) offers strolling musicians and a romantic atmosphere. With lighter food, the **Ocean Terrace** is also here.

SERVICES: For car rental in Dorado try Visa Dorado (☎ 796-6404).

PASO DEL INDIO

Unearthed during the construction of the expressway between Vega Baja and Vega Alta, the archaeological site of Paso del Indio contains traces of three cultures (Igneri, Pre-Taino, and Taino), which spanned 1,100 years. All three settlements were buried under floods, and as they are relatively well preserved they are easily studied. Researchers are analyzing tool use, age, and diet. Many of the remains are of children under age 12 who died from malnutrition.

Farther W

Reserva Forestal de Vega Alta is past Vega Alta on Carr. 2. **Hotel Cerro Gordo** (☎ 883-4370) here is on Carr. 690 at Km 4. You can camp at the *balneario* at Cerro Gordo at Carr. 690 in Vega Alta. Vega

Alta hosts the Piña festival every July; ☎ 883-5900. Vega Alta's claim to fame came a few years back when residents went on a spending binge after digging up steel drums – presumably buried by drug traffickers – which contained millions of dollars! Residents are believed to have made off with $11 million, which they used to buy everything from VCRs to new homes. In 1990, the FBI arrested 30 in the drug ring; they had been smuggling cocaine from Colombia via the Dominican Republic since 1985. **dining:** On Carr. 690, **Naborias** (☎ 883-4885) specializes in dishes such as *langosta rellena*.

Farther on is the town of **Manatí,** which was founded in 1738 and now produces the entire US supply of Valium and Librium. Here, the restored 2,265-acre **Hacienda La Esperanza** was once one of the largest sugar plantations on the island. It will be transformed into a living historical farm by the Conservation Trust of Puerto Rico and may be visited with their permission. It was one of the largest and most advanced of the island's sugar plantations during its years of operation (1804-1888). In addition to the colonial plantation house (listed as a historical monument in the National Register of Historic Places), the 19th-century sugar mill machinery is also being restored. Part of an alluvial plain (the Río Grande of Manatí), the estate has coves and dunes along its five miles of coastline, along with steep, conical karst formations. Gourmet dining is available at **Su Casa** (☎ 884-0047), Carr. 670, Km 1.0, and at **Manatubón** (☎ 854-8639) which is on Carr. 149 at Km 7.5. **Festival Playero Los Tubos**, a beach festival with music and water sport events, takes place in early July; ☎ 786-0062. On Carr. 149 at Km 7.5, **Manatuabón** (☎ 854-8639) serves gourmet specialties such as *berenjenas a la martebello* (eggplant with cheese). Leaving from Sector La Boca in Barceloneta, **Paseadora de la Boca** (☎ 858-4178) runs guided 20-minute boat trips on the rivers on weekends and holidays from 10 AM; group trips are available by reservation on Mon., Tues., and Wed.

Six beaches – Playa Mar Chiquita, Playa Tortuguero (which has a hideous *balneario*), Playa Chivato, Playa de Vega Baja, Playa Cerro Gordo, Playa de Dorado and a freshwater lagoon (Laguna Tortuguero) – lie along a series of winding roads running up the coast to the N. Find them using a good road map. **Laguna Tortuguero** has some 2,000 *caimanes* (caymans), a type of alligator indigenous to Central and S America. Disastrous to the ecosystem, their presence has proved a boon to nearby **Vega Baja** (pop. 30,000). The town's souvenir shops sell stuffed caymans and restaurants serve their meat as a delicacy. Prepared in stews, fried and put in salads, or deep fried in batter, the cayman reportedly tastes like rabbit or lobster. Released into the lagoon after a short-lived pet craze came to an end some three decades ago, the caymans have become pests, consuming dogs, cats, small pigs, yearlings, and the lagoon's wildlife (affecting its ecological balance). The caymans can grow up to six or seven ft and can live up to 20 yrs. Although generally timid, the females are the more violent of the two sexes and can be dangerous during egg-laying, which lasts from June to Sept. They grunt like dogs when disturbed or when fighting with each other. Hunting at night, locals trap the caymans in snares and then wrap their snouts with electrical tape. Meanwhile, Russian scientist Sergei Sktachkov, a researcher at Puerto Rico's Institute of Neurobiology, has been using cayman eyes to study their cells in an effort to better understand retina functioning.

Heading E

On the eastern outskirts of San Juan are the **Club Gallístico** (☎ 791-1557; open 2-9 on Sat; Carr. 888, Km 2.6), a cockfighting pit and public beach at Isla Verde and, farther on, the **Roberto Clemente Sports City**. Dedicated to the memory of the Pittsburgh Pirates baseball demigod who died in a 1972 aircrash, *Ciudad Deportiva* has facilities for teaching sports to deprived children. Open daily from 9-noon and 2-7, it's located on C. Icurregui off the Los Angeles Marginal Rd. in Carolina. Carolina is also noted for **Plaza Carolina**, a large shopping mall. Here, you can imagine yourself back home as you visit Sears, J.C. Penney, and The Gap. La Plazoleta here offers a wide variety of food shops. Also located in Carolina are the **Antigua Alcaldía de Carolina** (1872), C. José de Diego at Plaza de Recreo; the *second* **Antigua Alcaldía de Carolina** (dating from 1927), C. Arsuaga at De Diego; and the **Iglesia de San Fernando** (1860) on C. Muñoz Rivera. A bit farther near Piñones along Carr. 187 lies **Boca de Cangrejos** ("Point of the Crabs"), a fishing village. Birdwatchers here may see the common tern, the little blue, tricolored and green-backed heron, the black-necked stilt, and the spotted sandpiper.

BY *PÚBLICO*: *Públicos* leave from Old San Juan, Stop 18 in Santurce, and from Río Piedras. In general, it is easiest to head W towards Arecibo from Bayamón (Old San Juan), or Stop 18, and head S from Río Piedras or Caguas. To go E from Río Piedras is easiest. A bus leaves at uncertain intervals from the bus terminal in Old San Juan for Barranquitas. *Públicos* for Caguas leave from a stop across from the Teatro Tapia. Hitchers (keeping in mind that Puerto Ricans may be reluctant to pick them up, and it may be dangerous) will do well to take transport out of the urban congestion to a place where a thumb has room to breathe.

INTERNAL FLIGHTS: American Eagle flies to Ponce daily. Vieques Air Link flies from San Juan's Isla Grande to Vieques. Flamenco (☎ 725-8110/7707, 800-981-0212) flies to Culebra from Isla Grande (five flights daily; $30) and Fajardo (four flights daily, $20), and Carib (☎ 800-981-0212) flies to Culebra from the international airport.

FOR THE VIRGIN ISLANDS: Airlines flying back and forth change frequently. A new airline, Dolphin (☎ 800-707-0138) flies to St. Thomas, St. Croix, Virgin Gorda, and Tortola. Its aircraft have wonderfully wide windows. Be sure to bring along a copy of *The Adventure Guide to the Virgin Islands* by Harry S. Pariser (Hunter Publishing, 4th edition 1996). **for St. Thomas:** Dolphin, Carib (☎ 725-8110/7707, 800-981-0212), and American Eagle all fly. **for St. John:** Once in St. Thomas, take a ferry to St. John from Charlotte Amalie ($7) or Red Hook ($4). **for St. Croix:** Dolphin and American Eagle both fly, but you will likely have to stop and/or change planes in St. Thomas. From St. Thomas you can also take a catamaran (if it is running) and a seaplane. Vieques Air Link flies from Vieques. **for the British Virgin Islands:** LIAT, Dolphin, Carib, and American Eagle fly to Tortola daily, and Dolphin flies to Virgin Gorda daily. (Charters are also available and may be competitively priced). **excursions: Loose Penny Tours** (☎ 261-3333, 261-3030, 800-468-4786) offers one-day tours to St. Thomas for around $100.

FOR THE DOMINICAN REPUBLIC: The most reliable airline is American. Bring a copy of *The Adventure Guide to the Dominican Republic*, second edition, by Harry S. Pariser (Hunter Publishing).

FOR THE CONTINENTAL UNITED STATES: Most cities are readily accessible through direct or interconnecting flights. See "Arrival" in the Introduction. If traveling to the airport during rush hour, be sure to allow plenty of time.

FOR COSTA RICA: LACSA flies. See *The Adventure Guide to Costa Rica* by Harry S. Pariser (Hunter Publishing, 3rd edition, 1996).

Northeastern Puerto Rico

Loíza Aldea & Environs

Named after the Indian princess Luisa who died fighting beside her lover, the Spaniard Mejia, this area is the sole remaining center of Afro-Hispanic culture on the island. The *municipo* itself is divided into four parts – Piñones, Plaza, Mediana Baja, Mediana Alta. Its history dates back to the 16th century when African slaves were brought in to work the sugarcane fields and pan for gold in the river. They were supplemented by escaped and recaptured slaves from other islands. Today, the majority of its population of approximately 30,000 are freed descendants of these Yoruba slaves. The local leadership is trying to deny the presence of African influence in the area, attempting to substitute Indian instead, because there is no political capital to be gained from being black in Puerto Rico. The town of Loíza Aldea was founded in 1719, and its **Iglesia del Espíritu Santo y San Patricio** (begun 1646) in the Plaza de Recreo is the island's oldest active parish church. Its *fiestas patronales* of San Patricio take place around Mar. 17, and the **Festival de Burén** (named for a flat cooking stone) is held in Feb. Loíza is one of the three poorest municipalities in Puerto Rico.

GETTING HERE: Possibly the most exciting part of the trip. Take the A7 bus from Old San Juan's bus station to the end of the line in **Piñones** (Carr. 187) where many stalls serve traditional, African-influenced foods. The action here is at the **Reef Bar and Grill,** which offers a variety of American fare, often accompanied by live reggae or calypso music. Also in this area (Carr. 187, Km 5.4) is **Hemingway's Place** (☎ 791-4212), which serves a popular Sun. brunch. From Piñones onward the feel of Africa is in the air.

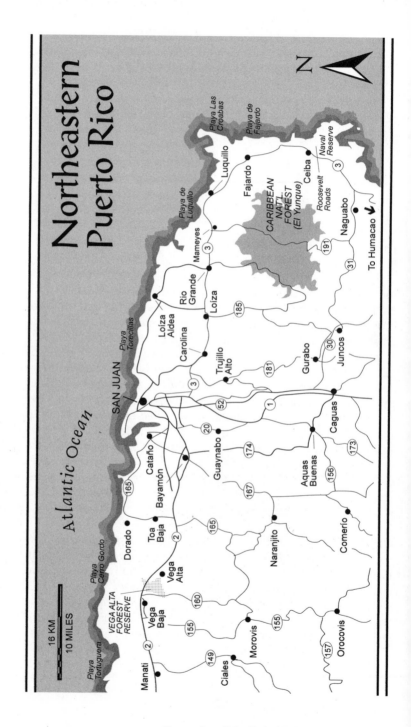

Northeastern Puerto Rico

Atlantic Ocean

16 KM
10 MILES

Playa Tortuguera

Playa Cerro Gordo

VEGA ALTA FOREST RESERVE

Playa Torecillas

SAN JUAN

Playa de Luquillo

Playa Las Croabas

Playa de Fajardo

Naval Reserve

N

Luquillo

Fajardo

Ceiba

Roosevelt Roads

CARIBBEAN NAT'L FOREST (El Yunque)

Naguabo

Mameyes

Rio Grande

Loiza

Loiza Aldea

Carolina

Trujillo Alto

Gurabo

Juncos

3

185

30

181

52

1

173

156

174

20

Caguas

Aguas Buenas

Guaynabo

Cataño

Bayamón

167

165

Comerio

Dorado

Toa Baja

2

165

Naranjito

155

157

Vega Alta

Vega Baja

160

155

Morovis

Orocovis

Manati

2

149

Ciales

To Humacao

191

31

3

Opposite: *Cabo Rojo* (© Harry S. Pariser)

Unfortunately, the area's distinctly laid-back and near-deserted ambiance has been continually threatened by a plan to build a housing development in its Vacia Talega section. The project, conceived more than three decades ago, would be known as Las Palmas. A 53-acre sprawl, it would incorporate 2,000 homes with a hotel-condo, eight pools, tennis courts, and underground parking. It is a scaled down version of the original plan, which would have built 8,000 homes while razing a mangrove swamp on 200 of the 1,200 acres it owns. The developer (the owner of ESJ Towers in Isla Verde) maintains that the project needs no environmental impact statement, and the Environmental Quality Board has gone along with them. This decison comes despite the fact that Piñones, the largest stretch of mangroves on the island, was designated as a critical coastal wildlife habitat by the Department of Natural and Environmental resources during the late 1970s. Residents and environmental groups are appealing and are likely to be triumphant as the decision violates local environmental law.

If you have a vehicle or don't mind hitching you can continue on the road, which runs six miles along unspoiled white sand beaches (nicknamed the lovers' lane of Puerto Rico). Then cross the Espíritu Santo River bridge which spans the Río Grande de Loíza, the island's roughest and only navigable river. An alternate but less spectacular route is to take a *público* from Río Piedras plaza. **note:** Avoid the Piñones area at night.

PRACTICALITIES: The only accommodations option is **Centro Vacacional UIA** (☎ 876-1446). **food:** Restaurants include **La Parilla** (seafood), Carr. 187 at Km 6.2 and **Doña Hilda**, at the corner of Carr. 188 and Carr. 951.

FIESTAS PATRONALES DE LOÍZA

Loíza's three-day tribute to Santiago (St. James) is the most famous fiesta on the island. St. James, first of Christ's disciples to be martyred, made a comeback during the Middle Ages when, descending from the skies on horseback, he slaughtered many Moors, thus ensuring a Spanish victory. His popularity with the *conquistadore* crowd confirmed by this action, he became their patron saint in the Old World as well as the New. Yoruba slaves were forbidden by their Catholic masters to worship the god of their choice, the omnipotent Shango, god of thunder, lightning, and war. Noting the resemblance between their god and the Catholic saint, they

Opposite: *Mayagüez* (Bob Krist, PRTC)

worshipped Shango disguised as Santiago. In the early part of the 17th century, a fisherman on his way to work found a statuette of a mounted Spanish knight hidden in a cork tree, and he took it home. When he came back later, the statue was nowhere in sight. Returning to the tree he again found it secreted, and brought it back home only to have the same thing happen once more. After the third occurrence, he took the statue to the local priest who, identifying it as Santiago, blessed it. The statue ceased wandering, and the local patron saint festivities commenced. Today, there are three images, the latter two brought from 19th-century Spain. Homage is paid to each image on separate days. The original, primitively carved statue, known as *Santiaguito* or "Little James," has been dedicated to children. The others are dedicated to men and women respectively. *Mantenedoras* ("caretakers") take care of each of the three statues; they organize raffles and collect donations. Strings of *promesas* (silver charms) hanging from the base of the statues are gifts from grateful devotees. These *promesas* are fashioned in the shape of the part of a body to be cured.

the festival: For nine days before the fiesta begins on the 26th July, the *mantenedora* of Santiago de los Caballeros holds prayer sessions at her house during which elderly women and children chant rosaries and couplets honoring the saint. On the first day of the festival, a procession led by a flag bearer proceeds to Las Carreras, the spot where the original statue appeared. Stopping at the houses of other *mantenedoras* along the way, the statues are brought out and both carriers and flag bearers kneel three times. The Loíza festival is famous all over Puerto Rico for the beauty and uniqueness of its costumes: *Vejiantes,* who represent devils, wear intricately crafted, colorfully painted coconut masks adorned with horns along the tops and sides. *Locas*, female impersonators with blackened faces and exaggerated bosoms, wearing clothes that don't match, pretend to sweep the streets and porches along the way. *Caballeros*, who represent Santiago, wear brightly colored clothes, ribbons and bells, and a soft wire mask painted with the features of a Spanish knight. *Viejos* wear shabby clothes and masks made from shoe boxes or pasteboard. Recently, the festival has been modified; outsiders, who know little of the traditions involved, now make up the majority of the participants. Consequently, the festival has become something of a carnival with salsa music replacing the indigenous *bomba y plena*. The festival is also becoming confused with Halloween; in 1982, E.T. won the prize for best costume.

CRAFTS: The Ayala family (☎ 876-1130), on Carr. 187 at Km 6 in Mediana Alta, make and sell the best festival *vejigante* masks. Before his death in 1980, the family patriarch Castor Ayala was the preeminent mask maker in Loíza. Another shop (☎ 876-7006) is on C. 5 off Carr. 187.

FROM LOIZA: Return to the plaza to catch a *público* back to San Juan, or cross the bridge to return via Piñones.

The Río Grande & Luquillo Areas

The main way out of San Juan to the east is by a highway with highly unpastoral surroundings: pharmaceutical plants and shopping malls galore. Near Fajardo and within easy reach of the side road to El Yunque, **Playa Luquillo** is the most famous beach in Puerto Rico. At the end of each day (5 PM) a white ambulance with screaming siren runs along the beach. Admission is free, but parking costs $2. The Balneario also offers showers (25¢). In town, at the traffic light where the banks are, you can head to the coast to find **Playa Azul**. There are no facilities on the beach but everything is a block away on the road paralleling Carr. 3. Further E near the Plaza you can find **La Pared** (The Wall), a surfing beach, although serious surfers will go to La Selva. **Playas San Miguel** and **Convento** stretch on to the E.

FESTIVALS AND EVENTS: Río Grande has a **carnival** celebration in mid-July that includes a traditional coastal burial of a sardine; events usually take place on weekday evenings and throughout the day and night on weekends.

SIGHTS: Luquillo has the **Alcaldía de Luquillo** (1925), C. 14 de Julio at C. Jesús T. Piñero on the Plaza de Recreo; it shows both neoclassic and neo-Spanish influences. In front of the Plaza, the Iglesia de San José dates from 1932. The abandoned 19th-century ruins of the **Panadería García** are in back of C. Fernando García 308, which is off of Carr. 3. In Río Grande is the **Iglesia de la Virgen del Carmen** (approx. 1880), C. del Carmen 55 at the Plaza de Recreo.

ACCOMMODATIONS: The **Grateful Bed & Breakfast** (☎ 889-4919; Box 568, Luquillo, PR 00773) is a great place to stay if you're interested in exploring El Yunque/Luquillo area as well as the island's eastern half. Proprietor Marty runs this small inn where rooms are free of charge. In lieu of a room rate you pay a flat daily fee for his help with planning your trip; breakfast is included, and other meals are inexpensive. Marty is well acquainted with the island and knows the hiking trails in El Yunque intimately. He can arrange horseback riding, snorkeling, and other activities in the area as well as advise you where to go islandwide while using the lodge as a base. The Grateful Bed is set on a tract of secluded acreage well away from it all and is very relaxing. It's not, however, for people who require anal-retentive orderliness. Marty says he would rather spend two hours with a guest planning a trip than on making the place immaculate. However, it is clean and comfortable enough to satisfy the average person, and Marty's hospitality is the major reason to come. There are two main houses. The principal house has a living space (with reading materials and musical instruments), a bar and tables where Marty serves meals, and walls of tapes including, as one might expect, a comprehensive selection of Grateful Dead tapes. The neighboring guest house has a few small, simple rooms and a lounge area. Two houses just down the road are also used to house guests. Marty sometimes serves delicious home-cooked meals, including black bean burritos. Because this place is so remote, it's definitely better if you have a car. Marty will make an effort to accommodate carless visitors, but he's not a taxi service. Rates at Marty's are $60 s, $15 add'l; camping is $15 pp pn, and you can rent a tent for $5 pn. When you write to Marty, he'll send you a vacation itinerary planner (which will help him plan how he can help you) as well as directions and a checklist of things to bring, which include your smile and a readiness for adventure. He has also organized the Grateful Bed & Breakfast Rainforest Action Group which is fighting environmental threats to El Yunque. Membership is $15.

Geared towards a somewhat different clientele, the **Casa de Vida Natural** (☎ 887-4359, 212-260-5823; Box 1916, Río Grande, PR 00745; e-mail, lacasa@universe.digex.net) is a combination spa, new age seminar center, and bed and breakfast. Managed by an intelligent and highly capable South African and English couple, the hotel was founded by entrepreneurial therapist and talk show guest Jane Goldberg. A variety of massages are offered, as are body wraps (mud, herbal), facial regeneration, and colon therapy ("the colon is gently irrigated using alternatively, warm and cool, pure filtered water"). Treatments run around $50, with one as low as $30 and another as high as $125. Packages include daily, weekend getaway, five-day stay, and bed and breakfast ($70 s, $90 d). Seminars in 1996 included one guided by a US-born "yogi" who teaches kundalini yoga as well as yogic rebirthing, a Taoist movement class, a Jane Goldberg seminar, and a Reiki workshop. Its rooms are quite attractive and some command great views, the proprietors go out of their way to cater to you (even taking you to El Yunque and coming back for you), and it's a great place to relax – especially if you enjoy vegetarian food. A trampoline is an on-site bonus. The hotel is off of Carr. 186 at Ramal 9960, Km 0.9.

Another, more staid alternative is the seven-room **Hotel Martorell**, 6A Ocean Drive in Luquillo (☎ 721-2884, 889-3975 in Luquillo; 800-443-0266 in the US; 889-2710 elsewhere in Puerto Rico). Rooms rent from around $65 s, $70 d. **Le Petit Chalet** (☎ 887-5802/5807; Box 182, Río Grande, 00745) offers a tranquil atmosphere that is ideal for birdwatchers. The **Río Grande Plantation Resort** (☎ 887-2779, fax 888-3239), a "Conference and Learning Center," has a pool, convention center, and a set of villas. Rates run from around $125 d. Other alternatives include the **Berwind Recreational Facilities** (☎ 256-3010; Carr. 187, Km 4.7) and **Motel Patria** (☎ 887-7763; Carr. 967, Km 1.1) in Río Grande. **Camping** is available at Luquillo's *balneario* at Km 35.4 on Carr. 3.

in Palmer: Set on 481 acres and reminiscent of a Caribbean great house, the 600-room **Westin Río Mar Beach Resort & Country Club** (800-4-RIOMAR) is a $178.5 million project that opened in 1996. It features a ballroom, casino, country club, business center, health club, beach club, sailing, boating, diving, surfing, windsurfing, horseback riding, hiking, two championship golf courses, and a mile-long beach. Dining is at your choice of 13 restaurants or lounges, which include an international café and bistro, **Palio** (Italian dishes), the **Grille Room**, **La Estancia** (Spanish), a tapas bar, a beachfront grill and bar, and the **Players' Lobby Bar**.

Casa Cubuy Ecolodge: On El Yunque's S side, this intimate guesthouse (☎ 874-6221; Box 721, Río Blanco, Puerto Rico) is at Km 22 on C. 191. It provides an ideal atmosphere for sunbathing, hiking, and relaxing. Some trails on the luxuriantly verdant property lead to pre-Columbian petroglyphs. Rates are $70 s or d. Both regular and vegetarian meals are available. Massages are $40. Visitors should note that there are no trails directly into El Yunque from this area so you will have to drive around to get into the park and access trails. The owners, Marianne and her son Mat, may be able to pick you up and put you on your way depending upon their schedule.

FOOD: Sandy's Sea Food Restaurant & Steak House (☎ 889-5765), C. Fernández Garcia 276 in Luquillo, offers fare ranging from a number of *asopaos* to *mondongo*, from lobster and shrimp dishes to poultry and meat. **Lolita's** (☎ 889-5770) is on Carr. 3 at Km 41.8 in Luquillo; it serves some mean nachos and offers tasty margaritas. **Back to Nature** (☎ 889-5560) is a health food restaurant and natural foods store. It's in Barrio Fortuna, Sector Villa Solís. At Jesús T. Piñero 2 on the main plaza in Luquillo, **Victor's Place** (☎ 889-5705) specializes in seafood. **Blue Jeans Bar & Grill**, next to the church and above the bakery in Luquillo, offers daily specials as well as Mexican, American, and traditional dishes. The **Brass Cactus** serves American food, and **Chianti Grill** offers Italian dishes. **El Rancho**, in Luquillo on Carr. 3 at Km 32, offers food ranging from fried rabbits to shrimp nuggets. They also have pony rides. On Carr. 191 at Km 1.3, **Las Vegas** (☎ 887-2526) serves Puerto Rican cuisine, including seafood dishes such as *salmorejo marino* (seafood stew). Offering a great view but slow service, **Restaurante Montemar**, on Carr. 969 off of Carr. 191, serves Puerto Rican dishes. On Carr. 187 at Km 1.6 in Río Grande, **Villa Pesquera** (☎ 887-9864) specializes in seafood. **Don Pepe** is located on Carr. 3 at Km 31.3 which is between Carr. 191 and 968 (near the entrance to El Yunque). It serves Tex-Mex dishes as well as international cuisine and has live music from Thurs. to Sun. nights.

SERVICES AND INFORMATION: La Selva Surf Shop (☎ 884-6205) is a block away from the beach near the plaza; you can find good surfing information here.

    golf: At Km 4.2 on Carr. 187, **Bahía Beach Plantation** (☎ 256-5600, fax 256-1035) operates an 18-hole course and offers rental clubs and lessons. **Berwind Country Club** (☎ 876-3056) has an 18-hole course in Río Grande

    horseback riding: **El Rancho** (☎ 889-6160, 860-7858; see above) has ponies and **Hacienda Carabalí** (☎ 889-5820, 887-4954; Carr. 992, Km 4) offers both trail and beach rides by reservation only.

El Yunque & The Caribbean National Forest

Forty km SE of San Juan, the Luquillo Mountains rise abruptly from the coastal plain. Although 3,526-ft (1,075-m) El Toro is actually the highest, the area is called El Yunque after the 3,493-ft (1,065-m) peak. The Taíno name *yuque* (white land) was transformed by the Spanish into *yunque* (anvil), which the peak does resemble when viewed from the N. Luquillo is a corruption of *Yukiyu* (the god of happiness and well being), who the Taíno believed lived amid the mountainous summits. The only tropical forest in the US National Forest system, its 27,846 acres contain 75% of the virgin forest remaining in Puerto Rico, the headwaters of eight major rivers, four distinct types of forest, and a wealth of animal and plant life.

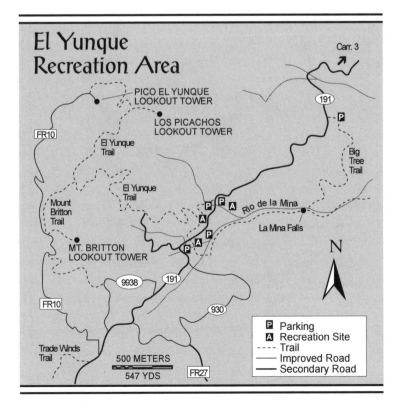

El Yunque
Recreation Area

Northeastern Puerto Rico

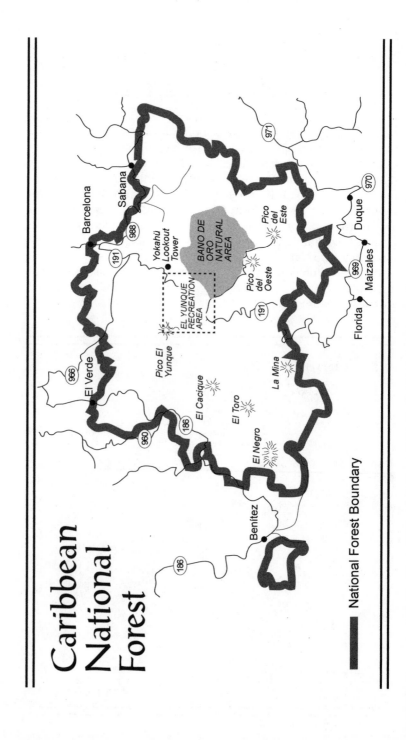

Caribbean National Forest

Barcelona

Sabana

988

191

Yokahú
Lookout
Tower

BANO DE
ORO
NATURAL
AREA

Pico
del
Este

971

970

Duque

969

Maizales

Pico
del
Oeste

191

Florida

EL YUNQUE
RECREATION
AREA

966

El Verde

Pico El
Yunque

El Cacique

La Mina

960

186

El Toro

El Negro

Benítez

186

National Forest Boundary

GETTING HERE: Easily accessible by car, it's less than an hour drive from San Juan. Follow Carr. 3, from which Carr. 186 and Carr. 191 branch off. While 186 traverses the W boundary of the forest, 191 cuts through its heart. Hiking trails branch off this road. A landslide has closed 191 to traffic at Km 13.5 so it's no longer possible to pass through to the S. Hitching along 186 and 191 can be slow (and possibly dangerous), and there's no public transportation through the forest. Sadly, the only practical way to visit is to have your own wheels or someone who will drop you off and then pick you up again.

tours: A large number of companies offer tours, but unfortunately do not do any serious hiking. If you'd like someone to show you around, **Elinor** (☎ 887-7789) gives private guided tours for up to three people.

HISTORY: First protected under the Spanish Crown, the 12,400 acres of Crown Forest were proclaimed the Luquillo Forest Reserve by President Theodore Roosevelt in 1903. Since the creation of the first Forest Service office in the area in 1917, the reserve area has continued to grow; the name was changed to Caribbean National Forest in 1935. It is now also known as the Luquillo Experimental Forest and Biosphere Reserve.

FLORA: Encouraged by the more than 100 billion gallons of water that fall on the forest each year, the vegetation is prolifically verdant. There are four different types of forest, which support 250 tree species – more than in any other National Forest. Only six of these 250 can be found in the continental United States. For more information about rainforests "What is a Rainforest" in this section.

forest ecosystems: On the lower slopes is the *tabanuco* **forest.** Nearly 200 species of trees can be found in this forest environment (with some 33 different kinds appearing within a single acre!) along with numerous small but lovely orchids. The dominant tree which gives this forest its name, the *tabanuco* can be recognized by its whitish bark which peels off in flakes. Contrary to what one might expect, these trees grow slowly: the circumference of their stems may increase only an eighth of an inch per year. Growing in valleys and along slopes above 2,000 ft is the *colorado* **forest,** called humid montane or montane rainforest elsewhere. The short, gnarled trees often have hollow trunks. Many are 1,000 years old or more. In one difficult-to-reach area is a 2,500-year-old *colorado* tree with a circumference of 23 ft, 10 inches. These aged trees house the nests of the Puerto Rican parrot. Curiously, these *palo colorado* trees are related to the titi bush, a shrub which thrives in coastal plain swamp from Florida to Virginia. The **palm forest**, at the next level, is composed almost completely of *sierra* palms (also known as cabbage or mountain palms) complemented by a few *yagrumos*. Masses of ferns and mosses grow underneath as well as on the trees. Limited to the highest peaks and ridges, the **dwarf forest** is composed of trees 12 ft high or less. Mosses and liverworts grow on the ground, on tree trunks, and even on leaves. Also known as elfin forest, dwarf forest is the result of a number of factors. The trees are continually buffeted by 32-mph trade winds and face a nearly permanent overcast sky, which hinders photosynthesis and other biochemical reactions. In better conditions (i.e., sun and shelter) at the same altitude elsewhere in the forest, normal tropical forest (montane thicket) containing many sierra palms replaces dwarf forest. Also, the soil – the result of weathering by rain on volcanic rock – is both boggy and highly acidic. The trees act as a filter to trap rainwater. Dwarf or elfin forest is found above 2,000 ft on Pico del Este, Pico del Oeste, Mt. Britton, and on El Yunque. The forest has 46 species of trees and shrubs.

epiphytes: Taken from the Greek words meaning "upon plants," El Yunque's luxuriant verdancy commonly associated with rainforests depends upon these hangers on. Although they can be found in other forests on the island, the combination of rain and warmth unique to this rainforest help them flourish here. Approximately 10% of the world's 250,000 kinds of vascular plants are epiphytes. Most tropical orchids are epiphytes. Don't make the mistake of thinking that these plants are parasitic. Although they are unwelcome guests, most do not feed on their hosts (as do the dodder and mistletoe). Generally, they arrive in the form of tiny dustlike seeds and establish themselves on moss or lichen, which serves as a starter. Unlike epiphytes, vines and lianas remain rooted in the soil.

What Is A Rainforest?

Rainforests, containing the planet's most complex ecosystem, have a richer animal and plant life than any other type of forest. Unlike other areas in which living organisms face conflicts in the face of a hostile climate, in the rainforest organisms struggle for survival against each other. Since the climate has been stable in this region for some 60 million years, each being – whether plant, animal, insect, or microbe – has been able to develop its specialized niche. Rainforests occur in regions without marked seasonal variation and which commonly receive more than 70 inches (1,800 mm) of rain annually.

COMMON MISPERCEPTIONS ABOUT RAINFORESTS

- ☐ Rainforests are not "the lungs of the planet." Mature trees produce as much oxygen as they consume. The danger in destroying rainforests lies with the effects on rainfall, flooding, and global warming resulting from increasing amounts of carbon dioxide being released in to the atmosphere.

- ☐ The rainforests are not bursting at the seams with colorful plants, wild orchids, and animals. The overwhelming color is green; flowers are few; and the animal you're most likely to encounter is the ant.

- ☐ Rainforests are not merely a source of wood. There are other values associated with them that must be considered.

- ☐ Once damaged, rainforest does not simply grow back as it once was. It may take centuries for the complex ecosystem to regenerate. Reforestation cannot restore the environment.

- ☐ Despite its verdant appearance, rainforest soil may not be fertile. Most of the nutrients are contained in the biomass.

- ☐ There is no need to "manage" a rainforest. They've been doing just fine for eons on their own. Everything in the rainforest is recycled, and anything removed has an effect.

- ☐ "Selective" cutting has detrimental consequences because it affects the surrounding soil quality and weakens the forest as the strongest specimens are removed. No way has yet been found to exploit a rainforest so that all species can be preserved.

- ☐ One "endangered" species cannot be effectively protected without safeguarding its ecosystem. Botanical gardens or seed banks cannot save important species. These are too numerous in quantity, seeds have too short a lifespan, and the species depend upon animals for their lifecycle equilibrium.

- ☐ Any reduction in consumption of tropical hardwoods will not preserve rainforests. The only effective method is formal protection of the forests in reserves and parks. The forests are falling at too fast a rate for any other methods to work.

Northeastern Puerto Rico

LAYERS: Life in the rainforest is stratified in vertical layers. The upper canopy layer contains animals that are mainly herbaceous. They rarely descend to earth. Typically more than a hundred feet high, these canopy trees generally lack the girth associated with tall trees of the temperate forest, perhaps because there are few strong winds to combat and each tree must compete with the others for sunlight. The next lower layer is filled with smaller trees, lianas, and epiphytes.

Some are parasitic; others use trees solely for support. The ground layer is littered with branches, twigs, and foliage. Most animals here live on insects and fruit; others are carnivorous. Contrary to popular opinion, the ground cover is thick only where sunlight penetrates sufficently to allow vegetation to grow; secondary forest growth is generally much more impenetrable. The extensive forest growth by the trees and associated fungi (*mycorrhizae*) form a thick mat that holds thin topsoils in place when it rains. If these are cut, the soil will wash away: the steeper the slope, the faster the rate of runoff. The land soon deteriorates after cutting. As the sun beats down on the soil, sometimes baking it hard as a sidewalk, the crucial fungal mat and other organic life die off. It may take hundreds of years to replace important nutrients through rainfall, and the forest may never recover.

VARIETIES OF RAINFORESTS

There is no single "true rainforest," and forest botanists have varying definitions of the term. It may be argued that there are some 30 types, including such categories as semi-deciduous forest, tropical evergreen alluvial forests, and evergreen lowland forests – each of which can be subdivided into three or four more categories. Equatorial evergreen rainforests comprise two-thirds of the total. As one moves away from the equator on either side, the forest develops marked wet and dry seasons. Cloud forest is another name for montane rainforest, which is characterized by heavy rainfall and persistent condensation due to the upward deflection of moisture-laden air currents by mountains. Trees here are typically short and gnarled. The so-called elfin woodland or dwarf forest is marked by the presence of extremely stunted moss-covered trees. Rainforest without as much rain, known as tropical dry forest, once covered Pacific coastal lowlands stretching from Panama to Mexico, an area the size of France. Today, they have shrunk to a mere 2% of the total area and only part of this is under protection; one of the world's best examples of tropical dry forest is found in the reserve at Guánica.

INTERACTIONS: As the name implies, rainforests receive ample precipitation, promoting a rich variety of vegetation to which animals and insects must adapt. Lowland rainforests receive at least 100 inches annually. Although some rainforests get almost no rain during certain parts of the year, these are generally cloaked in clouds from which they draw moisture. The high level of plant-animal interaction – taking forms such as predation, parasitism, hyperparasitism, and symbiosis – is believed by many biologists to be one major factor promoting diversity. The interactions are innumerable and highly complex: strangler figs steal sunlight from canopy trees; wasps may pollinate figs; bats and birds transport seeds and pollinate flowers. When a species of bird, for example, becomes rare or extinct, it may have an effect on a tree that depends solely upon that species to distribute its seeds. There is no such thing as self-sufficiency in a rainforest; all life depends upon its cohabitants for survival.

BIODIVERSITY: Those who are unfamiliar with the rainforest tend to undervalue it. Tropical deforestation is one of the great tragedies of our time. We are far from cataloguing the species inhabiting the rainforests; when cut down, they are lost forever. More than 70% of the plants known to produce compounds with anticancerous properties are tropical, and there may be many cures waiting to be found. One survey of Costa Rican plants found that 15% had potential as anti-cancer agents. Cures for malaria and dysentery have been found in the forests. Louis XIV was cured of amoebic dysentery by ipecac, a South American plant that remains the most effective cure. Cortisone and diosgenin, the active agents in birth control pills, were developed from Guatemalan and Mexican wild yams. These are some of the 3,000 plants that tribal peoples use worldwide as contraceptives. Continued research could yield yet other methods of birth control. Not all rainforest products are medicinal. Rice, corn, and most spices – including vanilla, the unripe fermented stick-like fruits of the Central American orchid *Vanilla fragrans* – are also medicinal. Other products native people have extracted from the rainforest include latex, resins, starch, sugar, thatch, dyes, and fatty oils. The rainforest also acts as a genetic pool, and when disease strikes a monocrop such as bananas, it's possible to hybridize it with rainforest varieties to see if this produces an immunity to pests or fungus.

GREENERY AND GREENHOUSE: Biodiversity is only one of many reasons to preserve the forest. Rainforests also act as watersheds, and cutting can result in flooding as well as increased aridity because much rain is produced from the transpiration of trees, which helps keep the air saturated with moisture. Although it is commonly believed that rainforests produce most of the earth's oxygen, in fact there is an equilibrium between the amount mature forests consume through the decay of organic matter and the amount they produce via photosynthesis. However, many scientists believe that widespread burning of tropical forests releases large amounts of carbon dioxide into the atmosphere. The amount of carbon dioxide in the atmosphere has risen by 15% in this past

Northeastern Puerto Rico

century (with about half of this occurring since 1958), and forest clearance may account for half of that gain. As carbon dioxide along with other atmospheric elements traps heat that would otherwise escape into space, temperatures may rise worldwide. Rainfall patterns could change and ocean levels could rise as the polar ice packs melt. In many areas, deforestation has already had an adverse effect on the environment. Although many questions remain about the "greenhouse effect," one probability is that by the time the effects are apparent they will be irreversible.

EDUCATING YOURSELF

Don't miss an opportunity to visit the rainforest while you are in Puerto Rico. When you return home, one of the best organizations to join is **Rainforest Action Network** (☎ 415-398-4404; fax 398-2732). Write to them at Suite 700, 450 Sansome, San Francisco, CA 94111. Another is **Earth Island Institute** (☎ 415-788-3666, fax 788-7324), which was founded by longtime environmental activist David Brower. Their address is Suite 28, 300 Broadway, San Francisco, CA 94133. A third is the **Rainforest Alliance** (☎ 212-941-1900, fax 941-4986), at 270 Lafayette Street, #512, New York, NY 10012. **Greenpeace** (☎ 202-462-1177) also has a rainforest program; write them at 1436 U St. NW, Washington, DC 20009. In Puerto Rico, contact Marty's newly organized **Grateful Bed & Breakfast Rainforest Action Group** (☎ 809-889-4919; Box 568, Luquillo, PR 00773), which is working to preserve El Yunque. If you want to inform yourself about the state of the US National Forests, you should join the **Native Forest Council** (PO Box 2171, Eugene, OR 97402). A donation of $25 or more gives you a subscription to their informative newspaper, the *Forest Voice*. If you're planning a visit to the Pacific Northwest and would like a guided tour, **Ancient Forest Adventures** offers both resort-based trips and less expensive backpacking trips. Call Mary Vogel at ☎ 503-385-8633 or write AFA, 16 NW Kansas Ave., Bend, OR 97701-1202.

FATE OF THE FORESTS: Just a few thousand years ago, a belt of rainforests covering some five billion acres (14% of the planet's surface) stretched around the equator. Wherever there was sufficient rainfall and high enough temperatures, there was or is rainforest. Over half that total area has been destroyed, much of it in the past few hundred years, with the rate accelerating after the end of WWII. Squatters and logging continue to cause deforestation throughout the region. At current rates, much of the remaining forest will vanish by the end of the century. One reason for the population expansion into the forests is the concentration of arable land among only a few owners. In El Salvador fewer than 2,000 families control 40% of the land. Another motivation is the desire to secure control over an area. Cattle ranching, logging, mining, and industry are other reasons to cut the forests. Forests do not recover soon. Depending on how much has been cut, recovery may take from centuries to eternity.

BIRDS: Many rare species are found here, including the green, blue, and red Puerto Rican parrot (*Amazona uttata*), a protected species (see the box below). Once common throughout the island, fewer than 50 now survive within the forest confines. It may be possible to spot one from either the patio next to the restaurant or in the picnic area behind the visitors' center. Other birds – like the Puerto Rican tanager, the bare-legged owl, broad-winged hawk, the quaildove, and the scaled pigeon – are common here, although rare elsewhere. You may be able to spot a green mango humming-bird near La Coca Falls or an elfin woods warbler along El Toro Trail and in the dwarf forest. Still other species include the Puerto Rican screech-owl, the Puerto Rican woodpecker, the Puerto Rican tanager, the Puerto Rican lizard-cuckoo, and the Puerto Rican bullfinch.

THE PUERTO RICAN PARROT

Known to the Taínos as the *iguaca*, the lovely Puerto Rican parrot stands in danger of extinction. The smallest species found in the West Indies, the parrot seldom reaches more than a foot in length. Colored green with flashes of blue and red, this gregarious frugivore nests in four- to five-foot-deep cavities found in palo colorado trees in the cloud forest.

Fewer than 50 remain in El Yunque (the Caribbean National Forest), with another 72 held in captivity. The parrot numbers as one of the 10 most critically endangered birds. Estimated to have numbered one million when Columbus invaded, their numbers plummeted to an all-time low of 13 wild specimens in 1975; half had disappeared with 1989's Hurricane Hugo. Birds are being bred at an aviary in the forest, and parrots have successfully been transplanted to Río Abajo Forest. Unfortunately, the issue of the bird's survival has become a political football with the Fish and Wildlife Service, the US Forest Service, and the Puerto Rico Department of Natural Resources all attempting to assert control.

OTHER ANIMALS: Snakes are scarce, poisonous ones nonexistent. There's the Puerto Rican boa, which may grow up to 13 ft, but you are unlikely to see one. *Coquí* frogs croak from every corner, and small fish, shrimp, and crayfish live in the streams. There are also tales of small green men living in the forest, undoubtedly an endangered species these days. You'll have to be either extremely lucky or have a hyperactive imagination if you expect to have an encounter.

ENVIRONMENTAL PROBLEMS: Ironically, the very means that gives visitors access to the forest has had detrimental effects. Cutting roads through steep terrain causes landslides. Accordingly, much controversy surrounds the possibility of reopening Carr. 191, which has been closed since Hugo. Perhaps not coincidentally, the parrot population, which had fallen from around 200 in the 1950s to 50, began to recover after the road's closing. Still, some people are pushing for the road's reopening.

HIKING: Among the 50 km of hiking trails, the principal ones include El Yunque, Mt. Britton, Big Tree, and El Toro/Tradewinds, which rises to the top of El Toro peak (3,533 ft). Trailheads are located on Carr. 186 at Km 10.6 and on Carr. 191 at Km 13.5. While La Coca Falls and Yohaku Lookout Tower are on or near Carr. 191, you must hike to reach La Mina Falls or Pico El Yunque and Los Picachos Lookout Towers.

hiking practicalities: The trails are well maintained, but no fresh drinking water or toilet facilities are available. Although locals drink out of the mountain streams, it's not advisable unless the water has been treated first. Bring food, waterproof clothing, hiking boots, and a compass. Long-sleeved clothing is advisable because there are some poisonous plants (and razor grass) along the trails. Although there are a number of food stands on the way up, Mameyes, along Carr. 3, is the last place to buy food.

trail details: Commencing just below the Yohaku lookout tower on Carr. 191, *La Coca Trail* is damp and leads through streams and near waterfalls. It's a rough and muddy trail; you need your hiking boots. A walking stick is recommended. Take the trail located between La Coca Falls and the Yohaku Lookout center downhill from Carr. 191; it descends until it crosses La Coca River twice and is preceded by a stream each time it crosses. La Mina River is next. It has a nice swimming hole. If you follow this trail uphill past another waterfall, you'll come to La Mina Falls. It's marked by a footpath over the river and is a popular bathing spot. From La Mina Falls, the *Big Tree Trail* passes through *tabanuco* forest to reach Carr.

191. This paved trail is located on the other side of the river. If you take it to the R, you will be on an interpretive trail, which has signs in both Spanish and English telling you about forest fires. This road will take you out to Carr. 191 at Km 10.4. Head downhill to return to your car. *El Yunque Trail* (2.6 mi, four hours RT) begins in the Caimtillo Picnic Area and ascends via sierra palm and *palo colorado* forests to the dwarf and cloud forests of Mt. Britton and El Yunque as well as to the top of Los Pichacos, Roca Maracas, and Yunque Rock. One way to hike it is to start from El Baño Grande, the upper ranger station, take El Yunque Trail (originating at the Palo Colorado Visitor's Center) to the R and head uphill. Passing several trails, you come to Los Picachos. Proceeding less than five minutes you come to a steep set of trails which leads to the top. The summit is some 20 ft in diameter and has a four-ft wall surrounding it. From the top of El Yunque on a clear day it's possible to see St. Thomas or even as far as the British Virgin Islands.

Heading down, backtrack to the other fork you passed earlier which heads towards El Yunque. Just before you come to the peak, there's an unmarked trail to the R, which will take you to nearby El Yunque Rock. It also has some great views. Backtracking, continue along the trail and then follow the road up to El Yunque Peak, which has high tech installations (antennas, satellite dishes and the like). Take the road downhill for about 15 minutes until you come to the paved *Mt. Britton Trail* on your L, which you take uphill until you come to **Mt. Britton Tower** – something straight out of a Monty Python set. A product of the Civilian Conservation Corps, it was built between 1930 and 1935 and is named after a famous botanist from the NY Botanical Garden who studied here. You can find this book in the gift shop along with a beautiful selection of postcards. Return on the same trail to the loop road. Either direction goes back to Carr. 191. If you started by the ranger station, take the loop road down to your L; make another L to get to your car. If you go to your R, it leads to Carr. 191 further uphill where the gate closes the road to vehicular traffic. Taking that road on foot you can head S to the landslide, where you'll come to the six-mile, 9.6-km *Tradewinds/El Toro Trail*. From this trail, which begins near the aviary and workers' housing area along Carr. 191 at Km 13.5, you can reach El Toro (392 ft, 1074 m), one of the most remote peaks in the area. At this starting point you will find yourself between two radio transmission towers. Follow the ridge W to the summit before descending to Cienaga Alta, a forest ranger station located along Carr. 186. Unpaved and beautiful, it's about seven or eight miles, and you need seven to 10 hrs. Start it from Carr. 186, which is the road that leads from Carr. 3 up through El Verde and heads towards Cotui.

It's advisable to start from this westernmost side of the trail because the first thing you'll do is climb El Toro Trail. As it's a steep ascent, you should not do it at the end of your hike. When you descend from the top, put on long pants and a long-sleeved shirt because you'll come across razor grass. As you proceed down the trail, you will traverse a number of hills. There's no dependable supply of running water so bring your own water with you. The trail ends again on Carr. 191; if you took it from El Verde side once you reach Carr. 191, you would make a L to the gate which closes it off; you would need two cars (one dropping you off and one picking you up) for this hike; it is very enjoyable, however, simply walking in for an hour or so from Carr. 191, then backtracking. An alternative is to begin hiking at Km 20, five or six km from Florida.

note: El Yunque area has a bad reputation regarding theft so leave *nothing* of value in your car, and exercise like caution while hiking in the area.

> ☞ Traveler's Tip. If you want to get away from the crowds
> but don't have a lot of time, try visiting the attractive falls
> at Juan Diego (at Km 9.8 on the R). You can easily hike
> in to two levels of falls; the third is a stiff hike up. It's
> truly an idyllic spot.

BICYCLING: The closed portion of Carr. 191 is the best bicycle path. Along the path you see hibiscus, coleus, and wandering Jew.

OTHER PRACTICALITIES: Best place to orient yourself is at El Portal (The Gateway), a visitor's center that opened in 1996. The 12,000-sq-ft center contains interactive displays as well as a video theater. It's just a few km in from the entrance road. Obtain additional information from Caribbean National Forest, Box B, Palmer, PR 00721; ☎ 888-5656. Topographical maps are available in the field office (open weekdays) at the base of the forest. Buy Puerto Rican snacks at stands along Carr. 191. The first kiosk to your L as you approach (at Km 7.8) is El Bosque, which has vegetable (and sometimes lobster, shrimp, or crab) tacos and soy or chicken *piñonos.* Camping is permitted in most areas of the forest; permits are available at the Service Center. Accommodations are listed under "Río Grande and Luquillo" above.

Fajardo

A small, sleepy town, Fajardo only comes alive during its **patron saint festival** (Santiago Apóstol) every July 25. It once served to supply pirates, and today it serves as a yachting haven. Offlying cays include Icacos, Palominos, Palominitos, Diablo, and Cayos Lobos. *Públicos* run to the outlying areas of Las Croabas and La Playa-Puerto Real from the plaza. There's nothing much in Las Croabas either except Soroco Beach and a few restaurants. Puerto Real has the **Casa de Aduanas** on C. Union, which dates from 1930. **La Playa** has a customs house, post office, and ferry terminal.

GETTING HERE: *Públicos* run from Río Piedras in San Juan. If you're planning to take a ferry, be sure to get one headed to La Playa. Otherwise, you may end up having to take another *público* from town. You can also charter a taxi from San Juan for around $50.

ACCOMMODATIONS: Pitch a tent within the confines of **Playa Soroco** for around $6 per tent. A comfortable and hospitable bed-and-breakfast, **Fajardo Inn** (☎ 863-5195, fax 860-5063; Box 4309, Puerto Real, PR 00740) offers a/c rooms with phones and cable TV; rates start from around $45 s or d. It's been recommended by a reader. To get here turn off Carr. 3 at the Esso station and head past the Amig store before turning R at the pharmacy, then L at the boat shop and R past the shops. Set on the waterfront, the 20-room **Delicias Hotel** (☎ 863-1818/1577; Box 514, Fajardo, PR 00740), Carr. 195 at La Playa, features a/c rooms from around $60. In Las Croabas and also known as La Familia, the **Family Hotel-Parador** (☎ 863-1193, fax 860-5345; HC 00867, Box 21399, Fajardo, PR 00648), Carr. 987, offers 28 a/c rooms with TV and refrigerators. There's a dive school as well as children's and adult pools. Prices start at $63 s and $73 d. For more information/reservations, ☎ (800) 443-0266 in the US or (800) 981-75 75 (or 721-2884 in San Juan) in Puerto Rico. In Ceiba along Carr. 977, the nine-room **Ceiba Country Inn** (☎/fax 885-0471; Box 1067, Ceiba, PR 00735) is a relaxed and personalized bed-and-breakfast set in the country. Rates run around $50 s and $60 d.

FOOD: On C. Las Croabas, expensive **La Fontanella** (☎ 860-2480) serves gourmet Sicilian dishes. Also expensive, **Restaurant Du Port** (☎ 860-4260) is inside the Puerto del Rey Marina and offers seafood, French, and international food. On Carr. 986 at Parcela 45 in Villa Las Corabas, **Anchor's Inn** (☎ 863-7200) opened in April 1994 and serves seafood dishes such as *filete de chillo tropical* (snapper filet); meals are expensive here as well. In Puerto Real, **Rosa's Seafood**, Tablazo 56, is a simple family-style restaurant; dishes here include lobster salad and other seafood dishes as well as seafood-stuffed *mofongo*. Two *arepas* (johnnycakes) are served with each meal. Offering free delivery within Fajardo, Luquillo and Ceiba, **Antonino's Pizza** (☎ 860-0070/0090) is set inside the Villa Marina Shopping Center. Mona's Mexican Restaurant (☎ 860-6300) is on Carr. 3 at Km 44.1.

EL CONQUISTADOR

Set on a bluff commanding a spectacular view of offshore islands, the $225 million El Conquistador resort is the largest self-contained "total escape" tourist resort readily available to upscale US travel groups. It opened in late 1993 with an initial 935 rooms; a total of 1,300 rooms are projected. The project was financed by the Kumagai Construction Company and Williams Hospitality. Promoting "instant gratification," golf, gambling, horseback riding, discos, health clubs and other activities are available. There's a 55-slip marina, five swimming pools, and 16 restaurants as well as shops, a large casino, an 18-hole golf course, and four different "villages," including an old colonial village. Off-lying Isla de Palominos, under lease from its owners, serves as a "fantasy island" which offers water sports from jet skiing to wind surfing. Transportation (bus, limo, or helicopter) is provided from a special reception lounge in San Juan's airport. One controversial aspect of the project is the proposal to establish an underwater park with underwater plaques and rest platforms and buoys above-water. Spear fishing would be banned, and the trail would run from Las Cucharas, Lobos, Palamitos, and a number of cays in the direction of Culebra. Curiously, the hotel's site has functioned in its past lives as a Maharishi Mahesh Yogi meditation institute and as an evangelical Christian mission. Restaurants here include **Blossoms,** which has both Chinese and Japanese dishes (including sushi). Rates start at $335 s, $455 d. If you are not staying at the hotel, a $4 parking fee is commanded. For more information, ☎ (800) 468-5228, (809) 863-1000, or fax (809) 791-7640.

MARINAS: Set on Demajagua Bay on the E shore, **Puerto del Rey Marina** (☎ 252-1250) has slips for 700 boats and can accommodate vessels up to 200 ft. It has a dive center, sailing school, haul-out facility, French restaurant, condos, and the Plaza del Puerto shopping plaza. **Tropic Key Charters** (Box 1186, Fajardo, PR 00738; ☎ 860-6100, fax 860-7592; 800-888-5186) is also here. Other marinas here are the **Villa Marina** (☎ 728-4250) and **Puerto Chico Marina** (☎ 863-0834).

diving: Offering scuba and snorkeling trips, **Sea Ventures** (☎ 800-739-3483) has been recommended by a reader. The **Caribbean Dive Institute** (☎ 860-2177), Av. Principal, offers certification and rentals. **note:** For other information on dive operations, charters, and excursions from Fajardo, see the "Vicinity of San Juan" section.

☞ **Traveler's Tip.** The best beach in Fajardo is at Seven Seas along Carr. 987.

FROM FAJARDO: For information about excursions by boat, see the "Vicinity of San Juan" section. *Públicos* for Luquillo, Río Piedras, Juncos, Humacao, etc. leave from the town plaza. **note:** Ferry departures may have increased by the time of your arrival. For information/reservations, ☎ 863-0705/0852 or (800) 981-2005. In case you wish to bring a car across, ferries also take cargo. Buy your ticket at the window to the R. Go around through the gate and to your L. **Culebra y Vieques Restaurant** is near the loading dock. Other places to eat are nearby, along with a PO and pay phones.

for Culebra: The ferry departs Mon. to Fri. at 4 ($2.25, two hours). On Fri., there are additional departures at 9 and 4. Sat. departures are at 7, 2, and 5:30, and ferries leave Sun. at 8 and 2:30. Flamenco Air (☎ 863-3366) flies to Culebra.

for Vieques: Ferries ($2, take 1½ hrs.) leave Mon. to Fri. at 7 and on Sat. and Sun. at 9, 3, and 6. A cargo ferry also runs. Vieques Air Link (☎ 863-3020) also flies daily.

for Icacos: Rent a sailboat or sail your own to this deserted island. Camping permitted.

☞ **Traveler's Tip**. From Vieques, you can continue on to St. Croix with Vieques Air Link (☎ 863-3020).

CABEZAS DE SAN JUAN NATURE RESERVE

(Reserva Natural de las Cabezas de San Juan)

Purchased in 1975 by the Conservation Trust for $5.7 million, the 316-acre Las Cabezas de San Juan nature reserve lies on the island's NE tip. It comprises a number of different ecological communities including mangroves, coral reefs, a dry forest and a series of lagoons; the largest lagoon (Laguna Grande) is seasonally phosphorescent. This wide variety of ecosystems in such a small area is part of what makes the reserve so special. It is the only place on the island where all but one of Puerto Rico's natural communities (the rainforest) can be viewed in a single area. The neoclassical restored lighthouse, El Faro, was constructed at the end of the 19th century. Formerly operated and still owned by the US Coast Guard, it now serves as a visitor's center and educational museum. It houses a nature exhibit, a small aquarium, and an observation deck with views of El Yunque and the USVI. It has been restored using 19th-century techniques.

visiting the reserve: Reservations (☎ 722-5882, 860-2560 on weekends) are required. Admission is $5 for adults and $2 for children under 12. Guided tours are offered daily at several times, but tours in English are available only at 2. A trolley takes you through the reserve, thus limiting environmental impact. There's a gift shop. To get here take Carr. 26 from San Juan to Carr. 3. where you head E towards Carolina and take the first Fajardo exit. Make a L from Carr. 3 onto Carr. 194. Turn L at the traffic light on the corner of the Monte Brisas Shopping Center and then turn R at the next traffic light. Continue until you hit Carr. 987 where you turn L and head straight until you reach the reserve.

Vieques

Set seven miles off the eastern coast of Puerto Rico, this special island possesses its own distinct magic. Its name comes from the Taíno word *bieques* ("small island"). Its nickname, La Isla Neña (Daughter Island), refers to its relationship with the main island. Horses roam freely all over the island, which is dotted with the ruins of pineapple and sugar plantations and more than 50 magnificent beaches. Undoubtedly, Vieques would have become one of the major tourist destinations in the Caribbean were it not for the fact that over 70% of its 26,000 acres was arbitrarily confiscated by the US military in 1948. Locals have suffered much at their hands. Noise from air and sea target bombardment, annoying in itself, was devastating when coupled with the structural damage to buildings and the dramatic decrease in the fishing catch caused by sea pollution. Population plummeted from 14,000 in 1941 to the present 9,000. Many left to find work in San Juan, St. Croix, or elsewhere. Bombing has now diminished, much of the land has been let out for grazing purposes, and military maneuvers have been substantially reduced (though Vieques was the site of a rehearsal for the 1983 Grenada invasion). Regrettably, the guise of National Security prevents the Navy from announcing when it is they will bomb. Pro- and con-Navy elements are both strong, and you'll note that *fuera la marina* is frequently stenciled on buildings.

FESTIVALS AND EVENTS: A **cultural festival** is held in the Fortín in Isabel Segunda (☎ 741-1717 for information) every February or March. It features music, theater, and a book and craft fair. Paired with the local carnival, the *fiestas patronales* are celebrated in mid-July. Centering around *bilí*, a drink made with *quenapas* (guineps) and rum, **El Festival del Bilí** takes place on Sun Bay Beach in Esperanza during Labor Day Weekend. Although it features music and sports events and should be a fun event in theory, it has turned into a big mess that makes money for out-of-town promoters. Taking place on Isabel Segunda's plaza in Nov., **El Festival de las Arepas** glorifies the local johnnycakes. **El Festival de la Langosta** takes place during the height of the lobster fishing season.

Northeastern Puerto Rico

HISTORY: The island was originally known as Bieques by its aboriginal inhabitants, but the first Spanish referred to it and neighboring islands as "Las Islas Inutiles" (The Useless Isles). The presence of land crabs caused the island to be dubbed Crab Island by the buccaneers, and Vieques later became known as one of the Spanish Virgin Islands. First explored in 1524 by Capt. Cristóbal de Mendoza, former governor of Puerto Rico, Vieques was occupied at various times by the British and French until it was formally annexed by Puerto Rico in 1854. Sugarcane became the major crop and, at its peak, the island had four sugar mills that processed 20,000 tons of sugar annually. In 1898, the gunboat *Yale* arrived, and Lt. Cont and his detachment landed. Tensions eased after it was realized that Cont and his men had no intention of eating babies as had been rumored and greatly feared. After the colonel commanding the Fortín explained that he could not surrender without firing a shot, Cont gracefully allowed him to fire off a volley.

As sugarcane continued to rise in price, the population grew – rising to 11,651 in 1920. The sugar economy began to decline during the 1930s. One project brought work for a brief period during the 1940s. Although Pearl Harbor would later serve to discredit the concept, a sea wall was planned that would stretch from Culebra on the N to Vieques on the SE to Roosevelt Roads on the main island. Fleets would be concentrated here. Work on a breakwater that would harbor the British fleet proceeded day and night. The Navy then abrubtly stopped work after it became strategically unnecessary. In 1948 the US Navy, acting on a 1942 authorization, took control of two-thirds of the island. An average of $47 per acre was paid out to eight owners for 21,000 acres where subtenants were living. Of the tenant farmers, 3,000 out of the 9,000 either left the island on their own initiative or were resettled on St. Croix. Some 4,000 were relocated elsewhere on Vieques.

At the end of the 1940s, 4,000 acres were put under the control of the Puerto Rican Agricultural Development Company (PRACO), which began cattle and dairy farming, egg production, and coconut and pineapple plantations. Employment rose but PRACO was replaced by the Land Authority of Puerto Rico in 1955, an agency which leases excess land to be used by a few landowners who have herds of Brahman cattle. On Feb. 6, 1978, 30 fishing boats protested joint exercises held between Brazil and the US, halting them for some hours. In 1975, Gov. Romero Barcelo sought an injunction against the Navy's use of the Vieques Weapons Range. Millions of dollars in legal fees later, the Vieques Accord was reached on Oct. 12, 1983. The Navy promised to create more jobs by attracting defense contractors, to reduce the size of its firing range, and to allow part of its land to be used for a forestry project that would grow 100 acres of mahogany trees. Although General Electric ("War is our most important product") and other firms have established plants here, the promises remain largely unfulfilled. Today, aside from tourism, there is little employment here, and welfare continues to be a major source of income. The military occupation continues to thwart development as well as the full utilization of the island's many resources.

FLORA AND FAUNA: Brown pelicans, other birds, and leatherback and hawksbill turtles are found on the island.

GETTING HERE: It's a bumpy but beautiful hour-long trip by launch from Fajardo. Pass by Isleta Marina, Palominos, Lobos, Isla de Ramos, and other small islands. Ferries ($2, take 1½ hrs) leave Mon. to Fri. at 7 and on Sat. and Sun. at 9, 3, and 6. A cargo ferry also runs. To get to Fajardo, you can either take a *público* (around $10) or charter a taxi (about $50).

   by air: Vieques Air Link (☎ 722-3736, 723-9882) flies from San Juan's Isla Grande daily, as well as from Fajardo and St. Croix. **La Parada del Viajero** is a small, attractive, inexpensive cafeteria across from the airport.

GETTING AROUND: There is limited service in shared vans from Isabel Segunda to Esperanza. Hitchiking is possible.

   car rentals: Contact **Dreda & Fonsin's Rent-a-Car** (☎ 741-8397/8163; Box 243, Vieques, PR 00765), C. AG Mellado 333; **Steve's Car Rentals** (☎ 741-8135); **VIAS Car Rental** (☎ 741-8173), C. 65th Infantería 186, which rents scooters and jeeps; **Island Car Rentals** (☎ 741-1666; Box 423, Vieques, PR 00765) on Carr. 201 next to Crow's Nest; and **Marcos' Car Rentals** (☎ 741-1388).

Isabel Segunda

Founded in 1843, Isabel Segunda is named after Spain's Isabel II, who ruled from 1833-68. It has the feel of a village. The main plaza has an antique church. Locals ride horses through the main streets while dogs sleep placidly under cars. Although none too attractive, the town does have a number of flamboyant trees which bloom in season. The town plaza has a bust of Simon Bolivar, who paid a visit to Vieques in 1816, and a 19th-century city hall.

Northeastern Puerto Rico

Isabel Segunda

1. Ferry Terminal
2. Puntas Mulas Lighthouse
3. Ocean View Motel
4. Lydia's Bakery
5. Supermercado Portela
6. Library
7. Gas Station
8. Catholic Church
9. Plaza
10. Alcaldía (City Hall & Tourist Information)
11. William's Pizza
12. Panadería Candy
13. Vieques Air Link
14. Farmacia Libertad
15. Post Office
16. El Fortín
17. Farmacia San Antonio
18. Gas Station

NOT TO SCALE

SIGHTS: There's not much to see in the town itself. On the main square is the **Casa Alcaldía de Vieques** (C. Carlos Le Brun at C. Benítez Guzmán), which dates from around 1845 and is still in use. The major thing to see is undoubtedly **Fortín Conde de Mirasol,** which dominates the town. The last Spanish bastion (1843) undertaken in the Caribbean, this fort was never finished. To get here turn R at the Muñoz Rivera Plaza and follow the hill up. It has been meticulously restored with beautifully finished wooden staircases, cannon, etc., and now serves as a small museum. It's open Sat. and Sun. from 10-4. Inside, you'll find exhibits relating to the indigenous peoples and archaeological digs on the island, agricultural tools, old maps, and the effects of the US military occupation and bombing on the island.

others: **El Faro de Punta Mulas** (☎ 741-5000) is right in town. Built in 1896, this white-painted stone lighthouse has a reflector (built in Paris in 1895) whose beam may be seen from as far as 16 miles away. **Casa Delerme** is an old house at C. Muñoz Rivera and C. A Mellado, built in the 1850s. The second house of the owner, **Casa de Augusto Delerme,** is at C. Benítez Guzmán 7 and dates from the same era. Both are private residences. **Davies Base** is just outside town. **Camp García Base** is the place to go for beaches. At the entrance obtain permission to visit the beautiful and isolated Red, Yellow and Blue beaches, imaginatively named by the Navy. **Red Beach** is near **García Beach,** which has a cave and and is popular with nudists. Spectacular **Green Beach** is in the Naval Reservation to the NW; sand gnats here can be a pain. **Purple Beach** is on the NW coast. Beaches also stretch along the road between town and the airport to the W. According to legend, a 16th-century island chief hid the sacred treasures of his tribe from the *conquistadores* in a large cave at the top of **Mt. Hirata**, highest point on the island. The roar you hear inside the cave is his ghost. Archaeological digs are being conducted at **La Hueca. Mosquito**, the long pier on the isolated NW coast, was built to shelter the British fleet in the event England fell to Germany in WWII. Once used to load sugar cane for transport to Puerto Rico, it is now used to bring supplies from Roosevelt Roads. The Vieques Conservation and Historical Trust (Box 1472, Vieques, PR 00765), a local conservation group, is endeavoring to preserve **Puerto Mosquito**, one of the world's last phosphorescent bays. See "Excursions" in the Esperanza section for information.

ACCOMMODATIONS: There are many small but not especially cheap hotels in town. The 35-room a/c **Ocean View** (☎ 741-3696/2175, fax 741-0545; Box 124, Vieques, PR 00765) is on Plinio

Peterson just minutes on foot from the ferry terminal. It has weekday ($179) and weekend ($134) specials that offer a variety of amenities including meals and some local transportation. Rates start from $50. Set on the N Shore Rd. past the ferry landing and the lighthouse, eight-room **Water's Edge** (☎ 741-1128, fax 741-0690; Box 1374, Vieques, PR 00765) offers a/c rooms with TV/VCR (free movies available), a restaurant/bar, and an oceanfront pool. All-year rates are $65 for courtyard rooms , $85 for oceanfront rooms, and $105 for superior rooms. There's also a two- to three-bedroon luxury villa ($1,800 and $2,500 pw) for rent. The **Cafeteria y Guest House Cayo Blanco** rents rooms for around $40. The **Depakos Hotel** (☎ 741-4126; Box 486, Vieques, PR 00765) has rooms with color TV. Rates are around $25 d for fan and $35 d for a/c rooms. The **Casa La Lanchita** (☎ 741-0023; Box 358, Vieques, PR 00765) has six rooms with kitchens.

near town: Set on a hilltop in Barricada Fuerte and commanding a spectacular view, the 16-room **Sea Gate** (☎ 741-4661; Box 747, Vieques, PR 00765) is run by the Miller family. They offer free transport to and from the airport and ferry, to and from Sun Bay, or to and from Red Beach. Rates run from $45 to $60 per room. They also have a cottage ($80) which can sleep four. It is, however, not for caninephobes: the Millers have a number of dogs. Offering 10 large rooms with kitchenettes, the **Crow's Nest** (☎ 741-0033) has a swimming pool, gazebo, bar and restaurant. A rec room has TV/VCR, games, and a library. Rates run around $60 pd d and $385 pw.

rentals: Connections (☎ 741-0023, 800-772-3050; fax 741-1228; Box 358, Vieques, PR 00765) is one major agency; it is located next to the Crow's Nest in Barrio Florida. They have an extensive list of rentals. Also contact **Island Vacations Rentals** (☎ 741-1666; Box 1508, Vieques, PR 00765), **Villa Estrella** (☎ 741-1228), **Laurel Real Estate** (☎ 741-6806; Box 1084, Vieques, PR 00765) or **Romero Real Estate** (☎ 741-8735; Box 1519, Vieques, PR 00765). Two-bedroom **Villa Vista Bella** (☎ 800-346-4205, 603-745-3365) sits atop a hill overlooking Isabel Segunda, with a panoramic view. It is completely furnished and has a pool. Write Tony McCann at the Kancamagus Motor Lodge, Pollard Road, Lincoln, New Hampshire 03251. Other listings are found under Esperanza.

FOOD: The **Wai Nam Restaurant** is in the Ocean View; it has lunch specials and is open daily, serving Chinese fast food, beer, and ice cream to the tune of salsa. Near the plaza, **Taverna Española** serves dishes such as *cazuela de mariscos* (seafood stew) and paella. Service can be slow. Right near the ferry, **Café Mar Azul** is a popular *gringo* hangout which has Mexican food on Sat. nights. **El Puerto** serves local food. Located above the fish shop ($2.75/lb.), **Johan's Bar & Restaurant** offers fresh fish, conch, and lobster. **The Green Palace** (seafood and daily specials) and **Willam's Pizza**, both on C. AG Mellado, serve pizza. In the Centro Comercial, **Nelson's Café** has burritos and tacos. In addition to catch of the day specials, **El Palomar** (☎ 741-8309) offers a special breakfast on Sun. Their reasonably priced dishes range from soups, salads, and focaccia for lunch to fish for dinner. Near the road to the airport, the a/c **Richard's Café** serves a variety of seafood dishes.

   near town: On the ocean at Playa Monte Santo to the W, the **Vieques Country Club** (☎ 741-1863) serves meat and seafood lunches and dinners in the open air. In Barrio Florida, the Crow's Nest has the **Spy Glass Bar & Restaurant** (☎ 741-0033), which dishes up three meals including dinner ($15 fixed price) plus Sunday brunch. Nearby, **The Galley** serves lunches daily; they specialize in pizza.

   bakeries and snacks: Panadería y Repostería Candy, C. AG Mellado 352, has breakfasts and sandwiches in addition to baked goods. Open daily from 5, **Panadería y Repostería Lydia**, C. Benitez Guzmán, also has sandwiches. Fenced in by a yellow railing, open-air **Coconuts** serves subs, large sandwiches, ice cream, and yogurt as well as breakfasts. The largest supermarket in town is **Supermercado Portela**, C. Baldorioty 15. **Supermercado Morales** is just outside town in Barrio Monte Santo.

SERVICES: Right inside the Alcadía (City Hall) on the main square, the **tourism department** (☎ 741-5000) has some information. Be sure to try and find a copy of *The Vieques Times* – a valuable resource. You might also try to find a copy of the *Vieques Visitors Guide,* which has some useful information. For taxis and tours contact **Vieques Tours** (☎ 741-8640). **Vieques Laundromat & Dry Cleaner** is on C. Victor Duteil. For your health care needs, **Grupo Médico Familiar del Este** (☎ 741-8569) is at C. Muñoz Rivera 112 and **Farmacia Libertad** and **Farmacia San Antonio** are on C. AG Mellado.

SHOPPING: Open from 9:30-1 Mon. to Sat., **Galería Isabela** is a small craft shop behind the PO. The **Second Time Around**, a thrift shop, sells Avon's Skin-so-Soft, an excellent sand flea and mosquito repellent, for $5/bottle. **Zona Tropical** sells reggae T-shirts. A flea market is held on the first Sun. of every month from noon-6 at

Coconuts (☎ 741-0033/1051) across from the Coliseum. The **Pelican Gift Shop** is on the Airport Rd. into town.

local specialties: While on the island, be sure to look out for the condiments made by the **Isla Vieques Condiment Company** (Box 1495, Vieques, PR 00765). They market their pepper sauce, jalapeño mango mustard, mountain herb sauce, and other spices and sauces for around $4/bottle. Another island product is the Miel Isla Niña ($7 for 2½ lbs.) produced by the Vieques Bee Farm.

ENTERTAINMENT: A popular watering hole, **Café Mar Azul** is set right on the ocean in town. For those craving a bit of blood and gore, **cockfighting** takes place at a mid-island arena, on Sun. afternoons during the winter months.

Esperanza

This is the island's second largest community. Taxis (around $3) meet arriving ferries. The 1963 film *Lord of the Flies* was filmed here; you can still see the hangar-like structure now incorporated into the grounds of a folded government-sponsored parador that remains. There's a *balneario* at Sunbe (Sun Bay) beach, a long, gorgeous stretch of palm trees and placid ocean. Hike to Navio and Media Luna beaches nearby. While Playa Media Luna has little surf and resembles a giant swimming pool, Playa Navio is a bit more turbulent. Although conditions here can be ideal for body surfing, the undertow is vicious so take care. One trail off of Media Luna goes to a cove with coral formations and a saltwater pond popular with seabirds. Crossing a promontory between Media Luna and Navio, another trail terminates at a boulder-strewn cliff with a great lookout point. Be sure to wear long pants on this trail or face the consequences.

There's also a dive shop and night excursions to the phosphorescent bay. The Vieques Historical and Conservation Trust (☎ 741-8850) operates the **Museo de Esperanza** here. Open Tues. through Sun. from 11-3, it features an archaeological exhibit as well as two aquariums. There's a gift shop, and their reforestation program distributes free trees.

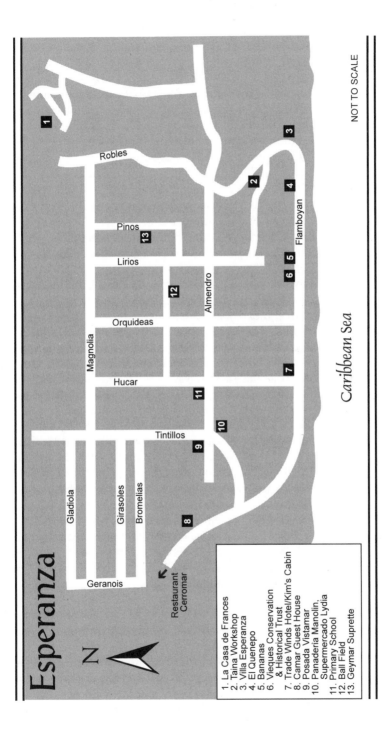

Esperanza

N

NOT TO SCALE

Caribbean Sea

Robles
Pinos
Lirios
Orquideas
Hucar
Tintillos
Flamboyan
Almendro
Magnolia
Gladiola
Girasoles
Bromelias
Geranois
Restaurant Cerromar

1. La Casa de Frances
2. Taina Workshop
3. Villa Esperanza
4. El Quenepo
5. Bananas
6. Vieques Conservation
   & Historical Trust
7. Trade Winds Hotel/Kim's Cabin
8. Camar Guest House
9. Posada Vistamar
10. Panaderia Manolin,
    Supermercado Lydia
11. Primary School
12. Ball Field
13. Geymar Suprette

ACCOMMODATIONS: It's possible to camp at the *balneario* at Sun Bay ($4 per tent). Note, however, that this beach is notorious for thieves – *never* leave anything unattended. **Posada Vistamar** (☎ 741-8716; Box 495, Vieques, PR 00765) has small rooms for around $40/d; a larger one is $45 d. **Banana's** (☎ 741-8700; Box 1300, Vieques, PR 00765) is another small guesthouse with an attached restaurant. Rooms have a/c or fans. Rates run from $40-$60 pd. **El Quenepo** (☎ 741-8541), C. Flamboyán, has four rooms with private baths, $30 and $40 (with a/c). The **Camar Guesthouse** (☎ 741-8604) has rooms, and also offers billiards and video games. The **Trade Winds Guesthouse** (☎ 741-8666; Box 1012, Vieques, PR 00765) has rooms from $35 on up and $3 breakfast specials. It has been recommended by readers. Set in an old plantation house which is a historical monument, **La Casa del Frances** (☎ 741-3751, fax 741-2330; Box 458, Vieques, PR 00765), on Carr. 996, has 18 rooms, a private pool, and restaurant. **La Piña Vacation Apartments** (☎/fax 741-2953; C. Acacia 222, Vieques, PR 00765) is another alternative. Inexpensive but spartan **Betty's Guest House** is behind Bananas. The **Esperanza Guest House and Cafeteria** (☎ 741-8722/2294; Box 204, Vieques, PR 00765) has three rooms (holding up to three persons each) for around $25. Nicknamed the **Chateau Relaxo**, a house at the corner of C. Magnolia and C. Robles offers rooms for around $50/wk. The owners also sell fish downstairs and cut hair. The "Italian Villa" on the water is being transformed and may have opened by your arrival. Currently bankrupt and closed, the Villa Esperanza has 50 rooms with private bath and ceiling fans, restaurant, swimming pool, tennis court, and a volleyball court. It will probably reopen sometime in the future in a new incarnation. Sandwiched between La Hueca and Esperanza, the **Inn on the Blue Horizon** (☎ 741-3318; Box 1556, Vieques, PR 00765) has a pool and offers massages. **rentals:** Contact **New Dawn** (☎ 741-0495; Box 1512, Vieques, PR 00765), **Marcos** (☎ 741-1388), or **Vieques Villa Rentals** (☎ 741-8888; C. Gladiolas 494). The latter has a wide variety of rentals ranging from coastal homes to ones commanding views from the inland heights.

FOOD: The **Villa Posada Parador** has delicious, authentic Puerto Rican dishes (like fish *asopao*). Fresh, piping-hot traditional Puerto Rican bread is available early mornings at **Gerena Bakery**. **Colmado Lydia**, next door, is well stocked with provisions. There are a number of food trucks here with local dishes. **The Esperanza** (☎ 741-8675) serves three meals daily and offers special activities such as a Wed. cookout and a Thurs. hermit crab race. **Kathleen's**

serves dishes such as falafel, *quesadillas,* and conch fritters daily from noon-5. Open from 11-9, **La Central** serves snacks such as *pastelillos* and pizza. **El Quenepo** (☎ 741-8541) serves seafood and Puerto Rican dishes. The **Trade Winds** has a restaurant that offers seafood dishes and fresh fruit. **Bananas** has good food in a terrace atmosphere. **Comidas China,** a greasy spoon on the main drag, has dishes like Chicken Cordon Bleu. Here, you can eat in the "dinning hall" and have ice cream in flavors such as "chery-vainilla." Other places to eat include **La Concha** and **El Gringo Viejo.** Set on the hillside of La Huce two miles W of Esperanza, **La Campesina** (☎ 741-1239) is open 6:30-9:30 from Wed. to Sun.

SERVICES: Dive shops include **18 Degrees North** and **Blue Caribe Dive Shop** (☎ 741-2522, fax 741-1313; Box 1574, Vieques, PR 00765). Blue Caribe also rents kayaks. **Caribbean Kites** (☎ 741-3260) offers a wide variety and also sells darts. Bike rentals are available for $10 pd from Inn on the Blue Horizon, or from **Don't Yank My Chain Bike Rental** (☎ 741-3042). Zoraida Morales (☎ 741-6031), C. Magnolias 425, offers **babysitting** services.

EXCURSIONS: Sharon (☎ 741-3751) has trips to the phosphorscent bay on *La Luminosa,* an electric launch. Other trips are offered by **Craig** (☎ 741-8675) and **Casey** (☎ 741-8542). Moonless nights are best. Offering day sails and moonlight cruises, the *Arawak* (☎ 741-8675) is based in Esperanza.

ENTERTAINMENT: Eddie's is on C. Flamboyan at Orquidea. **El Trapezon Oriental** has lots of flashing lights, chicken wire, and neon Budweiser signs. It has live music, which starts late.

SHOPPING: La Copa de Oro is next to the tennis courts. **The Mall** is at Casa de Frances. Behind **Kim's Cabin** which offers clothing and other items, **Peppers** has spicy condiments as well as crafts. Near Esperanza across from the pineapple factory, **Taller de Arte Taína** (☎ 741-0848) is a women's pottery workshop that recreates indigenous-style pieces. Constructing handmade works using the tried-and-true coil method, it has operated since 1991.

NEW DAWN

A spacious, fully furnished six-bedroom guesthouse set on five acres of land in the Pilón area, the **New Dawn Caribbean Retreat**

Northeastern Puerto Rico

& Guest House (☎ 741-0495; Box 1512, Vieques, PR 00765) is set on a hillside three miles from the nearest beach. Run by outgoing adventurer Gail Burchard, it caters to women and groups, but all are welcome. Simple and very practical in its construction, one of the nicest things about the house is its integration with nature. Small lizards come right in to visit you and birds nest by the porch. At night you have the 360° orchestral symphony of nature surrounding you. The sunrises here are spectacular; you truly wake up to a new dawn, feeling fresh and invigorated. Rather than being in a retreat, you feel more revitalized and connected with nature and with yourself.

The first floor consists of a kitchen, dining, and patio/living area. A bar/restaurant is open Dec. 15-May 14; the communal kitchen is shared off-season. There's a comfortable hammock and chairs and tables on the porch, a completely equipped large kitchen (refrigerators, microwave, range, oven, spices), washing machine, TV/VCR, a library, stereo, and large bulletin boards. Each room has a loft and queen-sized bed. The rent (May 15-Dec. 15) is $1,100 pw. Price includes utilities and caretakers. Cleaning is additional. Other rentals include a bunkhouse (sleeps six; only available if renting main house as well) and a three-bedroom house in Esperanza which is fully-equipped and near the beach. Household help and cooks are also available for hire as "island resource guides." Solar-heated showers and hammocks are available. Individual rooms ($40 s, $50 d) are also available as are bunkhouse beds for women ($18 pp) and tent spaces ($10).

FROM VIEQUES: There is no service to Culebra; you must return to Fajardo first. Ferries to Fajardo run from Mon. to Fri. at 7 and 3 and on Sat. and Sun. at 7, 1, and 4:30. For information ☎ 741-4761.

by air: Vieques Air Link (☎ 741-8331/8211) flies to Fajardo, St. Croix, and to San Juan.

Culebra

Set 22 miles to the E of Fajardo across a blue expanse of sea, this miniature archipelago consists of the seven-by-four-mile island of Culebra along with 23 other islands, cays, and rocks. This area still remains relatively unspoiled and set apart from the world. Much of its land, which includes dry scrub and mangrove swamps, has been designated a National Wildlife Refuge. Today, Culebra largely remains a neglected and forgotten backwater, to the point where it is sometimes maintained that the island is Puerto Rico's stepchild. The lack of rainfall not only ensures good weather but has the secondary effect of causing low sedimentation – thus producing healthy coral reefs and remarkably clear water.

Aside from tourism, the only business here is the R.D. Medical plant, which makes medical tubing for blood transfusions and injections. There's not much for a visitor to do except ponder what to eat next and which beach to go to. These are likely the biggest decisions you'll have to make during the day. The climate and easygoing atmosphere have attracted a large number of mainlanders, some of whom appear to be apt candidates for leading characters in a future Ann Tyler novel. Perspectives on life held by residents are best represented by their cars' bumper stickers, which run the gamut from "Support the Marines" to "I get my energy from the sun." Culebrans also express their sentiments by writing on boulders such sentiments as "CRISTO VIENE PRONTO. REPIENTENTE!"

The one thing that definitely binds both local and indigenous *culebrense* alike is that all smoke like chimneys from the time they are teenagers. The island is getting to be a busier place, and the *El Conquistador* is now ferrying visitors over for day trips.

GETTING HERE: The cheapest and best method is to take a *público* from the terminal in Río Piedras to the dock at Fajardo (You may have to change in the town to a car marked *playa*). Then board the ferry, which takes a scenic two hours to Dewey on Culebra. On the way, you pass Isla Marina to your R and Palomino and Icacos to your L; you can also see Cayo Bola de Funcé (Corn Flour Bowl) off in the distance. If you wish to bring your car, note that cars are not permitted on the ferry on weekends, so make plans accordingly. If the weather is good, the trip is remarkably beautiful. However, if seas are rough, it's soaking salt spray and barf bags galore. If the ocean appears to be rough, grab a seat downstairs, unless you relish getting soaked to your skin by salt spray. For ferry times, ☎ 742-3161. An alternative is the short flight with Flamenco (☎ 725-8110/7707 in San Juan, 863-3366 in Fajardo) from San Juan's Isla Grande Airport or with Carib (☎ 791-4115 in San Juan, 800-981-0212, fax 791-4115).

Northeastern Puerto Rico

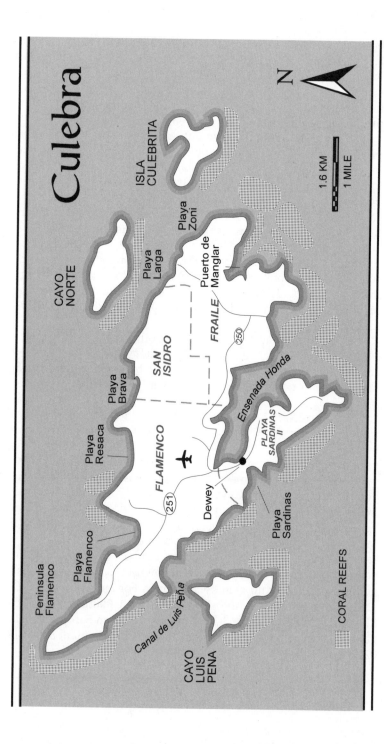

Culebra

N

ISLA
CULEBRITA

CAYO
NORTE

Playa
Zoni

Playa
Larga

Puerto de
Manglar

SAN
ISIDRO

FRAILE

Playa
Brava

Playa
Resaca

250

FLAMENCO

Ensenada Honda

251

*PLAYA
SARDINAS
II*

Dewey

Playa
Flamenco

Peninsula
Flamenco

Canal de Luis Peña

Playa
Sardinas

CAYO
LUIS
PENA

CORAL REEFS

1.6 KM

1 MILE

WHO SHOULD COME: Snorkelers will find great opportunities in the area, as will birdwatchers and hikers. It's not a place to come to if you're in a rush, nor is there much here to entertain children. It's not inexpensive, and there are no truly low budget accommodations, but the island provides value for money in terms of overall low-key ambiance. It isn't for people who wish to be catered to or who need all of the conveniences. Most of the hotels are fairly basic.

☞ **Traveler's Tip.** While many Culebrans can speak English, they will appreciate it if you try to speak Spanish with them. Remember that the island is no place for yuppies or those looking for nightlife and resort-style accommodation.

HISTORY: Under Spanish rule, Culebra and surrounding islands were designated as Crown lands. Transfer to the US in 1898 specified that these lands be used for their "highest and best use." Accordingly, an executive order Roosevelt signed in 1903 surrendered the lands to Navy control. Eight years later, Roosevelt, after reconsidering the matter, ordered that the lands serve the secondary purpose of a preserve and breeding ground for native seabirds. In 1936, the Navy (perhaps assuming noise improves fertility among nesting seabirds) began strafing and bombarding Culebra and surrounding islands. Despite long years of protest, both by locals *and* by the commonwealth government, the pigheaded military continued playing with their toys. The Culebra Committee, sponsored by the PIP in coalition with the American Friends Action Group, had constructed a chapel on Flamingo Beach. In 1975, the Navy discontinued firing. Since 1975, the local population has swelled to approximately 1,600. The island is gaining attention for its tourist potential, and the number of visitors is growing. The island was hit by 1996's Hurricane Marilyn (some 50 homes were destroyed and 200 more were severely damaged) but has nearly fully recovered.

FLORA AND FAUNA: The Culebra group has a huge sea bird population; several species have developed large breeding colonies on Flamenco Peninsula and surrounding offshore cays. Of the more than 85 species, the most numerous is the sooty tern, which arrives to nest between May and October. The sooty tern's eggs are highly prized by local poachers; they mainly breed on Cayo de Agua and Cayo Yerba off Culebra's W side. There are four other species of terns, three of boobies, the laughing gull, Caribbean

Northeastern Puerto Rico

martin, osprey, and other birds. Brown pelicans, an endangered species, live in the mangrove trees surrounding Puerto de Manglar on Culebra's E side. Small herds of cattle stroll amid the bombed wrecks of army tanks. The seldom-seen Culebra giant anole (a huge lizard), resides in the forested areas of Mount Resaca. Four species of sea turtles breed on Culebra's and Culebrita's beaches: the Atlantic loggerhead and green sea turtles, the hawksbill, and the leatherback. Leatherbacks may reach a length of 6½ ft (two m) and weigh up to 500 kg. These turtles have been exiled from one Caribbean beach to another by poachers and developers. Here too, despite the threat of stiff penalties under the Endangered Species Act, local poachers value the eggs as a protein source and an aphrodisiac. They nest from March to June.

As part of a well-developed, interdependent ecosystem, Culebra's flora is inseparable from its fauna. Mangrove forests surrounding the coasts provide a roosting ground for birds above the water while sheltering sea anemones, sponges, and schools of small fish among the tangle of stiltlike roots in the shallow water. Nearly 80% of Culebra's coastline is bordered by young and old coral reefs. Multicolored miniature mountain ranges of brain, finger, elkhorn, and fire corals shelter equally colorful and numerous schools of tropical fish.

ENVIRONMENTAL PROBLEMS: Unfortunately, increased touristic interest in Culebra is having deleterious effects. The island is battling to maintain its ambiance in the face of Mammon and his money. Enforcement of zoning regulations has been lax. One example is the Culebra Beach Resort, which has built a fourth floor, one floor higher than is permitted by rural building codes. In addition, eight houses have been constructed illegally by squatters along Ensenada Honda, the island's principal bay. The last land survey was done by the Spaniards in 1887 and is very inaccurate, which makes prosecution difficult. As there is no sewage system, much of it goes into the water. Two federal agencies have agreed to pay 75% of the $9 million cost of constructing a sewer system; the remaining funds will be loaned by the Aqueduct and Sewer Authority. Beach sand has been removed and roads illegally constructed. Turtles have vanished from Playa Tortuga on Isla Culebrita, victims of the dearth of sea grass, which has been killed off by boat propellors and anchors. In addition, fishermen have been illegally net fishing in turtle nesting grounds. The endangered West Indies whistling duck has disappeared from Laguna Flamenco.

BEACHES: The island's most famous beach is **Playa Flamenco**, a long stretch of beautiful sand which has only one hotel along its shores. On a weekday, this beach is wonderfully peaceful. As it's somewhat isolated, be sure to bring everything you need. Two wrecked tanks serve as reminders of the military occupation, as do a hilltop observation post and a set of stone piers on the E end. The calmest areas are to the L, and it's rather like being in a gargantuan shallow saltwater swimming pool. This long and lovely beach was temporarily closed to camping in 1993 because too many main islanders were coming here, drinking and using drugs, and getting bombed out of their skulls. The rumor mill had it that the last straw came when a prominent judge's 14-year old daughter was raped. Currently, you may camp on the beach but fees are $10 per tent, per day. It's a long walk from town, but there's irregular *público* service ($1.50) available. From the beach, you may head to the L on foot to reach Negro and Blanco beaches or head up the trail in back of the parking lot to reach several rough beaches with good snorkeling. To get to Flamenco from town you must turn L at the airport; you will pass the Ferretería González hardware store en route.

Visiting **Playa Resaca** is a true adventure. To get here you must hike a long way down through thorny brush. The only time this path is clear is during turtle nesting season, which is also when you aren't supposed to visit. It can be difficult to find your way toward the end. After emerging in a mangrove forest, a path leads down to the magnificent beach, which is generally deserted and without shade. It's like a tourist brochure, but without the hotel. Along the way you might see a hermit crab, a snake slither by, or a land crab. Be sure to bring a good supply of water, as none is available. Good shoes and long pants are strongly recommended. Allow about an hour to hike up the road to the starting point (unless you have a vehicle) and about half an hour down.

Playa La Brava (meaning "rough") is called that because of its continual heavy surf. To get here head out of town on Carr. 250; watch for the Km 4 marker and then turn L after you pass the cemetery. Park near the gate (around a mile further) and then walk. Both Brava and Resaca are leatherback turtle nesting beaches, and development on either would spell the end of the species on Culebra; even a small light can confuse hatchlings, who head into it instead of towards the sea. They may stumble into one of your footprints in the sand and become trapped. The road from the cemetery heads out here.

The main road on the island terminates near **Playa Zoni**, an important turtle nesting beach. This is a spectacular drive along an extremely bad road. From the road's end you can see St. Thomas. Offshore, there's good snorkeling, and you may hike up the N coast from this point as well.

Melones, a point rather than a beach, is well suited for snorkeling, fishing, and sunset photography. To get here take the road towards the hospital from town, pass the **Felipe Serrano Center**, and park before the hill leading to a private development.

Soldado, a stony beach best suited for snorkeling, is on the S side. Cross the bridge and head L until the end of the road, where you must hike in. Head to the R down the hill; the best snorkeling is to the SE (to your left); the majority of the reef is under 10-30 ft of water. Other beaches are on Luis Peña and Culebrita (see below under "Culebrita").

☞ **Traveler's Tip.** Visitors on Culebra may help out with nightly turtle watches from late Feb. until late July by calling Julian Howell (☎ 742-0057). In order to avoid harming turtle hatching, do not drive on the beaches or visit them during May, June, and July. Walking at the water's edge or near the trees will also help prevent any potential damage.

OTHER SIGHTS: Right in town is a drawbridge. Constructed by English engineers, it was designed to allow passage for two fishing boats. These boats have disappeared from the area, as the water is so shallow it only allows the passage of small motorboats. The bridge is useless and remains undrawn; indeed, it should never have been built. Another fiasco is **Cayo Pirata**, so named because it provided shelter to pirate ships, which was supposed to have been turned into a museum. The local government managed to run out of money before the project was completed, and it currently has some picnic tables that are accessible only if you have your own boat. It is used once or twice a year for a government party. As any visitor will soon learn, both God and the Puerto Rican government work in mysterious ways. Near Casa Llave and on the way to the airport, a house displays a wild lawn filled with coral lawn ornaments, painted tires, bombshells, and plastic black gorillas. A couple of miles out of town you come to the noisy desalinization plant to the R. Outside of town and back on the main road to the E at Barrio Los Frailes, the sole remaining structure from the **Antiguo Pueblo de Culebra** dates from 1889. It's currently closed and is not particularly impressive. Continuing on the same road you come to the Recursos Naturales. Further down, you pass mangroves with lots of birds. Epiphytes grow out of cacti, and you'll pass rusty barbed wire fences, dildo cacti, and Brahman bulls grazing.

DIVE SITES: At a depth of 14-45 ft, the reef called the **Impact Area** has a wide variety of fish as well as large sea fans. The 50-ft **Arch Dive** visits gigantic arch-shaped coral-covered boulders that host schools of gloriously colored fish. At 65 ft, the **Amberjack Hole** has an enormous boulder often saturated with colorful fish. An open water dive ranging from 50-75 ft, **Anchor Reef** was once used by the Navy as an anchorage. Artifacts to be found here range from an anchor and chain to a number of old bottles. There's good **snorkeling** at Punta Molinas at the NW and at Punta del Soldado to the S.

SNORKELING SPOTS IN CULEBRA

The west coast beaches are superior as they are coral and not sand.

❑ **Soldier's Point.** On the island's S tip, it may be reached by jeep or by boat. Snorkel here in the 15 ft-deep water along the S side of the bay at the road's end.

❑ **Melones.** Closest beach to town. Coral heads are found under 8-10 ft of water. Best snorkeling is found at end of beach. As you will see, the best-preserved coral is out of the beach's center. Reason for this is misuse by humans.

❑ **Tamarindo.** Take the road by the dump. Coral heads are found under 8-10 ft of water.

❑ **Carlos Rosario.** Near Flamingo and reachable on foot (or four-wheel-drive) from there. May also be reached by boat.

❑ **Playa Larga.** Good snorkeling. May still be blocked off by a gate (an illegal action).

❑ **Playa Zoni.** A remote snorkeling beach on the E end.

GETTING AROUND: In town, no spot is too far to walk. If you're staying outside of town, you may want to have a car ($45 pd) to get around. (You may ask your hotel to arrange a rental in advance). However, your feet or a bicycle can still take you to a lot of places. A *público* runs between the town, the airport, and Playa Flamingo. If you don't hitch or bike, you'll want to rent a vehicle for at least

Northeastern Puerto Rico

If you don't hitch or bike, you'll want to rent a vehicle for at least one day during your stay. To get to Culebrita or Luis Peña you'll need to charter a boat, which will run about $40 pp RT to Culebrita and $20 pp RT to Luis Peña.

> ☞ **Traveler's Tip.** Culebran beaches often offer little shade, so be sure to bring some cover-up clothes with you. Although the island is small, it can take a while to get places so allow at least a day to tour the island.

Dewey

When the Navy moved onto Culebra in 1903, locals living in settlements scattered all over the island were forcibly resettled in the newly created town of Dewey (or Puebla), built on what had formerly been a swamp. This small town has five *colmados* (grocery stores) and a couple of hardware stores. There're no movie theaters or (thankfully) video arcades. Dewey might best be characterized as an architectural hodgepodge. A clean, cutesy little Caribbean town filled with frilly white and pastel Victorians it is not. Some homes have been built over the water. Everything and anything can be called a "Villa" (or even a "Vlla"!), from a shack on up to a mansion. The only times the town comes to life are during the *fiestas patronales* of La Virgen del Carmen on July 17, Holy Week, and New Year's. Otherwise, the best entertainment is to be found at the local courthouse, where lawsuits may center around an inopportune sneeze by a visiting roof repairman or a dispute over moving a rock. Bring your mask and snorkel because the *real* life is under the water. A pair of binoculars will also come in handy for viewing bird life.

ACCOMMODATIONS: All hotels generally offer free airport pickup and delivery. There are no large hotels here as of yet, but none of the hotels are particularly cheap for what you get. For help with accommodations see Culebra Connection under "information" below. Set next to the drawbridge and convenient to town, **Posada la Hamaca**, C. Castelar 68 (☎ 742-3516; Box 338, Culebra, PR 00775) is an attractive Spanish-style nine-room inn. Rates run about $55/night for rooms and $65/night for efficiencies plus tax; weekly discounts are available.

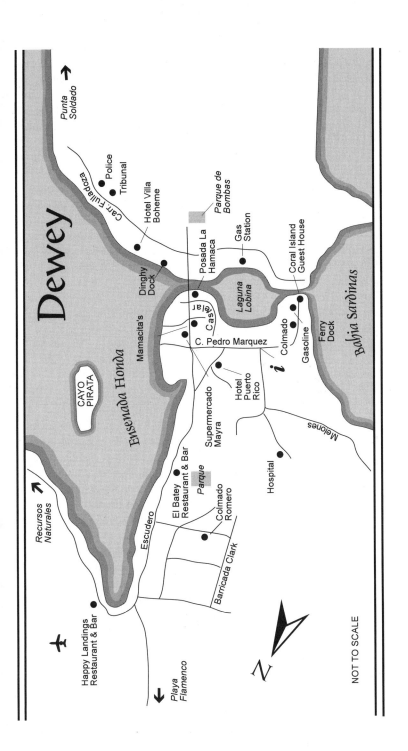

Attractive and a/c with balconies, **Mamacitas Guest House** (☎ 742-0090; Box 818, Culebra, PR 00775) has three small apartments. Rates are around $45-50 d and $65 for a room with a kitchen (holds three); if you pay for six nights, the seventh is on the house.

Set off of C. Escudero, **Casa Llave** (☎ 742-3559; Box 60, Culebra, PR 00775-0060) offers two rooms: a bedroom ($45 d with a/c and fan plus breakfast) and a studio (with a/c, fan and kitchenette for $60 pn or $350 pw). Each has an independent entrance, and there's a terrace and private dock in back. Older guests will feel most comfortable here. Right next to the ferry pier, the **Coral Island Guest House** (☎ 742-3177; Box 396, Culebra, PR 00775) has simple rooms and a shared kitchen. It is quite convenient if taking an early morning ferry, but luxury accommodation it is not. Prices run from $35 s, $40 d, and $75 quad. Less-expensive weekly rates are available. Also relatively near the pier and just off C. Tacita, the **Hotel Puerto Rico** (☎ 742-3372) is a true Caribbean classic; rooms rent for around $27 s and $38 d. For long term (around $100 pw), the **Jim y Mary Guesthouse** (☎ 742-3544) rents basic rooms out to men.

Overlooking the Bahía de Sardinas, **Harbour View Villas** (☎ 742-3855/3171, 800-440-0070; Box 216, Culebra, PR 00775) are completely furnished. There's a kitchen in each of the truncated A-frame-style units. Individual rooms may also be available. Rates are around $95 d; the "suite" (a unit with mini-kitchen and balcony) is $75. Extra adults are $15 each. **Villa Boheme** (Ensenada Honda, ☎ 742-3508) charges around $75. Facilities include use of kitchen. Renting efficiency apartments for a couple or a family of four, tranquil **Villa Fulladoza** (☎/fax 742-3756; Box 162, Culebra, PR 00775-0162) charges from $40-$60 per room. A phone and washing machine are available for use. Offering reasonably attractive villas that accommodate from two to eight people, **Villa Cielo y Mar** (☎ 742-3167; Box 292, Culebra, PR 00775) is located a mile from town and has private docks. **Tamarindo Estates** (☎ 742-3342/3343; Box 313, Culebra, PR 00775), with fully equipped a/c apartments way out at Playa Tamarindo off the road to Playa Flamingo, is another alternative. They have a pool and restaurant. You'll need a jeep if staying here. With two attractive attached cottages, the **Culebra School of Sailing** (☎ 742-3136) is seated above a private beach on the N side of Ensenada Honda within driving distance of Zoni; it's reached by a dirt road. Despite the name, you don't have to be in the "sailing school" to stay here. The studio-sized Coral Cottage rents for $50 pn with breakfast. The companion Cockatoo House ($75) has an attached living room.

BARRICADA CLARK ACCOMMODATIONS: Offering fully equipped apartments, the **Family Guest House** (☎ 742-3536) is often full with long-term tenants. Lacking a kitchen but offering a good view, **Tropical Garden Cottages** (☎ 742-3581/1922) is also nearby. **Tochi's La Vida Cottages** (☎ 742-3271; Box 606, Culebra, PR 00775) offers completely equipped cottages priced at around $45-$55 pn. Yoga classes are held here.

TOWARD PUNTA SOLDADO: Club Seabourne (☎ 742-3169, fax 742-3176; Box 357, Culebra, PR 00775) is the island's most deluxe accommodation; they have four rooms (from $65) as well as eight small villas ($110 d), a "Crow's Nest" ($110 d), and two cottages ($100 d). The last can house up to four for an additional surcharge of $15 pp above the double occupancy rate. The "club" also has a screened dining room, a pool, and a lounge/library. Rental yacht moorings are also available. Rates include airport pickup/drop-off and a continental breakfast; tax is additional.

PUNTA ALOE ACCOMMODATIONS: This area is also to the S of town. **Bayview Villas** (☎ 742-3392, 765-5711; Box 775, Culebra, PR 07775), a set of two 1,500-sq-ft villas, rent for $900 and $1,000 each out of season and for $1,000 and $1,200 each in season. The very attractive villas come fully equipped and sleep up to six. They each have a living/dining/sleeping area, phone, washing machine, and ceiling fans; attention is personal. They overlook the bay. **Culebra Island Villas** (☎ 742-0333; Box 596, Culebra, PR 07775; e-mail, 74743.364@compuserve.com) has fully-equipped houses that can handle up to six. Also here, **Villa Arynar** (☎ 742-3145; Box 744, Culebra, PR 00775-0744) is run by a retired Naval commander and his wife. Overlooking the water, one of the two bedrooms available has a balcony. There's a common room with refrigerator, books, and games. Rates start from $60 daily; reduced weekly rate is available. Packages are available, as are boat trips.

CAMPING: Camping is now available at Playa Flamingo for a charge of $10 pd, per tent. Keep in mind that the beach is remote from town, so you should try to bring as much as possible of what you need.

FOOD: Serving both breakfast and lunch, **Mamacitas** offers Puerto Rican and other Caribbean cuisine including fish steaks and pasta dishes. Vegetarian burritos are $3. A popular hangout for expats, **Chuck's Pizza** has Italian food including whole pizza pies ($6) and slices ($1.25), and eggplant parmesan. Near the canal, The **Dingy Dock** offers three meals daily (as well as daily specials) in an attractive setting. It has some specials. En route to the Fisherman's Cooperative, **El Edén** serves good local food; they also sell fresh baked baguettes. Set next to the PO, the **Culebra Deli** has sandwiches, hamburgers and other greasy fare, as well as ice cream. **Restaurante El Pesquerito** is near the canal. It's open daily from 8-4:30. Sandwiches and seafood dishes are available for lunch. **Café Galeria** is a gourmet restaurant across from the ferry dock.

out of town: On the road to Flamingo but not too far from the town center, **El Batey** (open Tues. to Sun. from 8-2) serves sandwiches (around $3) and lunch. If you wish to experience classic Puerto Rican greasy-spoon ambiance, **Tina's** (formally known as El Ceibo), reached by making the first L after El Batey, serves traditional, fattening Puerto Rican food platters. The absolutely unforgettable decor includes advertisements with girls in swimsuits, posters of jogging teddy bears, a photo of an egg-laying turtle, and plastic chairs – some of which have Good Housekeeping seals. At the airport, popular, and serving chiefly Puerto Rican food, the wonderfully named **Happy Landing** serves three meals daily. Other restaurants include **Maria's Deli**, and the more deluxe **Club Seabourne,** which offers gourmet dishes.

FOOD SHOPPING: As everything is imported and no fare discounts are given to trucks bringing in food on the ferry, prices are quite high. There are two food trucks that sell veggies, eggs, and the like near the dock. One usually sells on Tues. PM (by the Dinghy Dock, 6 PM) and Wed. AM (by the PO, 6-noon). Fishermen sell from the fishing dock at around 11 or so. You can try at the cooperative and see if they have any fish. In town, you can shop at **Suprette Mayra** (right near Mamacitas), **Colmado Esperanza**, and **Marco's Grocery**. Out of town is **Colmado Romero**. It carries the best selection of traditional mainland US supermarket items. In Barricada Clark, the **Vietnam Grocery** has good prices.

INFORMATION: Unless you're only staying for a night or so and want to be near the ferry, it's definitely preferable to stay out of town where you can really feel the breeze and see the stars. If you're looking for a place to rent on Culebra or just want a hotel that suits your needs, the person to talk to is Katherine West at **The Culebra Connection**, (☎ 742-3112; Box 509, Culebra, PR 00775). Affable Kathy will find the place for you. There's no charge to you. A small **information service** (☎ 742-3291; 9-noon and 1-3 weekdays) operates inside City Hall which is up on a hill overlooking the piers. A taciturn lady hands out a tourist guide and other information. For additional information on the island (including details on temporary rentals) write them at Box 189, Culebra, PR 00775. For information on visiting the Culebra National Wildlife Refuge, you can call 742-0115 or write in advance to Refuge Manager, Lower Camp, Fish and Wildlife Service, Box 190, Culebra, PR 00775-0190. Camping is currently prohibited on the island's beaches.

☞ **Traveler's Tip**. Keep an eye out for *The Culebra Calendar* (☎/fax 742-0079; e-mail, 76763.3420@compuserve.com; Box 761, Culebra, PR 00775), an informative bilingual monthly with a lot of useful information. It serves as a good introduction to the island. A copy through the mail may be had for $2 postpaid.

SERVICES: The **Post Office** is just around to the L from the pier and pay phones are just past it. The *San Juan Star* is available at the Paradise Gift Shop next to Mamacita's. Located out of town, **Casa Violeta** (☎ 742-1983) offers massage and sauna. Gasoline stations are **Garaje Ricky** (next to Coral Island Guest House) and **Gasolinera Villa Pesquera**, which is next to the fish market. **health:** A health clinic operates behind the City Hall. There is no pharmacy. Myrna Rodriquez (☎ 800-981-8124) offers Swedish and shiatsu massages.

MONEY: There is no ATH (instant teller machine) on the island as of yet. Some small hotels accept credit cards (a 5% surcharge may apply); others do not. You can draw a cash advance against your Mastercard or Visa at the **Banco Roig**; it's open 8:30-1 on Mon. and from Wed. to Fri. and from 8:30-noon on Sat.

CAR RENTALS: Unless you're staying in the boonies, it isn't really necessary to rent a car because of the island's small size. It's also expensive – around $45/day to rent a jeep. Contact **Culebra Car Rental** (☎ 742-3277), **Dick & Cathy** (☎ 742-0062), **Joe** (☎ 742-0587), **Kathy** (☎ 742-3112), **Prestige** (☎ 742-3242), **Randy** (☎ 742-3508), **Seaside Rentals** (☎ 742-3855), or **William Solis** (☎ 742-3537). Gas (around $1.65/gallon) is sold at the Fisherman's Cooperative's dock and at Garaje Ricky (see "Services," above).

BICYCLES: Because cars are so few and the topography so flat, cycling is an excellent way to see the island. Contact **Dick & Cathy** (☎ 742-0062).

Northeastern Puerto Rico

WATER SPORTS AND EXCURSIONS: The **Paradise** (☎ 742-0328) offers day sails for around $40 pp. The **School of Sailing** (☎ 742-3136) offers sailing lessons; around $200 for a four-day course. **Villas Arynar** (☎ 742-3145) offers turtle watching and outboard excursions for around $30-35 pp. **Druso Daubon** (☎ 440-0070) rents his 13-ft Boston Whaler for $75 pd. **Muff: The Magic Fun Boat** (☎ 742-3516) has water taxi services as well as snorkeling. Gene Thomas's **Caribbean Marine Services** (☎ 742-3555, fax 742-0036; Box 467, Culebra, PR 00775) offers snorkeling as well as dive courses (around $350) and dives (from $40) aboard his *Spanish Dancer*. It's quite popular and highly regarded. With offices in Mamacitas Restaurant, **Lana** charges $15/hour for a two-hour glass bottom boat trip. **Jim Peterson** rents kayaks for $25/half-day and $40/full day. **Culebra Marine Services** (☎ 742-3371) is in Barrio Sardinas. The **Sea Turtle** (☎ 742-0591) has snorkeling excursions and runs water taxis. The *Barefoot Contessa* (☎ 378-8908) will also take you out. **Tamaná** (☎ 413-0325: cellular) offers snorkeling, water taxi trips, and glass bottom boat rides. *Quarante "40"* (☎ 742-3569) has day sails and offers sailing lessons.

NIGHTLIFE: If this forms an important part of your vacation, you've come to the wrong place! Things are quiet at night, to say the least. The evangelical church hosts domino games on Thurs. nights, and you can watch the police drive around with their blue lights flashing as though to give thieves a chance to escape. Hoops are played at the court next to El Batey's at night. **Happy Landings** has dancing on Fri. and **El Batey** has the same on Sat.

SHOPPING: If you want to shop seriously, you should go to St. Thomas or do it in San Juan. There are a few alternatives, however. **Paradise Gift Shop**, **Mamacita's**, and **La Loma** are some of your shopping alternatives. **Ramona's Fashions** is next to Chuck's Pizza. **Liz Rivera** (☎ 742-2642) shows some of her woven art and sculpture by appointment. **Dave Moses** (☎ 742-3397) makes tin fish and will open his studio by appointment.

CULEBRA NATIONAL WILDLIFE RESERVE

One of more than 400 wildlife refuges administered by the US Fish and Wildlife Service, the Culebra Refuge covers some 1,480 acres, which includes four tracts on Culebra itself as well as 23 islands and rocks. It was established by Franklin Roosevelt in 1909 and is one of the oldest refuges in the entire system. Although ornithologists had surveyed the archipelago's birds early in the US occupation, the wide variety of nesting seabirds in the area became known only in 1971. The offshore islands (with the exception of Cayo Norte) were added in 1975 upon the Navy's departure. An additional 776 acres were transferred from the Navy in 1982. For information on wildlife, see "flora and fauna" earlier in this chapter.

regulations: Stay on existing roads and trails. In the unlikely event that you should come upon any ordnance, do not approach or disturb it; remember that hands and feet can be useful appendages. Do not hunt or molest any animals nor collect any living or dead coral or plant material. Do not litter, bring in pets, firearms, a car, or start a fire.

Culebrita

This lovely cay can be reached only by fishing boat or private yacht. Its century-old (1880) abandoned stone lighthouse overlooks a large bay and lagoon. Along with neighboring **Luis Peña Cay** (named after its second owner) to the W, it is a wildlife refuge site open to the public for daytime use. Other cays require special use permits available from the Fish and Wildlife Service, Box 510, Boquerón, PR 00622. A 1980 plan, now discarded, would have transferred ownership to the Puerto Rican government so that the island could have been converted to recreational use, a move which would have been ecologically disastrous. Luis Peña has a number of sandy beaches; a wonderful coral reef lies off its SW shore. On Culebrita, be sure to hike up to the lighthouse (tremendous views) and visit the area known as the "baths," a collection of huge boulders that entrap small pools.

flora and fauna: Heavily covered with vegetation including gumbo-limbo trees, frangipani, and bromeliads, the island provides haven for many rare and endangered species of animals and birds. Masked boobys, red-footed boobys, and brown boobys are found here. Red-billed tropic birds live in cliffs along the island's E shore, while mangrove swamps are home to birds and marinelife.

Northeastern Puerto Rico

THE OTHER RESERVE AREAS

An important nesting site for sooty terns, **Flamenco Peninsula** may be explored on foot. A special use permit is required to visit here. Protecting one of Culebra's remaining tracts of dry subtropical forest, the **Mount Resaca Unit** includes boulder-covered areas that host cupey and jaguey trees. Orchids and bromeliads cover the boulders. Providing a special habitat that fosters marine life (see "mangroves" in the Flora and Fauna section of the Introduction), the mangrove areas at **Ensenada Honda Unit** and **Puerto Manglar Unit** form a vital link in the conservation chain. Puerto Manglar's mangroves provide a roosting area for the endangered brown pelican and protect the bay's phosphorescent qualities by filtering sediments from runoff. **Cayo Lobo** is so named because its surveyor came from Tenerife in the Canary Islands where they have a similarly sized and shaped island.

FROM CULEBRA: Passenger ferries depart from Mon. to Fri. at 7, on Sat. at 7, 2, and 5:30, and on Sun. at 1 and 4:30. For information, ☎ 742-3161. Curiously, you buy your ticket at the window at the old terminal building and then proceed to the ferry, which is moored 300 ft to the R. Rather like a snake shedding its skin or a hermit crab outgrowing its shell, the current ferry can no longer fit into its berth. Walk straight on to board. **Flamenco Airways (☎ 742-3885)** flies daily to Fajardo and to San Juan's Isla Grande Airport. **Carib (☎ 742-1260, 800-981-0212)** flies daily to to San Juan's international airport and to Fajardo.

Southeastern Puerto Rico

Roosevelt Roads

Located near the town of Ceiba and Playa Naguabo, Roosevelt Roads is the most important American base in the Caribbean, home of the Atlantic Fleet Weapons Range, the most advanced technical training area in the entire Atlantic. "Springboard," the full NATO fleet annual exercises, are conducted from here.

Ciudad Cristiana

Partially funded with federal assistance, this "Christian City," past Roosevelt Roads at the Humacao River estuary, is the sight of a former low-cost housing project sponsored by an evangelical group. It was well known that mercury from a nearby industrial park had been dumped in a canal here (200 cattle died in 1977 after grazing in the fields where the town was located), and developers had been refused a building permit twice. Yet the development was approved and in 1978 the ground was broken by then Governor Carlos Romero Barceló; it came to house 451 families, who were largely attracted by low real estate prices. After arrival, the wives suffered miscarriages, the children were plagued with learning problems, and many inhabitants had skin rashes, hair and teeth loss, and tumors. The entire town was evacuated in 1985. Although many of the families concerned continued to endure health problems, the EPA has never discovered the exact cause of the problem. A nearby creekbed was found to be contaminated with mercury, but no traces were found in fish caught in the area or in the town itself. Amazingly, there is now talk of resettling the development! The FMHA auctioned off 166 mortgage debts in Aug. 1993.

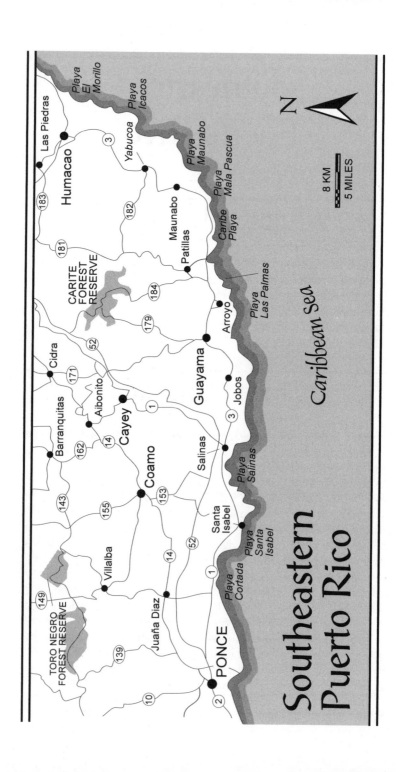

Southeastern
Puerto Rico

Caribbean Sea

N

8 KM
5 MILES

Las Piedras
Playa El Morillo
Playa Icacos
Humacao
Yabucoa
Playa Maunabo
Maunabo
Playa Mala Pascua
CARITE FOREST RESERVE
Patillas
Caribe Playa
Cidra
Aibonito
Barranquitas
Cayey
Playa Las Palmas
Guayama
Arroyo
Jobos
Coamo
Salinas
Playa Salinas
Villalba
Santa Isabel
Playa Santa Isabel
Juana Diaz
Playa Cortada
TORO NEGRO FOREST RESERVE
PONCE

183
3
182
181
184
179
52
171
162
14
1
143
155
153
52
14
1
149
139
10
2
3

Humacao

This small inland town is frequently visited by residents of Palmas del Mar; they put out a great map of the town, which you'll want to pick up if staying in the area. The town's *fiestas patronales* take place around December 8. A *pana* (breadfruit) festival occurs early Sept. in Barrio Matina.

SIGHTS: Downtown near Carr. 3, **Casa Roig** (☎ 852-8380) is open Wed. to Fri. from 10-noon and 1-4 and Sun. from 10-4. Constructed in the 1920s by Antonín Nechodoma, a local architect much influenced by Frank Lloyd Wright, it is now a small museum devoted to Necodoma and other local luminaries. You can also view the **Panteón de la Familia Guzmán**, C. Padre Rivera at C. Casillas, which dates from 1864. Its architectural style is best described as ancient Greek. At the Plaza Pública on C. Ulises Martínez, the **Antiguo Ayuntamiento de Humacao** dates from 1848. Now the City Hall, the **Antigua Corte de Distrito de Humacao** (1925) is on C. Dr. Vidal at C. Antonio López. Dating from 1869, the **Iglesia Dulce Nombre de Jesús** is at the Plaza de Recreo. You can see folkloric houses in architectural styles of the E on Callejón Trujillo. **Palmas Botanical Gardens**, 130 Candalero Abajo, has 208 acres (84 ha) of plants and trees plus a greenhouse. **Playa Humacao** is nearby.

OUTLYING SIGHTS: The abandoned **Antigua Aduana de Humacao** (1872) is at Punta Santiago near the NE. In Barrio Quebrada Arenas in Las Piedras, the **Cueva del Indio** has petroglyphs including the famous Sol Taíno. In the old sugar town of Yabucoa to the S, you can find the **Antiguo Hospital de la Caridad** (circa 1880), C. Muñoz Rivera 29, and the **Casa de la Cultural**, a gallery, museum, and library which in past incarnations has been a city hall and library. Plagued by a strong undertow, attractive **Playa La Lucía** is near town. The **Ruinas de la Hacienda Lucía**, the remains of an abandoned 19th-century sugarcane factory, is in Barrio Camino Nuevo off of Carr. 901. Off the same route, the 300-acre area surrounding Punta Yeguas has been titled the **Inés María Mendoza Natural Reserve** after the wife of a Governor who was a well-known conservationist. The **Antigua Hacienda Mercedita/Central Roig**, a still-operating sugar factory dating from 1870, is on Carr. 3 at Km 96. Constructed in 1892, **Faro de Punta Tuna** is operated by the US Coast Guard. It's off Carr. 760 to the S.

Beyond this point to the SW, the Sierra de Guarraya meets the sea at **Playa Mala Pascua** off Carr. 3. The most famous structures in Patillas are the **Iglesia de San Benito Abad** (1930), on the main plaza, and the **Antiguo Hospital Municipal** (1906), C. Muñoz Rivera.

ACCOMMODATIONS: Hotel Palace (☎ 850-4180), Av. Cruz Ortiz Stella, is right in town. Cabins are rented out at **Centro Vacacional Punta Santiago** by Fomento for $20 per night (see "Accommodations" under Introduction). **Palmas del Mar** to the S (see page 233) is the area's plushest accommodation. Set amidst 45 acres on Carr. 3 at Km 112 near Patillas and the village of Guardarraya, the **Caribe Playa** (☎ 839-6339, 800-221-4483, fax 839-1817; HC764-Buzon 8590, Patillas, PR 00723) faces a beautiful beach and is surrounded by coconut palms. There are 32 beachfront studios with kitchenettes – a series of breezy, attractive concrete structures with balconies and porches. Accommodating up to four, they are supplemented by hammocks, a restaurant and honor bar, a library/TV/music lounge, and plenty of parking. Guests may use facilities (golf, tennis, scuba) at nearby Palmas del Mar. Rates run from around $70 s or d; a $2.50 service gratuity is added. Discounts for longer stays. At Km 113 on Carr. 3 near Patillas, the 12-unit **Villa del Carmen Resort** (☎ 839-7536/4711; Box 716, Arroyo, PR 00714) faces the beach and has two pools. It has an a/c furnished studio, as well as one-, two-, and three-bedroom apartments. Rates start from around $50. At Maunabo and recommended by readers, **Playa Emajaguas Guest House** (☎ 861-6023; Box 834, Maunabo, PR 00717) has a/c rooms with sit-down full kitchen, pool table, playground, bar (BYOB), and tennis court. Rates run around $70. It's also right near the beach and the lighthouse.

DINING AND FOOD: There are a large number of restaurants in town. **Nutrilife**, a vegetarian restaurant, is at Av. Muñoz Marín and C. Miguel Casillas. A **Pizza Hut** is on Carr. 906 near Carr. 30.
  outlying dining: Overlooking the ocean at C. Marina 7 in Punta Santiago, **Daniel's Seafood** (☎ 852-1784) offers a variety of seafood specialties, including *pescado al Daniel*. **Tulio's Seafood** (☎ 850-1840), C. Isidro Andreu 5 in Punta Santiago, serves seafood dishes ranging from stuffed red snapper to grilled lobster and rice with crabmeat. Also in Punta Santiago on Carr. 3 at Km 70.3, **Marie's** (☎ 852-5471) serves gourmet seafood dishes. At Km 75 on Carr. 3, **Paradise Seafood** (☎ 852-1180) specializes in seafood. At C. Emilia

Príncipe 1 in Juncos, **Tenedor** (☎ 734-6573) is a steakhouse set in an old rum distillery.

shopping: The **Humacao Plaza** is a shopping mall.

> ☞ **Traveler's Tip.** If you happen to go through the Bosque Forestal Real de Patillas, an excellent place to stop in the area for a taste of Puerto Rican atmosphere is **Vega's Place,** a small bar in an attractive location.

Cayo Santiago

This small island off the coast contains a large colony of rhesus monkeys being specially bred for scientific experiments by the US Public Health Service. The monkeys were trapped in India in 1938 by C. Ray Carpenter, a pioneer in primate field studies, who recognized the need for a "wild" rhesus population in a controlled environment. Victimized at first by tuberculosis, the monkeys almost starved during the war when grant money ceased. In addition to providing a model for behavioral studies, the monkeys have provided clues in the fight against diabetes and arthritis. Over 300 articles have come from research and field studies performed here since 1978 alone. One of the monkeys bred here gained notoriety in 1996 when it escaped from a Florida research facility after being exposed to the herpes B virus. At present there are 20 scientists on the island. Unfortunately, no visitors are permitted.

Palmas del Mar

The island's largest resort (located just S of Humacao) and self-described "New American Riviera," the 2,750 acres of this former sugarcane plantation offer golf, riding, beaches, tennis, deep-sea fishing and, of course, dining and dancing. It's a great place to escape the island – and everything else, for that matter. It's worth a visit, even if you aren't staying here. The resort has 275 a/c rooms, suites, and villas with cable TV, plus the 27-suite **Palmas Inn & Casino** and the **Candelero Hotel**. There are seven restaurants and six pools. Its major restaurant is **Chez Daniel** (☎ 822-6000), which serves gourmet French and Spanish dishes.

DIVING: In Palmas del Mar, **Coral Head Divers** (☎ 850-7208, 800-635-4529; Box CUHF, Humacao, PR 00792) is one of the island's premier dive operations, according to no less an authority than Joyce Huber, co-author of *Best Dives of the Caribbean*. The shop has rentals (Sunfish, Boogie Boards, kayaks, snorkeling equipment), NAUI instruction, and offers trips to over 20 dive sites. Dive packages and special group rates are available.

Cayey

Founded in 1773, Cayey means "place of the waters" in the indigenous tongue. A former center of coffee and cigar production, the town now has a UPR campus as well as a variety of manufacturing operations.

events: Held on Aug. 15, the town's **fiestas patronales** are its major event. The traditional music group **La Tuna de Cayey** performs on the plaza or in the campus around Christmas.

sights: The 18th-century Catholic church **Nuestra Señora de la Asunción** is in the town square. At the local campus, the **Museo Ramón Frade** exhibits works by this artist. Off the Las Américas Expressway between Cayey and Salinas, the **Jíbaro Puertorriqueño** is a popular monument. The **sports complex** has a remote control racetrack.

dining: On Carr. 7737 at Km 2.1, **El Batey de Toñita** (☎ 738-1890) serves traditional Puerto Rican dishes. Across from Las Planicies, **Jardín de Chiquitín** (☎ 263-2800) offers a variety of seafood. It has an indoor patio garden. On Carr. 7737 at Km 2.8, the **Maramelinda** (☎ 738-9031/0715) serves seafood and gourmet dishes. Combining a Swiss chalet and medieval ambiance, **La Casona de Guavate** (☎ 747-5533), Carr. 184 at Km 28.5, offers a variety of gourmet items, including filet mignon stuffed with lobster. In Barrio Jájome Alto on Carr. 15 at Km 18.6, **Jájome Terrace** (☎ 738-4016) has cheese soup and Puerto Rican specialties. In Salinas, **La Barca** (☎ 824-2592) serves fresh seafood. Also here, **Ladi's** (☎ 824-2035) has Puerto Rican dishes, and **La Puerta de la Bahía** (☎ 824-1221), Principal 298 at la Playita, serves seafood prepared Puerto Rican style.

information: For tourist information, ☎ 738-3211, ext. 12.

Carite Forest Reserve (Guavate)

(Reserva Forestal Carite)

This relatively small (6,000 acres, 2,428 ha) but refreshingly cool (average temperature: 72° F) and moist forest reserve contains sierra palms, teak, and mahogany. It borders **Charco Azul**, a 30-foot-wide cool blue pool and undeveloped **Lago Carite** (which features a partially abandoned housing project and has good fishing: bring your equipment). A bit of dwarf forest surrounds the communication tower, an eyesore that mars the 3,000-ft Cerro La Santa peak. The reserve also includes Nuestra Madre, a Catholic retreat with lush gardens (the site of an Easter pilgrimage commemorating an alleged appearance of the Virgin Mary); Campamento Guavate, a minimum security penal facility; four picnic areas, and a camping spot. Permission to camp must be obtained in advance from the Department of Natural Resources in Puerto de Tierra, San Juan. Among the 50 species of birds found here are the Puerto Rican tanager and the Puerto Rican bullfinch (*como ñame*). **Lago Patillas**, in the area, is also worth a visit.

hiking: From the Charco Azul picnic site on Carr. 184, a path leads to Charco Azul; from there an overgrown path ascends **Cerro La Santa** (2,730 ft, 832 m), the reserve's highest point.

practicalities: The town of Carite has *lechonerías* galore; there's live music and a roasted pig on every spit on weekends.

Las Casas de la Selva

This 1,000-acre, 2000-ft-high reserve is N of Patillas in the Sierra de Cayey, which is next to the Carite reserve. A project managed by Richard Druitt, there are two trips offered here. The three-hour visit ($18 pp, which includes lunch) offers a 1½-hour walk on a loop trail with a possible stop at a small waterfall, where there is a swimming hole. The second trip ($50 pp) is to Hero Valley, one of three watersheds that intersect the reserve en route to Laguna Patillas and the Caribbean. Two hours from the homestead, your guide takes you down a steep path to a river, where you continue downstream. Sometimes you will jump from rock to rock, and a rope may be necessary. You picnic at one of the swimming holes and then continue downstream, where you meet a waiting vehicle; dinner back at the homestead is included. Depending upon the route, you will need 5-8 hours for the trip, and you should leave no later than 9 AM. Good shoes and long pants are recommended for this trip. Overnight camping can also be arranged. Near the lodge main building is a theater space, a waterfall and bathing pool, and a sweat lodge built by a Shoshone Indian; it's used on occasion. There's a hanging musical sculpture as well as an organic one created by British sculptress Sandra Boreham, a former resident.

One of the premier forested tracts still remaining on the island, the reserve was once a coffee plantation that held 30 families along with a coffee mill. Wild coffee trees and pineapples are still found. More than 40,000 trees have been planted on 220 acres – using a line planting method as opposed to monoculture – and the hope is eventually to maintain the reserve through sustainable tree farming. Research students (from as far afield as Yale) arrive on occasion. At night blinking fireflies and persistent coquis provide ambiance.

Very simple accommodations are offered at the guest house for $30 s, $40 d, and $10 each add'l person. Breakfast is included; other meals are $10. Richard also gives Tai Chi lessons. For more information write **Tropic Adventures,** HC 763, Box 3879, Patillas, PR 00723; e-mail 102534.72@compuserve.com; ☎ 839-7318. Be sure to call in advance as the front gate is generally locked.

GETTING HERE: To reach the reserve by road take Exit 33 (Carr. 184) from Carr. 52 and head through the Carite Forest Reserve towards Patillas. On the way you will pass a turnoff to the L, Carr. 179 to the R which heads to Guayama, and Carr. 7740 to the L which heads to San Lorenzo. From the latter, it's two miles to the woodyard at Km 16.1 on Carr. 184, which marks the turnoff to Las Casas.

Arroyo

This small W coast town was founded in 1855. C. Morse, the main street, was named for the inventor Samuel Morse, who arrived in 1848 to oversee installation of telegraph lines. His visit was undoubtedly the most thrilling event that has occurred here before or since the town's foundation. Several 19th-century houses, with captain's walks on the roofs, were built by New England sea captains who settled here. On C. Morse near the Alcaldía, the **Antigua Casa de Aduanas** (Old Customs House) is now used as the Centro Cultural; it dates from 1937. Also see the nearby old houses (from 1850) at C. Morse 67 and (from 1890) at C. Morse 92. A trolley (☎ 839-4963) tours the town of Arroyo from 8 AM on Sat., Sun., and holidays from the port. The **Auberge Olimpico**, off the Salinas toll booth on the Ponce Expressway, provides modern training facilities (including pool, track and field course, baseball and soccer fields, and a children's park) for Olympic athletes – facilities which visitors may use. The Central American Games were held here in 1993. It's open daily, 8 AM-10 PM, ☎ 724-2290.

In neighboring Guayama, the "City of Witches," you can visit the **Museo Casa Cautiño** (☎ 864-9083), which is open Wed. to Sun. from 10:30-noon and 1-4:30; $2 admission. Built in 1887, it is dedicated to the family that lived here and contains antique furnishings. This extremely *white* house, whose fancy grillwork and tall arched windows clearly set it apart, is set on a corner of the town's main plaza. Designed by Manuel Texidor, it is part French and part Puerto Rican in its design. The living room and bedrooms contain art deco and Victorian pieces. Persian carpets abound, and the large bathroom has a sparkling white bidet, shower, and bathtub. The Cautiño family made its fortune through exploiting sugarcane workers and dealing in tobacco and cattle. The home was forfeited to the government in lieu of back taxes in 1974 and was reopened as a museum in 1987. The nearby church, the twin-turreted San Antonio de Padua, is the town's oldest standing structure, having been rebuilt in the 19th century. There's a large sugar plantation windmill ruin on the outskirts of Guayama.

Over the opposition of the Association of Agronomists, the Environmental Quality Board has given its approval to the construction of a coal-fired energy plant in Guayama. It should be producing power in 1999, and it will take five of the 6.1 million gallons needed from the water-treatment plant. In addition, some 75-100,000 tons of limestone will be required on an annual basis. It will be mixed with the coal in order to neutralize the plant's sulfur emissions. It is not clear where the limestone will come from.

From the Salinas's *malecón*, it's possible to hike several miles E past Punta Figuras (swimming not recommended) to Punta Gullarte. Consisting of mangroves, salt flats, and estuaries, as well as a beach, the **Reserva Forestal Aguirre** (☎ 864-0105) is part of Bahía

Jobos to the W. Enter from Carr. 3 at Km 144.7; it's open from 7:30-4 daily.

events: The **Carnival Cristóbal L. Sánchez** takes place around mid-Feb. A *fiesta patronale* takes place in Guayama in July.

ACCOMMODATIONS: Cabins (and campsites) at **Punta Guilarte** are rented out by Fomento to bona fide family groups. There is a two-night minimum stay, and reservations must be made 120 days in advance. (For more information see "Accommodations" under Introduction). In Guayama you can stay at the 20-room **Posada Guayama** (☎ 866-1515, fax 866-1510, 800-443-0266; Box 2393, Guayama, PR 00785), Carr. 3 at Km 138.5, which has carpeted a/c rooms with TV. It features a pool, tennis court, and basketball court. Rooms run around $82 s and $87 d. Outside of town in Barrio Branderi, 22-room **Hotel Restaurant Brandemar** (☎ 864-5124) is off the road to Arroyo. It has a pool, seafood restaurant, and borders an attractive beach. Rooms rent for $50 and have a/c and cable TV. The **Cafeteria Vegeteriano** in the town has a health food store. The **Plaza Guayama Cinemas** (☎ 866-666; Carr. 3, Km. 134.6) consists of a six-theater complex.

Located next to the boat slips at Playa de Salinas, 33-room **Marina de Salinas** (☎ 752-8484, 824-3185, fax 768-7676; 8 Chapin, Playa de Salinas, Salinas, PR 00751) caters to both yachties and landlubbers. Free transport is offered to nearby islands. There's also a laundromat and a mini-plaza. Rates run from around $50 on up.

☞ **Traveler's Tip.** Manatees are sometimes seen feeding offshore along the mangrove coast near Salinas.

Aibonito

Aibonito (from *Artibonicu,* "River of the Night," the Taíno name for this region) is a small but colorful town set in a valley and surrounded by mountains. It has a Mennonite community, well-tended flower gardens, and boasts Puerto Rico's lowest recorded temperature (40° F in 1911). Once an important tobacco and coffee growing area, Aibonito is now known for its poultry farms and processing plants as well as its factories, which produce pharmaceuticals, clothing, electronic goods, and hospital equipment. The Seventh Day Adventists founded a high school here in 1920, the first of 19 academies all over the island that followed in its wake. Generally taking place around the beginning of June, the town's best known celebration is its traditional Flower Festival, in which colorful flowers (including gardenias, anthuriums, and begonias), gardens, and exhibits occupy 10 acres. There's also music, food stalls, and shows. It all takes place on Carr. 722 next to City Hall Coliseum; ☎ 735-4070.

SIGHTS: Standing next to the town plaza, the beautiful white **San José Church** dates from 1825. The twin-towered structure was reconstructed in 1978. The plaza's trees are trimmed in the shape of low-lying umbrellas. Now notable only for its spectacular view, **Las Trincheras** ("the trenches") marks the spot where the last battle of the short-lived American 1898 invasion was fought – a skirmish that took place the day after the armistice had been signed! Another famous panoramic landmark is **La Piedra Degetau,** a large boulder overlooking the town and on the site of the farm of Federico Degetau Gonzales, former Resident Commissioner in Washington, DC. If you see signs marked "Casa Manresa," they lead to the Catholic retreat center of the same name.

PRACTICALITIES: La Italiana, a pizzeria, and the **Tropical Surf Shop** are on a street running parallel to the plaza. There's also an attractive public library. At Km 0.8 on Carr. 7718, **La Piedra** (☎ 735-1034) serves traditional local dishes using area vegetables and spices; they also have a helicopter tour service.

Barranquitas

At 1,800 ft, Barranquitas is not only one of the highest towns on the island, but also one of the most beautifully situated. Viewed from the massive volcanic rocks that cradle it, the town resembles a Spanish medieval print. The Catholic church towers above houses that seem to have been built right on top of each other. Its chief claim to fame is as the birthplace of Puerto Rican statesman Luis Muñoz Rivera (see "History" under Introduction). At the **Museo** Biblioteca, in the wooden house where he was born in 1859, a small museum displays letters, pictures, newspaper clippings, a car used in his 1915 funeral procession, furniture and other items. Down the road is the **Mauseleo de Don Luis Muñoz Rivera**, C. Muñoz Rivera, located next to the tomb where Don Luis (1859-

1916) and his son Luis Muñoz (1898-1980) are buried. It documents his funeral vividly with objects and papers relevant to his demise. There are pictures of his life, his works, and bronze casts of his head and hands. Right in front of the entrance is the marble tomb. To the R are their wives. The pensive statue of Amistad, which gazes down at the tomb, is labeled "hoy y siempre," now and always.

   events: Barranquitas celebrates its **fiestas patronales**, that of San Antonio de Padua, around June 13. The **National Crafts Fair** is held here in mid-July in the town plaza; over a hundred artisans participate. ☎ 857-2065 for information.

FOOD: At Km 1.7 on Carr. 152 and commanding an impressive view, **Hacienda Margarita** (☎ 857-0414) serves steak and seafood dishes. On the same road, **El Coquí** (☎ 857-3828) is definitely not for vegetarians, let alone those shy of lard. Its *arroz con buruquena* features a crab that can only be captured in caves or on moonless nights. The shells are restuffed with the meat combined with spices and sticky rice. It must be ordered a few days ahead of time.

VICINITY OF BARRANQUITAS: Indian relics have been found in a number of caves near the town. Nearly inaccessible, the deep gorge of **San Cristóbal Canyon**, located along the road to Aibonito, is the most spectacular and deepest on the island. Precipitous cliffs, densely covered with vegetation (guava, shortleaf fig, and climbing bamboo), plunge 500-750 ft to a rocky valley where the Río Usabon races over boulders, dropping 100 ft at one point. Catch a glimpse from Carr. 725 (and side road 7715), 156, and 162. Best of these is from the San Cristóbal Development on Carr. 156, Km 17.7. An unmarked trail leads into the gorge from here (see below). Some 1,200 acres of this six-mile volcanic rift have been purchased during the past two decades by the Conservation Trust. An old refurbished house here hosts visiting artists, researchers, and scientists, and a five-acre tree nursery produces some 45,000 trees each year.

   hiking: This area was a former dump before its acquisition by the Conservation Trust during the 1970s, and some overgrown debris is still in evidence. It remains undeveloped for hiking. Entrances can be difficult to find so ask locals for help. Be sure to have good shoes and rain gear. One steep path branches off of Carr. 7725 between Aibonito and Barranquitas and leads to a 100-ft (30-m) waterfall, the nation's highest. Allow about 1½ hours RT. A second and yet steeper trail runs from Barrio San Cristóbal (Carr. 156, Km 17.7) down to the canyon floor (allow one hour), where you can explore the area by clambering over gigantic slippery boulders. Exercise caution while hiking here: in 1993, nine people were rescued from the canyon after being trapped by rising river waters. In Aibonito, the **Piedra Restaurant** (☎ 735-1034) offers free hikes through the canyon leaving at 8:30 AM on the last Sat. of each month; reservations are required.

Coamo

This small town has its old church set in a plaza enlivened by flowering bouganvillea. Once the site of two flourishing Taíno Indian villages, only a solitary Indian remained at the time of the town's founding in 1579. As the third oldest town on the island (after San Juan and San Germán), its name, San Blas de Illecas de Coamo, was derived from the patron saint of a major landowner – an expatriate from Illecas, Spain. Its *fiestas patronales* of San Blas/Nuestra Señora de la Candelaria take place in early Feb.

SIGHTS: The **Catholic church** is decorated with paintings by internationally renowned Puerto Rican artists José Campeche and Francisco Oller. The latter's Cuadro de las Animas features a blonde (rumored to be Oller's girlfriend) being tortured in purgatory. One of the church's three bells – said to have sounded so loudly that its vibrations killed fish off the coast and shattered lamps and glass in nearby homes – has been silenced by public pressure for over a century. An elegant two-story masonry **mansion** built by Clotilde Santiago, the town's wealthiest and most powerful farmer and entrepreneur during Spanish rule, still stands at one corner of the plaza. Converted to a museum, it now houses historical memorabilia, gold-plated bathroom fixtures, and mahogany furniture. Call the Alcaldía (City Hall, ☎ 825-1150) to make an appointment to see the museum.

The town's major landmark, however, is not a building but a group of **hotsprings**. First used by the island's indigenous inhabitants, the springs gained an international reputation by the end of the 19th century. Some assert that they are the Fountain of Youth Ponce de León had heard about from the Indians before taking off to search for it in Florida. To reach them, take the road outside of town going toward the Baños de Coamo Parador, a government-run inn built on the site of the Coamo Springs Hotel, which once sheltered the likes of Franklin Delano Roosevelt. Proceeding past the *parador*, turn R to find the springs. There are two large concrete pools. One is hot and the other is warm. The overflow from the hotter one flows down into the warm one. The ideal time to visit is right at dusk, but many Puerto Ricans also have the same idea.

WHERE TO STAY: The only choice is **Parador Baños de Coamo** (☎ 825-2186/2239, fax 825-4739; Box 540, Coamo, PR 00769) which is outside town on Carr. 546 at Km 1. One reader wrote "Our room was terrific and had a balcony with two rocking chairs. It was a beautiful place where we met a lot of interesting people." For reservations, ☎ 800- 443-0266 in the US; 800-981-7575 (721-2884 in San Juan) in Puerto Rico.

Ponce

Often neglected by visitors, the S coastal city of Ponce has much to offer. An impressive fine art museum, a restored historical district, a colorful firehouse set on the main plaza, free tram buses to take you around, and nearby historical and ecological attractions number among its many attractions. Though it's the second largest city in Puerto Rico, Ponce (pop. 191,000) has much more the feeling of a small town than bustling metropolitan San Juan. Set between the blue of the Caribbean and the green of the Cordillera Central mountain range, its central location makes it easy to visit other locales. It's just big enough to be fun to walk around and still small enough to allow for an easy escape.

Ponce is a city of many names. It is known as "La Perla del Sur" (The Pearl of the South), "La Ciudad Senorial" (Manorial City), and "La Ciudad de las Quenepas" (City of the Honeyberries). Ponce has played host to many prominent islanders, including opera tenor Antonio Paoli, composer Juan Morel-Campos, and painter Miguel Pou. *Ponceños* exhibit noticeably more civic pride than do residents of other urban locales. For example, you'll actually see city residents putting garbage in garbage cans, an act of civic pride rarely seen elsewhere.

HISTORY: Established in 1692, Ponce was named after Juan Ponce de León y Loaiza, the great-grandson of Puerto Rico's first governor, Ponce de León. Originally, Ponce was a town with only two entrances: one would enter either via a mountain road passing by the Church of La Guadalupe or along the road that borders the S coast. Point of entrance was La Ceiba de Cuatro Calles (Ceiba of the Four Streets) which led, as it still does today, to the main streets of Commercio, Cruz, Salud, and Mayor.

Plantation owners from S America, fleeing political unrest at home, arrived in Ponce in the early 1800s. These entrepreneurs founded coffee, tobacco, and agricultural plantations along the S coast. Plantations were worked by slaves who endured abominable conditions, but the town flourished.

In 1877-78, when it was granted the title of Ciudad (city) by royal decree, Ponce was already the social, military, and commercial center of the S coast. The city stumbled on into the next century. Briefly revitalized by the oil industry from the mid-1970s to 1980s, Ponce collapsed towards the end of the 1980s. Under the leadership of Ponce Mayor Rafael Cordero Santiago, downtown Ponce has been revitalized in recent years under the "Ponce en Marche" program (see box titled "The Renewal of Historic Ponce"). As Gov. Rosselló, the current governor, comes from the opposing party, the program has been put on hold. Thousands of *Ponceños* participated in a protest in San Juan in 1993. That same year Ponce hosted the 27th Central American and Caribbean Games. Those interested in learning in greater detail about the town's history should visit the Museum of the History of Ponce.

GETTING HERE: An expressway (Carr. 52) runs from San Juan to Ponce; every so often you must throw some change in the basket. You can also arrive via Guayama and Salinas (Carr. 1), Coamo and Juana Díaz (Carr. 14), Adjuntas (Carr. 10), and Mayagüez (Carr. 2). Ponce is approachable by bus from Utuado or Adjuntas, or by *público* from Río Piedras, Santurce, Mayagüez, or other neighboring towns. As you approach the town, you'll notice the urban sprawl beginning with Burger King, malls, and the like.

by air: American Eagle flies from San Juan's Muñoz Marín International Airport. Carnival Airlines flies directly from Miami.

GETTING AROUND: Ponce is small enough that any part of the main area may be reached on foot. Free trolley service, free train-cart, and free carriage rides (weekends only) start from Plaza Las Delicias. Running from 8 AM-9 PM, the trolleys are fun and allow you to get oriented, but they are slow. The nine trolleys have three routes; the train-cart takes around two hours and goes to the boardwalk. Trolley destinations may range as far afield as the ceiba tree and the cross. The best way to find out where it's going is to ask one of the friendly drivers. For taxis: ☎ 843-6000, 284-8248, 842-3370, or 840-9126.

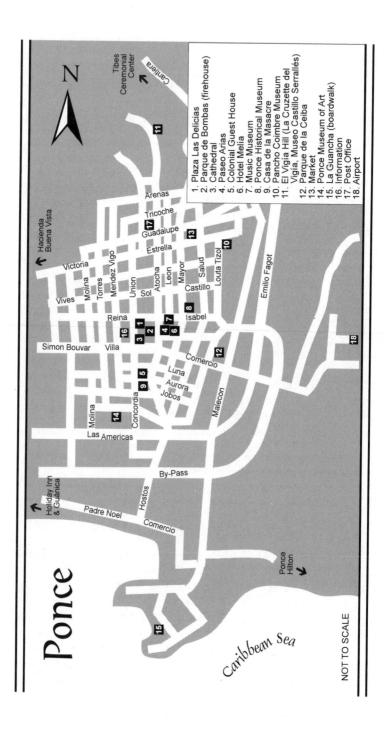

Ponce

N

Caribbean Sea

NOT TO SCALE

Tibes
Ceremonial
Center

Cantera

Hacienda
Buena Vista

Holiday Inn
& Guánica

Ponce
Hilton

Arenas
Tricoche
Guadalupe
Estrella
Victoria
Molina
Torres
Mendez Vigo
Union
Sol
Atocha
Leon
Mayor
Salud
Castillo
Louta Tizol
Emilio Fagot
Vives
Reina
Isabel
Simon Bouvar
Villa
Comercio
Luna
Aurora
Jobos
Malecon
Molina
Concordia
Las Americas
By-Pass
Hostos
Padre Noel
Comercio

1. Plaza Las Delicias
2. Parque de Bombas (firehouse)
3. Cathedral
4. Paseo Arías
5. Colonial Guest House
6. Hotel Meliá
7. Music Museum
8. Ponce Historical Museum
9. Casa de la Masacre
10. Pancho Coimbre Museum
11. El Vígia Hill (La Cruzette del Vígia, Museo Castillo Serrallés)
12. Parque de la Ceiba
13. Market
14. Ponce Museum of Art
15. La Guancha (boardwalk)
16. Information
17. Post Office
18. Airport

parking: A good multi-story parking area is on C. León between C. Sol and C. Isabel, on the E side of the street. Overnight parking is prohibited. Parking is also available under the new Parque Dora Colón on C. Marina.

Ponce Sights

In recent years, an intensive $440 million revitalization project has increased the city's historic area from 260 to 1,046 buildings. Electrical and phone wires have been buried and streetlights in the shape of 19th-century gas lamps installed. More than 200 of its buildings have now been restored, and many of them are on streets radiating from the main square.

the plaza area: Ponce's beautiful **Plaza Las Delicias** (Plaza of Delights), with its fountains and gardens, is dominated by the **Cathedral of Our Lady of Guadalupe**. Built in 1670, it has been destroyed several times by earthquakes, and this version dates from 1931. Painted baby blue and with beautiful stained glass windows, the cathedral's entrances house wooden choir boys who solicit for alms. Las Delicias is actually divided into two plazas. The first is Plaza Muñoz Rivera. In the plaza's center, the bronze statue of Luis Muñoz Marín, first elected governor of Puerto Rico and the son of Muñoz Rivera, gazes out over the banks, travel agencies, and stores that surround the plaza. On the S side, the Federico Degetau Plaza (named after the island's first resident commissioner in Washington who was born in Ponce) constitutes the other half. Ponce is renowned for its fountains and in the plaza's center stands the **Fountain of the Lions** (Fuente de los Leones), a monument dedicated to eight brave citizens who risked their lives in 1899 to extinguish a fire in the munitions depot that might have spelled disaster for the city. Purchased in 1939 at the New York World's Fair, it was restored in 1993 when its base was enlarged and a computerized lighting system installed. View it at night, when it becomes obvious why Ponce is famous for its fountains. There's also the obelisk to the Heroes of the Polvorín (Obelisco a los Héroes del Polvorín), which commemorates the seven firefighters and one local citizen who extinguished an 1899 fire that spread over the US Army powder magazine. It dates from 1958 and replaces the original, which was destroyed by the 1918 earthquake. A monument to Juan Morel Campos, known as the father of the Puerto Rican *danza* (see "Music and Dance" in the Introduction) also stands here. Born in Ponce in 1857, his *danzas* are still played in Puerto Rico, and many of his symphonic works have received international recognition.

Situated just off the plaza is Ponce's gaudy landmark the **Parque de Bombas** or firehouse. Painted red, green, black, and yellow, it has become the symbol of the city. Sole survivor of several buildings constructed for the Industrial Agricultural Exhibition held here on the plaza in 1882, it was donated to the homeless firemen in 1885 and was in active use until 1990. Restored to its original design, it now is a small museum housing a shiny fire truck that would've done the Beatles' firehouse on Penny Lane proud. The reverential first- and second-floor exhibits chronicle firefighting in Ponce; it's almost a shrine to firefighting. Objects displayed inside include various types of axes, brass nozzles, and a collection of firefighters' hats. It's open Mon. to Fri. (except Tues.) from 9:30-6; admission is free.

Across from the cathedral stands Ponce's **Casa-Armstrong Proventud**, a restored mansion housing a small museum. A two-story masonry building, it has stained-glass windows and parquet floors. It houses furniture and antiques that belonged to 19th-century statesman José de Diego, and is open Mon. to Fri. from 8-4:30. Also just off of the plaza, the **Fox Delicias Mall** was originally built as a theater in 1931; it now houses shops and eateries. **Casa Alcaldia** (City Hall) was built around 1840 and was first used as a prison. Its clock dates from 1877. Be sure to see the fantastic woodcuts representing popular songs, which hang in the main entranceway. Teddy and Franklin Roosevelt, Herbert Hoover, and even George Bush have paid their respects to local officials here.

Another beautifully restored area is **Paseo Atocha** along C. Isabel. It's chock-a-block with stores, and features a street fair every third Sunday of the month. Visit it at night when the walkway gleams from the streetlamps and a few romantic couples promenade.

nearby sights: After finishing with the plaza area, continue on to the surrounding area. As mentioned above, the area surrounding C. Cristina, C. Isabela, C. Mayor, and C. Salud have been transformed into a historical zone. At C. Mayor 14, the **Casa Paoli** was the birthplace of legendary operatic tenor, Antonio E. Paoli y Marcano. Born in 1871, Paoli was known as the "King of Tenors and the Tenor of Kings." Here you'll find a small museum, the headquarters of the Society for Folkloric Investigation, and a souvenir shop. Admission is free, and it's open from 10-noon and 2-4 from Mon. to Fri.

THE RENEWAL OF HISTORIC PONCE

The renewal of Ponce's historic district is a highly encouraging example of what a city can do when it listens to some of its more visionary citizens. Sadly, in these days of huge outlying strip malls and monotonous and tasteless chain architecture, Puerto Rico is losing much of the traditional charm that constitutes a large part of its appeal. In much of the world, a great deal of traditional architecture is not being maintained, and many historic structures have been demolished to make way for concrete and steel and plastic. Good global examples range from Singapore (which has destroyed much of its ambiance) to Beirut (where a massive urban renewal project has destroyed nearly all old buildings in its downtown area). As in the Virgin Islands, Barbados, and other areas in the world, conservation-minded locals with a vision are working to preserve these sites, repositories of local history and keepers of the as yet unlearned lessons of history.

Once a shining and bustling city of commerce, Ponce had nearly dipped during the mid-1980s down to the position of "historic ruin." Its historic zone was derisively referred to as the "hysteric zone." Ponceno-turned-governor Rafael Herdandez Colón issued an executive order in 1985 directing $600 million to be used in a program called "Ponce en Marcha," a massive urban development plan aimed at restoring Ponce's prominence.

Naturally, there was a lot of protest from other municipalities, but things moved right along anyway. Roads were constructed anew, water mains were replaced and power lines buried, and $200 million was spent to build a highway system on the city's circumference. Young architects were brought in to blueprint designs. The Institute of Puerto Rican culture assembled a 13-member group to research and survey what changes would need to be implemented, including zoning restrictions and restoration guidelines. Tax incentives were applied along with persuasion in order to get merchants to go along. Buildings were painted in pastels because architect Magda Bardina established that this was the area's original colors. Restoration of buildings on the main plaza – from the Fox Delicias (1847) to the City Hall (1847) – was paid for by the Government of Spain.

Urban renewal has been halted in recent years owing to lack of funds. A few museums have closed, and the entertainment district faltered. The main new change in the past few years has been a concrete-and-tree park named after Rafael Hernandez Colón's mama. The city still has major problems, ones shared almost universally with other cities in the States and worldwide, but the center of Ponce still shines. It's an excellent example of urban preservation, one which will hopefully permeate and transmute to other locales.

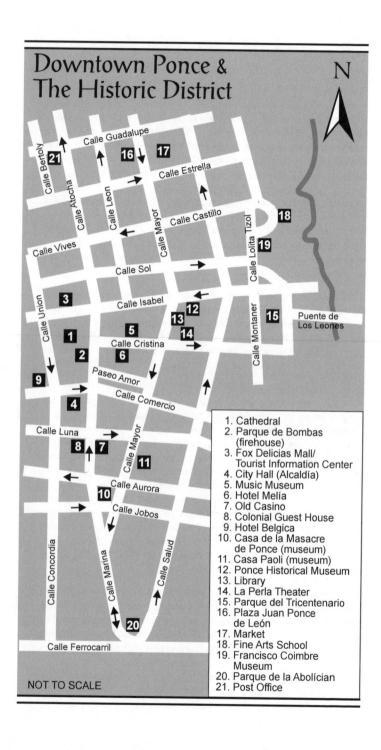

Downtown Ponce & The Historic District

N

Calle Bertoly
Calle Guadalupe
21
16
17
Calle Atocha
Calle Leon
Calle Estrella
Calle Mayor
Calle Castillo
Calle Vives
18
Calle Lolita Tizol
19
Calle Sol
Calle Union
3
Calle Isabel
12
13
15
5
14
Calle Montaner
Puente de Los Leones
2
6
Calle Cristina
9
Paseo Amor
Calle Comercio
4
Calle Luna
8 7
Calle Mayor
11
Calle Aurora
10
Calle Jobos
Calle Concordia
Calle Marina
Calle Salud
20
Calle Ferrocarril

NOT TO SCALE

1. Cathedral
2. Parque de Bombas (firehouse)
3. Fox Delicias Mall/ Tourist Information Center
4. City Hall (Alcaldía)
5. Music Museum
6. Hotel Melía
7. Old Casino
8. Colonial Guest House
9. Hotel Belgica
10. Casa de la Masacre de Ponce (museum)
11. Casa Paoli (museum)
12. Ponce Historical Museum
13. Library
14. La Perla Theater
15. Parque del Tricentenario
16. Plaza Juan Ponce de León
17. Market
18. Fine Arts School
19. Francisco Coimbre Museum
20. Parque de la Abolícian
21. Post Office

S OF THE PLAZA: Set at the corner of C. Marina and C. Luna, the **Antiguo Casino** (Old Casino) is a neoclassic structure that was designed and built in 1922 by a local architect. Its tapestries and other decorations were the creation of Miguel Pou, a local painter. Once the scene of some of the nation's most elegant parties, it now houses government offices on its first floor. Commemorating the massacre of Ponce (see "History" in the Introduction) the **Casa de la Masacre de Ponce** is at the corner of C. Marina and C. Aurora. At the time of the 1937 massacre, it held the local Nationalist Party's Assembly. This small museum may or may not be open; hours are irregular. Also on the same street, the **Holy Trinity Parish** was consecrated in 1874 and became the first Episcopal church in Spanish America. Queen Victoria intervened personally with the Spanish Crown in order to allow it to function, but for nearly its first quarter-century of operation the church's bell remained mute. It first sounded with the 1898 American invasion. Commemorating the abolition of slavery in 1873, the **Obelisco de la Abolición y Concha Acústica** (Abolition of Slavery Obelisk and Acoustic Shell) seats up to 2,000. It's on C. Hostos near Las Américas.

E OF THE PLAZA: Set in the first Puerto Rican House to receive telephone service and in the original home of the city's art museum, the **Museo de la Musica Puertorriqueña** (Puerto Rican Music Museum) is at C. Cristina 70, just down the street from the Hotel Melia and across to the L. This museum is a must-see for those interested in Latin and Puerto Rican music. In addition to presenting an overview of the island's music, it includes displays on such local luminaries as popular singer Ruth Fernández and composer Rafael Hernández. Its one drawback is that everything is titled in Spanish. As you come in, the first thing you see is a display of traditional instruments, including a reproduction of a Precolumbian tambor or log drum. A display on your L highlights instruments used to interpret indigenous music at the University of Cayey; they are based on a description by de Oviedo. There's also a woodblock print, various posters, pictures of musicians, and a collection of musical instruments such as the tiple, cuatro, maracas, and güiro. The *marímbola*, a large thumb piano that you sit upon and pluck, was used by the Blacks here during the 16th century. Entering the next room to your R, you find musical instruments, including a cello inscribed with mother of pearl in the shape of a butterfly. Here, there are some more old posters, a piano stand, and a piano. There's also an old jukebox with various hits such as *Lamento Boricano* and a display of old record covers. Also on exhibit are conga drums and masks. There's a good gift shop out front that has T-shirts, cassettes, and CDs for sale. Concerts are held on some Fri. evenings. Open Wed. through Sun from 9-noon and 1-5:30, the museum charges $1 for adults and 50¢ for children. If you're hungry **La Perla Sandwiches** is right across the street. **note:** This museum is currently closed for remodeling, but may have re-opened by the time of your visit. Check with the tourist office.

The **Museo de la Historia de Ponce** (Museum of the History of Ponce) was inaugurated on Dec. 12, 1992, the 300th anniversary of the city's foundation. Set at the corner of C. Mayor and C. Isabel, it occupies two old houses (Casa Zapater and Casa Candal Salazar) on C. Isabel adjacent to Teatro La Perla. The two homes are joined by a patio graced with a lime tree. The museum's 10 rooms illustrate important events in the city's history. The first shows the area's natural history. Another shows the roles played by the various cultural groups as well as the transformation undergone during the 19th and 20th centuries. Other rooms trace the evolution of daily life and the city's medical, educational, political dimensions. The museum publishes its own journal, and the gift shop sells books and crafts. Admission is $3 for adults, $2 for senior citizens, and $1.50 for children, and it's open Mon. to Fri. from 10-5, Sat. and Sun. from 10-6. Just next door, **Teatro La Perla**, a theater and cultural hub for over a century, is one of the area's highlights. It is a recreation of the original that was built in 1864.

Commemorating famous baseball player Pancho Coimbre, the **Museo Pancho Coimbre** houses memorabilia relating to the star as well as Ponce's Sports Hall of Fame. While not of great interest to outsiders, special exhibits are held here on occasion. It's open Tues. to Sun. from 9:30-4:30; free admission. Just up the street is the **Escuela de Bellas Artes** (Fine Arts School) which once functioned as the Spanish garrison headquarters as well as hosting the American Army, a court of justice, and a prison. Built in 1849 as El Castillo, it was transformed into the school in 1992 after an $8 million restoration.

N FROM THE PLAZA: Incorporating Byzantine and art nouveau styles, the **Iglesia Metodista Unida** (United Methodist Church) has remarkable stained glass windows; it was built in 1900 by a Czech architect and is located at C. Mendez Vigo and C. Villa. The **Nueva Plaza del Mercado** is at C. Estrella and C. Salud. Even as early as 7 AM you'll find a Jehovah's Witness holding up a copy of *Watchtower* at the door. Many sandwich and other food shops are here. Upstairs and accessed by an escalator, a smaller third level has check cashing, tailor shops, and *botanicas*. A narrow passageway originally used as a meat market, **Plaza Juan Ponce de León** was designed and constructed in 1926. It was informally known as Plaza de los Perros (Dog's Market) because of the hordes of dogs that once competed for scraps. Now housing a variety of stalls – which sell everything from drinking coconuts and magic tricks to crafts and musical instruments – it is one of the most pleasant places to visit. You will find it between C. Mayor and C. León near C. Estrella; the motorized trolley stops here for 15 minutes.

OTHER MONUMENTAL SIGHTS: Set in the town's NW at the intersection on C. Guadelupe and C. Torres, the **Panteón Nacional Baldorioty de Castro** (Baldorioty de Castro National Mausoleum) dates from 1843 and was converted into a park in 1991. A number of local notables rest here, and concerts and other activities are held regularly. Free guided tours are offered Tues. to Thurs. from 9-6, Fri. from 9-7, and on Sat. and Sun. from 9 AM to 10 PM. The three-plaza **Tricentennial Park** (Parque del Tricentenario) was completed in 1992 in time for the tricentennial celebrations. Its centerpiece is a fountain dedicated to the city's most illustrious citizens. Set on either side, two small sub-plazas honor Luis A. Ferré and Hernández Colón, two former governors who were born here. A second plaza honors the city's architecture and features a rotunda. The third honors Latin American statesmen. Spanning the Río Portugués, the **Lion's Bridge** (Puente de los Leones) is the gateway to the historical area. Two brass lions guard the entrance. The older one represents wisdom and experience, while the younger stands for the glorious future.

PONCE MUSEUM OF ART

The city's best known attraction is the Ponce Museum of Art on Av. Las Américas across from Universidad Catolica Santa Maria. Designed by architect Edward Durrell Stone and financed by conservative multimillionaire industrialist and former Governor Don Luis Ferré, this block-long building uses natural light to lend a spacious effect to its hexagonal galleries. It contains the best collection of European art in the entire Caribbean. From an original 400 works, the collection has grown to include more than 1,000 paintings and 400 sculptures. Three sculpture gardens branch off the main floor. Two dynamic 18th-century polychromed wooden statues carved in Toledo, Spain, representing Europe and America, greet the visitor near the entrance. Besides portraits and the representative works of Puerto Rican master painters like José Campeche and Francisco Oller, the first floor also contains a 15th-century Siamese Bodhisattva bust, intricate Incan pottery, and fine handblown decorated glass pieces. The second floor holds many fine sculptures and old European thematic religious paintings: plenty of blood, breasts, and skulls. See St. Francis at prayer and Pero feeding Cimon with her breast. The museum also houses works by masters such as Van Dyck, Reubens, Velazquez, and Gainsborough. There is a good gift shop. It's open daily 10-5; admission is $3 for adults, $2 children, $1 students. A good place to eat that features both Italian food and seafood, **Pizza Heaven**, C. Concordia, is within walking distance of the art museum. From the entrance, turn L and then head L again. A 99¢ breakfast place is located near the museum.

OTHER OUTLYING SIGHTS: **La Ceiba de Ponce**, an enormous 300-year-old silk cotton tree overhangs C. Comercio about a half-mile E of the plaza. Once a meeting place for the Taíno Indians, it was featured in one of Franciso Oller's paintings. **El Vigía Hill**, on Carr. 1 near C. Bertoly, is a famous lookout point surrounded by homes of the wealthy upper class. **La Cruzette del Vigía**, a gigantic 100-ft-high concrete cross, has been erected here. From Tues. to Fri. 9:30-6 and Sat. and Sun. from 10-5, it's possible to head for the top and check out the views; $1 admission is charged. In the distant past, a watchman, noting the arrival of a visiting merchant vessel, would raise a flag to indicate its nationality. To your L is the Serralés Mansion, which has been transformed into the **Museo Castillo Serrallés** (Serrallés Castle Museum, ☎ 259-1774). Built in the Spanish Revival style popular during the 1930s for the family that produces Don Q Rum, it now offers tours. The mansion includes a library, formal dining room, and living room, all decorated with period furniture. There's also a gift shop and coffee shop. It's open Tues. to Sun. from 9:30-5. Admission is $3 for adults, $2 for senior citizens, $1.50 for children and students. To get to these two sights by car, take Carr. 1 to C. Isabel, then turn R on C. Salud, L on C. Guadalupe, and R on C. Bertoly.

ART EXHIBITS: The **Casa del Abogado** (☎ 841-2123), a house built by a German architect in 1913, is run by the Ponce Historical Society and has art exhibits. Open Wed. to Sun. 9-5. Art is also exhibited in the Galerías inside the **Alcaldía** (City Hall) off of Plaza las Delicias.

FUTURE PROJECTS: These include the Parque Urbano y Planetario, the Museo de la Arquitectura, a trolley terminal, and the

Parque Lineal Acuático. Check with the tourist office to see if any of these have materialized yet.

Ponce Practicalities

DOWNTOWN ACCOMMODATIONS: Many inexpensive hotels are clustered around the main square. Right in town at C. Villa 122, **Hotel Bélgica** (☎ 844-3255; Ponce, PR 00731) has 20 a/c rooms with TV from around $50 s, $60 d (extra person: $5). Be sure to get a room away from the street. In front of the Old Casino at C. Marina 33, the **Colonial Guest House** (☎ 259-2463, 843-7585, 841-7134) includes breakfast in its rates. This relaxed, Puerto Rican-style managed inn is in a wonderful old building that has been restored by Roberto Porrata, a talented local artist who is responsible for the Rey Momo's papier-mâché head (see Carnaval in the "Events" section on page 256) as well as the annual Christmas decorations. The rooms and halls are beautifully decorated with works of art and antiques. This guesthouse is still under construction, so there are only a few rooms available. If you're noise-sensitive, avoid the rooms overlooking the street. Rates run around $65 d, $95 suite (holds four), and $125 (holds six). A restaurant is planned. The 78-room **Hotel Melía** (☎ 842-0260/0261, fax 841-3602; Box 1431, Ponce, PR 00733) is at C. Cristina 2. Facilities include a/c, phone, and TV in rooms. There's also a bar and restaurant. Rooms start at around $65 s, $70 d including continental breakfast.

OUTLYING ACCOMMODATIONS: The **Ponce Hilton & Casino** (☎ 259-7676/7777, fax 259-7674; Box 7419, Ponce, PR 00732) has 156 a/c rooms and suites, two restaurants, three lounges, jogging track, pool, Jacuzzi, and nearby beach. It charges from $170 s and $190 d. For more information ☎ 800-259-7676. The 120-room **Holiday Inn Ponce** (☎ 844-1200, fax 841-8085; Ponce, PR 00731), on Carr. 2 at Km 221.2 , offers 120 a/c rooms and suites with cable TV and balconies, two restaurants, disco, as well as Olympic and children's pools. Rates start from $124.50 s and $134.50 d. Directly off of Carr. 52 across from the Interamerican University, the two-story **Days Inn Ponce** (☎ 841-1000, fax 841-2560; Mercedita, PR 00715) charges from around $115 s and $120 d. It has 122 a/c rooms and suites with cable TV. Facilities include adult and children's pools, restaurant, nightclub, and nearby tennis. For reservations call ☎ 800-325-2525. The **Texan Guest House** is in the Sabanetas area. On Carr. 2 near town on the way to Guánica, oceanfront 27-room **Hotel las**

Cucharas (☎ 841-0620) charges around $40 and up. Rooms include a/c, TV, and phone, and there's a restaurant and bar.

in Juana Diaz: This small town on the way to Coamo has **Hotel Eden** (☎ 837-2075) on Carr. 149 at Km 4.6 in Barrio Guanabano. You can dine here at **R** (☎ 837-6638), Carr. 159, Km 5.7; it offers Italian, Spanish, and French dishes.

FOOD: Streets are literally packed with *cafeterias* and restaurants. Fast-food places are strewn along Av. Las Américas and the plaza. During the season in Aug. and Sept. vendors sell *quenepas*, a fruit similar to lychee. Right on the plaza, **Café Don Francisco**, C. Union 3, has inexpensive sandwiches, expresso, and capuccino. An old theater converted to an attractive mini-mall, **Fox Delicias Mall** contains a wide variety of inexpensive restaurants. Practically opposite the firehouse, **King's Cream Helados** has natural fruit-flavored as well as chocolate ice cream from 75¢ for a cone on up. **Panaderia Reposteria Suizeria del Sur**, across from the PO on C. Guadalupe, has sweets, a small cafeteria, and daily papers (behind the counter). **Ginorio's Pizza** at Paseo Atocha 97 offers slices ($1) as well as whole pies. It's open late. **Woa Kee** is a cheap Chinese joint across from the *público* station.

DOWNTOWN DINING: Set in a courtyard, **Lupita's** offers Mexican dishes and has mariachi from 8 on Fri. and Sat. nights. Specializing in international and seafood dishes for lunch and dinner, **Conda's** (☎ 843-9223) is at C. Comercio 28. The **Restaurant Hotel Melía** (☎ 842-0260/0261), C. Cristina 2, serves seafood and international dishes. Inside Hotel Bélgica At. C. Ferrocarril 15, **El Mesón de René** (☎ 844-6110) offers a variety of international foods. At. C. Isabel 56, **El Café de Tomás** (☎ 840-1965) has international food.

near La Guancha: With gourmet seafood, **Restaurant El Ancla** (☎ 840-2450) is at Av. Hostos 9 near the playa, as is **Restaurant El Naútico** (☎ 840-3044), which serves international fare. The Ponce Hilton (☎ 259-7676) has three restaurants: very expensive **La Terraza**, which has buffets (seafood on Fri.), and **La Hacienda** and **La Cava de la Hacienda**, which have international cuisine.

other dining: In the Urb. Santa María, **Pizza Heaven** (☎ 844-0448/3836) is an Italian steak house that features art exhibits by local artists. On Av. Pámpanos, **El Señorial** (☎ 844-1785, 842-1320) specializes in filet mignon. In Barrio Pámpanos, the **Tiara Seafood Restaurant** (☎ 843-5370; open daily) specializes in seafood, creole dishes, and sandwiches. With grilled steaks, **La Casa del Chef** (☎ 843-1298) is at C. Jón Fagot 23 in Barrio Cuatro Calles. Out at

Las Caobas Shopping Center, **Lydia's Restaurant** (☎ 844-3933; open daily) has seafood (including creole lobster) and creole steaks. In the Club Deportivo in Urb. La Alhambra, the **ND Restaurant** (☎ 259-8227) specializes in Puerto Rican and international fare. At Av. Las Américas 20, **Victor's** (☎ 841-8383) offers international and nouvelle cuisine. Hotel Days Inn, Carr. 1, Km 123.5, has the **Taíno Restaurant** (☎ 841-1000, ext. 1002) with international food. Off Carr. 2 in El Tuque at Km 255 in the Holiday Inn, the **Tamaná Restaurant** (☎ 844-1200) specializes in international cooking.

seaside dining: In the hotel of the same name out on Carr. 2, Km 218.1, **Las Cucharas Seafood Restaurant** (☎ 841-0620, 383-4073) serves a variety of tasty *mariscos*. Offering gourmet dishes, **Pito's Seafood Café** (☎ 841-4977) is in the vicinity, as is **Yeyo's Seafood** (☎ 843-7629), which is open daily.

MARKET SHOPPING: Ponce's modern *mercado* is an air-conditioned showplace with fruits and vegetables, spices, bottles of pure honey, gigantic avocados, and drinking coconuts (65¢). *Botanicas* (shops selling spiritualist literature and goods), tailors, and other shops are upstairs. There are a number of supermarkets in and around town. **Grande** and **Pueblo Xtra** are on the bypass. Sample prices in Grande: Brocoli, 97¢/ea.; mangos 50¢/lb.; small apples, $1/lb.; onions, 75¢/lb., white onions, 99¢/lb.; bulk cheese, $2.59/lb.; eggs, $1.29/doz.; tomato juice, $1.49/16 oz.; and Grande pineapple juice, $1.53/46 oz.

ENTERTAINMENT: To find out what's happening locally, consult the local weekly, the *Periodico La Perla del Sur*. At night the gleaming Paseo Atocha has a few couples strolling arm in arm, but is otherwise deserted. Inside the fire house, the engines shine. Illuminated by a constantly shifting array of colored lights, the fountain rises and then retreats. Its lions – seeming to spew out streams of water – appear at times to be escapees from a Stephen Spielberg movie. Cool dudes wearing sunglasses circle the plaza in their cars and blast hiphop. In the main square area, **Cafeteria Tompy** is the place to go for late night munchies. Discos are at the **Day's Inn** and at **Holly's** in the Holiday Inn.

Completed at a cost of $2 million, the **Paseo Tablado La Guancha**, a long and wide wooden boardwalk, is one of the most pleasant places to visit, especially at night when it comes alive. An open-air stage at one end features live music on occasion; *salseros* as venerated as Tito Puente have performed here. To get here take Carr. 14 S from Carr. 163 or Carr. 2. Keep straight ahead and ignore the L turn toward the Hilton. The street makes a R turn toward some big warehouses. After that R turn, make a L toward the ocean; La Guancha is at the end on the R. Park your car and walk in. You'll hear it before you arrive. Some toddlers receive their first dancing lessons here. At one end there's a video game center where you can play with the Teenage Mutant Ninja Turtles or test to see if you have "*la prueba cerebral de einstein*." At the other end, couples dance by the bandstand even when it is empty. In between, food stands sell everything from pastrami sandwiches to piña coladas. The choo-choo-train-style bus runs out here. Try the popular **Café de Puerto** here. Ponce's *fiestas patronales* are held here in Dec.

For **movies**, try **El Emperador** (☎ 844-2222) on the bypass, which has two theaters. The **Plaza del Caribe Cinemas** (☎ 841-6666) in the Plaza del Caribe has six theaters. The **Ponce** (☎ 843-7300), shows three films. Check *El Nuevo Día* for times and features.

concerts: One activity not to be missed is the **Banda Municipal de Ponce** (Municipal Band), which presents free concerts on the Callejón Amor on Sun. nights at 8. The band was founded in 1883 as the Banda del Cuerpo de Bomberos de Ponce. Arrive early to get a seat. Selections include everything from *danzas* to *boleros* to the Boogie Woogie Bugle Boy. **Teatro La Perla** (☎ 843-4080), near the plaza, presents plays in Spanish.

EVENTS: In Nov. an event entitled *"Descubre tus raíces,"* recreating indigenous island lifestyles, takes place at the ceremonial center in Tibes on the town's outskirts. **Carnaval** is held the week before Ash Wednesday, marking the beginning of Lent. Rey Momo leads the traditional parade. Probably influenced by the Carnival of Niza in Barcelona and introduced by Catalans who settled in Ponce, the Rey Momo is the King of Carnival, a comic figure sporting a giant papier-mâché head. Similar figures are found thoughout the Latin world, and he may be a remnant of Europe's pagan past. His identity remains secret until the final day, which is marked by the burial of the sardine. *"El entierro de la sardina"* is a Spanish tradition. Carnival's *vejigantes* sport colorful papier-mâché masks, which have an animal or devil design characterized by large, open fanged mouths and pointed horns. Held in May, the **Fiestas de Cruz** have a nine-step altar leading to a cross. Also taking place during May, the **Fiesta Nacional de la Danza** is the best place to see this traditional dance. The annual *fiestas patronales* of Nuesta Señora de Guadalupe, held from Dec. 6-16, centers on the main plaza. It includes a procession led by a mariachi band. *Salsa, merengue,* and jazz bands play, and *bomba y plena* dancing is supplemented by *aguinaldo* music. A variety of foods are served, and *artesanias* sell their wares. **Feria Regional de Artesanias,** a crafts fair, is held each Feb. or March, and the **Festival de Bomba y Plena** is held in the barrio of San Anton in June.

CRAFTS AND SHOPPING: Handicrafts – including crucifixes made from nails, weavings, and hammocks – are on sale during weekends in one corner of the plaza near the firehouse. All of the museums have good gift shops. Two shopping malls are the **Plaza del Caribe** and the smaller **Centro del Sur.** If you should be in Ponce during Feb. or March, an artisans' fair is held one weekend, offering music and a fine selection of crafts to choose from; prices are generally reasonable. There are also a number of small shops around, including a dollar store, **Todo a $,** on C. Union; a couple of record stores are up the street. **C. Atocha** is also a great place to shop for bargains. **Toda a Mano** here has a good selection of crafts. Another craft shop is found on the second floor of Plaza Las Delicias, and **Isabel 30,** C. Isabel 30, also has a good selection of crafts and art.

SERVICES: The **Ponce Tourism Office** (☎ 844-5575), located on the second floor of the Plaza Las Delicias, is open Mon. to Fri. 8-12, 1-4:30. The friendly staff do what they can to help. There's also a city government tourist office. It is cleverly hidden inside Citibank, across from the firehouse. You may be able to pry some information out of them, but they appear to be ill-equipped to deal with visitors. **Banks** offer a number of ATH (instant teller) machines; Citibank's is the most entertaining. There are four **post offices;** the most convenient is on C. Atocha. **Pharmacies** include Farmacias González (☎ 844-1475) on C. Cristina at the plaza, Walgreen's (☎ 840-6093) at 35 Av. Las Américas, and Farmacias Moscoso (☎ 842-1180) on Plaza Degetau. The best places to get a *San Juan Star* are at the **Farmacias González** on the square and (ask because it's behind the counter) at the **Panaderia Reposteria Suizeria del Sur,** across from the PO on C. Guadalupe.

TOURS: Turisla (☎ 843-6972), C. Comerico 88, offers tours and excursions. **diving and water trips: Marine Sports & Dive Shop** (☎/fax 844-6175; Box 7711, Ponce, PR 00732) will take you to Caja de Muerto or other locations.

CAR RENTAL: Rent cars from **Popular Ponce** (☎ 259-4848), **L & M Car Rental** (☎ 841-2482), **Avis** (☎ 284-4188), **Leaseway of Puerto**

Rico (☎ 843-4330), **Popular Leasing & Rental** (☎ 841-7850), **Thrifty** (☎ 284-5229), or **Velco** (☎ 842-9292).

FROM PONCE: Numerous *públicos* and very occasional buses depart from the Terminal Carros for local destinations – Mayagüez (around $7), San José ($9), Guayama, Yauco, Coamo, etc. Get an early start or you'll feel like a roast chicken while waiting for them to fill up. The terminal is right next to the United Evangelical Church. *Linea Atlas Trans Island* (☎ 842-1065/4375), with offices on C. Mendez Vigo, will take you to Río Piedras, Santurce, and directly to Isla Verde Airport. The first of nine *públicos* daily departs at 4 AM. Either reserve a seat or just hunt one up at the terminal when you're ready to leave. **by air:** American Eagle flies daily from Ponce's outlying Mercedita Airport to Luis Muñoz Marín International Airport, NYC, and Miami.

Vicinity of Ponce

Ponce is a good base for exploring the S coast as well as the mountains. You can head up into the mountains or along the coast in either direction. Watch out for vendors selling fruit along the highway as well as for the police, who are often out with their radar guns in search of a ticketing opportunity.

beaches: The nearest beaches are near Guánica. Caña Gorda is on Carr. 333 and Playa Santa is at Ensenada. Farther on, are Playita Roasada in La Parguera and a beach at Boquerón. To the W is El Tuque on Carr. 2 off the Guayanilla exit road.

CAJA DE MUERTOS

On a clear day, it's possible to see this mile-long (1.6 km) island offshore. It may be named either for its coffin-like shape or from the legend of a young Portuguese named José Almeida, who fell in love with a married woman on Curaçao. He returned to visit her after becoming a pirate, and her husband died of a stroke. They married, but she was killed in an attack shortly afterwards. Almeida had her embalmed and placed in a cedar coffin with a glass door. He secreted her in a cave on this island and came to visit her. Later, he was caught and hanged, after which his crew revisited the site believing that booty was buried there. When they came upon the copper box, the two crewmen murdered the boatswain;

then one crewman murdered the other. The remaining pirate jumped to his death in fright after viewing the contents of the coffin. When crew members came upon the corpse, they brought it to St. Thomas for burial. Some years later a Spanish engineer visited the island to survey it. When he found the copper planks that had been part of the coffin, he was told about the legend and gave the island its present name.

These days, its name may be more apt because the island has been found to host four endangered plant species (extinct on the mainland) and several endangered lizards as well. Cacti and small thorny bushes predominate here. The island is surrounded by coral reefs teeming with life. Its nearby neighbors are Cayo Morillito and Cayo Berberia. Restored by the Department of Natural Resources, the lighthouse (built in 1880) has a lookout and museum. **practicalities:** Ferries used to run out to the island on weekends. Unfortunately, the Commonwealth government carted the ferry off to Fajardo for the Vieques run. For trips here, call Rafí Vega or his son (☎ 844-6175).

TIBES INDIGENOUS CEREMONIAL CENTER

Marked by unlikely concrete buildings, this archaeological site is located in a suburb of Ponce. Drive or take a *público* from the vicinity of the *mercado* to get there. It's open Wed. to Sun. from 9-4; admission $2, $1 children. There's a small cafeteria here. The accompanying gift shop has some unusual items, including T-shirts with Taíno sun petroglyphs. There is also a small museum (see below); bilingual guides are available, as are special natural history tours that can be prearranged by appointment. **events:** *"Descubre tus raíces,"* a celebration depicting indigenous lifestyles, takes place here in Nov.

HISTORY: Predating the Caguana site near Utuado, Tibes was discovered in 1974, after a hurricane and subsequent flooding, by Luiz Hernandez, a local resident. The local government expropriated the 32 acres of land and Juan Gonzales, a local archaeologist, headed a dig. Tibes is the largest indigenous settlement and ceremonial center in the West Indies. Only some five acres have been uncovered; another 22 may be excavated in the future. Archaeological evidence suggests two distinct periods of occupation: during the latter phase of the Igneri culture from AD 400-600 and in the pre-Taíno period from AD 600-1100. Both cultures were similar in terms of diet and lifestyle; cultural differences were due to an influx of new blood from outside or transitions in style over time. The older Igneri period is characterized by animal-shaped amulets, ceramic vessels, and axes. The majority of the 182 graves excavated here, which were found to contain the remains of children along with ceremonial offerings, date from this period. Other ceramics and objects such as frog-shaped amulets, *cemi* figures, and adzes, are from the later pre-Taíno period. Moves are underway to declare the area a wildlife sanctuary, but political rivalries are holding up the process.

MUSEUM: If you have a wait before your tour, you can explore the museum, which compresses quite a bit of archaeology and ethnology into a small space. Ceramic reproductions are the first item to your R as you enter. *Dujos* (ceremonial seats), axes, *metates* (ginding stones), and stone collars are among the next exhibits. Another exhibit is devoted to the ritual surrounding the hallucinogenic *cajoba* seeds (see below). Continuing on, you encounter a burial site under glass. Found under the main ball court, these human remains date back 1,200 years. Other exhibits are devoted to Arcaicos, Igneri, Pre-Taíno, and Taíno. Around the corner are *cemis* and other clay stamps. The Igneri exhibit shows how their heads were purposely deformed. Taíno ceramics from E and W Puerto Rico are in two styles: *estilo capa* and *estilo esperanza*. While the former is near Utuado, the latter comes from Vieques. Another room contains temporary exhibitions.

BATEYES: Ten ceremonial *bateyes* have been reconstructed. Petroglyphs, with animal and human faces, have been chiseled on some of the stones, which delineate the *bateyes*. The largest *bateye*, measuring 111 by 118 ft, is bordered with walkways containing riverbed stones. The area of Tibes derives its name from these stones; tibes is the Taíno word for smooth riverbed stones. While some of these *bateyes* were used for a game resembling soccer, others were used for *areytos*, ceremonial dances in which Indians, drinking beer made from fermented cassava and inhaling hallucinogenic *cajoba* seeds through a two-pronged pipe, would commune with the gods. There are no records as to what they talked about, but presumably they touched on politics, food, and sex. One elliptical *bateye* is surrounded by triangles, which suggests that it represents the sun. One major archaeological find at Tibes, an adult male skeleton discovered within the foundations of a walkway bordering one of the *bateyes*, has been dated to A.D. 790, which pushes back the date of the earliest known indigenous stone constructions by 400 years. The horseshoe *batey* here is three times as long as it is wide. The *cemi batey* is shaped like its namesake and is the longest such court discovered in Puerto Rico and the longest pre-Taíno court to have been discovered in the Caribbean. Excavating underneath, archaeologists unearthed 11 human remains. One was a man who had had his head cut off and his arms securely tied behind his back. Another woman also had her arms tied behind her back. Dead were customarily buried in the fetal position, reflecting the belief that once a person passed on they returned to their mother's womb to face reincarnation. Wives would be buried alive with their husbands: such a fate was considered an honor and a privilege. Not just a sport, the games played on the *bateyes* were both a magic ceremony as well as a way of making important decisions. For example, a game might be played that would allow the winning team to decide whether prisoners of conflict should be set free or slaughtered. Besides the *bateyes*, a small Taíno village nearby has been faithfully recreated.

THE TOUR: The entire area of your tour has been cleared and the site is immaculately manicured. Your informative guide gives you a complete rundown on everything that the Igneris did and where. He will point out indigenous trees such as quenapa, spiny ash, and calabash; fruit trees such as the soursop and tamarind; endangered plants like the moralon; batata, manioc and century plants; and medicinal herbs. You learn of the uses for each and what they meant to the inhabitants. On the tour, you stop at a set of reconstructed huts (actually outside of the site's limits), which you are free to explore; the rectangular chief's hut is the best one.

HACIENDA BUENA VISTA

Restored by the Conservation Trust, this "Good View Estate," a former coffee plantation, contains slave quarters, a two-story estate house, and exceptional hydraulic machinery. Hacienda Buena Vista was founded in 1833 by Spaniard Salvador de Vives, who first emigrated to Venezuela. After Venezuela gained its independence, he, along with his wife, son and two slaves, migrated here in 1824. Purchasing 482 *cuerdas* of land, he named the estate Buena Vista because of its great natural beauty. Following in his footsteps, his son Carlos added hydraulic power to the estate along with a corn mill. His son Salavador, in turn, added the coffee depulping machine and a husking and polishing machine, which were placed in the corn mill's building and run off of the original water wheel. After the San Ciriaco hurricane struck, 60% of the coffee crop was destroyed and the world coffee market collapsed by 1900. Coffee was replaced by oranges until the Government of Puerto Rico expropriated the property in the 1950s and redistributed the land to local farmers. In 1984, the site was purchased because of its unique forest, river, and waterfall. Although the buildings had been largely consumed by termites and the machinery was covered with rust, it has been reconstructed through photos and other records. Carefully restored, it is truly one of the Caribbean's historical gems.

GETTING HERE: Set to the N of Ponce on the way to Adjuntas, the estate is located on Carr. 10 at Km 16.8; it's open to groups Wed. and Thurs.; general admission ($5 adults, $2 children) is on Fri. and Sat., with reservations required (☎ 722-5882, weekends 284-7020). Tours are at 8:30, 10:30, 1:30, and 3:30; only the 1:30 tour is in English, and you must request this.

touring: Arriving at the entrance, you park your car and then pay. Inside the first structure, the former family home, there are exhibits on coffee processing as well as on the different varieties of wood used. Upstairs there is a recreation of how the plantation owners lived. Rooms have been restored in late 19th-century style using original construction techniques and traditional materials; several pieces of furniture were donated by the Vives family. There's a parlor with a Victrola poised to play *La Traviata*, a sewing machine, a rocking horse, tables and chairs; a study with wire-rim glasses still on top of the ledger; a bedroom with shoes tucked under the bed; and a kitchen with coffee beans in various stages of processing. In short, it appears as if the family has either just stepped out for a minute or has been kidnapped by aliens. In fact, the Vives family never lived here full time, with the exception of a brief period during the American occupation.

Outside, you continue on a path, along which the water is channeled, and pass entranceways into which small slave boys used to crawl to clean the canal (the water must be returned without contamination). Passing a secondary forest, you come to a 100-ft waterfall at the path's end; this is the source for the hydraulic power. The next stop is at the hydraulic water wheel that separates the coffee beans from their chaff. This red water turbine is the only one of its kind still in existence: the water is fed in from the bottom rather than the top. The immense wooden wheels on top of the mechanism are what make it move. Invented by Sir James Whitelaw of Scotland and cast by the West Point Foundry in 1854, the impressive hydraulic corn mill is the last stop on the tour. When operating, it sounds like a rainstorm. You are then escorted to where you began the tour, treated to a cup of freshly ground and brewed coffee, and offered the chance to try cleaning and grinding your own coffee beans; small packets are on sale for $1.

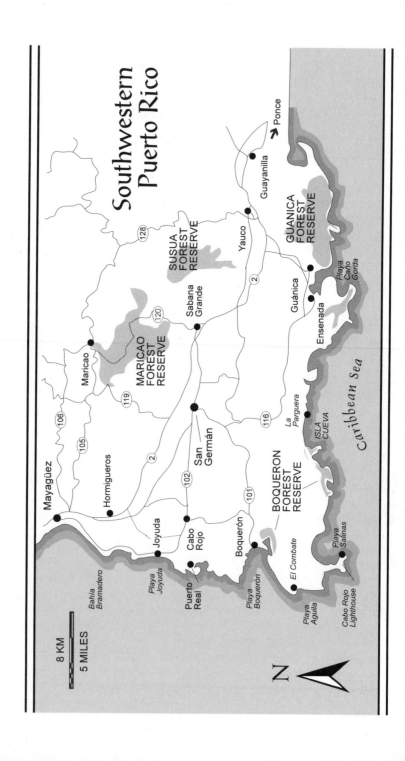

Southwestern
Puerto Rico

→ Ponce

Guayanilla

GUANICA
FOREST
RESERVE

Yauco

SUSUA FOREST
RESERVE

Playa
Caño
Gorda

128

Sabana
Grande

Guánica

120

MARICAO
FOREST
RESERVE

Maricao

Ensenada

119

106

105

Mayagüez

La
Parguera

ISLA
CUEVA

Caribbean Sea

Hormigueros

2

San
Germán

116

Joyuda

102

Cabo
Rojo

BOQUERON
FOREST
RESERVE

Bahía
Bramadero

Playa Joyuda

Puerto
Real

Boquerón

101

El Combate

Playa
Boquerón

Playa
Salinas

Playa
Aguila

Cabo Rojo
Lighthouse

8 KM

5 MILES

N

Southwestern Puerto Rico

Yauco

Built on a hillside W of Ponce, this small town still has its step streets, old houses, great coffee, and a distinctly Spanish-American atmosphere. Plaza de Recreo Fernando de Pacheco was reconstructed in 1993. Its **Festival del Café** (Coffee Festival) is held here in Feb., and the festival of patron saint **Nuestra Senora del Rosario** takes place around Oct. 7.

HISTORY: Originally known to the Indians as *Coayuco*, the surrounding area was settled by the Spanish, becoming an independent municipality in 1756. Haitian French, Corsicans, and other immigrants began arriving in the early 1800s. Sugarcane and cotton gave way to coffee cultivation. Low in caffeine but rich in taste, Yauco's coffee became famous in Europe for its exceptional quality and soon commanded a high market price. The loss of European markets after the Spanish-American War, combined with the devastation caused by a hurricane in 1899 and competition from mass-producing countries like Brazil and Columbia, led to the sad decay of the local coffee industry.

PRACTICALITIES: Camping is available at **Embalse Lucchetti**, an artificial lake dating from 1952. It has seven campsites, an information center, fishing, and a friendly flock of ducks. You will need to obtain a permit from *Recursos Naturales* in San Juan in advance. Dating from 1959, **Restaurante La Guardarraya** (☎ 856-4222), on Carr. 127 en route to Guayanilla, caters to meat-eaters. Its *chuletas can-can* are pork chops that are "frilly," thus resembling a can-can dancer's skirt. There's a movie theater in town. **Yauco Plaza** is a large shopping plaza just at the entrance to the town when coming from Mayagüez. From Ponce, Yauco is just off the expressway; you're welcomed by a Burger King sign. From here, *públicos* go to Ponce, Guánica, Guayanilla, and Sabana Grande.

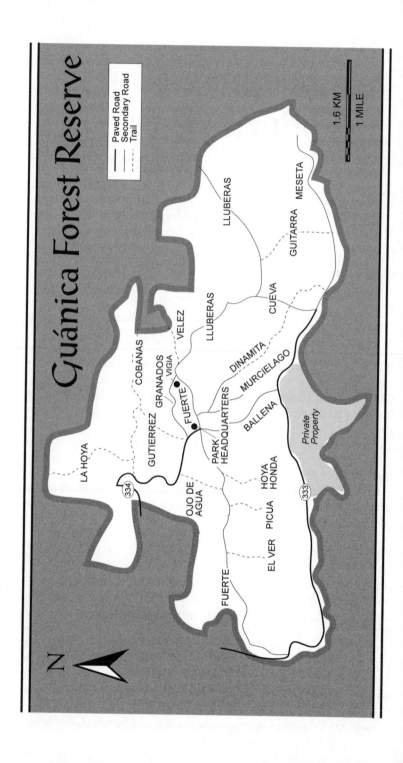

Guánica Forest Reserve

N

Paved Road
Secondary Road
Trail

1.6 KM
1 MILE

LA HOYA

COBANAS

GUTIERREZ

GRANADOS

VIGIA

VELEZ

FUERTE

LLUBERAS

LLUBERAS

DINAMITA

CUEVA

GUITARRA

MESETA

MURCIELAGO

BALLENA

PARK HEADQUARTERS

OJO DE AGUA

HOYA HONDA

PICUA

EL VER

FUERTE

Private Property

334

333

Guánica

Reserva Forestal Guánica, several beautiful beaches (Mangrillo Grande and Playa Jaboncillo), and the place where the Americans landed during the 1898 invasion are all situated around this pleasant town of 9,000. The small town has a nice boardwalk. Its ambiance is marred only by the chicken processing plant and the fertilizer factory. The reserve itself is one of the finest examples of cactus-scrub-subtropical dry forest in the world. It was designated by the United Nations as a Man and the Biosphere Reserve in 1975. Its dryness is assured by the Cordillera Central, which catches most of the rain before it reaches the coast. Encompassing over 1,620 acres (4,000 ha), it has 36 mi (57 km) of old roads and trails. Over 700 species of trees and plants are protected here, and vegetation inside the reserve includes *aroma* (acacia) and *guayacan* (lignum vitae) trees.

Adjoining the forest is 164 acres fronting the **Bahía Ballena,** which was purchased by the Conservation Trust and the Department of Natural Resources for $1.7 million in 1992. It had originally been slated for a $12 million Club Med resort. Local resident Miguel Cañas, leader of the fight, discovered that the *sapo concho,* a toad thought to have been extinct, lived in the area, and the planned resort would have restricted its movements and endangered its well-being. Plans are to develop tours and a variety of nature exhibits here.

GETTING HERE: Take Carr. 335 to the end of the road in Sector Jabonillo where there's a ranger station with information and restrooms. Carr. 334 leads NE from the town of Guánicato to the reserve and ranger station. Several dirt roads (no vehicles allowed) are the best place to hike from there. (See the "Hiking Trails" chart). Carr. 333 runs along the reserve's perimeter; an unmarked trail follows it to the ranger station. At the ranger station be sure to pick up literature, including the superb *A Guide to Trails of Guánica* by Beth Farnsworth.

FAUNA: The *guabairo* (Puerto Rican whippoorwill) survives on the island only in this reserve. Some of the other 40 species of birds found here include the troupial, the orange-cheeked waxbill (an introduced W African native), the Caribbean elaenia, the Puerto Rican bullfinch, the Puerto Rican nightjar (once thought to be extinct), and the Puerto Rican tody. The crested toad is born in pools but lives in limestone crevices. Green and leatherback turtles still lay their eggs along the coast, but mongooses are posing a threat to the eggs and hatchlings. The *Ameiva wetmorei* is a black-bodied lizard with racing stripes on its back and a blue iridescent tail. Also be sure to watch out for the "crazy ants" which are common.

HIKING TRAILS IN GUÁNICA FOREST RESERVE

This reserve contains a wide variety of trails – one for every level of hiker. Be sure to protect yourself from the sun, bring adequate food and water, and wear good shoes. Remember to avoid the *chicharron*, a poisonous shrub readily identifiable by its spiny reddish leaves.

BALLENA: Entrance at Carr. 333 near Punta Ballena. An easy walk along a two-km paved road heading through a mahogany plantation and deciduous forest that leads to dry scrub. After a km, follow a sign marked "Guayacán Centenario" to find a 700-year-old guayacán tree with a trunk six ft in diameter.

COBANAS: Enter at Carr. 334 (Maniel Rd.). This old road heads E 3½ km through a ridge covered with secondary deciduous forest to the reserve's end. At the three km point, it passes through an abandoned *campeche* plantation; these trees were once used to obtain a black dye as well as dysentery medicine. Just after the entrance to this trail is the start of the **La Hoya** trail, which heads 2½ km to the N. Traversing a verdant ravine, it passes through patchy thickets of evergreens that alternate with deciduous forest.

CUEVA: Enter from the parking lot at the end of carr. 333. This relatively flat and easy 1½-km trail heads N through a coastal forest to the Llúberas Rd.; orange and black troupials (onomatopoeically named after their "troo-pial" call) may be sighted en route. Owing to the ecological fragility of its ecosystem, the large cave near the path should be visited while in the company of a guide; permission should be obtained from the ranger station in advance.

FUERTE: Enter W of the ranger station at the end of Carr. 333. This 5½-km trail is of moderate difficulty; it leads along a ridge-top road to the ruins of a fort, where there's a lookout tower constructed by the Civilian Conservation Corps during the 1930s. Be sure to catch the spectacular view from here. A side trail, the **Hoya Honda,** heads down to a grove of mahogany trees; another trail to try is **El Ver.** Both pass through verdant ravines and old plantations. Also leading off of the Fuerte Trail at 1.2 km, the 1½-km **Ojo de Agua** heads N to Carr. 334 (Maniel Rd.). It passes through a spring-fed forest.

GRANADOS: Enter around a quarter-km N of the ranger station off of Carr. 334. Good for birdwatching, this one-km trail passes through deciduous forest on the way to the Llúberas Rd. (which you can take back to the parking lot). Watch for fossilized corals in the rocks along the trail.

GUTIERREZ: Enter at .5 km NW of the ranger station along Carr. 334; the one-km road heads NE to connect with the **Cóbanas Trail.** It passes through regenerating tropical forest that supported plantations 40 yrs. ago.

LLÚBERAS: Enter from the picnic area at the ranger station. This eight-km road passes through the gamut of the reserve's vegetative zones. You'll pass by limestone and matorral scrub as well as evergreen and deciduous forests. The remains of a sugar plantation and mill (which give the road its name) are near the E end. The **Cueva** and **Guittara** trails branch off of this road.

MESETA: Enter through the parking lot at the end of Carr. 333. This easy 3½-km trail follows the Guánica coastal dry forest with soaring sea birds, cactus scrub, sea grapes, and cliffs covered with dwarf white mangroves. It ends at the reserve's E boundary.

MURCIÉLAGO: Enter .2 km E of the ranger station by the picnic area. This 1.2-km trail heads off of the Llúberas Rd. and passes through a mahogany plantation, limestone bedrock (with nesting Puerto Rican todies), and deciduous forest before terminating in a moist ravine. The **Dinamita Trail,** which heads off to your L near the Murciélago's beginning, leads to Carr. 333; it is not maintained, so going can be rough at times.

VELEZ/VIGÍA: Enter one km NE from the ranger station on the Llúberas Rd. This one-km trail brings you up to **Criollo II,** the reserve's highest outlook. You can return via the Granados to make a loop.

Southwestern Puerto Rico

arboreal ecosystems: Comprising nearly two-thirds of the reserve's area, the **deciduous forest** contains mostly young trees. During the dry season (Dec. to April), almost half of the trees here shed their leaves, which release nutrients into the soil. At the end of the dry season, many of the trees flower and fruit. Check the trees for orchids and termite nests as well as the tiny green Puerto Rican tody and the brown lizard cuckoo (which can be spotted by its black and white tail).

Covering about a fifth of the reserve's area and largely confined to moist ravines, valleys, and sinkholes, the **semi-evergreen forest** contains plants more commonly found at higher and damper altitudes. The dry scrub forest contains stunted trees and cacti. Many of its shrubs are members of the *Rubiaccae*, the coffee family; they may be recognized by their thorns, small opposing leaves, and tiny white tubular flowers. The **coastal forest** endures low rainfall and salty wind spray. Its shrunken and twisted trees attest to the harshness of the environment. In this area you can spot buttonwood mangroves, sea grapes, and milkweed. Other parts of the reserve have been used as plantations and are in recovery.

ACCOMMODATIONS: Jack's Guest House (☎ 821-2738/5117; Box 988, Guánica, PR 00653) is along Carr. 333 on the way to Playa Gorda. Next door, there are apartments for rent (☎ 821-1168). **Mary Lee's By the Sea Cabañas** (☎ 821-3600) is at San Jacinto in Caña Gorda. You can **camp** at Caña Gorda's *balneario* (Carr. 333, Km 5.9). **Copamarina Beach Resort** (☎ 800-981-4676, 821-0505, fax 821-0070; Web site: www.copamarina.com; Box 805, Guanica, PR 00653), at Km 6.5 along Carr. 333, has undergone a $10 million renovation; it has expanded from 75 to 125 rooms, and added a marina and 15 privately owned villas. Rooms include a/c, cable TV, and phone. Its other facilities include tennis courts, swimming pool, and the nearby "Gilligan's Island," an offshore cay with mangroves and a beach. **LK Sweeny and Son** at Copamarina (☎ 800-468-4553 in the US; 800-981-4676 in Puerto Rico) is a gourmet seafood restaurant with rooms. Rates run about $135 s or d. Corporate, government, senior citizen, midweek, and other special rates are available, as are ecotourism and physical fitness packages. In Guayanilla to the E at Km 204 on Carr. 12, **Pichi's Hotel** (☎ 835-3335, fax 835-3272; Box 115, Guayanilla, PR 00656) has a/c rooms with satellite color TV, meeting rooms, and a pool. Rates start from around $60.

FOOD: You can buy inexpensive fish from Ameliana at the *pescaderia* just down the road from Jack's. **La Ballena** (☎ 821-0505) is a seaside seafood restaurant at Km 6.5 on Carr. 333. At C. Principal C-4 in Playa Santa, **La Cocha** (☎ 821-5522) serves gourmet Puerto Rican food and seafood. The upscale **Blue Marlin Restaurant** is at Av. Esperanza 59. The **Brisas del Mar Bar and Restaurant** is on the same seaside boulevard, along with other eateries.

Sabana Grande

Founded by Spanish nobility and members of venerable Spanish families, Sabana Grande set up its own government during the Spanish-American War. It lasted only days. The *fiestas patronales* of San Isidoro Labrador take place around May 15.

This small community is chiefly noted for the miracle that took place here. One day in 1953, a group of schoolchildren chanced upon the Virgin Mary while pausing at a brook near the town. She was wearing a blue robe, white tunic, a neck brooch, a sash, and sandals. After chatting a few minutes with the children, the Virgin promised to return on May 25. When a group of 130,000 devotees arrived on that date at the spot, the Divine Lady failed to show up. However, many of the chronic ailments and diseases of those present were reportedly cured on the spot. Many eyewitness reports attest to serious diseases cured by the healing power of the brook where the Virgin was seen.

Numerous small shrines and a large chapel have been erected to commemorate the miracles that took place here, and the anniversary of the sighting was celebrated by a Mass each year until 1989 (when the island's cardinal ordered a halt to the services). Hundreds of thousands attended, and calls continue for official recognition of the sighting by the Catholic Church. New plans call for the establishment of a multimillion-dollar theme park on the site, to be called Monte Mistico de Maria. It would include trams and a gigantic 25-story blue-robed statue of the Virgin Mary. Another noteworthy attraction near the town, though of a completely different type, is **Langostinos Del Caribe**, a shrimp farm; ☎ 873-1026 for reservations.

San Germán & Vicinity

San Germán

Second oldest and certainly the most attractive town on the island, San Germán retains its quiet colonial charm and distinguished architecture. The atmosphere is distinctly Mediterranean. Local legend insists that the swallows of Capistrano winter here.

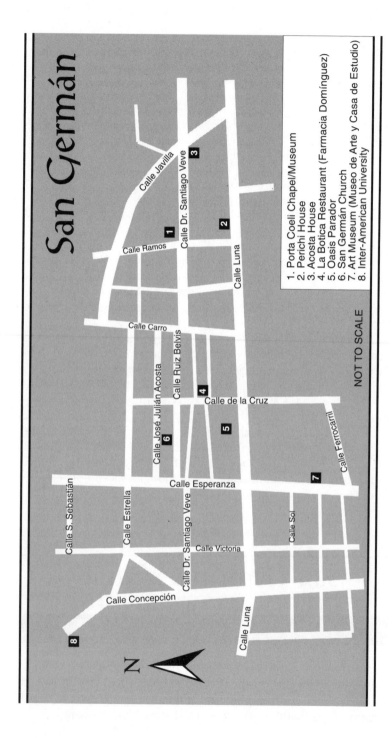

San Germán

1. Porta Coeli Chapel/Museum
2. Perichi House
3. Acosta House
4. La Botica Restaurant (Farmacia Domínguez)
5. Oasis Parador
6. San Germán Church
7. Art Museum (Museo de Arte y Casa de Estudio)
8. Inter-American University

NOT TO SCALE

Calle Javilla
Calle Dr. Santiago Veve
Calle Ramos
Calle Luna
Calle Carro
Calle Ruiz Belvis
Calle José Julián Acosta
Calle de la Cruz
Calle Ferrocarril
Calle Esperanza
Calle S. Sebastián
Calle Estrella
Calle Dr. Santiago Veve
Calle Victoria
Calle Sol
Calle Concepción
Calle Luna

N

The town is named after King Ferdinand of Spain's second wife, Germaine de Foix, whom he married in 1503. Its nickname is Ciudad de las Lomas ("City of the Hills"). Today's residents are descendants of the pirates, Corsicans, smugglers, poets, priests, and politicians of days past. Although the pirates and sugar plantations may be gone forever, a feeling from that era still lingers in the town.

SIGHTS: Two rectangular plazas in the center of town face each other, separated only by the city hall, a former prison. Martin Quinones Plaza boasts **San Germán de Auxerre Church**. Built in the 19th century, its wooden vault, painted in blue and grey, simulates a coffered ceiling. The second plaza, **Parque de Santo Domingo**, now bordered with black iron and wooden park benches, was originally a marketplace.

The Church of **Porta Coeli** ("Gate of Heaven"), the town's main attraction, rises dramatically from the end of the plaza (usually open Tues. to Sun. 9-noon, 1-4:30, but currently closed for restoration through 1996). Twenty-four brick steps lead up to the white walls of the entrance. Originally constructed by Dominican friars in 1606, it is believed to have been connected by tunnels to the main monastery, which no longer exists. It was used as a school in 1812, and almost became the district jail in 1842. In 1866 the monastery was razed and its beams and bricks were sold at public auction. In 1878, the chapel was restored and opened for services, which continued until 1949. Recognized as a historical monument in 1930, it was struck by lightning in 1948 and damaged.

The chapel was later sold by the Bishop to the commonwealth government for $1. Its most recent restoration was completed in 1982. While the palm wood ceiling and tough, brown ausobo beams are original, the balcony is a reconstruction. The structure is set up to resemble a working chapel rather than a museum, though Mass is held here now only three times a year. Treasures gathered from all over have been placed along its sides. Exhibits include choral books from Santo Domingo and a surly 17th-century portrait of St. Nicholas de Bari, the French Santa Claus. Others include a primitive carving of Jesus found in San Juan, several lovely 19th-century Señora de la Monserrate Black Madonna and Child statues, and a representation of San Cristóbal with a part from one of his bones inserted. To get here, keep to the R after you come into town.

Museo de Arte y Casa de Estudio (open 10-3, Mon. to Sun.), C. Esperanza 7, has a number of prints – most of them silkscreens. It also displays computer graphics and mixed media works. Particu-

Southwestern Puerto Rico

larly notable is José Alicia's mixed-media work *Niña con Granada*. It also has a cooling water fountain in back of the courtyard. Upstairs, you are taken back to earlier eras. The Sala Ramírez Arellano assembles a collection of 19th- and 20th-century furniture to resemble a living room. Sala de Arte Indigena holds a grinding stone, *cemi*, ax heads, and Taíno collars (which the chiefs used in a special ceremony). Across the hall is the Sala de Arte Religiosa with a crucified Christ and other ornaments and an old confession booth. Elaborate and placed on a pedestal, it dates from 1779.

NEAR PORTA COELI: At C. Santiago Veve 70, the art nouveau residence of Mrs. Delia Lopez de Acosta contains decorative murals inside. Built in 1911-12, it is a superb example of *criolla* architecture. The Perichi home, C. Luna 94, is another classic. Constructed in 1920, it is a fine example of Puerto Rican ornamental architecture. The lovely grounds of Inter American University are on the edge of town just off the road to Cabo Rojo. Founded in 1912 as the Instituto Politécnico, its name was changed in 1956.

ACCOMMODATIONS: The **Parador Oasis** (☎/fax 892-1175; Box 114, San Germán, PR 00683) is a classically styled hotel at C. Luna 4. Its facilities include 34 a/c rooms with private bath and color TV, a restaurant, and convention hall. Rates are $52/$54 s and $58/$60 d year round. For current prices and to make reservations, contact Paradores Puertorriqueños, Box 4435, Old San Juan, PR 00905; ☎ 800-443-0266 in the US, 137-800-462-7575 in Puerto Rico.

FOOD: At Dr. Veve 33, **Bótica** (☎ 892-5790) is a converted drugstore (Farmacia Dominguez); it serves seafood and other dishes. Open daily for lunch and dinner, it dates from 1877. Entrées range from $7 to $20. In the town center, **Antonino's Pizza** is a plush pizza joint. The **Sol de Verano** has Chinese food. The Oasis also has a gourmet restaurant.

PRACTICALITIES: The **PO** is right across from the terminal for *públicos*. The **library** is right on one side of Parque de Santo Domingo.

FROM SAN GERMÁN: La Parguera and other coastal sights are nearby. Ask a local how to negotiate the tricky transition from town to this road.

Lajas

Named after the slate deposits found in its vicinity, this small town dates from the early 19th century. Originally a part of San Germán, it became an independent municipality in 1883. Lajas's *fiestas patronales* (in honor of patron saint Nuestra Señora de la Candelaria) take place in the beginning of February, which is also the start of the *zatra* or pineapple season, for which the area is famous. There's a great view to be had from atop Las Animas mountain to the W.

LAGUNA CARTAGENA

This lagoon is off of Carr. 303 to the SE of Lajas. Overgrown to the point where it resembles more of a swamp than a lagoon, Cartagena is one of the island's two freshwater lagoons. Good places for a birder to spot water fowl, herons, ducks, cave swallows, common ground-doves and the northern mockingbird can all be found here. The sora, a marsh bird rarely seen outside Puerto Rico, and the American purple gallinule, can be found here as well.

La Parguera

Located off Carr. 304 is the eastern branch of **Bosque Estatal De Boquerón**, commonly referred to as La Parguera, after the town of the same name. The name itself derives from *pargos*, a type of snapper. This area contains what is probably the most famous marine attraction in Puerto Rico. **La Bahía Fosforescente** (Phosphorescent Bay) contains millions of luminescent dinoflagellates, a microscopic plankton. Any disturbance causes them to light up the surrounding water. Pick a moonless night and take one of the twice-nightly boats (times vary) departing from Villa Parguera's pier. Dip a hand in the water and watch as sparks of liquid silver run through it. Bahía Mondo José, nearby, also has a large population of dinoflagellates. In 1973 the Conservation Trust acquired some 400 acres in danger of development. This might have altered the drainage pattern, causing sedimentation, which would have played havoc with the bay's ecological balance. Also, the electric lights that go along with development would have competed with the bay's luminescence. The trust is seeking to acquire another 800 acres which will be used only for grazing cattle and for farming. The small town lights up on weekends when there's live entertainment. Offshore are more than 30 mangrove cays. Check on transport out to Mata de la Cay, two miles offshore. Visible from the outskirts of town is **Isla Cueva**. It's commonly known as Monkey Island because 400 monkeys reside there. Originally from India, they are allowed to pursue their favorite pastimes freely among the trees. Occasionally, a group of scientists arrives to check up on their habits. Rosada Beach is E of town.

ACCOMMODATIONS: All of the guesthouses and hotels listed here are within the heart of town. **Andino's Chalet & Guest House** (☎ 899-0000; HC-01, Box 4691, Lajas, PR 00667), which has been strongly recommended by a reader, has one-and two-bedroom apartments for around $35-45 pn. According to the reader, Ernesto Andino is a retired businessman who is "very knowledgeable" and can arrange boat tours. It's at C. 8 #33, right near Parque de Pelota in town. **Parador Villa Parguera** (☎ 899-3975/7777, fax 899-6040; Box 273, La Parguera, Lajas, PR 00667), Carr. 304, has 50 a/c rooms with private bath, restaurant, and swimming pool. Rates are $75 s and $85 d. ☎ 800-443-0266 in the US, 800-288-3975 in the US and Canada. The 18-unit **Posada Porlamar Parador** (☎ 899-4015, fax 899-6082; Box 405, La Parguera, Lajas, PR 00667), Carr. 304, is set in an old wooden building with balconies and a garden. Rates start from around $55. Contact ☎ 800-443-0266 in the US, 800-288-3975 in the US and Canada. The eight-unit **Guest House Viento y Vela** (☎ 899-4689/3030, fax 899-4698; Box 386, La Parguera, Lajas, PR 00667) is at Km 3.2 on Carr. 304. It's a wood-framed house with a/c and fan efficiencies. Rates start at around $30. Up to the R, the 40-room **Hotel Colónial Casablanca** (☎ 899-4250/0080; Box 481, La Parguera, Lajas, PR 00667) has a very attractive atmosphere, with a pool and restaurant; its off-season rates start around $50 s and $60 d. The **Parguera Guest House** (☎ 899-1933/3993; Carr. las Colinas, La Parguera, Lajas, PR 00667) charges about $60 s or d. The eight-room **Nautilus Guest House** (☎ 899-4565; Box 396, La Parguera, Lajas, PR 00667) has rooms with a/c and color TV from $55. **Gladys Guest House** (☎ 899-4678) is down a sidestreet; it has a/c.

FOOD: There are a large number of restaurants here, including the **Bahía and Restaurant Porto Parguera, Tony's Pizza, Café Vista al Mar, Mar y Tierra** (which features billiard tables), **Restaurant Reef Pop** (about the same price as the others but done up in fast food style), and the a/c **Shark Café**. **Los Balcones** has seafood and steaks served in a pleasant atmosphere. **La Palmita Cocktail Lounge & Café** has *sopa de pescado* and other seafood dishes; they charge $10-$15 for entrées. **Café Vista del Mar** has a fantastic selection of *empanadillas*. **Pargo Mar** has fish entrées for about $15. If you will be cooking your own food, there's also a *pescaderia* (fish market).

ENTERTAINMENT: La Playita offers live music on weekends. **La Tierra del Oz** has shuffleboard, pool tables, and video games. **Parador Villa Parguera** has a variety of live shows on Sat. nights.

KAYAKING: Kayaks are available for rent. A one-person kayak is $8 ph; a two-person is $15 ph. **diving:** Contact **La Parguera Divers** (☎/fax 899-4171; Box 514, Lajas, PR 00667). They run a number of trips. **glass bottom boats: Fondo de Cristal II** (☎ 899-5891/2972; box 427, Lajas, PR 00667) operates from the pier.

Cabo Rojo & Vicinity

Cabo Rojo

Founded in 1772, this small town is a convenient jumping-off point for Mayagüez or destinations to the S. Erected in 1783, the San Miguel Arcangel Church stands next to the plaza. Cabo Rojo reached its peak of prosperity in the 1800s when immigrants from Spain and other Mediterranean countries, fleeing revolutions in Europe, arrived to take up sugarcane cultivation. Today, the canefields have been displaced by pasture for cattle. Cabo Rojo's *fiestas patronales* take place around September 29.

ACCOMMODATIONS: For accommodations in the area see San Germán, Boquerón, La Parguera, and Joyuda. **Camping** is available around the Cabo Rojo area: **Villa Plaza** (☎ 851-1340) at Denigno Obejo Plaza is on Carr. 301 at Km 6.9; **Villa La Mela** at Carr. 307, Km 35, Cabo Rojo (☎ 851-1391/2067); and **Mojacascade Camp** (☎ 745-0305) at Carr. 301, Km 10.1, Playa Combate, Cabo Rojo.

Playa Joyuda/Punta Arenas

In an area also known as Punta Arenas, **Joyuda Beach**, with its numerous seafood restaurants, is off Carr. 102 to the NW. You can visit **Isla de Ratones** offshore. The town has been built up for tourism, but the beach can disappoint. It's not been the same since dredging for a landfill for a Mayagüez tuna plant impacted the area. **Tino's** here is famous for its *mofongo* with seafood. Other restaurants include **Restaurant Island View**, **Restaurant Brisas de Joyuda**, **Restaurant Brisas del Mar**, **Restaurant Costa del Sol**, **Restaurant El Bohio**, **Restaurante Vista Bohio**, and **Restaurant El Pueblito**. At Km 11.7 on Carr. 102, **Hotel/Parador Joyuda Beach** (☎ 851-5650, fax 265-6940; Box 1660, Mayagüez, PR 00681), a *parador*, has 43 a/c rooms with TV, phone, and bath; some suites have sunset views. Facilities include restaurant and beach bar, beach volleyball, small children's playground, windsurfing, canoeing, and golfing (at the Club Deportivo); cabins with kitchens are also available. Rooms run from around $65. Set in Joyuda on Carr. 102 at Km 14.2, **Parador Perichi's**, (☎ 851-3131, fax 851-0560; Box 16310, Cabo Rojo, PR 00623) has 30 a/c rooms with balconies, color TV, and phone. There's a pool, restaurant, banquet hall, baseball and basketball courts, and game room. Rates start at around $66 s and $70 d. For reservations for either of these two *paradores*, ☎ 800-443-0266 in the US and 800-462-7575 in Puerto Rico. Also here are **Hotel Antibes** (☎ 851-8800), **Cabañas Tony** (☎ 851-2500), **Cabañas Don Carlos** (☎ 821-9264/0976), which has a swimming pool, and other hotels.

To the W, nearly half the island's fish are caught at **Puerto Real**. When it served as Cabo Rojo's port (1760-1860), merchandise and slaves from St. Thomas and Curacao were off-loaded here. **Ostiones**, a point of land protruding to the N of Puerto Real, is the location of an important indigenous archaeological site. Of special interest to birdwatchers, **Laguna Joyuda** is 7½ km NW of town. Its 300 acres (150 ha) contain a vast variety of birds, including pelicans, martins, and herons. It is luminescent on moonless nights. Beachgoers will want to check out **Playa Buyé** and **Playa La Mela** to the SW on Carr. 307. At attractive and relatively uncrowded Playa Buyé, you can stay at **Cabiñas Playa Buyé** (☎ 851-2923), Carr. 307 at Km 4.8. **Restaurante Caribe** is at Km 4.3 on Carr. 307 here. **Puerto Real** is a very small and attractive fishing village; the neighboring lagoon at **Punta Guaniquilla** harbors strangely shaped boulders which protrude from and dominate the still waters of the sometimes dry lagoon. Birds squeal and cry overhead. Pirate Roberto Cofresi, who terrorized the coast during the early 19th century, hid out in a cave nearby.

AREA DINING: At Km 13.9 on Carr. 102, **Bohío** (☎ 851-2755) serves seafood and meat. **Brisas de Joyuda** (☎ 851-2488), at Km 14.2, offers a variety of reasonably priced seafood dishes. By the beach on C. Principal in Puerto Real, **Brisas del Mar** (☎ 851-1264) serves similar fare. At. Km 9.7 on Carr. 102, oceanside **Casona de Serafín** (☎ 851-0066) serves lobster and other seafood dishes. **Island View Restaurant** (☎ 851-9264), Carr. 102 at Km 13.7, also offers steak and seafood. Right next door, **Tino's** (☎ 851-2976) specializes in *mofongo relleno de mariscos en salsa.*

Boquerón

Located S of Cabo Rojo and W of San Germán is the small town of Boquerón and the western branch of the **Bosque Estatal de Boquerón** (Boquerón Forest Reserve). Herons perch on mangroves in the bird sanctuary here. The town itself is well known for its *balneario* (public beach), as well as its raw oysters with lemon juice and other types of seafood. The protected bay here is excellent for windsurfing, boating, and swimming. Its harbor once sheltered pirates like Roberto Cofresi. The US Border Patrol arrested 31 illegal immigrants here in March 1996. While 20 were from the Dominican Republic, 11 were Macedonian nationals who had paid $2,000 pp (plus airfare from Tirana, Albania) for the promised opportunity to enter the US.

ACCOMMODATIONS AND DINING: In Boquerón, off Carr. 307 and 103, **Parador Boquemar,** (☎ 851-2158, fax 851-7600; Box 133, Boquerón, Cabo Rojo, PR 00622) has 63 a/c rooms. Rates are around $60 s and $65 d. It has a pool, and its **La Cascada Restaurant** is well known for gourmet dishes. For reservations, ☎ 800-443-0266 in the US and 800-462-7575 in Puerto Rico. **Galloways** is a nearby restaurant right on the water. At Km 7.4 on Carr. 187, the 20-room **Hotel Cuestamar** (☎ 851-2819, fax 254-2019; Box 187, Boquerón, PR 00622) has a pool and coffee shop; rates start from around $60 s or d. Set at the town's entrance on Carr. 101, Km 18.1 is **Boquerón Beach** (☎ 851-7110, 254-3002; Boquerón, Cabo Rojo, PR 00622). You can eat at the **Fish Net Restaurant**, the **Restaurant Villa Playera**, or at a number of others.

The government agency Fomento rents out cabins here to "bona fide family groups" (i.e., parents and children). There is a two-night minimum stay, and reservations must be booked 120 days in advance. For more information see "Accommodations" in the Introduction.

El Combate

This small fishing village to the N of the salt beds has an unmistakable 19th-century aura about it. There are a number of restaurants and places to stay here. **El Combate Guest House** (☎ 747-0384) is near town. You can also try **Apartamentos Kenny** (☎ 851-0002), **Cabañas Marivan Playa Combate** (☎ 851-2433), **Cabinas Freddy** (☎ 851-7370), **Cabañas Miranda** (☎ 254-2992), **Cabañas Pou-Men** (☎ 254-2220), **Ranitt Cabinas** (☎ 833-2735), **Cabinas Cofresi**, **Cabañas & Restaurante Luichy's** (☎ 851-0206), and **Cabañas Villa Ranil** (☎ 851-4297). There are also some camping areas on the way out of town. **Annie's Seafood Restaurant** (☎ 851-0021) also has cabañas.

FOOD: Try **Santos Pizzeria, Restaurant El Combate**, or **Cafeteria Las Bohios**. **Willy's** (☎ 254-1111) rents jet skis and sells cooked chicken and pizza. You can buy basic items at **Colmado Chiquitin**.

CABO ROJO LIGHTHOUSE

This structure is on Carr. 303, standing along a spit of land between Bahía Salinas and Bahía Sucia. It's a really beautiful trip to get here. You pass the turnoff to El Combate (where there's a campground). The road turns to clay, and you follow it along past the salt processing fields to your R; a lagoon is on the L. On the way you pass mangroves. Keep going and you find one parking place; follow the other road which branches off to the L, park right by the beach and climb up. Once inhabited by the lighthouse keepers and their families who occupied the two wings at its base, it has been electrified and is now automatic. This lighthouse was built in 1881 under Spanish rule in response to pressure from local planters. Beneath the lighthouse, jagged limestone cliffs at Punta Jaguey drop sharply into the sea – an awesome sight to behold. The whole area has the feeling of being at the end of the world. There are large numbers of brown pelicans sitting on the rocks off the coast; it is a great place for birders. Behind it lies the Sierra Betmeja, low hills that date back 130 million years. The Salinas salt beds are nearby; salt harvested here is sent off to the Starkist plant in Mayagüez. The snowy plover can be seen in this vicinity.

Hormigueros

This town owes its name, meaning "ant hill," to the unique topography of the region. Originally a barrio of San Germán and later of Mayagüez, it became a distinct town in 1874. Hormigueros is home to the **Shrine of Our Lady of Monserrate**, a majestic yellow church that towers above the town. According to a 17th-century legend, a peasant working in the field where the church now stands saw an enraged bull charging toward him. He pleaded with Our Lady of Monserrate to protect him, and the bull stumbled and fell; the man managed to escape and the church was erected in thanksgiving. In commemoration of the miracle, the devout arrive for a religious pilgrimage and each Sept. 8 climb the long bank of steps leading to the church on their hands and knees. See the oil painting by José Campeche, which portrays the miracle, on a wall inside the church. There's a great view from the top of the steps.

FOOD: If you need a bite after your visit to the church, **Cafeteria María** or the **El Palacio de las Sandwiches** are near the base of the steps and next door to each other. Advertised by Bugs Bunny wearing a straw hat, **El Conejo Blanco** (☎ 849-1170/7744) is on Carr. 344 at Km 0. It specializes in Puerto Rican dishes such as *carne de conejo*.

Mayagüez

Despite its reputation as a center of industry, this western port, the third largest city on the island, still retains much of the grace and charm suggested by its lovely name, taken from *majagua* – the indigenous name for a tree plentiful in the vicinity. Although the city does have a fine collection of attractive homes and buildings, you have to look around for them. Many are in sadly deteriorating condition. Mayagüez made world environmental news in 1993

Southwestern Puerto Rico

after a grassroots movement triumphed and successfully rejected a 300-megawatt Cogentrix power plant. In addition to its zoo and agricultural research station, Mayagüez is a good place to base yourself for day trips to Maricao, San Germán, and the many beaches and small towns in the area.

GETTING HERE: Mayagüez is easily approached by *público* from San Germán, Ponce, San Juan, Arecibo, Aguadilla, or Rincón. American also flies daily from San Juan's Muñoz Marín International Airport.

SIGHTS: Almost completely destroyed by an earthquake in 1917, one of the premier sights in this largely rebuilt city is the impressive **Plaza de Colón,** with its monstrous statue of Columbus, surrounded incongruously by statues of Greek maidens. The old post office building is on C. McKinley nearby, as is the **Yaguez Theater.** In 1977 this theater was purchased by the federal government and declared a Historical Monument. Renovated, expanded, and modernized at a cost of $4.5 million, it presents all types of stage productions and is a center for artistic, cultural, and educational activities in the community. **Zoorico Park** (☎ 834-8110), the Mayagüez Zoo, is home of innumerable reptiles, birds, and mammals, presented both in cages and in simulated natural habitats. See everything from Bengal tigers to capybara (the world's largest rodents). However, conditions for the animals here are poor. It's located on Carr. 108 at Barrio Miradero; open Wed. to Sun. 9-4:30, $1 admission, 50¢ children; $1 parking.

Much closer to town is the **Tropical Agricultural Research Station** (☎ 831-3435, fax 832-3435; Box 70, Mayagüez, PR 00681-0070) on Carr. 65, between C. Post and Carr. 108, next to the University of Puerto Rico at Mayagüez. It's open Mon. to Fri. from 7:30-4 (free admission). Established at the beginning of this century on the site of a former plantation, its grounds present a dazzling array of exotic vegetation, ranging from a Sri Lankan cinnamon tree to pink torch ginger to the traveler's tree. The station researches agricultural techniques and breeds hybrid plants that are more productive. Research has focused on plantains, sweet potatoes, sorghum, casava, yams, bananas, beans, and tanier (taro root). Improved varieties of these crops have been developed or introduced to Puerto Rico here. "Improvement" in this case means greater yields and higher resistence to disease. Currently, research is ongoing with yam species imported from Southeast Asia; the hope is to develop a disease-resistant version that requires no fertilizer. Such a product would be a boon for the many people on this planet who are malnourished. Another attempt is to improve cassava, which is a problem-laden crop suffering from disease and poor crop management. Other projects involve tropical fruit trees.

While you're in the station's vicinity be sure to check out the **Parque de los Proceres** (Park of the Patriots) across the street on C. Luna. The old pink **Aduana** (Customs House) has also been restored.

EVENTS: Mayagüez's *fiestas patronales* honoring her patron saint, La Virgen de la Candelaria, held around Feb. 2 each year, is among the most spectacular of such events on the island. The annual **crafts fair** is held in the beginning of Dec. at the coliseum.

ACCOMMODATIONS: The **Hotel El Embajador** (☎ 833-3340, fax 265-5030), 111-E Ramos Antonini (near C. McKinley and the main plaza), has 28 a/c rooms and a restaurant. **La Palma** (☎ 834-3800, fax 265-6940), C. Méndez Vigo at Peral, has 47 a/c rooms (with TV and phone), restaurant, and bar. The **Parador El Sol** (☎ 834-0303, fax 265-7567), C. El Sol 9, has 52 a/c rooms, restaurant, bar, and pool. Rooms have cable color TV and phone; rates include continental breakfast. For reservations, ☎ 800-443-0266 in the US or 800-981-7575 in Puerto Rico (721-2884 in San Juan).

outside of town: The **Mayagüez Holiday Inn** (☎ 833-1100) on Carr. 2 has 154 a/c rooms with TV/VCR, am/fm clock radio, pool, bar, restaurant, cocktail lounge, and conference rooms. Rates start at $99 s and $109.50 d. The **Mayagüez Hilton**, Carr. 2, Km 149.9 in Barrio Algarrobo (☎ 831-7575; 724-0161) has 150 a/c rooms, pool, restaurant, bar, conference rooms, disco, casino, and tennis courts. Rates start at $105 s and $115 d. For more information ☎ 1-800-HILTONS in the US, 800-268-9275 in Canada, and 0800-289-303 in the UK.

outlying accommodations: Centro Turistico Rancho las Cuevas (☎ 831-0010), Carr. 352 at Km 2.8, offers cabins and a pool, and serves traditional Puerto Rican entrées as well as buffets.

FOOD: There are plenty of small, cheap lunchrooms, fast-food places, and restaurants. The expensive **Palma** is inside the hotel of the same name on Méndez Vigo, and **Perfect Nutrition Health Food** is next door. **El Estoril** is on Méndez Vigo. The **Restaurant Parador El Sol** is at 9 C. Riera Palmer. The **Pong Wai** is in the Guanajibo Shopping Center at Carr. 102, Km 6.3. Renowned for its sangria, **Fido's Beer and Wine Garden** is at C. Dulievre 90 in Barrio Balboa. **Franco's Confectionary** is at C. Manuel Piradillo 3 in Barrio

Marina Meridional. The Mayagüez Hilton has **La Rotisserie** (☎ 831-7575), which offers international cuisine. Overlooking the sea at Km 5 on Carr. 102, **El Mesón Español** (☎ 833-5445) serves Spanish dishes.

ENTERTAINMENT: It's pretty dull here even on weekends. The only thing to do is walk around and watch the kids hanging out, trying to be cool just as they do everywhere else in the world. Check to see if **Teatro Yaguez** has a show on. The **Mayagüez Hilton** has live music nightly and dance music Tues. to Sat. The **Mayagüez** (☎ 833-3335) shows three films daily.

SHOPPING: Mayagüez is a good place to shop for inexpensive bargains. Check the stores around the plaza.

SERVICES AND INFORMATION: The **Tourism Office** (☎ 831-5220, 833-9560, fax 831-3210) is inside the Citibank Bldg. at C. McKinley 53 on one side of Plaza Colón. They try their best to be helpful. **Conozcamos a Puerto Rico** (☎ 831-0865) offers island tours. Rent cars from **Popular Mayagüez** (☎ 265-4848).

FROM MAYAGÜEZ: *Públicos* leaving for surrounding towns depart from the area around the plaza. If heading for Maricao, get an early start.

Maricao-Monte del Estado

Maricao is a small coffee-trading center near Monte del Estado, a forest preserve which, confusingly, is also called Maricao. The preserve is one of the driest areas on the island. **events:** Its **Festival del Café,** which marks the end of the coffee harvest festival, is held here in late Feb.

SIGHTS: At the **Maricao Fish Hatchery**, more than 25,000 fish (such as black bass and tilapia) are reared and schooled yearly in preparation for their journey to lakes and fishponds. It's open Mon. to Fri. from 7:30-noon and 1-4 and on Sat. and Sun. from 8:30-4; reservations are required (☎ 838-3710). A trail, which begins at Km 128 on Carr. 120, leads from Maricao ridge down to the hatchery. Near the reserve's highest peak (2,625-ft, 800-m **Las Tetas de Cerro**

Gordo) a stone observation tower affords views of Isla de Mona as well as three of the four coasts.

FLORA AND FAUNA: Of the 278 species of trees found here, there are 123 endemic species and 37 that are found only in the area. Its serpentine soil derives from once-submerged bluish-green rock of volcanic ancestry. Despite the heavy rainfall, the area resembles karst rather than rainforest. Among the 44 bird species are the Puerto Rican vireo, the Puerto Rican lizard-cuckoo, the Puerto Rican tody, the Puerto Rican tanager, the sharp-shinned hawk, and the rarely spotted elfin woods warbler.

ACCOMMODATIONS: Apply for permission to camp (follow the sign to Casa de Piedra) at the Dept. of Natural Resources, Puerto De Tierra, San Juan, ☎ 724-3724, 724-3623. Cabins at the *Centro Vacacionales* hold six. Maricao or Monte del Estado also has picnic grounds, an observation tower, and a swimming pool. Climb the stone tower for a commanding view of SW Puerto Rico. On a clear day, you can even see the cliffs of Mona Island off in the distance. More expensive is the **Hacienda Juanita** (☎ 838-2550, fax 838-2551), Carr. 105 at Km 23.5. Set in a still-operating coffee plantation, its facilities include swimming pool, tennis and other ball courts, and hiking trails. ☎ 800-443-0266 in the US or 800-981-7575 in Puerto Rico (or 721-2884 in San Juan). Out in Las Marías to the N at Km 16.1 on Carr. 119, the 11-room **Gutierrez** (☎ 827-3100; Box 263, Las Marías, PR 00670) is set on top of a hill and is surrounded by great views on all sides. There's a pool, meeting room, large kitchen, and a bar. Rates start from $45.

Mona Island

Least known and least accessible of all Puerto Rico's offshore islands, seven-mile-long (11.2-km) Mona lies in the southern center of the Mona Passage. Viewed from the air, this 20-square-mile island situated 50 miles W of Mayagüez appears as a perfectly flat oval surrounded by offshore coral reefs. The only ways to reach it are by fishing boat from Mayagüez (six hours one way), by private plane, or by yacht. Nine miles of rough trails lead from the S shore through the dense foliage to the northern, rock-littered mesa, which gives way on three sides to a sheer 200-ft drop to the sea below.

FLORA AND FAUNA: The plateau is covered with low-lying trees and orchids, and the indigenous rock iguana (*cyclura*) scuttles furtively between rocks. Some grow as long as four feet. The only other land animals – wild boars, bulls, and goats – are descendants of livestock kept by the long-vanished pirates. Land birds include the yellow-shouldered blackbird and the pearly-eyed thrasher. While red-footed boobies nest on the N side, magnificent frigate-birds, white-tailed tropicbirds and other birds nest on the neighboring Isla de Monito. The beautiful coral reefs offshore have superb visibility and are said to number among Puerto Rico's best.

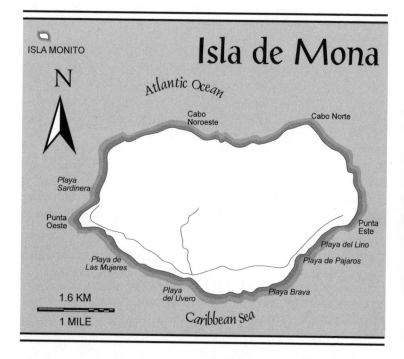

HISTORY AND SIGHTS: Mona's history is steeped in romance, much of which carries over into the present. Discovered by Columbus during his second voyage in 1493, it later became a port of call for Spanish galleons. Ponce de León stopped here to secure a supply of cassava bread on the way to take up his command of Puerto Rico. By 1584, most of the native Indians had been exterminated. A network of stalactite- and stalagmite-filled underground caves, containing pools of spring water used to supplement the average annual rainfall of 41 inches, served as a home for pirates over nearly three centuries. Fireplaces, cooking utensils, fragments of sabers, and chains have been found inside. In **Cueva Liria**, where guano was mined until 1927, you'll find tram tracks and the rusting remains of equipment. On the W end of the plateau are the ruins of a lodge dating from the 1930s and '40s when Mona was a popular weekend getaway for sports fishermen. Legend has it that the remains of a Spanish galleon lie just off the lighthouse and radio beacon manned by the US Coast Guard on the E end of the island. The most recent chapter in the island's history came in 1993 when groups of Cuban refugees seeking asylum were dropped off on Playa Mujeres by boats coming from the Dominican Republic.

PRACTICALITIES: Boats are usually chartered from Puerto Real. Camp at **Playa Sardinera** for a small charge. The Camino de Infierno ("Hell Road") connects it with Pájaros beach to the E; you may also camp here. Bring food and everything else you need, *and* take it out again. The only food you will find here is prickly pears. Water is in short supply so bring your own. For information on renting available cabins and on obtaining the reservations mandatory for camping, call the Dept. of Natural Resources, ☎ 723-1616, 721-5495.

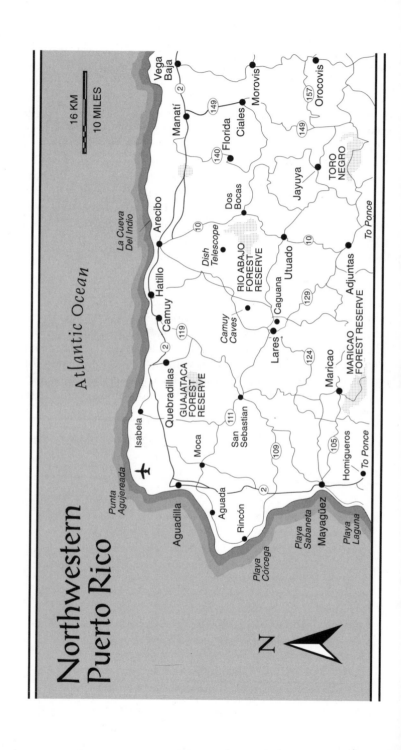

Northwestern Puerto Rico

This area is easily accessed from Mayagüez and the S and by heading W from San Juan. From the capital, the road is congested. After you pass Dorado, the traffic thins out. Housing projects with murals painted on their sides and shopping centers give way to trucks selling *lechon asado*, but there are still the ubiquitous McDonald's, Church's Chicken, and other delightful eateries. Just past Vega Alta you come to a string of roadside *chicharrones* stands.

Rincón

Although the name of this small town means "corner" (which suits its location perfectly), the town is actually named for Don Gonzalo Rincón, a 16th-century landowner. He granted a hill, known as *cerro do los pobres* ("hill of the poor") to local settlers. When the town was founded in 1772, they named it for their benefactor; its full name is Santa Rosa de Rincón. There are a half-dozen bathing beaches in this area, including Punta Higuero, where the World Surfing Championships were held in 1968. A reef to the N of town has a marina and charter boats available to take divers over to the National Wildlife Refuge surrounding Desecheo Island.

SIGHTS: Dating from 1798, Rincón's **Catholic church**, facing the E end of the plaza, is built on the very site which Santa Rosa de Lima, the town's patron saint, recommended when she appeared in a vision. A small chapel dedicated to her – containing plastic flowers and a model boat – stands on a ridge just beyond the intersection of Carr. 414 and Ramal 414. Her *fiestas patronales* take place during the last week in Aug. **Pico Atalaya** ("lookout peak"), easily recognizable because of its communication tower, commands a great view of the environs. A silver water tank, the sole reminder of a railroad that passed from San Juan to Ponce between 1907 and the early 1950s, stands on C. Cambija. The ruins of the storehouses and residences of the **Corcega Sugar Mill** (constructed 1885) remain behind trees where Playa Corcega meets Carr. 429. Rincon's **lighthouse**, rising 98 feet (30 m) above the sea at Punta Higuero, was built by the Spanish in the early 1890s. Today, the electric 26,000-candlepower rotating beacon is unmanned. It has a small museum. Both the lighthouse and the reactor (see below) have surfing beaches right by them. The "lighthouse beach" is also known as Maria's Beach. You may be able to spot humpback whales (during the winter season; see "Flora & Fauna" in the Introduction for information on the whales), as well as pilot and sperm whales, sharks, and sea turtles.

At the end of the road by the lighthouse are the rusting remains of the Boiling Nuclear Superheater Plant. "BONUS," as it was quaintly named, was the first nuclear energy plant built in Latin America. It began operation in April 1964. The $11-million, 16,300-kw facility was built with the intention of testing a new concept that would both reduce energy costs and train Latin American scientists and engineers (i.e., as a US government subsidy to the nuclear power industry). In 1962, seven reactor employees were exposed to contamination via irradiated fuel elements. The reactor failed in 1964 because of problems with its superheater assembly. In 1968, the plant was closed due to "technical difficulties." In 1969, it was sealed off; the Atomic Energy Commission announced that they had decommissioned and decontaminated the reactor in 1972. A 1996 investigation disclosed that radioactive materials were still present at the site, including 27 contaminated lead bricks, five 55-gallon drums of contaminated clothing, 11 contaminated radio-active warning signs, and seven lead shields. The municipality has plans to turn the plant into a museum, but this is on indefinite hold at present.

ACCOMMODATIONS: Many restaurants and guesthouses are open only during the surfing season, which runs from Oct. to April. The **Parada Muñoz Guest House** (☎ 823-4725; HC-01 Box 5266, Rincón, PR 00677-9725), Carr. 115 at Km 15, has a swimming pool; kitchens are $5 extra. **Beside the Point Resort** (☎ 823-0610/8550) is also outside of town at Carr. 413 at Km 4.5 in Barrio Puntas, as is the **Lazy Parrot** (☎ 823-5654) at Km 4 on Carr. 413. Open Thurs. to Sun., it serves fish, eggplant parmesan, and other dishes. (If staying here, dine at the bakery next door). The **Playa Corcega Beach Resort** (☎ 823-6140) offers tent and trailer camping areas as well as a cafeteria. The **Playa Real Guest House** (☎ 823-2800) is at Km 10.8 on Carr. 115 in Barrio Corcego. More expensive is **Parador Villa**

Antonio at Carr. 115, Km 12.3 (☎ 823-2645/2285, fax 823-3390; Box 68, Rincón, PR 00677). Facilities include 50 a/c rooms and apartments, two tennis courts, and swimming pool. Prices range from $70-$107. ☎ 800-443-0266 in the US or 800-981-7575 in Puerto Rico. The **Hotel Villa Cofresi** (☎ 823-2450, 823-2861) is next door. The area's most elegant hotel is the **Horned Dorset Primavera** (☎ 823-4030/4050, fax 823-5580; Box 1132, Rincón, PR 00677), which offers 24 suites with antiques and poster mahogany beds. Billing itself as "a place without activities," this is where you can escape from stress. There's no TV or rampaging children under 12. Rates start from around $135 s and $190 d; weekly package rates are available. Their six course dinner costs $40 pp. To get here, you must take Carr. 115 from Carr. 2 in the direction of Rincón for about four miles. Turn sharply L onto Carr. 429 after the "Kaplash" Restaurant. In another mile, you'll find the hotel on the L at Km 3.

camping: The nearest spot is Añasco on Carr. 401 at Km 1.

FOOD: Panadería la Estación and **Supermercado Paco** are on C. Luis Muñoz Rivera, and **Rincón Cash & Carry** is at the Plaza de Recreo across the street from the church. The **Pastrami Palace and Homemade Pies** (great breakfasts) is just near the main plaza. The **Lighthouse Café** is right out at the lighthouse. The **Kaplash Restaurant** (Carr. 403) and **El Bambino** (near the Parador Villa Antonio) offer seafood dishes.

SERVICES: The **public library** is on C. Nueva. The **Centro Cultural de Rincón** is open from Tues. to Sun. (9:30-3:30). **Savings Auto Rentals** (☎ 890-3203) is 1½ miles out of town outside Ramey's Gate 5. The **West Coast Surf Shop** is right in town. **Cap'N Bill's Dive Shop** (☎ 823-0390) is near the lighthouse. Operating during the high season, the *Viking Starship* (☎ 823-7010/7068) departs from Pescadería Rojas in town at 11:30 AM each Fri., Sat., and Sun.

ENTERTAINMENT: Tamboo Too! has live music, as does **El Nuevo Brisas** on Carr. 413. Whales can be sighted offshore from Dec. to Feb.

☞ **Traveler's Tip.** Although police monitor the beaches of Rincón, the best way to avoid theft is to leave all doors unlocked and leave nothing of value in your car.

Aguada

Settled in 1510, Aguada is the island's second oldest settlement. Another Columbus monument and park is near this town, as is **Balneario Pico de Pidera**.

PRACTICALITIES: On Carr. 416 and three minutes from Carr. 2, the **Hidden Village Parador** (☎ 868-8686/8687, fax 868-8701; Box 937, Aguada, PR 00602) has 25 a/c rooms with balcony and cable TV. Other facilities include pool, conference center (holds up to 300), and **Las Colinas** restaurant (seafood and other dishes). Built in 1990, its rooms start at around $70. **Aguada Seafood** (☎ 868-2136), C. Jiménez 103, offers *mariscada* and other specialties. The **Ann Wigmore Institute** is located in Aguada and set near the sea; this school specializes in raw foods. Developer of "Wheatgrass Therapy," the late Dr. Wigmore believed that "all disease is a result of toxicity and deficiency due to cooked and processed foods, drug, and negative mental attitudes." The curriculum includes internal cleansing, growing greens and wheatgrass, composting and soil management, indoor gardening, sprouting, food combining, energy soup, weight loss, and a 12-step program. Rates for a two-week program range from $600 for a day student to $1,750 for a private room with bath and meals. Monthly rates are slightly less than twice this amount. The school is located at Carr. 115, Km 20, Barrio Guayabo, Aguada, PR 00602. For more information write Box 429, Rincón, PR 00677; ☎ 809-868-6307.

Aguadilla

Located on Carr 111 along the W coast, this small town boasts fine beaches, intricate lace, and historical sites. Christopher Columbus first stepped onto Puerto Rican soil somewhere between Aguadilla and Añasco on his second voyage in 1493. Since then it's undergone numerous changes. For a while the population declined, owing to the economic depression caused by the phasing out of Ramey Air Force Base. However, recent census figures show a slight increase; the current population is about 67,000. Beaches (great snorkeling) extend from Crash Point to the N. Crash Point receives its name from the launches kept here to pick up crews in the event of a plane crash around Borínquen Point. Bosque Estatal de Guajataca and Lago de Guajataca are located 30 km to the E of Aguadilla. The town is famous for its *mundillo* (finely embroidered lace), first introduced to the area by immigrants from Belgium, Holland, and Spain.

EVENTS: The **Rafael Hernández Festival** is held yearly from Oct. 22 to 24 in honor of this world-famous composer. His music is interpreted by soloists and orchestras during the two days. Festivities surrounding the town's *fiestas patronales* go on for two weeks around the main feast day of Nov. 4 on the main plaza. Music is performed and local specialties are cooked. Another lively time is the **Velorio de Reyes** (Three Kings Celebration). Initiated 30 years ago by a wealthy local family, a religious ceremony with music, prayers, and chants takes place on the plaza the evening of January 6.

GETTING HERE: American Airlines flies to Aguadilla's Rafael Hernández Airport nonstop from New York and Miami.

SIGHTS: Ramey Air Force Base has been converted into **Punta Borínquen**, a tourist complex off Carr. 110 with complete sports facilities. To play at the **golf course** here, ☎ 890-2987. **Playuelas Beach** is divided by what was once the pier and docking facilities for submarines and fuel tankers. **Punta Borínquen Lighthouse**, located W of town, has been designated a historic site worthy of preservation by the National Register of Historic Places. Severely damaged by the 1918 earthquake, this tower, built in 1870, was incorporated into Ramey Air Force Base as a picnic area. Near the city's N entrance, between the foot of Cerro Cuesto Villa and the beach, lies the **Urban Cemetery**. This was established on what had once been a sugarcane hacienda. Although the 1918 earthquake destroyed many of the old tombs, those remaining are finely sculpted Italian marble. Borínquen Archaeological site, the only significant indigenous site in the region, was excavated by Dr. K.G. Lathrop of Yale in the 1920s. Objects found include human skulls, shells, animal bones, and shards of broken pots. **Fort Concepción** is the only remaining building from the Fuerte de la Concepción military complex, which was protected by a moat, walls, and guard and sentry houses. Extensively remodeled, it now houses schoolrooms. A statue of Columbus, built in 1893, stands within the seaside **Parque Colón** (Columbus Park). **Parque El Parterre** contains *ojo de agua*, a natural spring that once served as the water supply for arriving sailors. Isabel, to the NE, has great diving off of a beach called **The Shacks**. **Las Cascadas** (☎ 882-3310) is an aquatic park on Carr. 2 at Km 126.5. Admission is around $13 for adults and $9 for children. Group rates are also available. The park has such sights as a magic fountain," a "lazy river," a "fantasy oasis," an "astroslide," and an "aquatic tunnel."

ACCOMMODATIONS: Rent **cabins** at Punta Borínquen off Carr. 107 for $60 per night (☎ 890-6128/6330). **Camp** freely but insecurely at Playa Crashboat, Carr. 2 Salida 458, Aguadilla. The 50-room **Hotel/Parador El Faro** (☎ 882-8000, fax 882-1030; Box 5148, Aguadilla, PR 00605), Carr. 107 at Km 8.8 is a modern 32-room building dating from 1990. Set next to the former Ramey Air Force base (and its golf course), it has a restaurant (**El Caracol**), cocktail lounge, and pool. Rooms (from around $70 d) have a/c, cable TV, balconies, and phone. Also in Aguadilla, the 40-room **Cielo Mar Hotel** (☎ 882-5959/5960, fax 882-5577; Aguadilla, PR 00603) at Av. Montemar No. 84, Carr. 111 in Urb. Villa Lydia, has 40 rooms with a/c, cable TV, and private balconies. Facilities include a restaurant/cocktail lounge (live music on weekends), convention hall, and a pool. Rates start from around $75.

The a/c **Cima** (☎ 890-2016, fax 890-2017, Aguadilla, PR 00611) is set on Carr 110 within driving range of six beaches and has carpeted rooms with cable TVs and phones. Facilities and activities include sailing, surfing, golf, tennis, horseback riding, PO, pharmacy, and fitness center. **Hacienda El Pedregal** (☎ 891-6068, 882-2865, fax 882-2875; Box 4719, Aguadilla, PR 00605) has 27 rooms with a/c and cable TV. Facilities include restaurant, bar, and pool. Children under 10 (two to a room) are allowed to stay free.

In Isabela, **Costa Dorada Beach Resort** (☎/fax 872-7255; Isabela, PR 00662), Carr. 446 at Km 0.1, has 52 a/c units (rooms and suites), pool, restaurant, two tennis courts, basketball court, and meeting rooms. Rates start at $90 s or d.

COSTA ISABELA

This now-bankrupt project is an interesting footnote to tourism development on the island. Originally scheduled for opening in 1992, the first 650-room luxury hotel in this resort complex was axed after financing dried up and the project filed bankruptcy. Five other hotels had been scheduled for 3,000 acres and near Aguadilla's Rafael Hernández International Airport. Financiers of the project had included Takeshi Sekiguchi, chairman of TSA, a resort company that has developed hotels in Hawaii. The Resort's "Puerto Rican Village" was being designed as a tourist attaction in and of itself. Some 100,000 trees were to be planted, and the offshore breakwater was scheduled to be constructed in such a way as to enchance marine life. A transportation system was under development, along with an artificial lake, five electric power substations, water and waste treatment plants, helipad, small hospital, children's camp, and police and fire stations. The project would have also included 240 beach villas, 300 cliff villas, 25 golf villas, 270 duplexes, and 200 single-family lots. In its wake, another project has surfaced. The Columbus Landing Resort, a proposed $200-million project, has encountered stiff local opposition.

FOOD: Restaurant Ocean Front (☎ 872-3339), Carr. 4446 in Barrio Bajuras at Playa Jobo, serves seafood dishes such as *asapao* as well as meat. Offering Puerto Rican and international cuisine, **Darío's Gourmet** (☎ 890-6143), Carr. 110, Km 8, serves dishes ranging from *bouillabaisse* to lobster thermidor. Down the same road at Km 9.2, **Golden Crown** (☎ 890-2016) serves Chinese food. On Carr. 441, **The Shady Palm** is an oceanfront bar and restaurant which has a wide array of dishes, including Mexican. Recommended by readers, **El Yate** is set up above the bay and is a great place to watch a sunset. At C. Comercio 18-D, **Salud y Vida** (☎ 891-5755) has a veggie cafeteria as well as store; it has another branch in the Aguadilla Mall.

SERVICES AND EXCURSIONS: Aquatica Underwater Adventures (☎ 382-6437, ☎/fax 890-6071; Box 350, Ramey, Aguadilla, PR 00604) offers scuba and scuba instruction, fishing, and rentals. They're located on Carr. 110 at Km 10, just to the R of the Ramey Base entrance. Another operation is **La Cueva Submarina** (☎ 872-1094, fax 872-1447; Box 151, Isabela, PR 00662), which operates a full-service dive shop at Km 6.3 on Carr. 466.

ENTERTAINMENT: The **Twins I** and **II** (☎ 891-4421) show films. **Villa Ricomar** is a disco open on weekends in Isabela off of Carr. 459.

CAR RENTAL: Rent cars from **Sánchez Aguadilla** (☎ 891-7777). **L&M Car Rental** (☎ 890-3010) is at the airport.

Northwestern Puerto Rico

Moca

Known as the "Literary City" because some noted Puerto Rican authors have been born here, Moca's name is believed to come from the Taino word for the tree of the same name. It was founded in 1772. The town's *mundillo* festival takes place each Nov. on Thanksgiving weekend. Its *fiestas patronales* run in early Sept. If you're in the area, be sure to check out the procession for the Three Kings Festival, which takes place each Jan. 6.

SIGHTS: Hacienda Enriqueta is a small museum of colonial artifacts set at the town's entrance. **Palacete Los Moreau**, a French provincial-style mansion, is undergoing restoration and will have gardens and sports facilities. **Los Castillos Meléndez**, on Carr. 110 in Barrio Centro, resembles a medieval castle.

SHOPPING: Moca is famous for its *mundillo* lace. Shop at **María Lasalles'** store near the town plaza. **Artesania Leonides** is nearby at C. Ramos Antonini 114.

San Rafael de Quebradillas

This N coastal plain town (pop. 24,500) was originally founded by Spanish farmers and cattlemen. Popularly abbreviated to Quebradillas, its name derives from the *quebradas* (streams) that emerge when rain falls in this area.

events: The **Iglesia San Rafael Arcángel** attracts numerous visitors for its *fiestas patronales* on Oct. 24. A *carnaval* is held in Jan.

sights: The nearby **Playa Guajataca** is the area's scenic highlight. **Cueva Guajataca** is also in the vicinity and there's a statue of Mabodamaca, the Taíno chief who once controlled the area, at its entrance. Another place to visit is the **El Arca de Noé** (Noah's Ark), an aviary.

ACCOMMODATIONS: For local information, ☎ 895-2840/3088. On Carr. 2 at Km 103.8 near Quebradillas in Barrio Terranova, **Parador Guajataca** (☎ 895-3070/3074/3091; Box 1558, Quebradillas, PR 00678) offers 38 a/c rooms with cable TV, phones, and balconies facing the ocean. Facilities include a gourmet restaurant

(**Casabi**), pool, conference room, live music on weekends, and two tennis courts. Rates run from around $75. On Carr. 113 at Km 7.9, **Parador Vistamar** (☎ 895-2065, fax 895-2294; Quebradillas, PR 00678) has facilities including 55 a/c rooms with private bath, restaurant, swimming pool, game room, and tennis, volleyball, and basketball courts. It has a hilltop setting with great views. Rates start at around $65.

FOOD: Local restaurants include **Manny's Restaurant** (☎ 895-2717), C. Ramón Saavedra 105; **Lantern on the Green**, Carr. 119 in Barrio Guajataca; **El Soberau**, Carr. 113, Km 1.3; **Restaurant Brisas de Guajatacas** (☎ 895-5366), 750 C. Estación at Los Merenderos; and the aforementioned *paradores*. **Panadería Los Cocos** has bread baked in traditional ovens.

Camuy

This small town hosts its *fiestas patronales* on the last Fri. in May. It also hosts the **Carnaval del Río Camuy** in early Feb., the **Festival Playero Peñón Brusi** during the last weekend in June, the **Festival de la Cultura-Fería de Artesania** in Sept., and the **Paso Fino-Peñón Brusi** in Aug.

sights: In town, you can find the **Museo Histórico Cultural Camuyano** at C. Estrella Sur 6. Aside from the Camuy Caves (described below), the municipality contains the **Iglesia de Piedra**, a Methodist Church fashioned from stone and built in 1912, which is on Carr. 486 at Km 4.6 in Barrio Abra Honda de Camuy. Another sight is the **Calavario la Milagrosa**, a replica of Mt. Calvary created by a local artist. It's on Carr. 483 at Km 4.1 in Barrio Piedra Gorda.

ACCOMMODATIONS: Centro Vacacional Villa Brusi is on Carr. 485 at Km 1.8 in Barrio Puente and **Centro Vacacional Brusilandia** is also in Barrio Puente.

River Camuy Cave Park

(Parque de las Cavernas del Río Camuy)

Located on Carr. 129 at Km 19.8, Río Camuy Cave Park taps the island's extensive network of underground caves – the result of carbonic acid dissolving limestone over the course of thousands of years. Spelunkers Russell and Jane Gurnee explored and mapped the subterranean caverns in the 1950s and were the driving force behind the park's creation. A totally blind and previously unknown species of fish, which was discovered in a subterranean pool, was named *Alaweckelia gurneei* in their honor. **tours from San Juan:** A number of operators offer tours here including **Caverns Express** (☎ 791-0666), which has pickups in Isla Verde and Condado.

TAKING A TOUR: Arriving, you purchase a parking ticket ($1) and make your way to the entrance where you buy a ticket for the next tour. Admission to the Cueva Clara tour (45 min.) is $10 for adults and $7 for children 2 to 12. Senior citizens are charged half the adult price. The last tour is at 3:45. An optional trip to the **Tres Pueblos Sinkhole** is included. A gift shop is set near the ticket window. While waiting you can walk around the grounds; Kodak, in a gesture of disinterested corporate beneficence, has donated signs indicating when you should take a picture. You may exercise your free will if you disagree with their choices. There are covered picnic tables and a children's playground.

After viewing a film in the theater building, you take a tram bus down into the entrance to Cueva Clara. You descend along a concrete roadway through 200 ft of densely foliated tropical ravine and secondary forest, then proceed on foot down to the subterranean Río Camuy – one of the largest underground rivers in the world. The tour guide is well informed and helpful. The upper cave, Cueva Clara de Empalme, is a dry chamber carved out by the river sometime during the past million years. The cave is oriented from S to N. The stalactites and stalagmites are beautiful. It takes from 200 to 1,000 years for them to grow an inch. Dripping water is everywhere and one has the feeling of being in another world, as if a Venusian mold might appear and gobble you up at any moment. The giant boulders on the cave's floor fell from the ceiling. You will pass by the pool filled with microscopic shrimp on your way to the opening, which leads to the Sumidero Empalme – a 400-ft-deep, lushly vegetated pit open to the sky. The caves continue on from here for some 15 km but are inaccessible.

Returning up a side cavern, you can see the river flowing down some 150 ft, continuing inexorably to cut its channel. Bats are said to live down there. Similarly, the tour (optional, but included in your cost) of the Tres Pueblos Sinkhole (so named because it is between Camuy, Hatillo, and Lares municipalities) offers views from a walkway and two observation platforms. One traverses the Lares side and faces the town of Camuy while the other overlooks the sinkhole and the Río Camuy. The sinkhole measures 650 ft in diameter and is 400 ft deep. An elevator that will take you to the bottom is planned, and may be finished by the time of your arrival.

The caves are open Tues. to Sun. 8-4 and holidays from 8-5. If Mon. is a holiday, the caves will be closed that Wed. ☎ 898-3100 for more information and to confirm opening hours and tour times.

FOOD: There are two restaurants near the caves. The huge **Restaurante Las Cavernas** (☎ 897-6463) is on the L heading toward Lares (on Carr. 129 at Km 19.6) and the **Restaurante Vista Caverna** is across from the caves. The former is very plush and serves Puerto Rican dishes and seafood.

La Cueva de Camuy

Not to be confused with the above caverns, this small cave (☎ 898-2723), under private ownership, has ponies, go-carts, and a pool with a slide as well as bridges. On Carr. 486 at Km 11.1, it's open Mon. to Sat. from 9-5 and on Sun. from 9-8.

Hatillo

Meaning "grazing land," Hatillo was founded in 1823 and many of its early settlers came from the Canary Islands. It is noted for its dairy farms.

events: The town's **Festival of the Masks,** held annually on Dec. 26, commemorates the Slaughter of the Innocents detailed in the

New Testament. Costumes are abundant. Its *fiestas típicas* are held around the same time period. The *fiestas patronales* are held in mid-July, and the entire town turns out for the procession.

ACCOMMODATIONS AND FOOD: Camping grounds are at Punta Maracallo. Dine at the **Buen Café** (☎ 898-3495) at Km 84 on Carr. 2; it features Puerto Rican dishes including *mofongo*. **Plaza del Norte**, the island's fifth largest shopping mall, is just a few minutes drive from town. ☎ 898-3835/3840 for tourist information.

Arecibo & Environs

This simple but refreshing town on the Atlantic is more of a transit point or base for exploring the rest of the area than a destination in itself. The town comes alive during the annual feast of San Felipe Apóstol on or around May 1. It is a good jumping-off point for the beaches to the E or the mountains to the S.

GETTING HERE: Take a *público* from San Juan or Bayamón. Another approach would be from Ponce via Utuado, but allow plenty of time.

SIGHTS: The town's name is derived from Aracibo, an Indian chief who had a settlement here, and a cave (**La Cueva del Indio**) four miles E of town that was used for Indian ceremonies before the arrival of the Spaniards. To get here take a *público* marked "Isolte" four km, passing along a magnificent beach. Get off at the sign and the brown cement open-air igloo constructed with reinforced Coca Cola bottles. Turn L and it's a five-minute walk. Surf pounds on either side of the entrance. Descend the precipitous and makeshift staircase to view the petroglyphs adorning the walls. This area is spectacularly beautiful and well worth a visit. **note:** Park at the gas station nearby for safety. Readers have reported a case of attempted entry to their vehicle while parked near the entrance. It might be best to visit one at a time. Set just to the E of town on Punta Morrillo, the **Arecibo Lighthouse** (☎ 879-1625) has a small museum with rotating exhibits.

ACCOMMODATIONS AND FOOD: Hotel Plaza (☎ 878-2295), Av. José de Diego 112, is inexpensive. **Hotel Villa Real** (☎ 881-4134, fax 881-6490), Carr. 2, Km 67.2 in Barrio Santana, is one alternative. **Campsites** are at San Isidro Village, Carr. 2 at Km 85, Hatillo or at **Punta Maracaya Camping Area** (☎ 878-7024/2157), Carr. 2 at Km 84.6 . At Av. Rotarios 522, **La Parillada Restaurant Argentino** (☎ 878-7777) serves Argentinian meat and seafood specialties. There are plenty of *cafeterias* around.

ARECIBO OBSERVATORY

Don't miss visiting this amazing concrete, steel, and aluminum anachronism S of town. Tours are given Tues. to Fri. at 2. Visitors are also admitted (no tours) on Sun. from 1-4:30 (☎ 878-2612). Reach it via Carrs. 22, 651, 635, and 625 or via 22, 129, 134, 635, and 625; a special access road leads up to it. *Públicos* marked "Esperanza" also come here. The 600-ton platform, largest of its kind in the world, is a 20-acre dish set into a gigantic natural depression. Using this telescope, Cornell University scientists monitor pulsars and quasars and probe the ionosphere, moon, and planets. Unlike other radio telescopes, which have a steerable dish or reflector, the dish at Arecibo is immobile, while the receiving and transmitting equipment, which hangs 50 stories in the air, can be steered and pointed by remote control equipment on the ground. Although it costs $3.5 million annually to operate this facility, it has been responsible for several major discoveries, including detection of signals from the first pulsar and proving the existence of the quasar.

FOREST RESERVES NEAR ARECIBO

Lying to the E of Arecibo near Carr. 682, **Cambalache Forest Reserve**, a 914-acre (370-ha) subtropical forest, has 45 different species of birds. Great for hiking and picnicking. The same is true of **Guajataca Forest Reserve** with its limestone sinkholes and haystack hills. Sandwiched between Quebradillas to the N and San Sebastián to the S, Carr. 446 slices it in half. Cabralla, one of the longer of the 25 miles (40 km) of hiking trails, ends at Lago Guajataca (which is great for fishing and boating if you bring your own boat and rod). Maps may be available at the ranger station where a trail leads to a lookout tower and other trails. Camp Guajataca here may be rented on weekends when available; for information contact the Puerto Rico Council of Boy Scouts in San Juan (☎ 767-

0320). **Río Abajo State Forest** is S of Arecibo. Elevations reach 1,400 feet. Here, the most rugged karst formations are found. Old lumber roads and paths lead to them. Indigenous West Indian mahogany, teak, and balsa coexist here with introduced blue Australian pines, bamboo, and the SE Asian teak that dominates the landscape. This 5,080-acre forest was established in 1935. A recreational center and picnic ground is open from 8 to 6. In all of these reserves, camping is permitted with permission obtained from the Dept. of Natural Resources in San Juan 15 days in advance.

DOS BOCAS LAKE

This is located at Km 68 on Carr. 10 at the junction of the roads to Jayuya and Utuado from Arecibo. Its name means "Two Mouths." This long, beautiful, and winding reservoir was created in 1942. Three launches run scheduled two-hour trips around the lake at 7, 10, 2, and 5. Although these free trips are provided as a service for local residents, visitors are welcome to join. A one-hour trip to Barrio Don Alonso leaves daily at 12:40.

Utuado

This small, sunny mountain town is a stronghold of traditional *jíbaro* culture and is one of the best places to experience Puerto Rican mountain life. You could see anything here: from a man braking his horse at an intersection to young *evangelisticas* "singing in the rain," holding umbrellas over megaphones and shouting the praises of the Lord Jesus. Local buses run from Jayuya, Arecibo, and up from Ponce via Adjuntas. *Públicos* also ply these routes as well as connecting with other towns in the area.

SIGHTS: Near Utuado is **Caguana Indian Ceremonial Park and Museum,** the most important archaeological site in the Caribbean (open daily 9-5; museum open Sat. and Sun., 10-4). To reach it, take a bus or *público* ($1) or drive 12 km E along Carr. 111 towards Lares. Originally excavated by the famous archaeologist J.A. Mason in 1915, the park has been restored and established under the auspices of the Institute of Puerto Rican Culture. Don't expect much; although a loyal band keep up the grounds, the funds needed for guides and markers have not been supplied. The 10 *bateyes* (ball courts) are situated on a small spur of land surrounded by fairly deep ravines on three sides. Enter to find beautifully flowing arbors, roosters crowing, and mother hens tending their chicks. The largest rectangular *bateye* measures 60 by 120 ft (20 by 37 m). Huge granite slabs along the W wall weigh up to a ton. A few are carved with faces (half-human, half-monkey) that are typical of Taíno-Chico culture. One has deep, cup-like, haunting eyes. *La Mujer de Caguana*, most famous of all the petroglyphs, is a woman with frog legs and elaborate headdress.

Originally, all of the slabs were decorated with reliefs, but most of these have been lost due to erosion. The *bateyes* are bordered by cobbled walkways. This site dates from AD 1200. Although the ball game played in these arenas was indigenous to the entire Caribbean, the game reached its highest degree of sophistication in Puerto Rico. Two teams of players, thick wooden belts lashed to their waists, would hit a heavy, resilient ball – keeping it in the air without the use of hands or feet. These balls still survive in the form of stone replicas. Other examples of petroglyphs are found in Barrio Paso Palma and Salto Arriba, Utuado.

Lago Caonillas, an artificial lake near Utuado created by damming during the 1950s, came into the limelight a few years back when droughts caused it to recede, exposing the bell tower of a reinforced concrete chapel. Dating from the mid-1930s, it was built by an American Capuchin priest. Superstitious Puerto Ricans flocked by the thousands on weekends to the site, much to the bemusement of enterprising locals who charged entry to their property or took them out in boats. Visitors saw the re-emergence as some type of miracle or message from God.

FESTIVALS AND CRAFTS: The town holds its *fiestas patronales* on or around Sept. 29 every year, in honor of its patron saint, San Miguel Arcangel. On the main road at night you can find tents with Haitian women selling handicrafts from all over the world.

ACCOMMODATIONS: Hotel Vivi having folded, the only low-budget accommodation is offered by **Motel El Lago**. Right at the intersection of Carr. 111 and Carr. 140, you drive up the hill to the L. At the top, you'll find the entrance. After paying $15, you drive your car into a shed, close the sliding panel garage door, and enter the room, which consists of a bath with pink flamingos painted on the shower doors and a bed (with a plastic covered mattress) surrounded on all sides, including the ceiling, by mirrors. There's also a poorly functioning air conditioner. The a/c works better in the $20 rooms. Obviously, it's better to be here if you have someone suitably nasty to share it with. Throughout the night, alarms are set off periodically whenever a car enters or leaves. Other alternatives are **Cabañas Vall Rolando** (☎ 895-5648), Av. San Miguel, and **Cabañas Albarran Manuel** (☎ 894-4834), Carr. 10, Km 59.4 in Río Abajo. The nearest *parador* is **Casa Grande** (☎/fax 894-3939; Box 616, Utuado, PR 00761) on Carr. 612 N of Lago Caonillas at the site of a former coffee plantation. It has 20 rooms with fans, restaurant, and pool. Rates start at about $55.

FOOD: There are many places to eat in town, including the **Taco Rico Restaurant** along Av. Fernando L. Rivas, which serves Mexican food. A bit plusher is the **Aquarium**, Av. Esteres 29, which has entrées for $9-$11. Another alternative is **Café Borínquen** on Carr. 111 at Km 2.2. On Carr. 611 at Km 2.3, **Faro** (☎ 894-3206) serves Puerto Rican food such as *camarones al ajillo*. **Casa Grande** specializes in Puerto Rican dishes such as *piniono* and *filete de pescado en mojo*.

FROM UTUADO: Yellow buses and *públicos* ply over steep hills to Jayuya and, via Lake Dos Bocas, to Arecibo. The road to Jayuya is beautiful, with bamboo groves and rolling hills. **for Ponce:** A magnificent, steep and cool, lushly vegetated road leads through the mountain town of Adjuntas down to Ponce and the sea below.

Jayuya

This is another small mountain town with strong Indian cultural influences. Its moment in history came with the one-day "Revolution of 1950," in which *independentistas* proclaimed the Republic of Puerto Rico, burned police headquarters and held the town for several hours before being dislodged by air assaults from the National Guard. The revolt, which was to have been coordinated with the assassination of President Truman, was quashed elsewhere before it could make much of an impact. The only industry here is Travinol, an artificial kidney factory.

FESTIVALS: The town's **Fiesta Jíbara del Tomate** (Tomato Festival) takes place during the third week in Feb. Jayuya's *fiestas patronales* (Nuestra Señora de la Monserrate) take place on and around September 3. Held mid-Nov. in the public plaza since 1969, the **Festival Indígena Jayuya** (Jayuya Indigenous Festival) features parades, craft markets, presentation of Taíno sports and dance, plus a band that performs using indigenous musical instruments. On Dec. 18, the **Fiestas Canalianas** commemorates the life of renowned local man of letters Nemesio Rosario Canales.

INFORMATION AND SIGHTS: Be sure to obtain the map from the **Casa Cultural**, which is open Mon. to Fri. from 8-4:30. From the Catholic church you head up the steps past the **Tumba del Indio de Boriquén**, a locked structure containing Taíno artifacts and replicas of petroglyphs from Caguana. The Taíno buried under glass here has had samples of earth from the island's 78 towns placed by his side. The statue is a representation of the Cacique Hayuya. The Casa itself has an excellent collection of *santos* in the rear as well as a good gift shop with T-shirts, rocks painted with Taíno motifs, jewelry, and other memorabilia. You can sometimes see young girls taking dance lessons here. To visit the **Museo Cemí**, a museum shaped like a large fish and modeled after a *cemi*, you proceed along Carr. 144. It contains a number of artifacts on loan from the Institute of Puerto Rican Culture. None of them originally came from the area. However, there are photos from area archaeological digs. It's open daily from 8-4:30, and you must ask in the main building for someone to let you in. The main building has an exhibit of local crafts including *santos*. There are *cuatros* for sale, a gift shop, and a restaurant. The Casa Canales here is a recreation of the house of a famous local writer.

From the *parador* climb to the top of **Cerro Punta** inside Toro Negro State Forest. Small carvings of faces, frogs, and spirals are inscribed on the surface of a large boulder in the Saliente riverbed inside Barrio Coabey. **Sol de Jayuya** ("Sun of Jayuya"), found in Zama Province, is one of the most spectacular indigenous murals in Puerto Rico; it's essentially a sun equipped with eyes and mouth, which reflects surprise or fear. However, it's on private property and accordingly difficult to visit. **Los Tres Picachos** (3,952 ft, 1201 m), near Jayuya, is the second highest mountain in Puerto Rico.

ACCOMMODATIONS: Hacienda Gripiñas (☎ 828-1717/1718, fax 828-1719), Carr. 527, Km 2.5, is a very attractive *parador* set on the site of a 19th-century coffee plantation. Facilities here include 19 rooms with private bath (most with ceiling fans) in a 200-year-old restored coffee great house, pool, and restaurant. For current prices and to book reservations, contact Paradores Puertorriqueños, Box 4435, Old San Juan, PR 00905; ☎ 800-443-0266 in the

Northwestern Puerto Rico

US; 800-981-7575 in Puerto Rico (or 721-2884 in San Juan). **homestays:** *Hospederias* that provide simple lodging but a definite Puerto Rican experience include the **Hospedaje Viana** (☎ 828-0486) in Barrio Zamas off Carr. 528 near Carr. 144; **Casa Alfonso** (☎ 828-3742) in Barrio Coabey off Carr. 144 near Carr. 539; **El Cemí** (☎ 828-2164) also in Barrio Coabey off Carr. 144 near Carr. 539; and **Hospedaje Ché** which is in Barrio Coabey as well.

FOOD AND DINING: On the L hand side of the road coming into Jayuya, **Strubbe Delicatessen** has very friendly service. Other restaurants in and near town include **El Punto, Coré, Rivera's Café**, the **Naboria**, and **Rincón Familiar**. Offering gourmet Puerto Rican dishes, **El Dujo** (☎ 828-1143) is just about a mile past the gas station on the R side of Carr. 140 (at Km 82) heading to Carr. 10.

Lares

This *independentista* town is in the heart of coffee country, where the famous Grito de Lares rebellion (see "History" in the Introduction) was raised in 1848. A white obelisk in the plaza lists the names of the revolt's heroes. Annual *independentista* rallies are still held here on September 24 in commemoration of the event. Locked amidst limestone hills, the town is cool and relaxed. There's a waterfall on Carr. 446 near San Sebastián.

events: Lares' *Fiestas Patronales de San José* happens around March 19. In neighboring San Sebastián, the **hamaca (hammock) festival** is held each July. San Sebastián holds its *fiestas patronales* of San Sebastián on Jan. 20.

ACCOMMODATIONS: The nearest accommodation is in San Sebastián, where you can stay at the **Hotel El Castillo** (☎ 896-2365), Km 28.3 on Carr. 111, which is a kind of love hotel with mirrors, bidet, private drive-in entrances, and the works. It also has a pool.

Adjuntas

This small mountain town (pop. 20,000) lies on Carr. 10 between Arecibo and Ponce. *Fiestas Patronales* for San Joaquin and Santa Ana are held around August 21. Its name is short for "las tierras adjuntas" (attached lands). The area around the town has become the world's leading exporter of citron, a fruit which originated in Asia. Known since the Roman era, it may have been the first citrus fruit brought back from Asia. It is distinguished by its thick rind and small pulp, and its main use is as a candied ingredient in fruitcakes. After harvest, the fruits are fermented in brine-filled concrete troughs and covered by a wooden plank for up to 50 days. This process removes bitter oil, prevents spoilage, and softens the fruit, which enables it to absorb more sugar – one of the features that makes it attractive when candied. After removal by workers, the fruits are split in half (by a circular saw) and the central cavity of rind and seeds is removed (by passing it through a pulper). After having been cut into pieces and packed in barrels, it is exported, and the importing firm cooks the fruit in salt water until tender, then sweetens it and drains off the excess syrup. Ironically, it is difficult to find the candied fruit pieces in Puerto Rico. The main importers are Holland and the US. Corsicans, who arrived around the turn of the century, began cultivating the fruit.

ACCOMMODATIONS AND FOOD: On H Street in Adjuntas just one block S from the town square, **Monte Rio** (☎ 829-3705. fax 829-3705) rents 23 rooms for around $40 and up. Rooms have a/c, TV, and views. There's also a bar/restaurant. On Carr. 10 to the W of town, the 24-room **Villas de Sotomayor** (☎ 829-1774/1717, fax 829-5105; Box 661, Adjuntas, PR 00601) has rooms with color TV. On the premises are tennis courts, basketball and volleyball courts, swimming pools, and horseback riding as well as bicycles. Prices start from $90. An inexpensive Puerto Rican restaurant, **Monte Río** (☎ 829-3705) is in the center of town.

BOSQUE ESTATAL DE GUILARTE

Divided among six areas of land and located along Carrs. 518 and 525 to the SW of Adjuntas, this reserve has Monte Guilarte, which is one of the few peaks on the island remaining unmarred by radio

Northwestern Puerto Rico

or TV towers. The steep, unmarked path (1½ hrs RT) through rainforest extends to the top from the ranger station found at the intersection of Carr. 131 and Carr. 518. To the NE and off of Carr. 525, **Charco Azul** is the local swimming hole.

BOSQUE ESTATAL DE TORO NEGRO

(Toro Negro Forest Reserve)

Located to the E of Adjuntas en route to Barranquitas, this 7,000-acre (2,833-ha) reserve (open 8-5) is also known as **Doña Juana Recreation Center** and encompasses the Cordillera Central's highest peaks. These frequently remain shrouded by clouds in a perpetually cool and damp environment. Information is available from the Visitor's Center on Carr. 143.

HISTORY AND ECOSYSTEM: Set in the cool yet humid Cordillera Central, the forest's lower elevations formerly hosted coffee plantations. Most of the forest is secondary; only the highest peaks have never been cleared. Over three million seedlings and some 19,000 lbs. of seeds were sown in the forest between 1934 and 1945. Most of the forest is sierra palm, which dominates at higher elevations. *Tabonuco* (subtropical wet) forest is also present and comprises some 31% of the area. The cloud forest higher up differs from El Yunque's in that it faces a more benign environment. The shrubs are more erect, and there is less moss.

   hiking: Trails here are wet and slippery and only for the truly adventurous. Facilities remain underdeveloped, to say the least. It's possible to climb Cerro Doña Juana (3,341 feet, 1016 m) and Cerro de Punta, which, at 4,390 ft (1,338 m), is the tallest peak on the island. To get to the latter, drive or walk up a steep, short unmarked paved road on the N side of Carr. 143. Another approach is from Parador Hacienda Gripiñas on Carr. 527 in Jayuya. Expect to spend about six hours or more RT. **Cerro Maravilla** here is the place where Puerto Rico's Watergate took place (see "recent political history" under "Government"). Although it's difficult to reach, hikers can also trek to **Inabón Falls** in the heart of the reserve. Inside the main part of the reserve (enter from Carr. 143 at Km 32.4) is an often-dry swimming pool (filled only from May 15-Sept.), barbecue pits, and an observation tower. There are plenty of birds and the bamboo creaks eerily in the breeze. From the entrance, the trail goes past the pool and on ahead over two bridges (reduced by the elements to concrete beams), then up to the road. Head L and you will see a sign marked Tower No. 3, which you can climb for a view. Highest lake on the island, **Laguna Guineo** is set just off Divisoria, the junction of Carr. 143 and Carr. 149, which cuts through the forest E and W. A low temperature of 40°F (4.4°C) – a record for the entire island – has been recorded here.

ACCOMMODATIONS: Camping is permitted inside the reserve if applied for 15 days in advance at the Department of Natural Resources in San Juan. Rooms are rented on a daily, weekly, or monthly basis at **Quinta Doña Juana** within the reserve.

Northwestern Puerto Rico

Glossary

agregado – refers to the sugarcane workers who, up until the late 1940s, labored under the feudal system wherein wages were paid partially in goods and services received.

annatto – a small tree whose seeds, coated with orange-red dye, are used to color cooking oil commonly used in the preparation of Puerto Rican and other Caribbean cuisines.

areytos – epic songs danced to by the Taínos.

bacalao – dried salt cod, once served to slaves.

balneario – a government-administered beach area.

barrio – a city district.

bohio – Taíno Indian name for thatched houses; now applied to the houses of country dwellers in Puerto Rico.

bola, bolita – the numbers racket.

bomba – musical dialogue between dancer and drummer.

botanicas – stores on the Spanish-speaking islands that sell spiritualist literature and paraphernalia.

calabaza (calabash) – small tree native to the Caribbean whose fruit, a gourd, has multiple uses when dried.

callejón – narrow side street; path through the cane fields.

campesino – peasant; lower-class rural dweller.

cañita – the "little cane," bootleg rum (also called pitorro).

carambola – see star apple.

Caribs – original people who colonized the islands of the Caribbean, giving the region its name.

carretera – a road or highway (abbreviated Carr. in the text).

caudillo – Spanish for military general.

cassava – staple crop indigenous to the Americas. Bitter and sweet are the two varieties. Bitter must be washed, grated, and baked in order to remove the poisonous prussic acid. A spongy cake is made from the bitter variety as is *cassareep*, a preservative that is the foundation of West Indian pepper-pot stew.

cays – Indian-originated name that refers to islets in the Caribbean.

century plant – also known as karato, coratoe, and maypole. Flowers only once in its lifetime before it dies.

cerro – hill or mountain.

chorizo – Spanish sausage.

compadrazgo – the system of "co-parentage" that is used to strengthen social bonds in Puerto Rico.

conch – large edible mollusk generally used in salads or chowders.

cuerda – unit of land measure, comprising 9/10ths of an acre.

escabeche – Spanish and Portuguese method of preparing seafood.

espiritismo – spiritualism.

estadistas – Puerto Rican advocates of statehood.

Estado Libre Asociado – "Free Associated State." The Puerto Rican translation of the word commonwealth.

fiestas patronales – patron saint festivals that take place on Catholic islands.

guava – indigenous Caribbean fruit, extremely rich in vitamin C, which is eaten raw or used in making jelly.

guayacan – the tree lignum vitae and its wood.

guiro – rasp-like musical instrument of Taíno Indian origin, which is scratched with a stick to produce a sound.

independentistas – advocates of Puerto Rican independence.

jibaro – the now vanishing breed of impoverished but self-sufficient Puerto Rican peasant.

mundillo – Spanish lacemaking found in Puerto Rico.

naranja – sour orange; its leaves are used as medicine in rural areas.

Neoricans – term used to describe Puerto Ricans who have left for NYC and returned.

padrinos – godparents.

Paso Fino – developed over the past five centuries, these horses have a characteristic gait. Competitions are a national sport, and there are over 7,000 registered Paso Fino horses on the island.

pegado – from the verb pegar (to stick together); used together with nouns in Puerto Rico as an adjective.

personalismo – describes the charisma of a Latin politician who appears and acts as a father figure.

plebiscite – direct vote by the people on an issue.

plena – form of Puerto Rican dance.

poinciana – beautiful tropical tree that blooms with clusters of red blossoms during the summer months. Originates in Madagascar.

público – shared taxi found on the Spanish-speaking islands.

santos – carved representations of Catholic saints.

sea grape – West Indian tree, commonly found along beaches, which produces green, fleshy, edible grapes.

señorita – young, unmarried female, usually used in rural Puerto Rico to refer to virgins.

sensitive plant – also know as mimosa, shame lady, and other names. It will snap shut at the slightest touch.

star apple – large tree producing segmented pods, brown in color and sour in taste, which are a popular fresh fruit.

trigueno – ("wheat colored.") Denotes a mulatto and differentiates brunettes from blondes.

velorio – Catholic wake.

yautia – tuber also known as taro, dasheen, malanga, and elephant's ear.

zemi (cemi) – idol in which the personal spirit of each Arawak or Taíno lived. Usually carved from stone.

Spanish Vocabulary

Days of the Week

domingo	Sunday
lunes	Monday
martes	Tuesday
miercoles	Wednesday
jueves	Thursday
viernes	Friday
sabado	Saturday

Months of the Year

enero	January
febrero	February
marzo	March
abril	April
mayo	May
junio	June
julio	July
agosto	August
septiembre	September
octubre	October
noviembre	November
diciembre	December

Numbers

uno	one
dos	two
tres	three
cuatro	four
cinco	five
seis	six
siete	seven
ocho	eight
nueve	nine
diez	ten
once	eleven
doce	twelve
trece	thirteen
catorce	fourteen
quince	fifteen
dieciséis	sixteen
diecisiete	seventeen
dieciocho	eighteen

diecinueve	nineteen
veinte	twenty
veintiuno	twenty-one
veintidos	twenty-two
treinta	thirty
cuarenta	forty
cincuenta	fifty
sesenta	sixty
setenta	seventy
ochenta	eighty
noventa	ninety
cien	one hundred
ciento uno	one hundred one
doscientos	two hundred
quinientos	five hundred
mil	one thousand
mil uno	one thousand one
dos mil	two thousand
un millón	one million
mil millones	one billion
primero	first
segundo	second
tercero	third
cuarto	fourth
quinto	fifth
sexto	sixth
séptimo	seventh
octavo	eighth
noveno	ninth
décimo	tenth
undécimo	eleventh
duodécimo	twelfth
último	last

Conversation

¿Como esta usted?	How are you?
Bien, gracias, y usted?	Well, thanks, and you?
Buenas dias.	Good morning.
Buenas tardes.	Good afternoon.
Buenas noches.	Good evening/night.
Hasta la vista.	See you again.
Hasta luego.	So long.
¡Buena suerte!	Good luck!
Adios.	Goodbye.
Mucho gusto de conocerle.	Glad to meet you.
Felicidades.	Congratulations.
Muchas felicidades.	Happy birthday.

Feliz Navidad.	Merry Christmas.
Feliz Año Nuevo.	Happy New Year.
Gracias.	Thank you.
Por favor.	Please.
De nada/con mucho gusto.	You're welcome.
Perdoneme.	Pardon me.
¿Como se llama esto?	What do you call this?
Lo siento.	I'm sorry.
Permitame.	Permit me.
Quisiera...	I would like...
Adelante.	Come in.
Permitame presentarle...	May I introduce...
¿Como se llamo usted?	What is your name?
Me llamo...	My name is...
No se.	I don't know.
Tengo sed.	I am thirsty.
Tengo hambre.	I am hungry.
Soy norteamericano/a	I am an American.
¿Donde puedo encontrar...?	Where can I find...?
¿Que es esto?	What is this?
¿Habla usted ingles?	Do you speak English?
Hablo/entiendo un poco Español	I speak/understand a little Spanish
¿Hay alguien aqui que hable ingles?	Is there anyone here who speaks English?
Le entiendo.	I understand you.
No entiendo.	I don't understand.
Hable mas despacio por favor.	Please speak more slowly.
Repita por favor.	Please repeat.

Telling Time

¿Que hora es?	What time is it?
Son las...	It's...
... cinco.	... five o'clock.
... ocho y diez.	... ten past eight.
... seis y cuarto.	... quarter past six.
... cinco y media.	... half past five.
...siete y menos cinco.	... five of seven.
antes de ayer.	the day before yesterday.
anoche.	yesterday evening.
esta mañana.	this morning.
a mediodia.	at noon.
en la noche.	in the evening.
de noche.	at night.
a medianoche.	at midnight.
mañana en la mañana.	tomorrow morning.
mañana en la noche.	tomorrow evening.
pasado mañana.	the day after tomorrow.

Directions

¿En que direccion queda...?	In which direction is...?
Lleveme a... por favor.	Take me to... please.
Llevame alla ... por favor.	Take me there please.
¿Que lugar es este?	What place is this?
¿Donde queda el pueblo?	Where is the town?
¿Cual es el mejor camino para...?	Which is the best road to...?
De vuelta a la derecha.	Turn to the right.
De vuelta a la isquierda.	Turn to the left.
Siga derecho.	Go this way.
En esta direccion.	In this direction.
¿A que distancia estamos de...?	How far is it to...?
¿Es este el camino a...?	Is this the road to...?
¿Es...	Is it...
... cerca?	...near?
...lejos?	...far?
...norte?	...north?
... sur?	...south?
... este?	...east?
... oeste?	...west?
Indiqueme por favor.	Please point.
Hagame favor de decirme donde esta...	Please direct me to...
... el telephono.	... the telephone.
... el excusado.	... the bathroom.
... el correo.	... the post office.
... el banco.	... the bank.
... la comisaria.	... the police station.

Accommodations

Estoy buscando un hotel....	I am looking for a hotel that's...
... bueno.	... good.
... barato.	... cheap.
... cercano.	... nearby.
... limpio.	... clean.
¿Dónde hay hotel, pensión, hospedaje?	Where is a hotel, pensión, hospedaje?
Hay habitaciones libres?	Do you have available rooms?
¿Dónde están los baños/servicios?	Where are the bathrooms?
Quisiera un...	I would like a...
... cuarto sencillo.	... single room.
... cuarto con baño.	... room with a bath.
... cuarto doble.	... double room.
Puedo verlo?	May I see it?
Cuanto cuesta?	What's the cost?
Es demasiado caro!	It's too expensive!

Booklist

Travel & Description

Arciniegas, German. *Caribbean: Sea of the New World*. New York: Alfred A. Knopf, 1946.

Babin, Theresa Maria. *The Puerto Rican's Spirit*. New York: Collier Books, 1971. Excellent information regarding Puerto Rican history, people, literature, and fine arts.

Blume, Helmut. (trans. Johannes Maczewski and Ann Norton) *The Caribbean Islands*. London: Longman, 1976.

Bonsal, Stephen. *The American Mediterranean*. New York: Moffat, Yard and Co., 1912.

Caabro, J.A. Suarez. *El Mar de Puerto Rico*. Río Piedras: University of Puerto Rico Press, 1979.

Creque, Darwin D. *The U.S. Virgins and the Eastern Caribbean*. Philadelphia: Whitmore Publishing Co., 1968.

Fillingham, Paul. *Pilot's Guide to the Lesser Antilles*. New York: McGraw-Hill, 1979. Invaluable for pilots.

Hanberg, Clifford A. *Puerto Rico and the Puerto Ricans*. New York: Hippocrene, 1975. Survey of the Puerto Rican historical experience.

Hart, Jeremy C. and William T. Stone. *A Cruising Guide to the Caribbean and the Bahamas*. New York: Dodd, Mead and Company, 1982. Description of planning and plying for yachties. Includes nautical maps.

Holbrook, Sabra. *The American West Indies, Puerto Rico and the Virgin Islands*. New York: Meredith Press, 1969.

Kurlansky, Mark. *A Continent of Islands*. New York: Addison-Wesley, 1992. This suberb book by a veteran journalist is one of the best books about the Caribbean ever written, a must for visitors who wish to understand the area and its culture.

Lewis, Oscar. *La Vida*. New York: Irvington, 1982. The famous (1966) chronicle of Puerto Rican life.

Lopez, Adalberto and James Petras. *Puerto Rico and the Puerto Ricans*. Cambridge, MA: Schenkmann-Halstead Press, 1974.

Morrison, Samuel E. *The Caribbean as Columbus Saw It*. Boston: Little and Co., 1964. Photographs and text by a leading American historian.

Naipaul, V.S. *The Middle Passage: The Caribbean Revisited*. New York: MacMillan, 1963. Another view of the West Indies by a Trinidad native.

Perl, Lila. *Puerto Rico, Island Between Two Worlds*. New York: William Morrow and Co., 1979.

Radcliffe, Virginia. *The Caribbean Heritage*. New York: Walker & Co., 1976.

Robinson, Kathryn. *The Other Puerto Rico*. Santurce, Puerto Rico: Permanent Press, Inc., 1984. Guide to the natural wonders of the islands.

Samoiloff, Louise C. *Portrait of Puerto Rico*. San Diego: A.S. Barnes, 1979. Descriptive and comprehensive profile.

Steiner, Stan. *The Islands*. New York: Harper & Row, 1974. An in-depth living journalistic portrait of the Puerto Ricans – on their island and in the mainland barrios.

Van Ost, John R. and Harry Kline. *Yachtsman's Guide to the Virgin Islands and Puerto Rico*. North Miami, Florida: Tropic Isle Publishers, Inc., 1984. Where to anchor in the area.

Waggenheim, Kal. *Puerto Rico: A Profile*. New York: Praeger, 1970. A revealing if dated survey of Puerto Rico's economy, geography, and culture.

Ward, Fred. *Golden Islands of the Caribbean*. New York: Crown Publishers, 1967. A picture book for your coffee table. Beautiful historical plates.

Flora & Fauna

Humann, Paul. *Reef Fish Identification.* Jacksonville: New World Publications, 1989. This superb guide is filled with beautiful color photos of 268 fish. Information is included on identifying details, habitat and behavior, and on reaction to divers.

Humann, Paul. *Reef Creature Identification.* Jacksonville: New World Publications, 1992. The second in the series, this guide covers 320 denizens of the deep. Information is included on abundance and distribution, habitat and behavior, and identifying characteristics.

Humann, Paul. *Reef Coral Identification.* Jacksonville: New World Publications, 1993. Last in this indispensable series (which is now available boxed as "The Reef Set"), this book identifies 240 varieties of coral and marine plants. The different groups are also described in detail.

Kaplan, Eugene. *A Field Guide to the Coral Reefs of the Caribbean and Florida.* Princeton, NJ: Peterson's Guides, 1984

Little, Elbert L., Jr., Frank J. Wadsworth, and José Marrero. *Arboles Comunes De Puerto Rico y las Islas Virgenes.* Río Piedras: University of Puerto Rico Press, 1967.

de Oviedo, Gonzalo Fernandez. (trans. and ed. S.A. Stroudemire.) *Natural History of the West Indies.* Chapel Hill: University of North Carolina Press, 1959.

Riviera, Juan A. *The Amphibians of Puerto Rico.* Mayagüez: Universidad de Puerto Rico, 1978.

History

Bonnet, Benitez and Juan Amedee. *Vieques En La Historia de Puerto Rico.* Puerto Rico: F. Nortiz Nieves, 1976. Traces the history of Vieques over the centuries.

Cripps, L.L. *The Spanish Caribbean: From Columbus to Castro.* Cambridge, MA: Schenkman, 1979. Concise history of the Spanish Caribbean from the point of view of a radical historian.

Deer, Noel. *The History of Sugar.* London: Chapman, 1950

Golding, Morton J. *A Short History of Puerto Rico.* New York: New American Library, 1973.

Hovey, Graham and Gene Brown, eds. *Central America and the Caribbean.* New York: Arno Press, 1980. This volume of clippings from *The New York Times,* one of a series in its Great Contemporary Issues books, graphically displays Amnerican activities and attitudes toward the area. A goldmine of information.

Knight, Franklin W. *The Caribbean.* Oxford: Oxford University Press, 1978. Thematic, anti-imperialist view of Caribbean history.

Lewis, Gordon K. *Puerto Rico: Freedom and Power in the Caribbean.* New York: Monthly Review Press, 1963. Dated but still the most comprehensive general work in existence on Puerto Rican history and economics.

Mannix, Daniel P. and Malcolm Cooley. *Black Cargoes.* New York: Viking Press, 1982. Details the saga of the slave trade.

Mendez, Eugenio Fernandez. *Historia Cultural de Puerto Rico 1493-1968.* Río Piedras, Puerto Rico: University of Puerto Rico Press, 1980.

Silen, Juan Angel. *We, the Puerto Rican People.* New York: Monthly Review Press, 1971. Analysis of Puerto Rican history from the viewpoint of a militant Puerto Rican nationalist.

Wagenheim, Kal., ed. *Puerto Rico: A Documentary History.* New York: Praeger, 1973. History from the viewpoint of eyewitnesses.

Williams, Eric. *From Columbus to Castro: The History of the Caribbean.* New York: Random House, 1983. Definitive history of the Caribbean by the late Prime Minister of Trinidad and Tobago.

Politics & Economics

Anderson, Robert W. *Party Politics in Puerto Rico.* Stanford, CA: Stanford University Press, 1965.

Barry, Tom, Beth Wood, and Deb Freusch. *The Other Side of Paradise: Foreign Control in the Caribbean.* New York: Grove Press, 1984. A brilliantly and thoughtfully written analysis of Caribbean economics.

Bayo, Armando. *Puerto Rico*. Havana: Casa de las Americas, 1966.

Blanshard, Paul. *Democracy and Empire in the Caribbean*. New York: The Macmillan Co., 1947.

Cripps, L.L. *Human Rights in a United States Colony*. Cambridge, MA: Schenkmann Publishing Co., 1982. Once one gets past the ludicrous paeans to life in socialist countries, this contains valuable information concening matters one never hears about stateside: Cerro Maravilla, the Vieques and Culebra takeovers, police brutality, etc.

Diffie, Bailey W. and Justine Whitfield. *Porto Rico: A Broken Pledge*. The Vanguard Press: New York, 1931. An early study of American exploitation in Puerto Rico.

Johnson, Roberta Ann. *Puerto Rico, Commonwealth or Colony?* New York: Praeger, 1980.

Langhorne, Elizabeth. *Worlds Collide On Vieques*. New York: Rivercross Publishing, 1992. An excellent book and a must read for any interested visitor to Vieques.

Lewis, Gordon K. *Notes on the Puerto Rican Revolution*. New York: Monthly Review Press, 1974. A Marxist analysis of the past, present, and future of Puerto Rico.

Matthews, Thomas G. and F.M. Andic, eds. *Politics and Economics in the Caribbean*. Río Piedras: Institute of Caribbean Studies, University of Puerto Rico, 1971.

Matthews, Thomas G. *Puerto Rican Politics and the New Deal*. Miami: University of Florida Press, 1960.

Mitchell, Sir Harold. *Caribbean Patterns*. New York: John Wiley and Sons, 1972. Dated, but still a masterpiece. The best reference guide for gaining an understanding of the history and current political status of nearly every island group in the Caribbean.

Petrullo, Vincenzo. *Puerto Rican Paradox*. Philadelphia: University of Pennsylvania Press, 1947.

Roosevelt, Theodore. *Colonial Policies of the United States.* Garden City: Doubleday, Doran, and Co., 1937. The chapter on Puerto Rico by this ex-governor is particularly fascinating.

Tugwell, Rexford Guy. *The Stricken Land.* Garden City, New York: Doubleday & Co., 1947.

Vieques Conservation and Historical Trust. *Vieques: History of a Small Island.* Vieques, Puerto Rico: Vieques Conservation and Historical Trust, 1987.

Wells, Henry. *The Modernization of Puerto Rico: A Political Study of Changing Values and Institutions.* Cambridge, MA: Harvard University Press, 1969.

Sociology & Anthropology

Abrahams, Roger D. *After Africa.* New Haven: Yale University Press, 1983. Fascinating accounts of slaves and slave life in the West Indies.

Acosta-Belén, Edna and Elia Hidalgo Christensen, eds. *The Puerto Rican Woman.* New York: Praeger, 1979.

Brameld, Theodore A. *Remaking of a Culture: Life and Education in Puerto Rico.* New York: Harper & Brothers, 1959.

Horowitz, Michael H. (ed) *People and Cultures of the Caribbean.* Garden City: Natural History Press for the Museum of Natural History, 1971. Sweeping compilation of social anthropological essays.

Mintz, Sidney W. *Caribbean Transformation.* Chicago: Aldine Publishing Co., 1974. Includes an essay on Puerto Rico.

Mintz, Sidney W. *Worker in the Cane: A Puerto Rican Life History.* New Haven: Yale University Press, 1960.

Rand, Christopher. *The Puerto Ricans.* New York: Oxford University Press, 1958.

Steward, Julian W. *The People of Puerto Rico.* Urbana: University of Illinois Press, 1956. An early and thorough social-anthropological study of Puerto Rico.

Art, Architecture, & Archaeology

Buissert, David. *Historic Architecture of the Caribbean.* London: Heinemann Educational Books, 1980.

Fernandez, José A. *Architecture in Puerto Rico.* New York: Hastings House, 1965.

Kaiden, Nina, Pedro John Soto, and Vladimir Andrews, eds. *Puerto Rico, The New Life.* New York: Renaissance Editions, 1966.

Rouse, Benjamin I. *Puerto Rican Prehistory.* New York: Academy of Sciences, 1952.

Willey, Gordon R. *An Introduction to American Archaeology, Vol. 2, South America.* Englewood Cliffs, New Jersey: Prentice-Hall, Inc., 1971.

Music

Bergman, Billy. *Hot Sauces: Latin and Caribbean Pop.* New York: Quill, 1984.

Language

Rosario, Ruben del. *Vocabulario Puertorriqueño.* Sharon, MA: Troutman Press, 1965. Contains exclusively Puerto Rican vocabulary.

Literature

Babin, Maria Theresa. *Borinquen: An Anthology of Puerto Rican Literature.* New York: Vintage, 1974.

Baldwin, James. *If Beale Street Could Talk.* New York: Dial, 1974. Novel set in NYC and Puerto Rico.

Howes, Barbara, ed. *From the Green Antilles.* New York: Crowell, Collier & Macmillan, 1966. Includes four stories from Puerto Rico.

Levine, Barry. *Benjy Lopez: A Picaresque Tale of Emigration and Return.* New York: Basic Books, 1980.

Sanchez, Luiz R. *Macho Camacho's Beat.* New York: Pantheon, 1981. Novel set in Puerto Rico.

Index

Update: Hotels Opened in 1997

The Centro (☎ 751-1335, fax 751-0930, 724-4920; e-mail: 102451.3026@compuserve.com), located in the heart of Rio Piedras in San Juan, has a/c rooms with color TV. Conference rooms and a business center are available.

Hampton Inn (☎ 800-HAMPTON), across from the El San Juan and Ritz Carlton hotels, offers suites, a business center, meeting rooms, health spa, concierge floor and pool. Complimentary local phone calls; Continental breakfast included in the rates.

The **Colony San Juan Beach Hotel** (☎ 253-0100, fax 253-0220), C. Tartak 2, Isla Verde, has 71 units; rates are from around $150 d.

Hacienda Tamarindo (☎ 741-8525, fax 741-3215; Apdo. 1569, Vieques, PR 00765), Carr. 996 at Km. 4.5 on Vieques, has 16 units. It may be distinguished by the large tamarind tree rising through its center atrium. The imaginatively designed rooms and common areas feature art and antiques. Rates start at around $105 d and include a full breakfast.

The **Palmas de Lucía Hotel** (☎ 893-4423/0291, fax 893-0291; Apdo. 1746, Yabucoa, PR 00767), south of Humacao, is located right on the beach at Playa Lucía, E of Yabucoa, off Hwy 901 on Carr. 9911. Rooms have a/c, color TV, private baths, and balconies. Facilities include a pool, game room, restaurant, children's playground and basketball court.

The **Buen Café Hotel Parador** (☎ 898-1000, fax 820-3013) is a new parador near Arecibo (Carr. 2, Km. 84). It has a restaurant; rooms have cable TV and a/c. Beaches are nearby.

New Web Sites

Many new Puerto Rican Web sites have started up. Here are some useful ones:

- ❑ **www.pdnt.com/cutpo/inforpr.html** – Official Visitors Guide of the Puerto Rico Hotel & Tourism Association.
- ❑ **www.naic.edu/** – Arecibo Observatory.
- ❑ **www.nps.gov/saju/**– San Juan National Historic Site.
- ❑ **www.geocities.com/CapitolHill/1033/queeni.html** – Salsa 101.
- ❑ **www.prol.com/hotels/index.html** – Hotels, paradores and guesthouses.